50 Teams that Mattered

by

David Hartrick

Published by Ockley Books Ltd

First published 2012

ISBN 978-0-9571410-0-1
Front cover designed by Proworx

Printed by Riley Dunn & Wilson Ltd.
Red Doles Lane
Huddersfield
West Yorkshire
HD2 1YE

www.ockleybooks.co.uk

For my wife Penny who has not only given me Beau,
our beautiful daughter, but also makes every day better than
yesterday by simply being a part of today.

Contents

Introduction

You can blame the Football Ramble I guess.

It was listening to their podcast and host Marcus Speller's Hall of Fame profile on Pro Vercelli that finally got me to put pen to paper (or more accurately fingers to keyboard) and begin writing this book. A little club in Northern Italy had left such an indelible mark on the game that there should be footballing works of art raised in their honour but yet, there remained something so beautifully humble about their story.

I knew of Pro Vercelli and had vague recollections of some tale about Internazionale stealing a title from them, but I began to look further and slowly a plan began to form. I always had an idea of the football book I wanted to write but it emerged from a simple tome talking about a couple of club's histories, into the piece you hold in your hands today. Pro Vercelli really mattered to the game in Italy and Europe and it made me realise that football is littered with the stories of the great and the good, but it also owes some smaller clubs a huge debt for moments in history that still echo today.

Don't get me wrong, the usual suspects are covered here as any great club is great for a reason and their moments in time are often longer and shine brighter than most, but also it's important to acknowledge the contribution a club like Exeter City have made in igniting a passion for a truly national team in Brazil, or how romantic a team like Millonarios can make football to those in love with the sport. What this book represents is a look behind the curtain at several stories you may or may not be aware of that have really mattered for all the best, and in some cases all the worst reasons. They are snapshots in time and I hope you will read and enjoy them but most of all, not forget them.

Now to address the elephant in the room – the selection process.

This book is titled '50 Teams That Mattered' for a reason and not 'The 50 Teams That Mattered Most', or 'The Only 50 Teams That Mattered'. Every football fan can give you a reason why their team matters locally, nationally, and some cases globally. Those selected in this book are purely here on the basis of my own personal choices and there are some very obvious and what will be to some, glaring omissions.

Where are the Aston Villa side that helped form the inaugural football league with William McGregor at its head?

What? No place for the all-conquering and breath-taking St Etienne side that swept all before it in the late sixties and seventies?

Manchester United's 1999 treble-winners are here but the European Cup winners of 1968 aren't?

The answer to all these questions and the many, many more levelled at me for the choices in here can all be put to bed very simply.

I had to stop somewhere.

This book could have been '75 Teams That Mattered' quite easily, or a 100, or 250 in all honesty. Football's story is so rich that nearly every major club in world football have a team that at one point of another can lay claim to a place in the sport's history. To back that up, try talking to football fans whilst preparing a book such as this and record how many times the phrase 'I know I'm biased but...' comes up. It's that deep-rooted and engrained sense of pride in our chosen club's efforts that continues to make football such an all-consuming global force.

So relax and hopefully enjoy having a read of a collection of stories that make up a single love letter to the game I adore. This has been a life-changing experience to write and within I hope there's at least one story that will stay with you long after this book has been and gone in your own footballing history.

And if your club isn't in here?

Relax, I'm a Brighton and Hove Albion fan and I couldn't sneak my own club in here let alone yours and who knows, whoever you've chosen, been forced to or fell into supporting, they'll probably make the sequel...

David Hartrick
October 2011

Foreword

When David asked me to write this foreword, I had just two questions. How much do I get paid and how much of the book is given over to Southend United? Disappointingly, he gave me the same answer to both questions. Nevertheless, I shall continue with great stoicism and a rigid upper lip, for it is a great honour to write the opening remarks for a book that I am sure you will enjoy as much as I will.

In this brave new world of modern media, David is one of the pathfinders. For the first time in many years, independent writers are finding footholds on the mainstream, using the internet, social networking, raw talent and desire to fight their way to recognition. You'll know David already, I'm sure, as one of the founding fathers of the intellectual bric-a-brac shop that is 'In Bed With Maradona'. In that pleasingly musky corner of the internet, he provides a nook for nostalgia, a cranny for curiosities and, most importantly, a chance for this future generation of writers to shine. It is a website that I've had the great pleasure to write for in the past, and the exposure I enjoyed there helped boost my profile, turning me into the hapless jobbing columnist you see twitching before you today.

Now David has turned his hand to the printed press, and typically he's done it with no small amount of style. I've seen a few chapters and this is an absolutely corking collection of writings. Pleasingly, he hasn't limited his selection to the winners, preferring to add a few of the more interesting, but less successful tales to the mix. Leeds United, I'm looking in your direction.

Who were my favourite team of all time? How kind of you to ask. Well, disregarding the Barry Fry-led, Stan Collymore-infused Southend United side of 1993, I'd have to plump for Kevin Keegan's Newcastle. The first time around, obviously. Poor Keegan will be forever inextricably linked with that 'I'd Love It' speech, but history would do well to treat him with more respect. Those free-flowing, fleet-footed mentalists will be remembered for coming second long after the title-winning Blackburn Rovers side of 1995 have been forgotten. Keegan made football fun again. In those less cynical times, Newcastle genuinely were the second favourite team of many football fans. More than that, that Newcastle team lured my father back to the game and that took some doing. Disenchanted with football and disgusted with the violence of the 1980s, Keegan had him on the edge of his seat again in the 1990s. Some things are more important than silverware.

But that, I'm sure you'll agree, is more than enough from me. Make yourself a cup of tea, rip open a packet of hobnobs and settle into a comfy chair. Young or old, veteran or newcomer, I promise you, you're going to like this.

Iain Macintosh
September, 2011

Iain writes for (amongst others) The New Paper, The Irish Examiner, The Blizzard, Sports Illustrated and BT's 'Life's a Pitch', he is also one third of the 'Red, White and Blue' podcast and website.

Sheffield FC 1857

Honours

Awarded FIFA Order of Merit in 2004

Entered into English Football Hall of Fame 2007

Married Men v Unmarried Men

Professional Occupations v The Rest

Fixtures organised by members in the absence of opponents in 1857

On Thursday 20th May 2004, dignitaries gathered in Paris for the 54th annual FIFA Congress. This event carried an extra significance, as a gala held at the same time would celebrate FIFA's 100th year since formation. Over fifteen hundred people, including Prime Ministers and the footballing elite, gathered to join in with the centenary celebration. FIFA decided to mark the event with the award of several 'Centennial Order of Merits', one for every decade of existence across ten different categories. Covering all aspects of the global game, from players to the organisation's economic partners, the awards for the clubs themselves were amongst the highest prized on offer. It was decided only two Orders would be given to football clubs – one to a giant who had helped shape the modern game, and one to a team few people in the room would've even heard of.

The first would go to Real Madrid. A highly decorated club with a rich history of success, domestically their hand had been felt in all aspects of the Spanish game from the original founding of the country's football association. Beyond that they had helped to shape European competition during Santiago Bernabéu's reign as President of the club and attracted some of the world's greatest players to play for them in Madrid. In 2001 FIFA had voted Real 'Most Successful Club Of The 20th Century', so at football's governing body's centenary just three years later the award was almost inevitable.

The second team to receive the honour couldn't boast the record of their Spanish counterparts; they couldn't even claim to be in the top two most successful teams in their home city. Sheffield Football Club received exactly the same accolade as Real Madrid for one important reason – they are recognised by both the English Football Association (the FA) and FIFA as the first and therefore oldest football club in the world.

Nathaniel Creswick and William Prest originally organised a version of what would be recognised as 'mob football' in 1855. Played between members of the same cricket club, their main aim was to engage in a sport that would keep their fitness levels for the summer's cricket season high during the winter. Eventually they adapted and formed their own set of rules drawn from the various codes by which football was played to at the time, mostly in public schools. Officially founded in 1857, Sheffield F.C, or 'The Sheffield Club' as some would know it, became the first football club in recorded existence.

In the absence of opposition games were organised amongst themselves. At the club's annual general meeting in 1858, Creswick and Prest settled on a set of laws that would become known as the 'Sheffield Rules'. They had no offside as such but introduced many elements we recognise in the modern game today. It was the first code to over time introduce free kicks for foul play, throw-ins, corner kicks and the idea that a solid cross bar was better than a length of rope. Also heading or 'butting' as it was known was allowed and encouraged as part of play, something which when playing London City at Battersea Park in 1866 caused the opposition players and crowd to laugh at their Northern opponents strange way of playing the game. It is alleged that modern day Australian Rules Football carries many of the features of this Sheffield code and despite joining the English Football Association in 1863, they continued to play by their own laws until 1878 when they adopted the FA's code.

By 1860 Sheffield F.C had an opponent and local bragging rites to play for. Two former members – Thomas Vickers and John Shaw – formed Hallam Football Club. The oldest recorded derby game in the world first took place on Boxing Day 1860 and within two years, nearly twenty recorded clubs had been formed in the Sheffield area alone. In 1867 a local theatre owner sponsored the Youdan Cup and as the competition would be focused towards the Sheffield area, therefore took the preferred local rules as the code for the tournament. The first recorded competition took place and after a series of games, Hallam FC were crowned champions.

Despite the local prestige on offer and the use of 'their' rules, Sheffield F.C did not take part. The decision had been taken to only play teams outside of the Sheffield area to seek a greater challenge. Bringing their own brand of football to various locales around country, the people in charge of the team were liaising with the FA to try and change the national rules to mirror Sheffield's. The FA continually refused and in 1867 things came to a head when the London based committee refused to organise any more fixtures for the Yorkshire club unless they adopted the FA's code. It would be eleven more years before Sheffield F.C would finally give in totally to FA rule but this was perhaps the era when they exerted most influence over the national game, as many of the Sheffield Rules had been included, refined and taken into the FA's standards.

Over the years professionalism confined Sheffield F.C's amateurs to the lower levels of English football. Instrumental in so much of the game's early groundwork, they also helped to form the professional club known today as Sheffield United and launch the FA Amateur Cup in 1893. Official honours have been sparse, a single FA Amateur Cup in 1904 is their only national competition win, but hopes remain that one-day they will play at a level that befits their history.

Despite the lack of success if there was any doubt to their importance it can be dismissed by the regard in which the club is held by the football world. On top of the official recognition in the form of the Order of Merit, FIFA supported Sheffield F.C's 150th anniversary celebrations in 2007 by sending its president Sepp Blatter to attend a celebratory banquet. Also in attendance from the football world were names like Sir Tom Finney, Sir Dave Richards, Bryan Robson, Gordon Taylor and former Spain manager and Inter Milan player, Luis Suárez Miramontes. As well as some of the sport's leading figures, several local dignitaries and Director of the National Football Museum Kevin Moore also attended the celebration. After the banquet, Sheffield F.C took part in a friendly against Italy's Internazionale to mark the occasion in November 2007, with guest of honour for the day none other than Brazilian legend Pelé. Over 18,000 fans attended the game held at Bramall Lane to see the club honoured for their place in world football history. Out of respect for being invited to take part in such a prestigious occasion, Sheffield F.C were then invited to send a representative to Internazionale's own centenary celebrations just a year later.

Sheffield F.C only matter for one reason but being the original football club, it is perhaps the biggest reason of all. The influence of the brand of football they played in those early days is now taken for granted – the modern game still carries some of the hallmarks of Sheffield F.C's very own rules and in hindsight, that's some achievement for a group of men who were only trying to stay fit for the cricket season.

The Queen's Park Football Club 1867–93

Honours

Scottish Cup Winners
1874, 1875, 1876, 1880, 1881, 1882, 1884, 1886, 1890, & 1893

FA Cup Runners Up
1884, & 1885

'Ludere causa Ludendi'

Queen's Park's motto – 'Play for the sake of playing'

When a 'Scottish' method of playing football first emerged few would have guessed its influence would run through the game all the way to Hungary's Mighty Magyars and beyond. It was seen as a radical new style and touched some of football's most forward thinking coaches but to understand the revolution it must first be said that at the modern game's birth in England, football was about attack through physicality and dribbling. The idea was simply to get the ball as close to the goal as often as possible. While individual ability was still prized in the Scottish game, a different approach was taken and as their country's oldest and once highest profile club, Queen's Park became its flag bearers.

Formed in 1867 as Scotland's first Association Football club, the inaugural meeting of 'The Queen's Park Football Club' did little more than settle on the name. Based in Glasgow, the club took their moniker from the Queen's Park Recreation Ground where several of the members had met to practice athletics. Football in Scotland had been a pursuit of the educational system where just as it had in England, the rules could differ from school to school. Queen's Park's formation brought with it an agreed set of standards but aside from games amongst themselves, they had to wait for real opposition.

Several decisions were taken early in Queen's Park's burgeoning life as a football club that still hold true in its running today. The most significant of all was the agreement that Queen's Park would be an amateur club throughout their existence. As admirable as that commitment remains, it is of course also what eventually left them trailing behind Scotland's newer professional clubs. Queen's Park remains an amateur club to this day and along with Sheffield F.C, perhaps do not enjoy the status their entry in football history deserves.

Over the next two years from Queen's Park's formation, football clubs slowly began to emerge across Scotland giving them sporadic opposition. Naturally they proved to be the strongest side in the country but they were also focused in helping football grow. Several exhibition games were played where great pains were taken to explain the separate rules and phases of play to teams and spectators alike, the idea being that a uniform version of the game was left as a legacy. With Scottish teams emerging but requiring time to reach Queen's Park's level of ability, they needed to look further a field for a level of opposition that would improve their own game and spread their method of 'combination football'.

There are several theories as to how their 'combination' style came into being. Despite their amateur status, the team practised religiously where games were organised amongst themselves in the same fashion they had been in Sheffield – Smokers v Non Smokers, Light v Heavy Weights etc. It could be argued that the overly physical approach and the practise of 'hacking' at your opponent to win the ball so common place in the game elsewhere, would not have been as well received in games between friends taking place regularly in the face of no regular opposition clubs to compete with. With an initial lack of opposition the group of men who played for the club became close, bonded by their sport, the idea of injuring a colleague and possibly friend may have lead to a different approach being taken.

Queen's Park developed a style of play where by they passed the ball between their front and back lines, combining the dribbling so valued previously with an ability to move the ball sharply between themselves – essentially a passing game. With dedicated practise their game evolved without interference, the players becoming just as skilful as their English counterparts but with a mind to shift the ball amongst themselves and then around their opposition.

As Queen's Park continued their missionary journeys around Scotland, so they left a style for the burgeoning clubs to take and mould for themselves. What started as a method specific to Queen's soon became a symptom of a 'Scottish' way of playing the game. This Scottish game went on to influence such footballing revolutionaries as Hugo Meisl and Jimmy Hogan, whose

Austrian 'Wunderteam' took the 'pattern-weaving' of the style to its next level. By the time Gusztáv Sebes was in charge of the legendary Hungarian national team of the 50's, the Scottish style was well on its way to evolving into a 'total' football of short passing and constant movement.

The first real exposure outside of Scotland for the combination style came in 1872 with the first international match in the history of the game. Queen's Park had joined the English FA in 1870 as it was the only governing body available, therefore they became the de facto heads of Scottish football. When the question was raised of a game between representative Scotland and England teams, Queen's simply played their first team as 'Scotland' and even wore their club kit of the time – the dark blue shirts that survive as Scotland's colours to this day.

The game was played at Hamilton Crescent in Glasgow and a slightly surprising 0-0 draw ensued. While the English had the physical advantage in comparison to their 'light-weight' Scottish opponents, the passing and greater movement proved to be the equal of the English dribbling. The game had generated a great deal of interest and the newspapers carried stories of the difference in approach. A huge crowd of 4,000 had also gathered to observe the game proving there was a real interest in the sport, and in possible future internationals. 'Scotland' had emerged with great credit and the world had now had its first look at a different way of playing the game. Such was the impact of the Scottish style over the next decade, the migration of talented Scottish players to England (nicknamed 'professors', prized for their ability and mined for their knowledge) in part caused the clamour for professionalism in the game.

Queen's Park led the march for a Scottish Football Association and in 1873 representatives of Scotland's foremost clubs met and formed the organisation to govern the Scottish game. Where they had been essentially doing the job anyway, Queen's Park were now able to concentrate solely on their own game.

Free of any organisational responsibility Queen's Park flourished and with 'official' competition to compete in, their chance to win national honours was now the prize. The Scottish Cup tournament was immediately formed to provide a national rather than regional reward. Queen's Park dominated the early competition and took the first three trophies, only Third Lanark managing to take them to a replay in that time. After three years of Vale of Leven winning until the turn of the decade in 1880, Queen's would then take seven of the next thirteen cups, their last trophy coming in 1893 with a 2-1 victory over fellow Glaswegians Celtic. That Scottish Cup would also mark the club's last major honour of their era of domination, as the professional game began to leave them behind. During that spell they had left another note in the football record books, competing in a second national competition with some success. As dual members of both the Scottish and English Football Associations, they had been allowed to compete in the FA Cup.

Queen's Park had been entered in the first ever FA Cup in 1872, receiving a walkover though to the semi-finals to be played at the Kennington Oval. After playing out a 0-0 draw with Wanderers, financial constraints meant the Scottish club simply couldn't afford to play a replay. Wanderers received a bye to the final in the light of Queen's Park's enforced withdrawal and went on to defeat the Royal Engineers 1-0 to become the competition's first winners. Over the next ten years Queen's Park could only take part when financially able to do so but in 1884, they not only competed in the competition, they reached the final.

The previous year's FA Cup had seen its first northern winners, Blackburn Olympic, and 1884's tournament looked to be even more open to another winner from north of London. Queen's Park began with a 10-0 drubbing of Crewe Alexandra away from home and even more impressively, defeated Manchester 15-0 in the second round. Their imperious form continued as they beat Oswestry away 7-1, and then Midlands club Aston Villa 6-1. The quarter-finals brought a tighter contest with Old Westminsters but once again, Queen's emerged triumphant to set up an even tougher tie against holders Blackburn Olympic in the semi-final. What looked like being a close game was in reality a comfortable 4-1 victory to put Queen's Park through to the final.

The Kennington Oval played host to the Scottish club for the second time in its history and for the second time, the result went against Queen's Park. After shading the first half but finishing 2-1 behind, they struggled to make any impact against opponents Blackburn Rovers in the second half. Unable to force an equaliser, Rovers held off the Scottish challenge to take the trophy. Queen's Park had been impressive throughout but ultimately, failed at the final hurdle.

The following year saw Queen's Park set about trying to atone for their loss. In the largest ever field for the cup – 114 teams accepted the FA's initial invitation – they were awarded a walkover in their first game as Stoke couldn't fulfil the fixture. The second round saw a rematch with Crewe Alexandra still smarting from the previous years 10-0 mauling but a much tighter game saw Queen's Park win 2-1. They marched on all the way to the final following wins over Leek, Old Wykehamists, Notts County and Nottingham Forest, the last two ties requiring replays to settle them.

The final gave them the chance to avenge the previous years loss as they faced Blackburn Rovers once again. Queen's Park took their nerves into the game and struggled right from the off with Rovers taking the initiative and scoring twice in the first half. Despite a huge effort from the Queen's Park players to get back into the game, Rovers held out and had repeated their triumph of the previous year. The Scottish FA banned their clubs from competing in the English FA's premier tournament in 1887 and Queen's Park's FA Cup history ended. The prestige of being runners-up twice lives on but the disappointment of never having taken the FA Cup back to Scotland remains one of football's great missed (and perhaps deserved) opportunities.

Queen's Park's latter achievements or lack there of have all been dictated more or less by their amateur status. They were the instigators and innovators at Scottish football's birth and still play at Hampden Park, the country's national stadium. They may never have been truly successful in the modern era as professionalism has marginalised them more and more, but they remain a club rightly proud of their place in football history.

The Queen's Park Football Club's reasons for appearing in this book are obvious. They created a passing game that would eventually reach across the breadth of the football world in part as a result of their willingness to spread it. Their style of play created a 'Scottish' method that in time would influence some of the greatest football teams in the game's history. Aside from 'combination' football, the impact they had on the Scottish and English game at domestic and international level should not be underestimated either.

Darwen Football Club 1878–79

Honours

First Northern Club to reach the F.A. Cup Quarter Finals

First Game under lights played in October 1878 at Darwen's Ground, Barley Bank

1st Round Proper					
Darwen	W	v	W	Birch	Home Walkover
2nd Round Proper					
Darwen	0	v	0	Eagley	
Darwen	4	v	1	Eagley	Replay
3rd Round Proper					
Remnants	2	v	3	Darwen	
Quarter Finals					
Old Etonians	5	v	5	Darwen	
Old Etonians	2	v	2	Darwen	Replay
Old Etonians	6	v	2	Darwen	Replay

Darwen's F.A. Cup Results 1878-79

On New Years Day 1878, Darwen Football Club played Partick Thistle in what was a largely uneventful game. Thistle had journeyed down from Glasgow to play some of the better English teams from the north of the country in a short tour. The day after the game at Darwen's home ground Barley Bank, Thistle went on to play against Blackburn Rovers and the games could have been lost to the history books without incident. However, two of Partick Thistle's players had enjoyed the trip so much they were unwittingly about to write themselves into the football folklore. Although Darwen FC had no idea at the time, they were about to help change the game forever.

Playing for Thistle that day two attacking players were impressed with the set-up at Darwen – James 'Jimmy' Love and Fergus 'Fergie' Suter. The Lancashire team formed part of a combined cricket and football club playing in a joint ground at Barley Bank. Founded in 1870 by the coming together of two local mill teams, the owners of the larger Orchard Mill retained the controlling interest of the club and provided financial backing as and when required. They had quickly risen to become one of the leading teams in the North West of England and the friendly against Partick carried a certain amount of prestige as they had been specifically selected as a challenge.

Love and Suter played in the friendly and then wrote to Darwen FC, Suter explaining that they had been impressed with the area and were thinking of relocating. Keen to carry on their playing careers both men wanted to move and the club immediately responded positively to the idea of them joining.

Scottish players had already built up a reputation for technical ability that surpassed their English counterparts and both players exemplified this. Suter was one of the best of his generation and his interest in playing for Darwen would be rewarded with a first team place immediately. Within weeks the move was done and Suter, a stonemason by trade, settled in Darwen straight away. Love also moved and took a job at the Orchard Mill, helped by the club's owners who controlled both organisations. Both men began playing for Darwen as soon as their moves were complete but soon they would be mired in controversy, as rumours of professionalism spread.

Suter was never seen carrying out any of the stonemasonry he claimed to be working on. Within weeks of his move he had given up stonework all together, claiming that English stone was too difficult to work compared to the Scottish granite he was used to. Speculation was rife as the improbable situation of a player moving from Scotland, and then remaining in the area with no source of income pointed to only one thing – Darwen Football Club were paying Suter to play. The same accusation was levelled at Love but his job at the mill seemed to provide adequate explanation for most observers. Some still believed that neither player would have moved to the area without some sort of inducement from the club, a charge Darwen FC would strenuously deny.

History never proved conclusively that these two Scottish players were the first professional footballers but the evidence is damning. Darwen would continue to deny the allegations of professionalism but it was widely known that both men would often 'find' money in their boots on match days. The game was suddenly awash with stories of players signing for clubs and receiving a fee for doing so or a well-paid job in the local area. There was also talk of expenses payments that varied greatly from player to player.

What is clear is that whilst playing for Darwen, Suter would never pursue a career in anything other than football. In later life he would go on to admit he'd 'interview the treasurer as the occasion arose'. He had also flirted with professional football before the move with reports of an alleged £3 payment to play for Turton Football Club in a cup competition surfacing earlier in his career. Love would never stir the same controversy as after two seasons at Darwen, he took the decision to join the Royal Navy. Tragically he never returned to the area, dying in the bombardment of Alexandria in 1882.

As well as the constant allegations off the pitch, 1878-79 would also find Darwen making headlines on it. They would become the first Northern club to reach the quarter finals of the FA Cup after a turbulent campaign, eventually losing after two replays to Old Etonians who would go on to win the cup. After a walkover in the first round, Darwen were drawn against a very good Eagley side in round two. After a goalless draw in which Darwen played with only ten men for the whole game, the replay saw Love score a hat trick before half time and Darwen run out 4-1 winners. After an away victory at Remnants, Darwen took on the highly fancied Etonians on their home ground and played out an incredible five-all draw. Etonians had asked for Love and Suter to be withdrawn as they were sure Darwen were fielding them as paid professional players. In the light of no hard evidence of the claim and Darwen's continued rebuttals, the request was denied and another draw was recorded taking the tie to a third game. Despite holding them twice, Etonians took the upper hand early and Darwen never recovered, eventually losing 6-2.

Darwen also initiated the formation of a Lancashire Football Association in October 1878 and in the same month, took place in one of the first recorded football games to be played under lights. Borrowing two 'magneto electric engines' from the Orchard Mill, Barley Bank played host to three thousand spectators as Darwen defeated an invitational Blackburn Olympic side 3-0.

Despite the relative F.A. Cup successes, technical innovations and administration advances made by the club, it was professionalism that would be Darwen FC's legacy. By 1885 the Football Association had to embrace the top clubs willingness to pay their players and legalize professionals in the game. By this time Suter had gone on to become a highly controversial figure in the area. Moving to Blackburn Rovers in the 1880/81 season, he had once more come under the spotlight for claims of professionalism. The first game between the two sides after his move had to be abandoned in the second half, the fights breaking out on the pitch after an incident involving Suter spread to the crowd and the referee gave up trying to regain control. The atmosphere had been stoked by Darwen's somewhat hypocritical announcement that they would only field players that were 'Darwen born and bred' in an attempt to embarrass Blackburn for turning Suter's head.

Nowadays, Darwen Football Club is no more. The phoenix club AFC Darwen was raised in 2009 in the light of the financial collapse of the old team. Whilst originally embracing professionalism, Darwen never really sat at the top table with the biggest teams in the country. The high points in the clubs history were an FA Cup semi-final appearance in 1881 and election into the Football League in 1891. Some sporadic local success throughout the twentieth century and a third round FA Cup tie against national champions Arsenal in 1931 seem scant reward for a team so important in the formation of the professional game.

In reality if Darwen FC hadn't been the first to pay their players for playing for the club, someone else would have. Football was on the rise nationally and the crowds it was now drawing meant the game was already becoming a profitable business. James Love and Fergus Suter might have been the first but the change to professionalism was inevitable, Darwen FC was just the first club to realise it.

Blackburn Olympic 1882–83

Honours

First Winners of FA Cup to come from North of London

1872	Wanderers	1	v	0	Royal Engineers	
1873	Wanderers	2	v	0	Oxford University	
1874	Oxford University	2	v	0	Royal Engineers	
1875	Royal Engineers	2	v	0	Old Etonians	⋆
1876	Wanderers	3	v	0	Old Etonians	⋆
1877	Wanderers	2	v	1	Oxford University	⋆⋆
1878	Wanderers	3	v	1	Royal Engineers	
1879	Old Etonians	1	v	0	Clapham Rovers	
1880	Clapham Rovers	1	v	0	Oxford University	
1881	Old Carthusians	3	v	0	Old Etonians	
1882	Old Etonians	1	v	0	Blackburn Rovers	

⋆ = Replay, ⋆⋆ = AET

First eleven FA Cup finals, all winners from Southern England

For football to become a global game it needed to be truly national within England. While pockets of teams and rules existed all over the country, it needed a unifying competition from one association to marshal the various different forms of the game. As football emerged a north-south divide also arose, the northern mill and factory teams deemed as working class compared to southern university 'gentlemen' playing the game. The FA Cup would provide the impetus for football to change those perceptions but the trophy would remain in the South of England for over a decade before Blackburn Olympic finally managed to take it north in 1883.

The Football Association first came into being in October 1863 after a meeting at the Freemason's Tavern in London. With twelve local clubs and schools present, a set of 14 laws was agreed that set the framework the game would take in the future. After losing one of their representatives straight away due to the decision to outlaw 'hacking', the eleven left now became the founding members of the FA. With areas playing football throughout the country but to their own rules, the FA now provided an organisation for teams to join and play in a codified fashion. With Ebenezer Cobb Morley installed as the first Secretary of the FA, the first game under the new 'Football Association Rules' took place weeks later in the January of 1864.

At first the FA members and rules remained very much localized to the London area. As football grew across the country clubs remained initially resistant to the idea of joining a London based organisation, whose rules they had to adhere to when they could have been very different in their local area. The FA continued to refine and change the laws of the game, introducing a designated goalkeeper and offside laws for instance, but as the game's popularity grew so did the divisions between groups of teams playing to their own code.

Football had become the spectator sport of the masses and the FA was keen to capitalise on this popularity. By 1871 plans were in place, proposed principally by then secretary Charles Alcock, for a Challenge Cup between all members. Taking the knockout form of many local and interschool competitions nationally, the rules were agreed and members invited. A trophy was ordered from Martin, Hall, & Co for the price of £20 and fifteen clubs accepted the chance to play for what would become known as the FA Cup.

The first cup was won by a team who would dominate the trophy's early years. The Wanderers were based in London's Wandsworth with no fixed home ground and at the time had a huge influence within the game and the FA. Captained by Charles Alcock who had proposed the tournament itself, Wanderers took the first ever FA Cup after defeating the Royal Engineers 1-0 in a final played at the Kennington Oval. The Oval would remain predominantly the home of the final until 1892 when it began a pilgrimage that would eventually lead it to Wembley in 1923. Wanderers would go on to win five of the first seven competitions, taking it three times in a row between 1876 and 1878. As the tournament grew and newspaper coverage became more widespread, entrants began to emerge from far and wide wanting to compete in the national competition.

By 1882, Northern England had embraced both the FA and it's cup. Football in the north had been heavily influenced by the Scottish game and its popularity had continued to grow to almost unprecedented levels. Whereas southern clubs were largely made up of university teams, former school players, and so called 'gentleman' footballers, northern clubs were birthed from the mills and factories and largely made up of the workers therein. Blackburn Rovers had provided the north with it's first ever FA Cup finalists and despite the Old Etonians ultimately triumphing 1-0, there was a general feeling that the balance of power on the pitch was shifting towards teams based north of London.

The 1883 FA Cup competition began with 84 teams accepting the invitation compared to the 15 who entered the first ever tournament in 1871. Along with Blackburn Olympic and Blackburn Rovers, teams from Blackpool, Nottingham, Sheffield, Manchester, Grimsby, and Liverpool would all take part. In the previous year's final Rovers had been heavy favourites but had fallen at the last: this time they were expected to see it through. Blackburn Olympic were considered a good if not great side, a distant second to Rovers in the area but ambitious. In reality Olympic were about to make their own footnote in football history, with an inspirational character driving them forward and an almost unparalleled work ethic.

Olympic had only come into being in the late 1870's, as Blackburn became a hotbed for football's growth. By 1877 the area boasted a thriving league with twelve major clubs vying for local honours. While Rovers were acknowledged to be the largest club in the area, there was still space for others to emerge and become competitive. Olympic formed as two smaller clubs decided to pool their talents in order for a greater chance of success. Black Star and James Street became Blackburn Olympic and took place in their first competitive games in early 1878. Two years later they took part in their first ever FA Cup competition, losing 5-4 in the first round having been drawn away to Sheffield. The following year they watched Rovers reach the final from afar as once again they suffered a first round defeat, this time to local rivals Darwen. By 1883's competition there was little to suggest on paper Olympic were about to have any sort of run in the competition, let alone win it.

However the results didn't tell the full story. The previous years away draws at Sheffield and Darwen would have been a tough start for any team in the country, let alone such a new one in an area where the search for players was so competitive. Lancashire was also at the hub of many of the controversies surrounding the emerging 'problem' of professionalism, and Olympic were still a relatively small fish in a large pond. In 1882 in a major coup they attracted one Jack Hunter to the club as a player in the dotage of his career, but also as a forward thinking coach. The move would be significant as he revitalised the club on the pitch and took huge strides to help his players off it.

Hunter was a former England international and captain who had spent the largest part of his career playing for clubs in the Sheffield area. After moving to Blackburn for work he was contacted by Olympic and accepted the chance to coach and play for his local side. Playing in defence had given him the ability to see the game as a whole and he immediately coached Olympic to play in the passing style of the Scottish teams. Hunter had been suspected of taking payment for playing previously and had been in contact with the Scottish 'professors' around whom the professionalism rumours began. He had been influenced by the short passing and high fitness levels of those he'd seen and now had a chance to form a team in his own image. Dropping a man back from the front line to link play between the defence and attack, he concentrated on getting his Olympic players as fast and fit as possible. The gentlemen of the south with largely better diets and facilities would have to compete with the pace and passing of the northern mill workers.

With Hunter leading the team Olympic's amateurs set about achieving what had been seen as almost impossible. Boasting mill staff, a plumber, a picture framer, a foundry worker, a dental assistant, and pub landlords in their side, the first round draw was slightly more favourable than it had been previously and pitted them at home against fellow Lancastrians Accrington. After a good game between two sides both trying to adopt the passing style, Olympic triumphed with a convincing 6-3 victory although locally they were completely eclipsed by Rovers resounding 11-1 victory over Blackpool St. John's.

The second round threw up a huge clash between Darwen and Blackburn Rovers. A tight game saw the previous year's finalists Rovers lose 1-0 in somewhat of a shock as they were widely considered to be northern football's best chance to win. As Darwen celebrated their progress Olympic also progressed in a local derby, this time with Lower Darwen who were put to the sword with an 8-1 romp at Olympic's home ground – the Hole-i'-th'-Wall – named after a local public house. Rovers shock exit received most of the local press but Olympic it was noted, were making tidy progress. The third round draw gave them a home tie against another side from Darwen, the Ramblers. Olympic romped to an 8-0 win and were now just beginning to look like possible contenders.

Still led by Hunter and playing a fast passing game at odds with many of their opponents, another local rival – Church – were swiftly beaten 2-0 to see

Olympic into the quarterfinals. This time the draw put them against Welsh side Druids, easily the strongest team they'd faced, and despite another home tie it was widely expected that their campaign was about to end. In front of their biggest crowd to date Olympic played superbly. After taking a first half lead they never looked back and dispatched Druids 4-1. Many were quick to cite a poor performance from the Welsh side but Olympic had made their point, they had taken their biggest test so far and passed.

A semi-final against Old Carthusians was won in similar fashion, 4-0 with Olympic never looking in danger. Almost without anyone noticing, they were heading to the Oval for the final. Their opponents would be Old Etonians, conquerors of Rovers the previous year and holders. Hunter took his team to Blackpool to prepare, a move that caused some consternation in the strictly amateur climate. While there his team lived and trained together, Hunter controlling their activities, diet and drinking. By the time they took the pitch on the 31st March 1883, despite a hugely partisan crowd cheering for the gentlemen from Eton and all pre-game articles and comment making them heavy under dogs, Olympic knew if they played to their best they could take the FA Cup north for the first time in its history.

Etonians were playing in their third successive FA Cup final and started much the better, taking the lead through forward Harry Goodhart. Olympic were not to be overawed by the occasion though and in the second half equalised through Arthur Matthews. With full time up both sides agreed to play half an hour of extra time and Olympic's superior fitness turned the tide in their favour. Olympic nudged ahead through Jimmy Costley's volley and never looked back, seeing out the 2-1 victory that no one had expected. They returned to a heroes welcome in Blackburn, their victory standing for more than just Olympic fans. Northern working class teams had finally made an inroad in to the dominance of the southern gents. Football had become the game of the people, and now it ran the full length of the country.

Blackburn Olympic opened the door, Blackburn Rovers then kicked it through in fine style with three successive FA Cup victories in 1884, '85, and '86. It was then the Midlands turn as Aston Villa and West Bromwich Albion took the trophy. What had once been seen as a game for the establishment was now a truly national pursuit.

Olympic's time in the sun was brief, dissolving in 1889 in the wake of the newly formed Football League's decision to take Rovers as Blackburn's entrants. Despite their brief tenure as a football club, Olympic had managed to matter to English football for helping to change the perception of the game. From the moment the perceived aristocrats were defeated for the first time, the artisans of the north never looked back.

Corinthian FC 1882–1939

Honours

Sheriff of London Charity Shield Winners 1898 (Shared with Sheffield United), 1900, & 1904

24.08.1910	Fluminense	1	v	10	Corinthians
26.08.1910	Rio XI	1	v	8	Corinthians
28.08.1910	The Brazilians	2	v	5	Corinthians
31.08.1910	Palmeiras	0	v	2	Corinthians
02.09.1910	Paulistano	0	v	5	Corinthians
04.09.1910	Sao Paulo AC	2	v	8	Corinthians

Details of 1910 Tour to Brazil, Corinthian finished having played 6, won 6.

On the 18th November 2009 at the Stade de France in Paris, a play-off game between France and the Republic of Ireland moved into extra time. The prize for the winner was a place at the 2010 World Cup in South Africa. In the 102nd minute France won a free kick and took the opportunity to load the Irish penalty area with blue shirts. With plenty to aim for, Florent Malouda played the ball to the back post where striker Thierry Henry was lurking.

After slightly misjudging the bounce Henry tried to bring the ball under control with a deliberate touch on his left forearm. After an unsuccessful first attempt, Henry then flicked out his hand to bring the ball back into his path. Despite the double infringement the expected referee's whistle never came and a grateful William Gallas bundled the ball home from Henry's pass. The goal would prove to be decisive, causing a storm in Ireland, Henry was accused of bringing the game in disrepute and demands were made for a rematch. Despite the outrage and controversy the result had to stand, France had qualified for South Africa and Henry had managed to cheat successfully.

Football's littered with stories that are used to point to a supposed lack of morals within the game. Henry's handball joined Maradona's 'Hand of God' as an infamous and quite deliberate example of cheating. From diving becoming more prevalent in the game globally to the use of intimidation to influence a referee, on the pitch there is more than enough evidence for those wishing to disparage the game. As football comes under a more intense media spotlight than ever before, so it attracts negativity and controversy as every action and decision is analysed by a raft of pundits. Off the pitch a new level of celebrity and 'wag' culture means that many of football's biggest headlines have nothing to do with a ball or even a referee.

In the face of the growing army of football's detractors it's important to remember the game can also be a positive influence. Many football related charities and organisations operate successfully and help people of all ages across the globe. Sport is often a unifying force and its power to heal should not be underestimated. The game has an almost unique ability to generate vast income and many clubs now have their own foundations and support events such as Football Aid and Kick4Life. Barcelona recently paid UNICEF nearly $10m over five years for their shirt sponsorship in a uniquely structured deal, where the club paid for the privilege to use their name. Tournaments such as the Homeless World Cup are receiving more coverage than ever before and football's ability to give has never been greater.

One club took this to an extreme long before the media spotlight burned so bright – vowing to remain an amateur side and only compete for competitions with charitable aims. They became a 'missionary' team, travelling the world to take on all comers and leaving a legacy wherever they went. What is all the more extraordinary is the standard of football they were able to achieve even with amateur status. They regularly played fully professional sides in Britain and around the world and beat them convincingly, taking on FA Cup winners and even national sides on occasion. Above all though the team stood for what they believed was the right way to play football, refusing to even take or save a penalty as they believed no player would deliberately set out to commit a foul on another. The team was the London based Corinthian FC and they would leave a mark on football from the shores of Brazil to the Madridistas of Spain.

Corinthian were formed in 1882 by a group of like minded individuals desperate to build a team who could challenge what was then Scottish dominance. It was decided the club would never compete in competition and the very highest standards of sportsmanship would be upheld at all times. The team would compete largely in the London area in 'challenge' matches and try to retain a pool of players who could regularly play and train together. The ultimate aim was to mirror the Scottish success achieved by having a group of players largely from Glasgow who could regularly get together. Many of their players would also play for various universities and institutions at the same time as keeping their place in the Corinthian's playing pool, another reflection of the staunchly amateur status valued so highly by the club.

As a result many of their players had dual affiliations throughout their careers, including when playing for England. In 1894 and 1895 in games against Wales, the England team was made up of players who all had an allegiance to Corinthian. Despite essentially supplying the entire national side, Corinthian couldn't claim this as a record due to the players differing club associations. The club supplied a vast number of England internationals before the professional game raised standards across the country significantly, and the national team's performances improved as a result. The ultimate aim of overcoming Scotland's superiority was achieved, as England became football's real powerhouse in the early 20th Century.

The club's results over its existence are the smallest part of its history. The first competition they officially competed in was the 1898 Sheriff of London Charity Shield, the forerunner of today's traditional Community Shield season opener. Approving of the charitable aims of the game, Corinthian would take the shield three times – particularly impressive when you consider the game was between the best amateur side in England and the best professional. The competition ran from 1898 to 1907 when three years of professional dominance meant the game had lost its edge.

With the formation of a new AFA (Amateur Football Association) after a growing unease over professionalism in 1907, the Sheriff of London Shield became the Football Association's Charity Shield prohibiting the now AFA affiliated Corinthians from playing. A return to the professionals versus amateurs format for a spell in the 1920's saw Corinthian lose 2-1 to FA Cup holders Cardiff City, and they regularly supplied players for several English Amateur XI's in the competition.

After the First World War Corinthian broke with tradition and entered the FA Cup. While they never achieved huge success in the competition, they did take part in some memorable games against their professional counterparts. Throughout their history they had been England's unofficial 'best' team and games against FA Cup winners had often been cited as proof. After winning the 1884 cup final with a tense 2-1 victory over Queens Park, Blackburn Rovers played Corinthian at home and were thrashed 8-1 to the amazement of the newspapers. In 1903, Bury turned Derby County over 6-0 to take the cup, and were then promptly taken apart by a rampant Corinthian side 10-3. A year later they recorded another huge victory over a professional side, beating Manchester United 11-3.

By the time they entered the FA Cup in 1923 professional football had advanced but Corinthian still took Brighton and Hove Albion to two replays before losing 1-0. The following year they beat Blackburn Rovers before losing to West Bromwich Albion. Corinthian's status in the English game was cemented in 1925 when in a drastic reorganisation of the tournament they joined teams from England's top two divisions in being granted a bye until the third round proper. Now they were only joining the competition when the best professional clubs in England did. Without the aspect of league participation it seemed there was now a barometer to measure their standing in the game.

Their real legacy came as a result of their decision to take to touring the world. The split and formation of the AFA initially prohibited Corinthian playing professional sides domestically. After a hugely successful tour of Northern England in 1884, Corinthian realised the trip had massively advanced their standing and ideals in the game as a whole. Now aware of the huge impact the experience had on their game and those who they played against, Corinthian became one of the most travelled teams in the world. Between 1897 and 1939 they took part in tours of South Africa (3 times), Hungary, Scandinavia, North America (3 times), Germany (twice), Holland (3 times), Brazil (twice), Paris, Switzerland, Prague (twice), Denmark (twice plus two games against Copenhagen in their Scandinavian tour), France and Belgium.

From these tours their sportsmanship and style of play left a huge impression in many areas of the world. A 1904 tour of Scandinavia saw them spend much of their time in Sweden where they became so fondly remembered, a cup competition beginning in 1906 was named 'the Corinthian Bowl' in their honour. They left such an impression on ex-patriot Arthur Johnson they'd become his favourite club back in England. Now in Spain and playing for Real Madrid where he would later become manager, Johnsen became famous for not only scoring their first ever goal against Barcelona in 1902, but also suggesting Madrid take the same team colours – all white with blue trim – as his favourite team Corinthian. He'd studied the English team and admired their dedication despite amateur status. The reasoning behind taking their colours was by extension a move towards taking their work ethic and attitude. Real Madrid now have many nicknames but among the most prominent are Los Blancos (the whites) and Los Merengues (the meringues), both references to the now legendary white shirts that they have worn ever since.

The 1910 tour of Brazil saw Corinthian leave perhaps the biggest single legacy that remains in the game today. Not only did they play brilliantly against all comers, including a Brazilian team drawn from the best players in Rio, they played in a style that inspired as much as it surprised. Five spectators had been so impressed by the touring English team that they decided to form their own club named Sport Club Corinthians Paulisto. Taking the team's white shirts as well as their name, the São Paulo version of Corinthians are not only one of the biggest teams in Brazil, but in 2000 won the FIFA Club World Championship to give a famous name global recognition. They have become known as a team of the people and attract vast support, numbering among their ex-alumni Garrincha, Zé Maria, Carlos Tévez, Serginho, Rivaldo, Marcos Senna and perhaps their two most revered graduates – the brilliant Rivelino and the inspirational Sócrates. In 2010 the first team squad could boast both legendary attacking fullback Roberto Carlos, and three times FIFA World Player of the Year Ronaldo for their centenary year. The 'gentlemen' from England had birthed a great club bearing their name.

Corinthian's achievements in taking the English game to all corners of the world far outweigh anything a bulging trophy cabinet could have proved. Despite providing over 100 full England internationals and gaining limited success as an amateur side in the Shield and FA Cup, worldwide they are remembered for so much more. In 1939 with fortunes declining and professionalism fast increasing the gap between the AFA and FA at an unstoppable rate, Corinthian merged with another great amateur side – The Casuals – and their era of contributing to football's emergence had ended. The game had arrived worldwide and with it unfortunately, a professional approach that the amateurs just couldn't keep up with.

The Corinthian Casuals website still bears the hallmark of the club's conception. On the home page you are greeted with the statement *'The aims of the Club are to promote fair play and sportsmanship, to play competitive football at the highest level possible whilst remaining strictly amateur and retaining the ideals of the Corinthian and the Casuals Football Clubs'*. While they have never reached the standards they once achieved, no one can deny their history.

If you wanted to ask why Corinthian mattered I would give you a choice. They could be in here because they gave Real Madrid a key part of their identity – who can think of Los Blancos without thinking of those famous white shirts? They could also be in here because of the fact they gave birth to a Brazilian football club with a reported 25 million supporters, and who went on to nurture the talent of several of the world's greatest ever players. If you wanted to keep things completely domestically centered, you could point to the achievements and recognition they gained while remaining amateur, including the huge amount of England internationals that could claim allegiance with the club. They are in here for all of the above and more, a club who took a moral stance to the game and kept their standard unashamedly high. They were and are a truly great club who inspired and played in a 'Corinthian Spirit' that claimed global recognition. Their time might have passed but they will never be forgotten, here or in the football world as a whole.

Middlesbrough F.C. 1904–05

Honours

Finished 15th in the English First Division

1905	Alf Common	*Sunderland to Middlesbrough*	£1,000
1928	David Jack	*Bolton Wanderers to Arsenal*	£10,890
1957	John Charles	*Leeds United to Juventus*	£65,000
1961	Denis Law	*Manchester City to Torino*	£100,000
1977	Kevin Keegan	*Liverpool to Hamburg SV*	£500,000
1979	Trevor Francis	*Birmingham City to Nottingham Forest*	£1,180,000
1991	David Platt	*Aston Villa to Bari*	£5,500,000
1996	Alan Shearer	*Blackburn Rovers to Newcastle United*	£15,000,000
2006	Andriy Shevchenko	*AC Milan to Chelsea*	£30,800,000
2009	Cristiano Ronaldo	*Manchester United to Real Madrid*	£80,000,000

Evolution of transfer record involving British clubs since Common's £1,000 move

Since professional football began, players have always moved from club to club creating equal quantities of delight and despair for fans and chairman alike. Transfers have always been littered with controversy, excess, and sometimes the downright bizarre. From Cristiano Ronaldo's record-breaking transfer fee in 2009, to Tony Cascarino moving to Gillingham from Crockenhill for a set of tracksuits in 1981, player's movements always generate interest. While the transfer windows now provide only a limited time for the speculation, acquisition, and idle gossip to occur, the amount of money passing between clubs continues to outstrip inflation with no ceiling yet in sight.

Managers and players have always approached the transfer system from very different viewpoints. Managers can become renowned for their 'wheeling and dealing', achieving the ultimate by buying a fleet-footed diamond for peanuts and depending on the ambitions of their club, either selling for a huge profit or enjoying a long and successful career from the player involved. For example, when Alex Ferguson paid Leeds United just £1.2m for Eric Cantona in 1992, he signed a player who would become a catalyst for the greatest era of success in the club's history. Similarly, when Liverpool manager Bob Paisley paid a reportedly record fee (£300,000) for a teenager named Ian Rush, he paid them back with a career spanning over six hundred games and just shy of three hundred and fifty goals. Some players even enjoy the weight of expectation a record transfer fee brings – Alan Shearer smashed the British transfer record in 1996 with a £15m move to Newcastle United and repaid a huge chunk immediately by finishing as the league's top scorer with twenty-five goals.

Just as a transfer can inspire and motivate, the stigma of an over inflated fee can become a burden – Kevin Davies (Southampton to Blackburn in 1998, £7.5m), Garry Birtles (Nottingham Forest to Manchester United in 1980, £1.25m), and Albert Luque (Deportivo La Coruña to Newcastle United in 2005, £9.5m) all laboured to live up to the amount of money paid for their signature. While Manchester United won with the Cantona transfer in 1992, they lost in 2001 by paying £28.1m to Lazio for Juan Sebastian Veron's services. Veron failed to justify his price tag and was sold to Chelsea for a near fifty percent loss after just two seasons at Old Trafford.

The transfer system is a gamble with as many triumphs as spectacular failures. So many factors contribute to a player's success that most football fans can tell you a story of a striker who blew most of their transfer budget and never performed, just as they can tell you of a player they virtually stole from another team who surpassed their transfer fee so far they became a club legend. While fans will debate and celebrate their club's transfer history in equal measure, they also know there is another side to the system – controversy –

that means certain deals will go down in infamy regardless of a player's performance.

When Jean-Marc Bosman changed the face of the transfer system in 1990 by creating the law that allowed players to move for no fee once their contracts had expired, a sixteen-year old Tottenham Hotspur youth team player named Sol Campbell might have not paid much attention. Eleven years later however and after thirteen seasons on Spurs's books, with his contract drawing to a close Campbell had remained hesitant to talk about his future throughout the 2000-01 season. Many of Europe's top clubs circled the England international and Spurs resigned themselves to losing a player they had raised through the ranks for no fee. As his contract ended Campbell rocked the English football world by moving on a free transfer to Tottenham's closest and most hated rivals Arsenal. Apoplectic with rage, Spurs fans labelled Campbell 'Judas' and he remains a hate figure for the club's fans today.

Just as controversial but for different reasons was the transfer of Carlos Tévez to West Ham United in 2006. Arriving in a joint deal with Javier Mascherano from Brazilian club Corinthians, the structure of Tévez's deal was murky due to the issue of 'ownership' of the player. Rather than a simple transfer from club to club it emerged that Tévez's playing contract was in part owned by a sports investment company. After being found to breach Premier League rules in signing the players, West Ham were fined over £5m but crucially didn't receive the points deduction that had been suggested. Regardless of the controversy Tévez became a key figure for West Ham, contributing hugely to the clubs relegation battle and scoring the only goal in a final day win at Old Trafford that sealed their safety. As the season ended relegated Sheffield United challenged the Premier League ruling and demanded to be reinstated in West Ham's place, arguing they had in large survived thanks to a transfer that shouldn't have been allowed to happen. After a two year legal battle between the clubs, West Ham United agreed an out of court settlement of £20m to be paid to Sheffield United in compensation for Tévez's transfer. Tévez himself had moved again at the end of the season to Manchester United in a deal originally structured as a loan to avoid similar pitfalls.

So how does all this link to Middlesbrough's team of the 1904-05 season? Well, before Sol Campbell there was a highly controversial figure involved in a well-publicised transfer that outraged fans. Before Trevor Francis became the first one million pound footballer in England in 1979, a player broke the £1,000 barrier to the disgust and outrage of the public and football's authorities. Lastly, before Carlos Tévez helped West Ham avoid relegation in controversial circumstances, a player had been signed long before for the same purpose and also succeeded despite the vitriol from the press.

Alfred Common had already enjoyed a colourful career up until the 1904-05 season. Alf, as he was known, had begun his playing career in the amateur leagues of the North East of England before signing for Sunderland. After breaking into the first team in 1900 as both centre forward and at times outside right, Sunderland finished the season in second place just two points behind Liverpool. Common had become one of the most noted young players in the English game and in October of 1901, he was transferred to Sheffield United for £325.

Whilst at Sheffield United Common had a huge impact. In his first season he scored in the FA Cup final against Southampton and helped his club lift the trophy for the second time in their history. Now recognised as one of the best young goal scorers in the country, he also contributed to a tenth place league finish. In 1902/03 they failed to defend the cup but finished a more than respectable fourth in the league, a finish marred only by local rivals The Wednesday winning the title. In the 03/04 season United finished seventh but it was a landmark season for Common. On the 29th February 1904, Common represented his country for the first time in a 2-2 draw with Wales at the Racecourse Ground in Wrexham. Whilst he failed to get on the scoresheet he was instrumental in getting England back into the game after being 2-0 down at halftime. Twelve days later he earned his second cap in Belfast in a 3-1 victory over Ireland. Common produced a man of the match display and scored in each half to add to Aston Villa's Joseph Bache's twelfth minute goal. Amid rumours of homesickness Common told Sheffield United he wouldn't be playing for them in the 1904/05 season and moved back to Sunderland for a reportedly record fee of £520.

Common struggled to settle back at Sunderland. By now he was known for three things – his obvious talent, his love of practical jokes and his strength thanks in no small part to his 'robust' frame. Common would struggle with his weight throughout his career and obvious parallels with Paul Gascoigne aside, his second spell with Sunderland was making headlines in the North-East as he failed to live up to the fee and expectations.

Meanwhile in Teesside, Middlesbrough Football Club were struggling. Formed in 1876, the 'Boro turned professional in 1889 only to revert to amateur status just three years later. The club had enjoyed mild success; two F.A. Amateur Cup wins in 1895 and 1898 preceded a further move to professionalism in 1899. Promoted by the football league into Division Two, it took only three seasons to achieve a second place finish and entrance to English football's top tier. Up until the 1904-05 season they had enjoyed lower mid-table finishes and relative safety, but an awful start in 1904 saw them staring relegation in the face. This was an unthinkable result given the size of the clubs expenses, not least of which their new stadium Ayresome Park which had opened the previous season.

Drastic action was required. Middlesbrough's biggest problem was a lack of goals and or a proven goalscorer. Negotiations began with Sunderland about the possibility of bringing Common to the club. In February 1905, Middlesbrough created a maelstrom in the press and at the FA as they paid Sunderland what was viewed as an astronomical fee of £1000 for Common's services.

In footballing terms Common went on to become a success for the club. His first game was ironically an away fixture against one of his previous clubs, Sheffield United. Common scored a second half penalty to earn Middlesbrough a 1-0 win, their first away from home for nearly two years. His goals would steer the club away from the relegation and keep their place in the division. Middlesbrough finished fifteenth and the calculated gamble of paying such a huge fee for one player had paid off. Ironically the two teams who finished in the relegation places, Bury and Notts County, were not relegated due to the resizing of the league from eighteen to twenty clubs. Common would go on to play 168 league games for 'Boro, scoring 58 times for the club. He continued to struggle with his weight and courted controversy, becoming club captain and then being stripped of the honour as a punishment for drunken behaviour. In 1910 he moved to Woolwich Arsenal for no fee, and after two relatively successful seasons he was sold to Preston North End for £250. After 9 goals for the club over the course of the next year, Common retired from football after nearly 400 league appearances, over 120 goals, 3 England caps, 2 international goals, and over £2,000 in transfer fees.

Back in 1905 the shockwaves from Common's move reached the highest echelons of the game. The press seized on the 'disgusting' sum paid for one player, describing the transfer as everything from 'flesh and blood for sale' to raising the debate that money was ruining football. The players were compared to 'thoroughbred yearling racehorses in the market', the transfer system was even called a 'new type of white slave trade'. The Football Association immediately launched an investigation into the transfer and Middlesbrough's finances. They found nothing illicit in the financial aspect of Common's transfer but they did find records of illegal bonus payments made to players in the past. Common never played for the national side again and while the FA had struggled to find evidence of wrongdoing specifically, it's hard to see this as anything other than an unofficial punishment directly to the player.

Sheffield United were outraged at the profit Sunderland had achieved in such a short space of time on a player they had sold. There were calls to cap transfer fees just as the FA had attempted to impose a salary cap previously.

It was argued that the transfer system was unfair and what's more, unsportsmanlike, the ultimate indictment on a sport now making strides towards being considered the national game. The FA met and agreed to implement a transfer fee cap of £350 for any player purchase or sale. The ruling first came into effect in January 1908 and lasted just three months as the FA struggled to bring the clubs to task. The Common transfer had opened the door and clubs were now buying and selling players for bigger and bigger fees.

In 1913 George Utley broke the £2,000 barrier by moving from Barnsley to Sheffield United. In 1922 Syd Puddefoot moved to Falkirk from West Ham United for £5,000. When David Jack moved south to Arsenal from Bolton in 1928 for £10,890, the floodgates had been well and truly opened. To date the transfer fee has peaked at Christiano Ronaldo's move to Real Madrid for £80,000,000 but history predicts that it won't be long before we have the first £100million transfer in football. One wonders what the outraged journalists would have made of the sums paid today after the rage Common's fee had provoked.

Common himself left football and became a publican and local celebrity in Darlington. He died in 1946 at the age of 65 years old. Middlesbrough struggled for major honours during Common's time and found themselves yo-yoing between divisions in the twenties. The latter part of the century saw Middlesbrough earn their place in the Premier League and go to a UEFA Cup final in 2006. Their transfer record today stands at the reported £12.7m paid for striker Afonso Alves in 2008. Whilst a far cry from the £1000 that took Common to Teesside, the parallels drawn from that deal to the game today are obvious. Transfers will always generate controversy, hundreds of words in the sports pages, and it seems fees that will continue to rise as long as clubs believe that one player can make all the difference to their season.

S.G. Pro Vercelli Sezione Calcio 1907–22

Honours

Italian National Champions, 1908, 1909, 1910-11, 1911-12, 1912-13, 1920-21, 1921-22

'Football is not a game for little girls'

Italian football cliché, originally attributed to Guido Ara

U.S. Pro Vercelli Calcio's current status as a mid-table side in the midst of Italy's lower leagues belies a legacy that ensures their place as one of the most important teams in Italian football history. Between 1907 and 1922 Pro Vercelli not only dominated the country's football landscape in every conceivable way, they also revolutionised the way the sport would be approached forever.

Formed in 1892 as a branch of the city's gymnastics society, the authorities didn't establish its soccer team as a separate entity until 1903. Their first match under the name SG Pro Vercelli Sezione Calcio took place in August 1903, and by 1904 they were wearing the legendary white shirts that would become their hallmark. By 1907 they had worked their way into and then won the Italian Subs Division, therefore granting admittance into the top tiers of Italian football for the first time. Made up of regional competitions, then a play off league system for the winners of each, the Italian National League had been dominated thus far by the 'Cricket and Football' clubs of Genoa with 6 Championships, and Milan with 3. The only other team to challenge either Genoa or Milan's dominance was a Juventus side that took a single title in 1905, although this was in part due to F.C. Torinese forfeiting their fixtures as the club imploded to make way for Torino Football Club to emerge.

Pro Vercelli had by now built up the reputation in regional competition that they would go on to earn nationally. Nicknamed the 'Bianche Casacche' or 'White Shirts' by some, they had also earned the more telling 'Leoni' meaning 'the Lions'. Playing with the famous 'Midfield Line of Wonders' consisting of Guido Ara, captain Giuseppe Milano I, and Leone, they developed an aggressive playing style and were noted for their tough tackling and constant pressure on the ball. Coupled with this robust approach was the sheer athleticism of a team still made up of members of the gymnastic society.

With an average age of just twenty, almost instantly they became revered as the fittest and quickest team in the country. Eager to couple reputation with success, Pro Vercelli began to actively work on specific conditioning and fitness training for football. The stamina and speed advantage made them difficult for every team in the league to live with as general football training up until this point consisted of simply playing the game. After the established clubs had become accustomed to a reasonably universal pace, suddenly there was a team that they struggled to keep up with, let alone go stride for stride for the full length of the game. This athleticism, enthusiasm and at times outright aggression stood them well apart from their contemparies.

Not content with just the physical advantage, Pro Vercelli also became the first team to realise the importance of tactical training. They began regularly training for set pieces at either end of the pitch. Generally speaking, most Italian teams had little in the way of a strategic plan from game to game – it was simply a case of getting the ball as close to the opposition goal by any means possible. Pro Vercelli played a different style, they realised that possession was the key to victory. An ability to keep the ball in tandem with extra speed and energy made them unplayable at the end of games.

Physically and mentally better prepared than most they were eager not to waste the opportunity of a league ill equipped to deal with them. The top tier of Italian football was now waiting for Pro Vercelli just four short years since their first official fixture. Their success was inevitable and instant, their first two national titles coming in their first two years in the competition, 1908 and 1909.

The 1908 title win came via a 3-1 victory in their local championship play-off over the already established Juventus, then an undefeated record in the final round of games against U.S Milanese and Andrea Doria. In 1909 they beat Torino 3-1 on aggregate to earn a place in the national semi-finals, where after beating Genoa 4-3 they defeated U.S Milanese convincingly to retain their title for the first time. By now Pro Vercelli had a fervent support that made home games intimidating for visiting teams. Due to their provincial status and a team made up of local Italian players as opposed to the larger city teams that contained foreigners, they became a club followed by ardent Italian and Vercelli citizens. This small town club was taking on the larger established teams and winning, aggressive on the pitch and wildly partisan on the terraces.

They felt untouchable going into the 1909-10 season that would become notable and notorious in equal measure. A more natural league system consisting of 9 teams from around the country was adopted but the Italian Football Association (the FIGC) had no idea the controversy it would create.

Pro Vercelli predictably finished the season at the top of the league but Internazionale who finished level on points at the top had run them close. Both teams had an identical record – played sixteen, won twelve, drawn one, lost three. Two goals better off then the Milan side; Pro Vercelli claimed the title via a system of goal difference until the Italian Football Association decided to change the rules. The FIGC ordered the teams to meet in a play off to decide the actual league winners and Pro Vercelli immediately launched a protest that was promptly ignored. After an alleged conference with Internazionale the Football Association set a date for the play-off game.

The date fell at a time when any Pro Vercelli player with military connections would be committed to take part in an army tournament. At the time and with their all-Italian side it meant a virtual decimation of their squad. Despite numerous and reasonable requests to change the date, the Football Association dismissed them all and threatened Pro Vercelli with various sanctions including a lengthy ban if they didn't comply. Faced with no other option and with nearly all of their players committed elsewhere, a furious Pro Vercelli sent their fourth team to face Internazionale for the title of National Champions. Reports from the time suggest that the Pro Vercelli side contained players ranging in age from as young as ten to fifteen years old. Against the second best team in the country they really had very little chance. Losing the game 10-3 the trophy officially went to Internazionale but Pro Vercelli would forever protest that without interference, a third title in a row should've been theirs. The Italian F.A. banned Pro Vercelli in response to the appearance of their forth team but eventually relaxed their ban and allowed them to enter the following season as normal.

The 1910-11 season saw a wounded Leoni roar back and take the title, losing only once in the process. The following year the winners of two regionally classified and expanded leagues played off for the national title. Pro Vercelli defeated Venezia 13-0 on aggregate to take a fourth championship with ruthless efficiency. Destined to take a third title in a row – officially this time – the 1912-13 season saw teams from Southern Italy admitted into the competition for the first time and an unbeaten Pro Vercelli won nine out of ten fixtures in their regional qualification league. Progressing into another group stage for Northern Italy, Pro Vercelli remained unbeaten winning seven out of the eight fixtures, scoring twenty-one goals and equally as impressively, only conceding one. Facing Lazio in the National Championship final, Pro Vercelli won 6-0 and their reputation as possibly the best team in the world was now set in stone. Before the war took hold the team was invited to tour South America and play Flamengo and Botafogo in the belief that they were the best team in Europe.

In the following three seasons Pro Vercelli lost players to the Italian military including Guido Ara's brother Felice, who would tragically never return. They narrowly missed entry to the Northern Italian qualification league by one point in 1913. In the 1914-15 championship they achieved qualification but in a reduced league, they missed out to Torino at the semi-final stage. The National title was officially postponed between 1916 and 1919 as the war took hold in Europe but in 1919-20 the championship returned and a Pro Vercelli team in the middle of rebuilding itself once again fell at the semi-finals.

In the 1920-21 season Pro Vercelli became the premier club in Italy once more. In their regional classification league they qualified in second place for the semi-final leagues. Winning five out of their six fixtures they then faced Bologna in the Northern Italian final. A deserved 2-1 victory earned them their place in the National final against the Southern Italian champions Pisa, another 2-1 victory meant they had now taken their sixth title and once more looked untouchable. Playing in a vastly expanded Northern League Group after a change in Football Associations in 1921-22, they finished first with the stand out result of a 10-0 romp against Vicenza. In the game against the winners of Northern Group B Genoa, a 2-1 aggregate win saw them through to a national final against Southern Italian champions Fortitudo. A convincing 8-2 score line over two legs saw them crowned champions for what would be the last time to date and their legacy was almost complete.

There was no official European competition at the time of the great Pro Vercelli side but is in this era Liverpool toured Europe as English Champions and took on the best teams on the continent. They defeated all but one easily, touring from country to country and playing the national champions of each. When they came face to face with Pro Vercelli they could only struggle to a draw in a match billed as taking place between the two best teams in the world.

Between 1907 and 1922 Pro Vercelli rose to worldwide prominence, dominated the Italian National league and birthed three of the foundations of the country's modern game – tactical preparation, conditioning training and fervent support. Such was the influence of Pro Vercelli in the Italian game at the time, in 1910 the Italian national side played their first official fixture wearing white shirts in tribute to their country's most successful side. As well as copying the kit of the national champions they also fielded nine Pro Vercelli players in the staring line up, cementing their place as the number one side in Italy.

Unfortunately for the Leoni the years that followed brought a spectacular decline. Professionalism favoured the bigger sides that could attract bigger crowds and pay larger wages. After seven league titles and the controversy of 1910, the only honours of note for Pro Vercelli in the modern era have been two Serie D titles in 1983-84 and 1993-94. Despite these meagre latter day honours their importance and legacy still echo in the game today, particularly in their home country, and for that they will always matter.

Exeter City 1914

Honours

First team to take part in a high profile overseas tour of Argentina and Brazil

'They will never achieve real success until they recognize that it takes eleven men to score a goal,'

Exeter trainer speaking after a friendly game against Brazil

On Sunday 30th May 2004, Exeter City walked out onto the turf at their home ground St James Park for a game they would never forget. Packed to its 9,000 capacity, they were playing host to a rematch ninety years in the making. To celebrate their centenary year the Grecians were playing a team made up of ex-Brazilian internationals, mainly from the 1994 World Cup winning squad. Officially named the 'Brazil Masters', Dunga, Jorginho, Branco, Careca and Paulo Sergio all lined up in the yellow and blue for the national anthems. Undaunted despite only just labouring to a win over Bideford Town days before, Exeter City's players sang 'God Save The Queen' as if they were on the hallowed Wembley turf itself. A fiercely competitive game ensued, the atmosphere nearly boiling over after a poor tackle in the second half. The Brazilians would run out 1-0 winners thanks to a first half penalty from Careca but both teams had made a good account of themselves, one made up of players who have held the World Cup, one made up of players who would go on to finish sixth in the Conference National the following season.

The reason an officially sanctioned Brazilian exhibition side had made the journey for the game was in recognition of a voyage made in the other direction ninety years earlier. At the end of the English football season in 1914, Exeter City travelled to South America to tour Argentina and Brazil. The tour would eventually go down in football folklore for the last of their eight games abroad. Exeter City provided the opposition for the first ever fixture of the team that would become Brazil's national side.

Exeter City had only been in existence for ten years when put forward by the FA for the overseas trip. Formed by the amalgamation of Exeter United and St Sidwell's United in 1904, Exeter City only turned professional in 1908 after replacing Tottenham Hotspur in the Southern League. At the end of the 1913-14 season Exeter had finished an unremarkable twelfth, still competing in Division One of the Southern League. When the FA received a request from the Argentine and Brazilian football authorities for a 'typically English' side to tour their countries, it was the perfect marriage for a side keen to up their profile and struggling to do so on the pitch. The Southern League put Exeter forward as possible candidates and just a few weeks later a party made up of players, wives, club officials, and FA representatives set sail from Southampton for the two-week voyage to Argentina.

Once there eight games were agreed to fit with the English party's travel schedule, the last three games to be played in Brazil. It was decided the tour would end with match against a national side made up of players from Rio and São Paulo. Until this point any 'Brazil' team had been made up solely of players from one city, this was to be the first time a team would be able to be considered truly 'national' in any regard. As City began with games in Argentina, a hype machine went into effect in Brazil and a nation began to take notice of a very interesting fixture up ahead.

Reports of the tour vary greatly in everything from order of teams played to the results of the games. In the first game against Argentine Norte, legendary goalkeeper Dick 'Pincher' Pym suffered broken ribs after a 'robust' challenge from an Argentinean forward. Played just hours after arriving in the continent, Pym would play no further part on the pitch for the rest of the tour. In the game against Racing Club de Buenos Aires, City scored and the home side's club secretary drew a gun and threatened to kill the referee. When playing Rosarian League, a goal from the home side prompted a band to march on and play the Argentine national anthem an alleged six times in a row. If Exeter City had needed any reminding they were a long way from home, these incidents and generally rabid crowds armed with fireworks and flares were more than enough to do so.

Moving onto the Brazilian leg of the tour Exeter opened with a game against some English expatriates. In a more sedate atmosphere and playing a style of football they were accustomed to, City won 3-0. The game marked the first appearance of a professional football club on tour in Brazil. Shortly after, City's players were briefly arrested for indecent exposure after removing their tops in the heat of a training session on the beach in Santos. Anxious to cool off, a dip in the sea turned into a stay in the cells. Writing it off as a cultural misunderstanding, the Brazilian Police let the team go to play a Rio XI. Exeter played up to their professional status and won convincingly 5-3. The last game of the tour beckoned and Exeter travelled to Laranjeiras Stadium in Rio not quite sure what to expect.

The small stadium, home of Fluminense Football Club, was packed to the rafters. A crowd of 6,000 Brazilians had taken a national team instantly to their hearts and Exeter found themselves in a surprisingly hostile atmosphere. Some reports give the score as a 3-3 draw but most agree the game ended with a 2-0 win for Brazil, Osman and Oswaldo the scorers. The game was fired by occasion and atmosphere and the match itself is remembered as a heated one. The legendary Arthur Friedenreich played for Brazil and had two teeth knocked out by his marker after a strong tackle, he would finish his career with over twelve hundred goals in Brazilian football. After the second goal was scored the stadium erupted, spectators waving sticks and hats in the air and shouting 'Brazil' but Exeter felt cheated. Two players left the pitch in protest at the referee who they felt had been heavily influenced by the crowd's raucous support. City captain Jimmy Rigby talked them into finishing the game but at the final whistle, Exeter had lost.

In the process of defeat they had unwittingly ignited a passion in the Brazilian public to follow a national team. A year later Brazil would play Argentina and local rivalry would add even more to the excitement. As the history of football unfolded they would be rewarded for that support with five World cups, eight Copa América titles, three Confederations Cups, two Panamerican championships, and some dazzlingly talented footballers in their national side. What a group of footballers from Devon had started, Brazil would embrace and make a matter of national pride.

Returning home was as eventful as the tour itself for Exeter. During the journey growing tensions in Europe forced the ship to change routes and twice shots rang out across the bow as a course was plotted in league with the allied warships in the area to avoid German cruisers. Once docked safely back on English soil, much of the journey having been spent at full speed with all lights extinguished to avoid detection from hostiles, they discovered that Britain had officially been at war with Germany for the last five days. The following season was the last for three years as the First World War suspended professional football in Britain. Exeter improved slightly and finished eleventh. In 1920 they would become one of the founding clubs in the Football League Third Division but while the team they had played that day in Rio would go on to become the most successful side in world football, Exeter would continue play in footballs lower leagues right up until the present day.

Despite the relative lack of success their entry in football history is a significant one. The willingness of the Brazilian Football Association to send their exhibition side to Devon bears out the place they hold in their eyes. The tour had been a difficult undertaking but ultimately very successful for both South America and Exeter City. It is worth noting that even with officials being threatened with guns, injuries, arrests and biased refereeing, City finished the tour with the impressive record of played eight, won five, drew one, and only lost two.

Arsenal FC 1925–35

Honours

First Division Champions 1930-31, 1932-33, 1933-34 & 1934-35

FA Cup Winners 1930

Charity Shield Winners 1930, 1931, 1933, & 1934

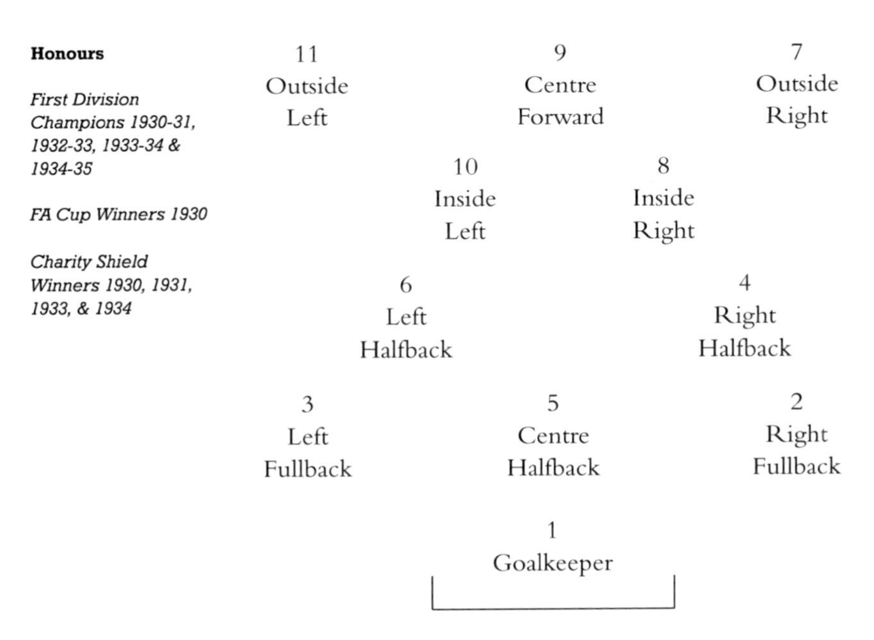

Herbert Chapman's 'WM' formation

By the time you've finished reading about this era of Arsenal's history, you might think it a slight misnomer to say that they mattered. It's not that they didn't change football's landscape and transform their club because this team absolutely did. This was the era that Arsenal won their first major trophy and pressed themselves onto English football's landscape permanently. It was a time where they played in a unique way that would soon become a blueprint for English football until the 1950s. It is not that this period of Arsenal's history didn't matter to the game but in reality it's the story of how just one man's vision changed it as a whole – manager Herbert Chapman.

Chapman, like so many of football's genuinely great managers, had only a middling career as a player. Raised in the northern mining town of Kiveton Park, his gritty upbringing and work ethic reflected in his playing style as a methodical but limited inside forward. He could've perhaps progressed as a player but the majority of his career was spent as an amateur meaning a life split equally between working and playing dictated several decisions and moves between clubs. Chapman was a keen student and spent much of his playing career studying mining and engineering but as his mind progressed off the pitch, on it he realised the general disorganisation and lack of tactical thought left a vacuum for someone innovative enough to exploit. He moved around the north predominantly, playing for Rochdale, Grimsby and Worksop Town amongst others before Tottenham Hotspur lured him south in 1905. Chapman drifted into Spurs's reserve side but his ambitions now seemed to lie away from the pitch. A chance recommendation got him his first stint in management with Northampton Town, a team he'd briefly played for and who were currently struggling at the bottom of the Southern League.

As was to become typical, his spell at Northampton was a success and began to earn him the reputation that would eventually take him to Arsenal. After failing to turn the club around immediately, Chapman realised a new approach was required to playing the game. His response was to develop an early counter attacking system and encourage his players to pass in the Scottish style, quickly and along the ground, making them as willing to sit and retain the ball as continually attack. After an initial culture shock, Chapman led his Northampton Town team to the Southern League title and four consecutive top-four finishes. His tactical breakthrough had inadvertently created a team ethic at a time when football was largely about an individual's ability to dribble. Northampton Town's approach was different and their results proved the merit of an unusual style.

With no structure set for promotion from the Southern to the Football League, Chapman put forward a rejected proposal to set up two-tiers with promotion and relegation to the Football League the prize at its top level. Frustrated at being unable to take his talented and attacking team into national competition, Chapman was left with little option when given an opportunity in 1912 to further his career. Football League Second Division side Leeds City offered him the chance to become their manager and leaving behind a legacy of success and a talented team, Chapman headed to Yorkshire.

His time with Leeds City ended up blighted by a life-ban from football in 1919. His spell in charge was interrupted by the war and Chapman himself took a dual role as Leeds's head coach and a munitions factory manager. Leeds were poorly supported and despite a change in fortunes under Chapman, promotion remained out of reach. Chapman resigned in 1918 and as rumours of financial irregularities involving the club began to circulate, his absence was seen as proof of guilt. Although the Football League could find no concrete evidence of what had been alleged – that during the war Leeds City had been paying 'guest' players to play for them – Chapman's resignation, a general stone-walling by the club to any line of questioning and a blanket refusal to allow anyone to view the club's accounts led to the League expelling them in 1919. An ugly auction of the club's players and assets took place and along with several other club officials, Chapman was handed the ban.

His early career had taught him several key things but it looked like he may never be given the chance to further his ideas. He had already realised the value of buying talent that could improve the side. At Northampton a sprinkling of players Chapman believed to be intelligent enough to see his vision through had been the final piece of his tactical puzzle. At Leeds City he had realised that a football club was more than just what happened on the pitch on a Saturday afternoon. When he was approached by Huddersfield Town with a proposal to come back into football as assistant manager to Ambrose Langley in late 1920, he realised he still had a lot more to give the game.

On appealing to the FA, backed and funded by his potential new club, he put to them that the resignation they had seen as a sign of guilt actually meant that Chapman had been away from the club at the time of the alleged misdealing. The FA allowed him to take the post at Huddersfield and within a month, Langley had left and Chapman was manager once again.

His time at Town was an unqualified success. Learning from his early days in management, he inherited an inexperienced but skilful team and immediately bought some new faces to gel them together. From Aston Villa came Clem Stephenson for what was seen as a huge fee for an aging player but then throughout his career, Chapman would never be afraid of spending his club's money. Stephenson became captain and a huge figure at the club, Chapman realised the importance the player and praised him personally and through the press almost continually. He adapted his playing method to keep the counter attacking and passing, but ensured that the reserve sides mirrored the system so he could place players into the first team without any need or time for adaptation. He also had the Leeds Road pitch fully re-laid so that his style of passing and quick dribbling inside from wide positions would not be hampered by the playing surface.

The emphasis was still on attack, even if predominantly done on the counter, and Chapman had learnt two things from this approach. Firstly, it filled the terraces as goals meant fans through the turnstiles. Secondly, it had just as much potential to fill the trophy cabinet as the stands. The defensive responsibilities were far from neglected however, Chapman encouraged a tight unit where every player had his role in defending in their part of the pitch. It was at Huddersfield where he first struck upon the idea of playing his centre half, then the term for the central player in the three-man midfield of a 2-3-5 formation, deep enough to break up play and cover his defenders if they chose to get tight to a player. While he had yet to fully convert to a 'W-M' formation, he was certainly laying the groundwork for the full move in his next role to create a 'stopper'.

Huddersfield Town under Chapman became the best team in England and one of the most progressive football clubs in the world. He'd realised the benefit of a match day 'experience' and knew everything from favourable local press, to establishing firm connections with the local community bolstered the crowds which was his main source of generating the clubs income to sign further players. The press box was immediately revamped with Chapman's eye firmly fixed on making life as comfortable as possible for the gathered journalists, the hope being that even a poor performance would pail against the club's hospitality. Then he moved towards the crowd and decided to entertain them on match days with music over the public address, as well as announcements regarding team news and selection. The move was designed to make them feel as involved as possible with 'their' team. By 1925 he had bought the club unprecedented honours in front of a regularly capacity crowd, taking them from a lower mid-table team to FA Cup winners in 1922, Charity Shield winners in the same year and Football League First Division winners in 1924 and 1925. By the time Town took a remarkable third league title in a row in 1926 and became the first team to do so, Chapman had been tempted by both a large salary and by what he saw as even larger opportunity in London with Arsenal.

Arsenal had been formed in 1886 and their most notable history up until Chapman's arrival was a litany of name changes. Originally named Dial Square after the workshop at the Royal Arsenal in Woolwich, South London whose workers made up the team, they quickly became known as both Royal Arsenal and the Woolwich Reds thanks to a donated set of shirts bearing the colour they played in. By 1891 they took the name Woolwich Arsenal but in 1914 finally dropped the monikers to become simply 'Arsenal'. The name change had come a year on from a move north of the River Thames to their new home at Highbury and by the mid 1920s, the club was ripe and ready for a revolution.

Arsenal were currently being led by chairman Sir Henry Norris, a committed football fan who like Chapman had realised there was more to a football club than just the games. Although he'd been known for an autocratic and meddling style, Norris wanted to allow Chapman the free reign and support he'd enjoyed at Huddersfield to turn Arsenal into more than just a struggling football club. Chapman responded by setting about the task in the manner he'd employed before – by signing a player who could help his vision come through on the pitch. Charles Buchan came in a uniquely structured deal and immediately broke the club's transfer record. Arsenal paid Sunderland £2,000 plus an additional £100 for every goal scored in his first season. Buchan was a difficult character and at 33 coming to the end of his career, but it was the first sign that Norris had turned complete trust over to Chapman despite the obvious questions raised by the signing.

Buchan was installed as captain just as Clem Stephenson had been at Huddersfield. He worked closely with Chapman at recognising the need to adapt the current pattern of Arsenal's play to something more progressive. With a change to the offside law came both men's realisation that more defensive cover was needed in the centre of a team's back line. There was now a reduction in the number of players needed between an attacker and the goal line – previously an attacker had needed three players (including the goalkeeper) between himself and goal to be 'onside'. With a huge drop in the amount of goals scored and a general decline in entertainment, the authorities reduced it to two in an effort to encourage attacking play.

The rule meant a new defensive strategy was needed as strikers now had the opportunity to lurk higher up the pitch to capitalise on an attack. Chapman's thoughts immediately went back to his deep-lying midfielder at Huddersfield and after discussion with Buchan, a new system was devised and refined over time into the 'W-M'. In a radical break from the established 2-3-5, Arsenal would now play with three recognised defenders, the centre half from midfield now permanently deployed at the back to cover the advancing opposition. Two lines of two now made up the midfield ahead and in attack, three players would line up making the symmetrical 3-2-2-3 formation. It was immediately christened 'W-M' for its likeness to the shape of the letters. The system provided the triangles and squares of players needed to encourage retention of the football and Chapman's preferred base to counter attack. Playing in the short passing and pacy style he'd created at Huddersfield, he was now on the way to creating his second team to sit at the very head of the English game.

W-M was a football revelation. While some teams had experimented with playing a deeper midfielder or 'stopper', Arsenal were the first to use it to great success and use the three man defence long term. Chapman took a team with a wholly unremarkable history to date, and turned them into FA Cup runners up in 1927, FA Cup winners in 1930 (the club's first ever major trophy) and then delivered their first title success in 1931. The title of 1931 was worth noting for the nature in which Arsenal had crashed through the opposition, racking up 66 points and scoring 127 goals in 42 games. A second place in 1932 would then lead onto three consecutive First Division titles from 1933 to 1935. He had turned Arsenal into a great success story and one of England's biggest clubs, and he had mirrored then bettered his success with Huddersfield Town.

The FA Cup final on April 26th of 1930 had seen Arsenal line up against Chapman's old employers with both teams bearing hallmarks of his reign. Huddersfield couldn't match up to the refinements Chapman had made to his system during his time in London and in front of 92,488 fans packed into Wembley, they lost 2-0 to an emerging Arsenal side. A goal in each half was enough to give Chapman the trophy and after declaring in 1925 that it would take five years to build a side capable of winning major titles, he'd delivered on his promise and now stood poised to take them onto even bigger success in the league.

Chapman had developed the system but he'd also made sure his team was staffed by some of England's best players to implement it. In 1929 a teenage left-winger was signed from Exeter City after only 17 appearances for the first team. After being personally checked by Chapman, he would go on to score 178 goals for the club – a record that would stand until 1997 when Ian Wright broke it. Cliff Bastin was not only one of the greatest players of his era, he was one of the greatest players Arsenal ever had. Bastin was often the profit of Alex James work, a player with wonderful passing ability and unmatched speed of thought. It was James who would sit and create chances for his strikers and after also joining in 1929, formed a partnership with Bastin immediately. He also became a huge source of the great Ted Drake's goals after the striker joined in 1934. In his first season Arsenal took their third title and Drake scored an incredible 42 goals. As well as Bastin, James, and latterly Drake, Arsenal also had David Jack and his signing gave the world a great story that summed up Chapman's approach to the game.

Jack was signed for £10,890 in 1928, a world record at the time and a figure seen by many as obscene for a 29 year-old footballer. Chapman had always been unafraid of paying for players who he believed fitted his vision and his pursuit of Jack would become the stuff of legend. With his current club Bolton

Wanderers quoting £13,000 as a fee and Chapman believing the minimum Arsenal would have to pay for Jack would be £12,000, he travelled with his assistant Bob Wall to a hotel to negotiate with the Bolton board. Making sure he arrived early, Chapman grabbed the waiter who would serve them all evening and instructed him he would drink gin and tonic, while Wall would drink whisky and dry ginger. The stipulation two pound-notes in the waiter's pocket earned was that while the Bolton board would be served whatever they chose to drink as a double, Chapman's gin and tonic would contain 'no gin', and Wall's whisky and ginger would contain 'no whisky'. After a suitably alcohol soaked evening ensued, a sober Chapman negotiated a still record fee but some £2,110 cheaper than had been first feared. True to form Jack slipped into Chapman's system and became an important part to the Arsenal first team.

Chapman's legacy didn't end at a new formation and the first major trophies in Arsenal's honours room. It was Chapman who orchestrated North London's Gillespie Road Underground station changing its name to Arsenal, arguing nobody knew nor cared where Gillespie Road was, everybody wanted to go to Arsenal. Despite the change of timetables, ticket, and signage across the breadth of the network, LER agreed and duly changed to give Chapman a real publicity coup. In Highbury itself it was Chapman who oversaw a full-scale redevelopment of the ground to befit their new status. He suggested they install the famous clock on the south terrace and build the countries first permanent floodlights. He designed the club's scoreboard that would be copied throughout the footballing world over the following decade, and suggested the system that would late become the electric turnstile. He also openly courted movie stars and the famous to come and watch Arsenal and with each news worthy visit, the club's profile increased incrementally.

Just as Arsenal mined his ideas off and on the pitch, so the kit eventually fell under Chapman's gaze. Arsenal's cranberry red shirts, the colour copied in the kit used by Arsenal's first team for Highbury's last season in 2006, were changed to a lighter red with white sleeves. This and some new-hooped socks made team mates easier to pick out when passing in the manager's eyes. Chapman had first had the idea when sporting a pair of pale yellow boots during his playing career, believing the contrast served the same purpose. Now he was in almost sole control of the football club following Sir Henry Norris's departure in 1929, Chapman was free to bring his every idea to fruition.

In recognition of his status in the English game, in 1933 Chapman took charge of the England side for a brief tour of Europe. The position was yet to be permanent and was given to club managers depending on timing and location. Chapman took a spine of Arsenal players and led his team into a draw with a strong Italy side in Rome, and then a comfortable 4-0 victory in

Switzerland. Cliff Bastin scored in each game and Chapman's reputation in Europe grew. Already counting Hugo Meisl among his friends Chapman was a huge studier of European football and to put England's result in Rome in perspective, just a year later Italy would win the World Cup.

In 1934 tragedy struck and football lost one of its greatest ever innovators. After attending a game in Bury with a heavy cold he ignored his doctor's insistences to rest and watched Arsenal's reserves while struggling with a fever. Days later pneumonia had taken hold and as a game against Sheffield Wednesday loomed, Chapman died. His team would go on to take the title still playing in his style and the W-M he had created, also winning a further two more in 1934 and 1935 under George Allison's management, but English football had lost a man who had given it so much.

The list of Chapman's ideas – some implemented, some ignored – was extraordinary. Not only did he shape Huddersfield Town and Arsenal into something more than 'just' a football club, he created the modern realisation of what a manager should be. Once considered a secondary but necessary figure, Chapman had become the most pivotal person in the entire football club. From minor but long lasting changes such as introducing tactical discussion with the team using boards and models to explain his point, to renaming tube stations or suggesting an additional referee, Chapman was to football what others have been to the worlds of science and technology.

I stated that it might be a small misnomer to suggest Arsenal mattered when in reality the key figure was Herbert Chapman himself. What has to be noted is that Arsenal gave Chapman what he had nearly achieved at Huddersfield – virtually sole control over the club. It is not enough to suggest that Arsenal may not be the club they have become without Chapman. It is more accurate to say English and arguably football as a whole would have suffered for not having benefited from Chapman's involvement in the game. Just as an Oscar winning actor needs the script to provide him with that opportunity, so Arsenal gave Chapman his chance to really flourish.

Uruguay 1930

Honours

First Winners of the FIFA World Cup

Pool 1	Pool 2	Pool 3	Pool 4
Argentina	Bolivia	Peru	Belgium
Chile	Brazil	Romania	Paraguay
France	Yugoslavia	Uruguay	USA
Mexico			

First World Cup Group Stage Pools

The South African World Cup of 2010 was a mammoth event orchestrated by a vast organising committee. The tournament was a huge economic commitment requiring not just the building of new stadiums to accommodate games, but vast improvements to the countries travel networks and hospitality industries. With 64 games attended by an estimated 3.18 million people, billions more watched live as the tournament unfolded on television coverage worldwide. The Cup bought the host country into the focus of the world and suddenly South African music and imagery was used to evoke anything even remotely World Cup related. 204 countries set out to qualify for the finals, taking part in a combined 853 games to whittle it down to the last 32. It had now become a huge undertaking to stage the month long tournament and any country with the privilege is left a legacy that extends far beyond the sport itself.

On its conception there was no real understanding of the monster the World Cup would become some eighty years later in 2010. FIFA always had dreams for their premier tournament but as football has become a truly global pastime, so the World Cup now enjoys the levels of sporting interest that once the Olympic Games alone could generate. Part of the reason for FIFA's formation in 1904 was for football's growing status in the game to be reflected in its own world title away from the constraints of Olympic football. 26 years later they had their tournament and shortly after, their first world champions.

When Jules Rimet ran for FIFA's presidency in 1920, the only measure of the best team in world football was the poorly supported Olympic tournaments. The format was problematic, football had only moved from 'exhibition' status at the Olympics in 1908 and the first official Gold Medallists had been Great Britain. With just eight teams entering the competition overall, all of them from Europe and two dropping out before a ball had been kicked, any aspirations of the medal bringing immediate attribution as the 'best' team in the world was heavily tempered.

Up until 1928, thanks to the war's interruption, only four more gold medals had been awarded. Great Britain retained the title in 1912, Belgium won in 1920, and then the South Americans had shown how they were developing with Uruguay's two gold medals in 1924 and '28. Uruguay showed greater skill and passed the ball over shorter distances than the Europeans but still their success was met with doubt. The 1928 tournament saw Egypt, Uruguay, and the USA make up the only non-European contingent in the tournament and no involvement from a Great Britain side historically regarded as the best in the world. The other question mark was the amateur status the games demanded to fit with the Olympic ideal. In countries where the best players were all professional, the medal was regarded as pointless.

However, it was still the only technically global football tournament in existence. FIFA existed as the governing body of a game growing in popularity in nearly every continent. With Jules Rimet now installed at its head, it was time to see through one of the key objectives of his presidency. After announcing the plans a year earlier, at a meeting in Barcelona in 1929 Rimet's 'World Cup of football' became an official event scheduled for 1930. The tournament would take place in Uruguay who were using the showpiece to celebrate one hundred years of independence. The Uruguayan bid to host was almost too good to be true in FIFA's eyes as the country offered to pay for the competing teams travel and hotel expenses, and build a new showpiece stadium in Montevideo. As European football was still manacled by the continent's economic problems, the comparatively rich Uruguayans would have no serious competition to become hosts.

Invitations were sent to FIFA regulated countries to participate in the tournament. Immediately this gave the organisation its first criticisms as England had opted out of FIFA rule in 1928 over a row about the status of amateurs at the Olympics. England were still widely regarded as the game's leading light and had a difficult relationship with an overall governing body for a game they felt they'd given to the world. Regardless of their absence FIFA hoped the rest of the invitees would be as excited as they were about their new venture, particularly as they wanted to generate revenue for the game as a whole from the tournament. While Uruguay as hosts would take the bulk share, FIFA made a point on accepting their bid that they would be entitled to 10% of all profit from 'their' tournament. The money was to be used to continue the game's growth and allow FIFA to move with it but that success was dependant on countries becoming passionate about their involvement. As determined to put the tournament on as Uruguay were, the quality of opposition had to be as high as possible despite the British not being involved.

Much to Rimet's disappointment the reception was luke warm. Professionalism was still to reach many European countries and the idea of amateurs, many with jobs to maintain as well as their sporting 'hobbies', setting sale for South America for up to three months was unrealistic. Rimet was both FIFA president and chairman of the French federation so he was assured of at least France's involvement as long as the rest of the federation shared his vision, but a spate of teams declining the offer threatened to derail the World Cup before it had even begun.

Germany, Italy, Spain, Sweden, and Holland all declined to take part despite some having offered to host the tournament. Many used the three-week voyage to Uruguay as reason for their withdrawal but some were irked that the tournament should take place in anywhere other Europe in the first place. With just two months to go before the World Cup would begin only France, due to Rimet's involvement but still not definite attendees, had accepted the opportunity to enter in theory from all the European teams invited.

Eventually Belgium and Romania agreed to travel with the French to South America and Yugoslavia would also make the journey due to King Carol's direct involvement with the team. He still had to negotiate with the oil companies the players worked for to release them for the full length of time potentially involved. On June 22nd 1930, a liner named the SS Conte Verde departed for South America with the French, Belgium and Romanian teams on board, as well as various European based football officials including Rimet himself. He travelled with the statuette of the Greek Goddess Nike that would be awarded to the winners, at the time named 'Goddess ofVictory' but destined to become the Jules Rimet trophy in 1946.Yugoslavia travelled separate to the main party on the MS Florida and despite being slightly disappointed with the European malaise that had generally greeted the World Cup, Rimet had his wish that the continent would be represented.

Joining Europe's contenders were a group of teams travelling to Uruguay from less of a distance. Accompanying the players already on the Conte Verde were South America's second entrants after the hosts, Brazil, who were picked up on a stop in Rio. The continent also provided beaten Olympic finalists Argentina, Chile, Bolivia, Peru and Paraguay. With seven representatives from South America and four from Europe, teams from Mexico and the USA would make up the rest of the thirteen teams to compete in the first ever World Cup. With all the games set to take place in Montevideo in just three stadiums, the groups were drawn and despite the reluctance from elsewhere, expectation and excitement in Uruguay was beginning to build.

The first game on the 13th July saw France take on Mexico and Lucien Laurent's volley take the honours as the first ever goal in a World Cup game. Rimet's dream had officially become a reality and fittingly, it was the country of his birth that won the first game as France ran out 4-1 winners. Drawn into the only group to contain four teams – Pool 1 – with Argentina and Chile, neither France nor Mexico would make the semi-finals as group winners. That honour went to Argentina who lived up to their reputation as one of the favourites by winning all three of their games.

Group 1 was rife with incident. The first game had seen France have to play with ten men and an outfield player in goal after goalkeeper Alex Thepot had to leave the field after a kick to the jaw. In a time before substitutes the French had still had too much for the Mexicans. Two days later in the game with Argentina, a late free kick from Luis Monti had the South Americans in front. With six minutes left to play Brazilian referee Almeida Rego blew the final whistle, much to the disgust of the French who were not only being denied the time to fight back, but also as Marcel Langiller had dribbled past Argentina's defensive players to be clean through on goal at the time the game was ended prematurely. After a pitch invasion from the Argentinean fans and the French players pleading with the officials to restart the game, Rego eventually relented after realising his mistake. France couldn't find the equaliser despite incessant pressure in the delayed closing moments and Argentina took a 1-0 win. Argentina then beat Mexico 6-3 in a game where five penalties were awarded to set up a 'group final' with Chile. They were too strong and won 3-1 to secure their passage to the first ever World Cup semi-finals.

Group 2 was a more straightforward affair. Yugoslavia won both games against Brazil and Bolivia to qualify. The Yugoslavians were somewhat of an unknown quantity, even in their own continent, but were impressive against a

Brazil who had yet to blossom, and a limited Bolivian side yet to become professional. Group 3 had also gone to script as Olympic champions Uruguay won both games against Romania and Peru without conceding a goal. Only Group 4 had provided a slight shock as the USA had beaten both Belgium and Paraguay 3-0. The USA were strong, hard working, and noted for their stamina, as well as their ranks being bolstered by six British professional players.

The USA would play Argentina in their semi-final while Uruguay would play Yugoslavia. Both games finished 6-1 and saw interest explode in the tournament. A reported 80,000 people packed into the Centenario Stadium to watched Argentina destroy the USA's decision to counter attack in the light of several fitness issues. After another injury forced the Americans down to ten men as Raphael Tracey suffered a broken leg, they did well to get to halftime having just conceded one Luis Monti goal. The second half saw an inevitable collapse and goals from Alejandro Scopelli, Guillermo Stabile with two, and Carlos Peucelle with two, saw the Argentines through to the final in hugely impressive form.

The second semi-final for the right to face Argentina was similarly one sided. An estimated 93,000 spectators roared the hosts to a crushing win over an exposed Yugoslavia. After taking a surprise lead in just the fourth minute through Branislav Sekulic, Uruguay responded with a Pedro Cea hat-trick, two from Juan Anselmo, and a goal from Victor Iriarte. The final would be a repeat of the 1928 Olympic final between the two favourites, hosts Uruguay against old rivals and neighbours Argentina.

The game on the 30th July captured local imagination and Argentineans began to enter the country hopeful of watching their team lift the World Cup. Reports vary as to whether 15,000 or 30,000 Argentina fans crossed the River Plate to journey to Montevideo, but hundreds of boats had to be specially chartered to cope with the migration. With kick-off set for 15:30 the stadium was full hours beforehand. Rimet's World Cup had finally gained the levels of public interest he knew it could but also taken on the importance it needed to survive.

The first half saw the home team take the lead to the delight of the Uruguayan contingent in the crowd. Pablo Dorado nudged the Celeste in front but then Peucelle and eventual top-scorer Stabile struck back to give the Argentineans a 2-1 lead. The final had a slightly bizarre feel about certain aspects and the free-flowing first half had seen mistakes, injuries, players wearing hats and a referee officiating in a jacket, tie and plus-fours. Even the ball itself had caused controversy as both teams wanted to play with a ball designed and made in their own country. The Argentineans had won a coin toss and their ball had been used for the first half. 2-1 down and unable to find their top gear yet, the Uruguayans needed to raise their game.

Fortunately for the home crowd the Celeste did just that and overturned Argentina's lead with just twenty minutes to go. Pedro Cea scored a brilliant solo goal after a mazy run in the fifty-seventh minute, and then Iriarte smashed in a strike from the edge of the penalty area for the lead. Despite Argentina rallying and pushing for a winner, Uruguay held firm and in the last minute scored a fourth as Hector Castro, a forward who had lost his right forearm in an accident with an electric saw in his teenage years, headed in the goal that sealed the trophy.

Uruguayan captain Jose Nasazzi lifted the World Cup aloft and football had its first world champions. The host country immediately declared a national holiday and celebrated its triumph. Argentina on the other hand reacted by smashing the windows at the Uruguayan embassy in Buenos Aires. The reaction from both showed what the World Cup had become instantly and what the Olympics had never achieved. They were football's own world champions, recognised by the game's governing body without the questions the gold medallists had traditionally raised.

While participation had been limited, the precedent had been set and four years later at the second World Cup the interest levels raised even higher. Uruguay refused to defend their crown in the light of the bigger European teams snub in 1930, but the tournament was contested between an expanded sixteen teams and in front of full stadiums again. While it was yet to become the behemoth it is in the modern era, the World Cup had established itself very quickly as international football's premier tournament.

I concede that Uruguay matter not because of what they did on the pitch or any great revelation in playing style or tactics, but their 1930 World Cup winner's status shouldn't be diminished in anyway by that fact. Uruguay took a fledgling FIFA tournament seriously when others treated it with distain. The organisers invested heavily in turning it into a spectacle and the team didn't let them down. They may not have radically altered the way the game was played but they were football's first truly global champions and no one can take that away from them.

Austria 1930–36

Honours

4th at 1934 World Cup in Italy

12.04.31	Austria	2	v	1	Czechoslovakia
03.05.31	Austria	0	v	0	Hungary
16.05.31	Austria	5	v	0	Scotland
24.05.31	Germany	0	v	6	Austria
16.06.31	Austria	2	v	0	Switzerland
13.09.31	Austria	5	v	0	Germany
04.10.31	Hungary	2	v	2	Austria
29.11.31	Switzerland	1	v	8	Austria
20.03.32	Austria	2	v	1	Italy
24.04.32	Austria	8	v	2	Hungary
22.05.32	Czechoslovakia	1	v	1	Austria
17.07.32	Sweden	3	v	4	Austria
02.10.32	Hungary	2	v	3	Austria
23.10.32	Austria	3	v	1	Switzerland

The Wunderteam's 14 game unbeaten run

The story of Austria's Wunderteam is one of triumph and ultimately tragedy, a team whose legacy was almost completely swallowed by a war. Brilliant and innovative in equal measure, the side was moulded by one of football's greatest ever managers – Hugo Meisl. Meisl and his hugely influential relationship with English coach Jimmy Hogan gave football a stylish makeover. They created a blueprint for a successful passing game, proving a series of short passes could triumph over the kick and dribble style employed by most of the international footballing world elsewhere. While Austria's Wunderteam may have fallen just shy of taking a major international trophy, they were without doubt one of the best sides in world football at their peak.

It all began with a bank clerk in Vienna and a passionate and outspoken Englishman. Hugo Meisl turned his back on his family wishes for him to move into the world of banking to concentrate on football. After a brief and unsuccessful spell as a player, he'd moved to Italy to continue his training for a career in finance. Called back to Vienna by national service, despite the training for his proposed trade he was still harbouring his true sporting love. Even with a lucrative position as a clerk secured and a path to bank management clearly laid out for him, Meisl left it all behind as his role in football grew, eventually leading to the job as General Secretary of the Austrian Football Association. Originally employed for his financial leanings to help with fund raising and administration, Meisl spent his most productive time studying the game.

He devoured football's patterns and rhythms and a vision of a 'new' way to play formed in his mind. His background in academic study gave him a different approach to digesting football's idiosyncrasies. He was soon considered a leading authority and after moving away from administration to pure coaching, he was installed as the man in charge of the national side in late 1912. The First World War would take Meisl away for five years in 1914 but he returned in 1919 to take up the position once again. On his return he set about continuing to create what his brother would record as the 'whirl', a new style of playing the game for the continent. It involved a skilled, more technical approach with a series of short passes taking precedence over speed and power. The passing game he now desired had been in part inspired by working with a man who would also become synonymous with the Wunderteam's success – Jimmy Hogan.

Hogan had enjoyed a reasonable career as a player and moved from his hometown of Burnley to success with Fulham. He developed a reputation for being outspoken but inventive, often questioning a manager's ideas in training and during a game. As a player he became obsessive about improving every facet of his own play, realising technique should play as great a part as condition. In a world where training was almost totally about building strength, speed, and stamina, Hogan's approach was radical.

As injury all but curtailed his career as an inside-right, he looked to coaching and the opportunity it presented to pursue his ideas about footballing method. He'd already become obsessed with the style that would become part of his legacy. Whereas English football was about physicality and pushing the ball long for forwards to dribble as close to goal as they could, Scottish football had emerged with a 'pattern' for short passing between players to attack. Hogan had fallen in love with the Scottish method and believed it was football's future. His desire to grow players ability in line with their endurance would fit with Meisl's growing philosophies and the two seemed fated to meet.

Hogan became aware of Europe's growing footballing interest on a pre-season tour with Bolton Wanderers to Holland. Now into the beginnings of his coaching career, his willingness to work abroad led to a recommendation from a friend to meet Meisl. The Austrian manager had identified the lack of technical ability in his players and knew he needed to take his country's football in a new direction. After a meeting of like minds led to some radical ideas, Meisl recognised the merit of Hogan's direction. Possession and passing were the key to mastering the game and as the war took Meisl from his position, he retained influence in the Austrian FA and employed Hogan to continue his good work with both the national side and Vienna's top teams. Hogan became a popular figure but war interrupted everyone's plans and he had to leave the country to continue his football career.

As Meisl returned in 1919 he had a vision in his mind of where Austrian football's future lay. Guided by the legacy of his brief time with Hogan, Meisl began to create a side to live up to their ideals. His ideas were not just restricted to the Austrian game, as he recognised the need for European club competition to increase exposure to different forms of football for all involved. In 1927 with Meisl as the architect, the Mitropa Cup was formed and open to teams from Hungary, Austria, Czechoslovakia, and Yugoslavia. Meisl also devised the system of teams playing a home and away leg, therefore reducing the advantage familiarity would afford.

Meisl's ideas were now beginning to benefit the wider football family as well as his own national team. The Mitropa Cup expanded and grew in stature until the Second World War ended the tournament for a decade. In his own domestic game Meisl had pushed for the move to professionalism to enable greater efforts to be made to grow players abilities. The change was slow moving but evident and results were not far from proving the benefits of his approach.

Throughout the twenties Austria occasionally sparkled but struggled for consistency. Their football grew and occasionally they simply blew teams away but they lacked the thread that would pull them together permanently. The game had become enormous in the country and interest in the national team was huge. Meisl was not immune to criticism but his goals were slowly being realised. As much as possession and passing between his attacking players was key, defensively Austria were improving and the changes to the offside law meant that their ability to hold the ball high up the pitch allowed them to exploit the ruling when defending. Come the end of the decade, Austria were on their way to becoming the Wunderteam and had found the final piece of the puzzle.

Matthias Sindelar collected nicknames almost as readily as he scored goals. Because of his slim build he became known as the 'wafer', the 'paper man', the 'paper-dancer', and the 'Mozart of football'. He was cut from a different cloth to the usual forwards of the day who even Meisl had advocated should have a physical presence at the forefront of their game. An intelligent player, his immense movement was what set him apart from his contempories. Sindelar would regularly move along the front five and play well in any position, he would also drop deep to receive the ball and pull an opposition's defensive players from their positions. Given a chance as early as the mid 1920s, it wasn't until the beginning of the thirties when he became a regular fixture in the side, replacing the all together more robust Josef Uridil.

Sindelar was the attacking intelligence around whom the team could revolve. Meisl still subscribed to the 2-3-5 formation but looked for adaptability from his players. Josef 'Pepi' Smistik provides a good example, as he was adept as both cover for his defenders and a supply line for Austria's attacking players. Along with Walter Nausch and Adolf Vogel, Meisl had the spine of greatness so key to any successful team. The final element in creating the Wunderteam was the return of Hogan who had continued his coaching career and tour of European football. He returned to work with Meisl at a crucial time with Austria approaching the peak of their powers. After a 14 game unbeaten run they faced England, considered by most and Meisl himself to be one of the best teams in the world. The game offered an opportunity for Austria to show that their new brand of football was superior to the established English method, and they were now on the back of an incredible run.

The Wunderteam's reputation for free flowing attractive football was established in that undefeated sequence that began in April of 1931. At times they routed their opposition into submission and taking Scotland's prized scalp in particular caused huge waves in the European game. Whilst they were traditionally seen as weaker than England, Scotland had never lost an international in Europe. After travelling to Vienna they were torn apart by Meisl's team, their own passing and movement left behind by Austria's new version. They had been beaten, quite literally, at their own game. The 5-0 win was the moment when people started to believe in Meisl's system, the 6-0 and 5-0 routs over Germany confirmed their affirmation. The game against

England was going to be a watershed moment, the oldest guard of all in world football playing the new school. After scoring 51 goals in those 14 games, the Wunderteam were to be feared and admired in equal measure.

72,000 fans packed into Chelsea's Stamford Bridge in anticipation of a great game. They weren't disappointed as a seesaw match saw England eventually triumph 4-3. The Austrian team acquitted themselves well and earned the moral victory in the morning press, lauded for their new 'revelation' in football. England had moved into a 2-0 lead at half time and their direct style had overwhelmed the Austrians at first. In the second half Karl Zischek pulled a goal back for Austria and their confidence grew. They couldn't peg England back enough not to concede twice more but two goals from Sindelar made the game close. They left the pitch in London with heads held high. They may not have beaten England but they had shown them there could be more to football than power and pace.

Over the next two years the Wunderteam continued to dazzle at times and were installed as favourites along with hosts Italy for the 1934 World Cup. In reality many of Austria's best players had aged and this would be their best chance at lasting glory. The format was a straight knockout and the first round saw France take them surprisingly to extra-time. Sindelar managed to get himself on the score sheet but it was Josef Bican who would score the decisive goal. The quarter-final drew Austria with perennial opponents Hungary and an ill-tempered game ended with a 2-1 win. The Wunderteam had yet to really play to their full potential but maybe that would come in the semi-final against Italy, managed by a good friend of Meisl's – Vittorio Pozzo.

Pozzo's team played an intelligent pressing game. Austria had played them not long before the tournament began and triumphed 4-2 but on the 3rd of June 1934, everything seemed to conspire against them. The bruising game against Hungary had left a few of his players carrying injuries and Meisl knew Italy had the capacity to be just as physical. On top of his worries regarding the fitness of his players, the pitch on which they would be playing was a muddy bog and as kick-off approached a deluge of rain ensured there'd be little chance of Austria's slick passing being given the chance to shine. The final nail in the coffin was the intimidation referees had felt when refereeing the host nation. The crowd animosity to any call against Italy had produced some extraordinary decisions, particularly in a quarter-final against Spain that had collapsed into violence. Sure enough Austria struggled to get anywhere near their best and lost 1-0 thanks to a scrambled goal from Enrique Guaita. Still carrying injuries and with the Wunderteam effectively at an end, the third-place playoff against Germany ended in a surprise 3-2 loss and the decline that had begun at Stamford Bridge in truth now began in earnest.

The Olympics in 1936 saw Austria take silver but in reality the whole competition had been mired in controversy and politics. After overcoming Egypt in the first round, Austria played and lost their second round game against Peru. The game had moved into extra time and would go down in infamy as a farce. Peru scored five goals and had all but two scratched off. Their fans invaded the pitch several times and there were reports that some Austrian players were threatened with guns. On top of the obvious intimidation Austria complained that the pitch hadn't been fit to play. A rematch was granted but Peru withdrew in protest, citing Nazi Germany's involvement as the real reason for the granted rematch. After that drama a win against Poland in the semi-finals and a loss to Italy again in the final paled into insignificance.

The story of the Wunderteam then descended into tragedy and controversy as the 1938 Anschluss of Austria into Nazi Germany created a unified team and effectively ended Austria's participation. The Wunderteam's time had ended, Meisl had passed away in 1937 and most tragic of all, Sindelar died with his new Jewish girlfriend in January of 1939 aged just 36. His death was officially put down to a faulty heater in his apartment causing carbon monoxide poisoning, but his refusal to play for the unified Germany team and democratic leanings gave birth to conspiracy theories varying from murder by Nazi soldiers, to a suicide in the face of the growing darkness.

The Wunderteam, Meisl, and Hogan's place in football history was secured. They had taken the 'Scottish' way of playing and perfected it. They may have fallen short of coupling the revolution with a trophy but they mattered because their legacy was set to run on and on. Not only had they given the world a reason to doubt the kick and run sensibilities of the English, in Hungary they'd watched keenly on and had been a much beloved part of Jimmy Hogan's European tour. Once the war had finished and the football world began to find it's feet again, Hungary's Mighty Magyars would draw direct inspiration from Meisl and the Wunderteam's method.

A.C. Torino 1942–49

Honours

Serie A Champions 1942-43, 1945-46, 1946-47, 1947-48, & 1948-49

Coppa Italia Winners 1942-43

Torino, the other Turinese team, have had a history of triumph *and* tragedy. Theirs is a story of a small club that became unbeatable, and then vanished in a disaster that transformed Italy. Torino's history can only be written with reference to one date. Everything revolves around that moment: *before*, and *after*.

John Foot writing in 'Calcio: A History of Italian Football'

4th May 1949. The squad of AC Torino sat aboard an Avio Linee Italiane Fiat G-212 plane returning from a friendly testimonial game in Lisbon. Played in honour of Benfica legend Xico Ferreira, Torino had been invited due to their status as the best team in Europe and probably the world. A friendship between Torino president Ferruccio Novo, club captain Valentino Mazzola and Benfica's Ferreira himself had made the organisation relatively trouble free. There were strong rumours a transfer bid had been accepted and Ferreira was about to become a Torino player in his swansong years. Flying through some terrible weather conditions around the mountains of Turin, pilot Pierluigi Meroni appeared to lose his bearings momentarily. Reports indicated that the plane was seen circling though the fog while trying to find the right path to begin a descent.

Through heavy rain and low-hanging dark cloud, Meroni attempted to drop altitude to try and improve visibility. On the hill at Superga sat an 18th century basilica, often used by pilots as a landmark and well known in the area as a point of local interest. Investigators concluded that the pilot must have seen the building late whilst flying too low. The small aircraft crashed into a wall at the back of the church and exploded into a huge ball of flame. Luggage and wreckage lay strewn across a huge area and fires burned on in defiance of the driving rain. Initial reports suggested there were no survivors and they would be proved correct.

With many of the victims only identifiable by documents or personal effects due to the intense fire, the realisation that 'Il Grande Torino' (the Great Torino) were no more slowly spread across Italy. Late editions of newspapers carried the story and the impact of losing their champions spread across the nation. Rivalries were set to one side in mourning not just Turin's but the whole country's loss. They had become a symbol of Italy's regeneration after the curse of Fascism and the ghost of war had loomed so large in recent history. Within that Torino side laid the heartbeat of the national side and now both teams had been all but decimated. With the Italians heavily favoured for the upcoming World Cup in Brazil in 1950, the Torino side would have provided the majority of its playing staff and most probably its captain – the great Valentino Mazzola.

Mazzola had been a legendary figure in the game, captaining Torino to four consecutive Serie A titles and just about to complete a fifth. An Italian international midfielder playing mostly at inside-left, he had scored 4 goals for his national side – a relatively poor return for a player so prolific domestically. Moving to Torino from Venezia in 1942 after rising to prominence in Venice, his leadership and partnership with Ezio Loik was often cited as the beginning of Torino's dominance of the Italian game. In five title-winning seasons Mazzola would score over a hundred goals for Torino from an attacking midfield position. In the 1946-47 season he finished as the league's top scorer comfortably. A complicated character, Mazzola remained an inspiration on and off the pitch throughout his career. It is said that in a moment of high drama, when Mazzola looked around and rolled up his sleeves it was a sign to his team mates and the supporters that 'Captain Valentino' was signalling to attack and more often than not, he led by example.

And attack they did. Torino's success was based on a blistering goal-scoring record. In the season before 'Il Grande's' first triumph they had finished second, three points behind Roma. In a thirty game season they had scored 60 goals, 5 more than the champions, 20 more than third place Venezia. In their first title-winning season in 1942-43 Torino improved on that total by 8. Playing with a revolutionary loose 4-2-4 formation years before Brazil would use it to win a World Cup, and adopting the principals that would later become the 'total football' that the Dutch fell in love with, AC Torino were years ahead of their time and an irresistible force.

As well as being tactically ahead of their opponents, Mazzola and Loik were not Torino's only great players. Both men would take part in every one of the five title winning campaigns along with several other genuinely talented footballers. Guglielmo Gabetto played as a striker and was famed for his athleticism and balance. A lithe and talented player, Gabetto won the title with both Juventus and Torino and earned full international honours with the Italian side. Winger Franco Ossola defied his fragile frame and became a favourite with the fans thanks to his superb ball-control and raw pace. Like Mazzola, Ossola scored freely as well as supplying crosses and momentum. Defender Giuseppe Grezer was a full international who made over 150 appearances for Torino and earned eight caps for his country.

These five key players won all five titles with Il Grande Torino and all died in the Superga tragedy. Over their glorious run Torino could also boast Valerio Bacigalupo in goal after his move from Genoa in 1944. Bacigalupo won four titles and five caps whilst in goal for Torino. In defence Aldo Ballarin also won four titles and died in the crash with his brother Dino, Torino's back-up keeper for the trip. Romeo Menti scored the last goal in Lisbon and turned out 131 times for Torino, winning three titles in the process.

AC Torino played many more who would make up the bulk of the national side in the latter part of the decade. Regularly contributing as many as eight of the starting line-up, on one famous occasion in a friendly against Hungary every outfield player played for Il Grande. President Ferruccio Novo had created a legacy and he desperately fought to keep them together, even telling authorities that every player worked at his FIAT plant on one of the many production lines to prevent call-ups to the war efforts.

In that first title-winning season in 1942-43, the Second World War heavily affected the championship. Winning by one point from Livorno, the highlights of the season had been home and away wins over local rivals Juventus. AC Torino had originally been formed by a breakaway group of Juventus fans and officials who had objected to the running of the club. After a bitter split the derby between the two clubs – the 'Derby Della Mole' (derby of the mole after one of the symbols of Turin) – had become a heated affair on and off the pitch. The double over their rivals who had finished third seven points behind Torino, had been particularly sweet. Fittingly the title had been sealed by Mazzola, grabbing the only goal late in the last game of the season against Bari.

In the same season Torino also won the Coppa Italia at a canter, scoring twenty goals in five games and conceding none. It would be the last time the tournament was played until 1958 due to the initial suspension of the cup due to the war. Opening up with a 7-0 win against Serie B Ancona, Torino then beat Atlanta, AC Milan and Roma before the final against Mazzola's old team Venezia. Any sentiment between captain and team was quickly forgotten as Torino slammed four past their opponents and took the cup as ruthlessly as they had been throughout the campaign.

The 1943-44 season was a non-event for the same reasons the Coppa had been called off. Torino finished second in an unofficial and mainly localised championship not recognised by the Italian FA. By the time the competition proper began again in the 1945-46 season, many teams had lost or gained players due to the machinations of the war. Circumstance dictated that the league would be split into a Northern Italy and Central & Southern Italian Championship, the top four from each meeting in a final round of games. Torino won their group and scored thirteen more goals than the next highest scorers, Internazionale and Juventus. Torino scored four or more in six of their 13 home games.

In the final national round of games, Torino were once again imperious. Winning 11 of 14 games and scoring over 40 goals in the process, satisfyingly they took the title by a point from Juventus. On the last day of the season Torino needed a win to take the title at home to Pro Livorno. They responded by putting nine past their visitors to take another Scudetto.

After two narrow league victories the 1946-47 season was a watershed moment. Il Grande truly earned their name, taking the title by 10 points from Juventus in second place. Losing only three games in the 38 game season, Torino scored an incredible 104 goals. Almost as impressively was their defensive record, conceding just 35 – less than a goal a game. Torino's home form was the foundation of their season, in 19 games they remained unbeaten and regularly recorded heavy victories, scoring six no less than three times.

Mazzola had finished as top-scorer and stand out player by some way. He had played every minute of every game and become well aware of his value to the team. Whilst remaining an inspiration he could be a thorn in the side of club directors and officials, argumentative and repeatedly asking for more money to reflect his value to the side. He was outspoken but genuinely brilliant and Torino's management repeatedly caved to his demands fearful of losing their leader and the uproar it would create amongst their fans.

If that title had been emphatic, the 47-48 season would be absolutely devastating. Torino would break their own records by earning two more points and scoring an incredible 125 goals in 40 games. The average of over three goals a game was earned courtesy of some huge victories, including a 10-0 against Alessandria. In 20 home games Torino only failed to score three or more four times and won all but one fixture, a 1-1 draw against Juventus. They finished a huge 16 points ahead of joint second placed Milan, Juventus, and Triestina. In reality 16 points may as well have been 16 light years. Mazzola had contributed another 25 goals, Gabetto 23. Incredibly in the 40 game season, Torino had only used 15 players in the first team in total.

Going into the fateful 1948-49 season it was difficult to look past Torino for the title again. Up until the beginning of May they had comfortably led the league and looked to be heading for their fifth straight championship. Whilst not quite hitting the heights of the previous season, they remained unbeaten at home and lost only three times away. After the Superga tragedy the remaining four games were fulfilled by Torino's reserve and youth team players. With the country still reeling from such a high-profile national tragedy, their opponents fielded their own reserves as a mark of respect to the great Torino side that had passed. The Italian Football Federation had awarded them the title anyway but in the first game after the crash, Torino beat Genoa 4-0 to retain their unbeaten home record. In an emotional atmosphere a capacity crowd wept and sang together. The greatest Torino side of all time and the core of the Italy squad had been taken cruelly. Whilst tragedy can often exaggerate greatness, this side had earned their plaudits in life and death.

Italy would take a boat to Brazil rather risk flying for the 1950 World Cup. After two turbulent weeks at sea, the Italians lost to Sweden and played out a dead rubber against Paraguay before returning home. Sadly robbed of the opportunity to see how the Torino-led Azzurri would have faired, Italian football remained also-rans for the next four World Cups before a final appearance in 1970.

Torino would never again hit the heights their great side had achieved. The following season marked their decline as Juventus took the title and Torino finished sixth. A single further title in 1976 proved to be their last to date. The day after the league title had been won there was a spontaneous march up to Superga by the club's fans to pay their respects. The tradition continues today every May 4th and the site of the crash has become a shrine to those that lost their lives.

Sporadic cup success in the late sixties and a UEFA Cup final appearance in 1992 proved to be their only other real high points since 1949. Relegations and financial difficulties have blighted Torino in recent times. Declared bankrupt in 2005 a phoenix club was raised into Serie B and renamed Torino Football Club. After achieving promotion via an extraordinary play-off final win on away goals in 2006, their most recent relegation from Serie A came in 2009.

31 victims died on that day in 1949 along with a country's dream of possible World Cup glory. Torino and Italy had lost its footballing heartbeat in one horrific tragedy. Several myths and even conspiracy theories arise from that day and the players have passed into folklore as the fans that witness the great side have aged and passed away themselves. In those five glorious seasons Torino set record after record, took five Scudettos, one Coppa Italia, and showed the world a new way to play attacking and successful football. While it's true that the Superga crash robbed the world of one of its greatest club sides ever, it is important to note that 'Il Grande Torino' matter because of what they achieved in life, not their tragic deaths.

Club Deportivo Los Millonarios 1949–53

Honours

Dimayor Champions 1949, 1951, 1952, & 1953

Dimayor Runners Up 1950

'The Municipalistas have become the Millonarios'

Journalist Camacho Montayo gives birth to the name change from Deportivo Municipal to Deportivo Millonarios in a 1938 as the amateur club stood at the forefront of a movement to professionalism.

In the summer of 2000 Real Madrid president Florentino Pérez embarked on a project that became known as 'Zidanes y Pavones' (Zidanes and Pavóns). The idea was that each year Real would buy one of the biggest names in world football, a Zinedine 'Zidane' for instance, but also promote youth players to surround them, the 'Pavones' being a reference to Real youth player Francisco Pavón who was making his way into the first team via Madrid's development structure. First to come in 2000 was Luis Figo, a huge coup as he was signed from bitter rivals Barcelona. Over the next three years they did indeed sign French playmaker Zinedine Zidane, as well as Brazilian striker Ronaldo and the most marketable player in the world in David Beckham to put Pérez's grand plan into action. As Real Madrid's transfer policy made headlines the 'Zidanes y Pavones' project was given a simpler name by the press – 'Los Gálacticos'.

Pérez's plans were designed to have two effects on the club as a whole. The first was to grow 'Real Madrid' the brand by creating the most popular football club in the world. The signing of football's most exalted players, David Beckham in particular, ensured that the attention levels every time they took the pitch were huge. This led to increased sponsorship, merchandise and endorsement deals as companies clamoured to be associated with the club.

The second effect was that Pérez believed the best players should guarantee success on the pitch. All the attention that the Gálacticos could generate would be for nought if the team couldn't win the silverware that proved the validity of the approach. At first Pérez's scheme seemed to ring true as Real won two La Liga titles and the European Cup in the first three years of the project. Real's fans could not only boast about watching the best players join their club every summer, but they were challenging for the biggest trophies season after season.

After the initial vindication, the next three years were to expose the flaws in the Gálacticos ideal. Players were picked regularly for the first team on their reputation rather than their form. When English striker Michael Owen signed in 2004, his appearances were sporadic over the course of the season despite playing well and outscoring 'homegrown' Gálactico Raúl. Pérez demanded that his superstars should take the pitch at every available opportunity, an example of the perceived interference that contributed to seven managers taking charge of team affairs at the Bernabéu stadium in just seven years of the project.

The final nail in the coffin of on-pitch affairs was the lack of adequate defensive reinforcement. Pérez believed that defenders didn't fit with the Gálacticos ethos. Famously on selling defensive midfielder Claude Makelele he remarked that Real wouldn't miss the player and that his passing all went sideways or backwards. Without the cover players such as Makelele had once afforded them, the attacking unit struggled to compensate for their frailties as the back. By the time Fabio Capello brought them the title at the end of the 2006-07 season, their first trophy since 2003, the era of Los Gálacticos was over. Only Beckham remained and he'd spent much of the season out of the first team after sealing a move to the LA Galaxy at the end of his contract. Capello had won the title by creating a team who were the antithesis of the superstar policy, turning them into a side that could grind out ugly wins when required. Zidane had retired, Figo and Ronaldo moved to Italy, and Beckham's imminent move to America was seen as the last vestige of Pérez's plan gone.

What Florentino Pérez and Real Madrid didn't realise at the time was that they'd merely walked along a well-trodden path. Years before this era of Gálacticos, and even before Real's first attempts to bring in superstars in the mid-1950s, a league was attracting the best players in the world and one team in particular was using this to achieve great success. Thanks to a disagreement with the footballing authorities and a huge amount of investment, Colombia's Dimayor league of 1949 to 1954 had an El Dorado, becoming home to some of the world's best players. At its head was it's most successful team, Millonarios of Bogotá, home of Argentina's best players and in particular home to one Alfredo di Stefano. The striker would go on to easily occupy the same conversational space as Pelé, Cruyff, and Maradona and would move to Real Madrid himself in late 1953.

Millonarios were originally formed as amateur side Club Deportivo Los Municipal in 1938. Based in Bogotá their potential was huge as football began to sweep the country as the new pastime of choice. Currently a staunchly amateur sport, the club's board knew there was potential for more. They'd been originally formed by the students of two schools in the city wanting to start a football club as a means of exercise and enjoyment. By 1945 the groundswell of popularity meant the push for a change to professionalism and a professional league was being led by the club. The backing was in place and the club were rich with both money and ideas, prompting the official change to drop the Municipal and become Millonarios in 1946. The movement to change was led by Alfonso Senior Quevedo, club president and a man destined to become a huge figure in Colombian football.

All over the continent of South America countries had embraced and benefited from a move to professionalism. Argentina had first formed its professional league in 1931 and two years later both Uruguay and Brazil had followed suit. Colombia were not only in danger of being left behind in sporting terms but there was a world of revenue opportunities currently lost. As if to prove the massive interest the sport in Colombia was now generating, a tournament played at Sante Fe with professional Argentine side Velez Sarsfield present generated a huge amount of interest. The grounds were packed with fans eager to get a look at professional footballers playing in their own country. The matter was all but sealed in the minds of a group of club presidents and entrepreneurs – it was time to take advantage of the popularity of the sport and force the change. Alfonso Senior took a leading role in the movement and set about gathering support and funding for the proposal. His club Millonarios would be one of the founding members of the league and in 1947, he successfully approached the ten others who would form the proposed División Mayor del Fútbol Colombiano.

Colombia suffered as the country descended into La Violencia. Supporters of differing political parties were at war with one another as attack was countered with revenge attack. The country hung dangerously in the shadow of an all out civil war. As the violence increased so football's popularity swelled. It became an escape from the danger of life in Colombia's rural areas. The bigger cities and their football clubs remained relatively conflict free and games became an oasis of passionate support without fear of reprisal. The media could also cover football without the threat of censorship or even terrorist attack that reporting of La Violencia could bring. Even in the face of mounting unrest, football represented opportunity. Having firmly grasped the fact, Alfonso Senior was desperate to make sure Millonarios were in the driving seat of any change.

A meeting was called between representatives of the proposing clubs, the Colombian Football Federation, and Adefútbol – the Colombian amateur football association. The clubs all stated their intention to withdraw and form a professional league – the Dimayor – with Humberto Salcedo Fernandez, president of Cali based club Corporación Deportiva América, at it's head. They repeatedly stated that they wanted to work with Adefútbol to make sure the change was as efficient as possible and beneficial for all, even to the point of negotiating cheap chartered flights for all teams to move around the country to away games. The move was to improve Colombian football as a whole and it was billed in the proposal as the next and only logical progression. Pleased that they had covered all angles, Alfonso Senior and his cohorts waited for Adefútbol's expected approval.

The support never came even though moves were taken to begin the league in 1948. Adefútbol took great exception to the proposals and felt it was coup attempt by the biggest clubs and their owners to take over Colombian football. Not only did they refuse to approve the move, they reported the newly formed league to FIFA. After an impassioned campaign to convince football's governing body that the league was not to the benefit of anyone but the owners, Adefútbol had their victory as FIFA withdrew any affiliation to the Dimayor and promptly suspended the national team from all international competition.

A choice now had to be made by Alfonso Senior and his fellow club presidents as to their next move. The country needed a professional league and had proved the support was there to sustain it – dare they form a 'pirate' league outside the bounds of FIFA rule? In reality it was always more of an economic decision than a sporting one and the money that the Dimayor could potentially generate far outweighed any risk of reprisal from FIFA. The motion was taken and the Dimayor professional football league came into existence in 1948. With ten clubs fighting for the title, Colombian professional football now existed outside of the game's established regulatory body.

Fernandez was installed as president of the Dimayor and together with Alfonso Senior immediately spun FIFA's absence as the moment Colombian football was entering its 'El Dorado'. The league took steps to ensure that it existed outwardly as an entertainment product above all else. Free of FIFA's shackles, several rules were installed including the allowing of two substitutes per team per match. This reduced the penalty to either side due to injury, something that had been a real issue in the midst of the ill discipline of the country's amateur game.

To combat other issues dragged over from the amateur era, English referees were imported and professionalised. English officials were seen as beyond reproach and high wages and expenses were offered to ensure they would not be subject to bribery. Also shirt numbers were printed on the backs of player's kit for the first time to allow the crowd to easily identify individuals. This encouraged the idea of teams having 'star' men that the fans could idolise. Unfortunately the current level of quality available was not all it could be but Alfonso Senior and his Millonarios team were about to change that.

The Dimayor league rules, contrary to FIFA's, contained no restrictions with regard to transfers or the number of foreign players. With this in mind and as his team finished in fourth place in the league's first season, Senior sent his head coach Carlos Aldabe to Argentina – a country whose professional football was in turmoil. The lack of FIFA affiliation meant that no transfer fee had to be paid between clubs – they were from different footballing worlds. Argentina was in the middle of a nationwide player's strike and their clubs were only fulfilling fixtures by using amateurs. With no transfer fee involved it was simply a case of offering a wage structure that would lure footballers to the Dimayor. Having realised this stroke of fortune Senior awaited his coach to return, hopefully with an Argentinean star in tow.

Millonarios already possessed Alfredo Castillo, the league's top goalscorer, and Pedro Cabillón in what was a fine attacking pair. On his return Aldabe had achieved everything he'd been asked and had pulled off perhaps more than Senior had dared wish for. He'd managed to tempt Adolfo Pedernera into joining Millonarios, one of the greatest players in the world and still regarded as one of the best footballers Argentina has ever produced. He had been part of the famed La Máquina (the machine) forward line of River Plate's magnificent team of the early forties. Pedernera became an integral part of Millonarios's success, as it was he who was tasked with not only playing but also recruiting the cream of Argentinean football to play in Bogotá. On his arrival he was greeted by a sea of Millonarios fans and it was a truly a before and after moment for the Colombian game. Senior's team had taken advantage of their situation and pulled off a remarkable and technically 'free' signing.

Within weeks a migration of Argentinean footballers had come to the league. The Colombian Football Federation had joined Adefútbol in not recognising the Bogotá based Dimayor, and now cut any remaining ties in the light of a wave of foreigners joining clubs. Rather than suffering any ill effects clubs began to look elsewhere to recruit players more aggressively. Soon different nationalities of players, tempted over to clubs for vastly improved wages compared to their former employers, began to form communities around the cities they had been recruited by. Players from Peru, Hungary, Brazil, Costa Rica and England found their way to Colombian clubs. Even eight of the 1950 World Cup winning Uruguay squad moved to the league flushed with success. At its peak 320 foreign nationals plied their trade in Dimayor, many clubs becoming associated with certain countries. Independiente de Medellin for example became nicknamed the Sun Dance in reference to their Peruvian imports. Millonarios used Pedernera to become home to Argentina's best players, and it was after a process of recruiting such that the 'El Ballet Azul' (the Blue Ballet – so named for Millonarios's blue shirts and playing style) was truly formed.

In the five seasons of El Dorado in Colombian football between 1949 and 1953, Millonarios took four titles. They became the best team in the most competitive league in the world. Pedernera became head coach in 1950 on the retirement of Aldabe and had already enticed some of the best players in Argentine to Bogotá. Nestor 'Pipo' Rossi came shortly after Pedernera and played for Millonarios for six seasons. Predominantly a defensive player, he and Julio Cozzi in goal gave them a platform at the back to build on. His greatest piece of recruitment was to persuade his replacement in River Plate's forward line to join him in Colombia – Alfredo di Stefano.

Di Stefano had started as a winger but on his move to centre forward his skill had really come to the fore. Right from the off Di Stefano was different, from his blond hair that earned him the nicknames 'the German' and the 'blonde arrow', to the playing style that saw him capable of taking the ball from the feet of his defenders to marauding through the opposition penalty area. Di Stefano was a supreme athlete who would be still be sprinting in the last minute when many had flagged long before. In a new league now packed with star names, Di Stefano was the crowning glory. It was he who had the ability to bring the best from those around him. The term 'Ballet Azul' was coined for the way di Stefano and his team mates would weave amongst each other and destroy any defensive structure. To illustrate their superiority he admitted in later life that Millonarios had a 'five and dance' policy. This meant that when they moved five goals into the lead, they would stop and play the ball amongst themselves so as to avoid any further humiliation for their opponents unless provoked.

Millonarios were free scoring in each of their four title wins. In 1949 when they took their first championship they scored 99 goals in just 26 games. In 1951 when they won their second it was 98 in 34 games as the Dimayor expanded to 18 teams. They were entertaining and rewarded their fans with success, attracting huge crowds to the El Campin stadium to watch them in full flow. With Di Stefano as the fulcrum and a myriad of quality imports surrounding him, they became the dominant force in Colombian football and the most talked about team in South America.

El Dorado and Millonarios's glory days were not to last but the club was to leave Di Stefano as its legacy in world football. After the initial celebration of Dimayor and Colombia's glorious new football, it was quickly realised that long-term success could only be achieved with FIFA affiliation. Not only did it bring Colombia under the world football umbrella, it also restored their national team to competition. As the Colombian government and La Violencia pushed the country towards a potential economic meltdown, the excesses of Dimayor were looking less and less like a sustainable product. After negotiation it was agreed Dimayor would move under FIFA's jurisdiction and rejoin their country's football federation in 1954. This allowed the current contracts held by imported players to be run down and ownership would revert to the clubs who held the player's original contracts. A predictable exodus meant that El Dorado was over, Colombian football had reached its rebellious peak and now had to tow the line.

The agreement softened FIFA's stance towards Dimayor clubs and Alfonso Senior saw one last chance to use his Millonarios side to generate income and interest in Colombian football. With Colombian teams now allowed to participate in friendlies with sides from FIFA's approved leagues, an arranged tour of Spain in 1952 brought Di Stefano into the spotlight of European football. Millonarios were selected as the best side in South America to play in a tournament to mark Real Madrid's 50th anniversary and Di Stefano was exceptional throughout. Standing out even amongst his talented peers, both Barcelona and Real Madrid identified him as the man their squads desperately needed.

Di Stefano's move to Spain was horrifically complicated due to both River Plate and Millonarios's claim to ownership of the player. After one of the most protracted transfer sagas in history, Di Stefano eventually signed for both Barca and Real on the agreement he would have to play for one for a season, then the other the following year. Eventually and largely thanks to the negative reception of the Catalan public to such a situation, Alfredo di Stefano agreed to become solely a Real Madrid player.

Alfonso Senior's legacy was not complete either. With his passion and eye for an opportunity he had briefly created the strongest league in the world, all without FIFA's blessing. Millonarios had become known throughout the football world – their selection for the tournament in Madrid confirming their meteoric rise – and Senior had been the driving force. After working outside of the accepted norms, Senior eventually became part of the system as he rose to become Colombia's FIFA representative, masterminding his country's ill-fated but successful bid to host the 1986 World Cup.

Millonarios mattered because briefly they became the most romantic of footballing notions – a fantastically entertaining team living outside of the game's rules both on and off the pitch. Beautiful to watch and led by one of the game's truly progressive owners, the Ballet Azul hit sporting peaks that Colombian football would struggle to reach again. A true Gálactico long before Florentino Pérez's 'revolution', Di Stefano's story was far from done once he left Colombia as he was about to become integral to Real Madrid's greatest ever side.

Uruguay 1950

Honours

World Cup Winners at Brazil '50

'Only three people have, with just one motion, silenced the Maracanã: Frank Sinatra, Pope John Paul ll and me.'

Alcides Ghiggia speaking about his winning goal

On July 16th 1950, the largest crowd ever assembled for a football game filed expectantly into Brazil's newly built Maracanã stadium in Rio de Janeiro. Nearly 175,000 tickets had been sold but some 25,000 more would be present for what had effectively become the World Cup final. The competition thus far had been following a unique league format but thanks to results, the last game of the 1950 World Cup was now a winner-takes-all affair, played between two of the biggest footballing sides in South America – the expansive and flamboyant host nation Brazil against the hard-working and technical Uruguay. Despite the 'cup final' nature the odds were anything but even and the huge crowd reflected that. Playing on their home soil with a partisan crowd roaring them on, all Brazil needed was a draw to become World Champions for the first time.

Robbed of European sides to compete against since the beginning of the war, both Brazil and Uruguay were well acquainted with one another. Recently they had played a series of three games against each other in Rio,

Uruguay winning one, Brazil the other two. However history and past results were to have no bearing on what was now a one off game for the trophy. So far Brazil had delighted a vociferous home support that had in turn embraced them, believing destiny had pre-ordained that Brazil would take the trophy whilst in their homeland.

The best-attended tournament in the competition's history, the success of the hosts had played no small part. Brazil had been sensational at times, scoring 21 goals in the five games leading up to the 'final'. When attacking at their best it was thought they could be almost unplayable, their flair and athleticism building relentless pressure as games wore on. Uruguay in contrast had made steady, stumbling progress up until this point. Much to Brazil's chagrin, la Celeste (meaning Sky-Blues – Uruguay's given nickname) held the honour of winning the first ever World Cup in 1930. Despite history and with their form unspectacular to say the least, very few gave them even half a chance against the destructive Brazilians.

That presumption had already reached all corners of Brazil, not least the Brazilian Football Association who had the commemorative winner's medals made and then embossed with the Brazilian players' names. As well as this a victory song had been composed ready for its first performance at the final whistle, and many of the national newspapers had already printed their headlines for the following morning – 'Brazil, Champions of the World' or a variation of it. Even FIFA had joined in with the assumption, Jules Rimet only preparing his trophy presentation speech in Portuguese to be able to congratulate the Brazilians on their victory fittingly.

There was just one problem standing in the way of this supposed destiny – no one had told the Uruguayans that they were just there to spectate. After a goalless first half Uruguay manager Juan Lopez delivered an uninspiring team talk warning of an onslaught in the second half. Taking everything into account, captain Obdulio Varela gathered his players together on the pitch before kick off. He immediately dismissed everything their manager had just said, telling them all they needed to do was stay calm, stick to their natural game and the win was there for the taking. Before kick off Varela had already delivered one inspirational speech in the changing room, telling the team not to adopt the defensive approach Lopez was favouring. After the first forty-five minutes he knew in his heart he was right, there was only one way to approach playing the Brazilians and that was to attack them. This had already boiled over in the first half, an alleged punch between Varela and Brazilian left-half Bigode had shown everyone involved the Uruguayan captain was in no mood to just roll over. Now with the second half ahead, Varela was keen to instil that same desire to win in his team mates.

Even with their inspirational captain's words ringing in their ears, on forty-seven minutes Uruguay fell behind. Brazil winger Friaça picked the ball up from Ademir and his run and cross shot just beat keeper Roque Máspoli. Unrelenting in his approach Varela grabbed the ball and disputed the goal, stating it should have been judged offside. The goal was clearly legitimate but the act was purely to instil a sense of injustice in his team mates. After marching the ball back to the centre circle he turned to each of his players and demanded 'Now, it's time to win!' Despite Varela's belief he was almost a lone voice in the stadium. A rabidly biased crowd had now whipped themselves into a frenzy, the stadium erupting into a 200,000 strong party. Brazil now believed they had both hands on the trophy and it looked like the newspaper headlines were about to come true.

Long before this moment the atmosphere during the World Cup in Brazil had been electric. The first tournament for twelve years due to the Second World War, the trophy had spent much of that time under the bed of the Italian Vice-President of FIFA. Anxious to restore the competition, FIFA chose the football mad Brazil as host country for the restored tournament. But for the war, Brazil would have held the World Cup in 1942 anyway. The authorities were keen to reinforce what they felt was the most prestigious football tournament in the world, bigger even than the other 'world' crown on offer – the Olympic Gold Medal. Brazil had submitted an impressive bid to host, promising to build a new national stadium in particular, but it hinged on FIFA delaying their proposed date in 1949 to allow them time to do it. Recognising a genuinely football hungry nation, FIFA had no qualms about giving them the extra year and the 1950 World Cup Finals had become one of the most eagerly anticipated tournaments ever.

The hosts were immediately installed as one of the favourites along with England who were making their debut at the World Cup. Originally the tournament was designed to include sixteen teams, the winners of four groups going into a final group of four. Several teams immediately withdrew from qualification for economic or political reasons. The world was still finely balanced after the war and as keen as FIFA were to put on a tournament with the best teams in the world competing, they could do nothing about some countries prevailing situations. While nations like Germany were missing due to obvious political reasons, others like France dropped out because they were unhappy with the host nation's organisation after qualification. They felt that the World Cup venues were too far apart and the travelling unrealistic, especially as the draw was to be made with no geographical significance. This meant that teams could be feasibly expected to travel over three thousand kilometres between group games. Despite these problems and even India withdrawing due to FIFA's refusal to let them play in bare feet, 13 teams did travel to Brazil and every one of them felt they had a realistic chance to win it.

Despite the absence of three qualifiers, FIFA and Brazil wanted to keep the four-group format the finals had been designed around. Other national teams were invited to make the numbers up but all would decline. Undeterred, four groups were still drawn and the winners of each would enter a final group with a round robin of games against each other. Group 1 was drawn with the hosts Brazil taking on Yugoslavia, Mexico and Switzerland. Immediately the favourites imposed themselves with a 4-0 over Mexico in the opening game. Ademir scored twice and would eventually claim the golden boot with eight in the tournament. Yugoslavia beat Switzerland and Mexico convincingly and after a surprise draw with the Swiss due in part to some drastic team changes, Brazil went into the their final game needing a win to progress. An injury to key man Rajko Mitic walking up the stairs that led to the Maracanã pitch gave Brazil a one-man advantage at kick off, the Yugoslav forward receiving treatment and then playing heavily bandaged for the rest of the game. Ademir gave Brazil a third minute lead and they eventually finished with a 2-0 win that saw them qualify for the final round.

In Group 2 joint favourites England were joined by Spain, Chile and the USA. As talented as the Spanish side was, England were expected to progress easily from the group. On the 25th June they beat Chile 2-0, a result that belied a general lack of preparation. Spain won their opener against the USA despite going behind in the first half, and then matched England's 2-0 result against Chile. England arrived in Belo Horizonte for their game against the USA expecting to breeze past them and set up a winner takes all game against Spain three days later. An England side containing future World Cup winning manager Alf Ramsey, Tom Finney and Billy Wright lost 1-0 thanks to Joe Gaetjens first half header and never recovered. Losing by the same score line to Spain in the final game England were out, finishing level on points with Chile and the USA. Spain on the other hand had qualified into the final group with a perfect record and with brilliant striker Telmo Zarra at the top of his game, scoring in every game so far.

Group 3 had been reduced to three teams in the light of India's withdrawal. Italy were the holders of the World Cup but had been robbed of the core of their side in 1949 by the Superga air crash. The tragedy claimed the lives of 18 of the great Torino side that made up the bulk of the national team. A seriously weakened Italian side lost to Sweden in their first game and playing in a three team group, knew their fate was already out of their hands. Sweden went on to draw 2-2 with Paraguay and qualification was secure. Despite missing three of their greatest ever players in Gunnar Gren, Nils Liedholm and in particular Gunnar Nordahl, Olympic champions Sweden now joined Spain and Brazil with a real chance to win the trophy.

The final group could hardly have been described as such due to the withdrawal of Scotland and Turkey who would have made it up to four. Scotland felt they didn't deserve to be there after losing the British Championship to England. Turkey withdrew after qualifying for a combination of economic and political reasons. This left the group with one game for the chance to progress, held between Uruguay and Bolivia. Uruguay had pedigree and a reputation as a steady if unspectacular side. Influential and brilliant captain Obdulio Valero was far from their only good player, Óscar Míguez in particular would go on to become one of the all time top goal scorers for Uruguay and remains their top goal scorer in World Cup competition. Playing in attack with Míguez was Pepe Schiaffino, a talented striker who would go on to move to Europe and play over 150 games for A.C. Milan. Also going on to make a name for himself in Europe was Alcides Ghiggia, widely considered one of the best wingers of the time and eventual AS Roma club captain, making over 200 appearances for the Italian side. Ghiggia remained very much the creative influence, Varela the driving force and inspiration from midfield with partner Julio Pérez providing work rate and support for the attackers. Centre back Eusebio Tejera was tough and uncompromising in defence and sweeper Matías González would play every minute of the tournament behind him. Whilst nowhere near as attractive as Brazil, Spain or Sweden, going into the only game in Group 4 Uruguay had a more than capable side. Bolivia were 3-0 down inside the first twenty minutes, 4-0 down by half time. They went on to concede another four in the second half, Míguez finishing with a hat trick, Schiaffino with two. After the crushing 8-0 win, Uruguay entered the final group ready for the much tougher tests ahead.

The final group opened in breathtaking fashion in Rio. In front of nearly 140,000 supporters Brazil ripped Sweden apart, putting seven past the Olympic champions. Ademir in particular was in spectacular form, scoring four at the head of the forward three with Jair and Zizinho. Scintillating going forward, Sweden had simply melted away in the face of wave after wave of Brazilian attack. Playing at the same time in São Paulo, Uruguay struggled to a 2-2 draw with Spain. Despite taking the lead they found themselves 2-1 down at halftime. Captain Varela's late second half goal earned a point but neither side looked a match for the brilliant Brazilian machine on this evidence.

Playing in Rio again four days later Brazil put Spain to the sword who fell away 6-1, Jair, Zizinho and Ademir all finding themselves on the score sheet. Once more Uruguay were less than convincing despite beating Sweden 3-2 in São Paulo. Behind early to Palmér's fourth minute goal, Ghiggia equalized with five minutes of the first half left. Just a minute later Stig Sundqvist put the Swedes back in front and again the Uruguayans look laboured. With just thirteen minutes left on the clock Míguez made it 2-2 and then went hunting for a winner, Varela driving the team forward. With five minutes left to play Míguez got his second and Uruguay closed the game out to come away with an unconvincing win.

Brazil sat atop the group in exhilarating form, Uruguay a rather flimsy second. Sweden would go on to beat Spain 3-1 in their final game leaving them in third and the Spaniards in fourth place respectively. Events had now conspired to give the tournament a 'final' to be played out in front of the largest crowd ever assembled for a football game at any level. Lining up for the national anthems Julio Pérez admitted to wetting himself in fear at the noise and the occasion. Now back in the second half and 1-0 down, Uruguay needed to up their game and go on the attack if they were to have any chance of lifting the trophy.

Led by Valero, a new sense of focus descended over Uruguay and was to prove the difference over the rest of the game. On scoring the opener, Brazil manager Flavio Costa had ordered his players to curb their attacking instincts and sit back holding onto what they had. Either through naivety or ignorance, Brazil ignored the instruction and continued to push forward looking for a more convincing scoreline. On sixty-six minutes Schiaffino dampened the celebrations as his first time finish past a despairing Barbosa in the Brazil goal brought the teams level. Ghiggia's run and cross had supplied the goal and he was just beginning to get on top of his markers. Cracks in the Brazilian armour began to appear as suddenly a team known for its lightening quick attacking had to defend. Now caught in a no-mans-land of pushing for another or settling for the draw, Brazil started to give the ball away in key areas.

Uruguay's game plan was simple, they had to score again to take the trophy. Now pressurising the Brazil defence, the stadium had suddenly become a hive of nervous energy as opposed to the noisy support of the previous hour. With eleven minutes to go the unthinkable happened as the reinvigorated Ghiggia outpaced Bigode on the right and broke into the area. From a tight angle he squeezed the ball past Barbosa and his near post and wheeled away celebrating his fourth goal of the tournament. Now 2-1 down and ten minutes from an unthinkable defeat, the Maracanã fell silent as Brazil struggled to break down the resolute Uruguayan defence. Jules Rimet himself described the sudden silence of 200,000 supporters as 'morbid'.

As time crept on the defeat loomed larger on the horizon. On ninety minutes English referee George Reader drew his whistle to his lips and it was all over, Uruguay were crowned champions for the second time and the Brazilian players collapsed in tears onto the sun drenched pitch. A silent stadium watched Valero accept the trophy from Rimet with no ceremony or fanfare, everything that had been organised had been dependant on a Brazilian victory. In Montevideo reports state that three Uruguayans died of heart failure in shock at the result. Back in Brazil it was reported that several suicides were attributed to the defeat. Some newspapers simply refused to accept the defeat and a nation lay in agony at the failure.

The magnitude of reaction to this defeat cannot be overestimated. The echoes can still be felt today with several outlets in Brazil selling video and DVD copies of the game, edited to show Brazil actually winning 1-0. Brazilian goalkeeper Barbosa had gone into the game with a reputation as possibly the best in his position in the world, he left a villain and spent the rest of his life receiving the brunt of the abuse and blame of the Brazilian fans. Considered a jinx, he was banned form Brazil's training sessions and in 1993, forty-three years after the defeat in Rio, the President of the Brazilian F.A. wouldn't allow Barbosa to commentate on a Brazil international match. Shortly before dying in 2000 he was quoted as saying 'the maximum punishment in Brazil is 30 years imprisonment, but I have been paying, for something I am not even responsible for, for 50 years'.

Brazilians have obsessed over the defeat ever since. Thousands of words have been dedicated to the subject, whole books devoted to the game itself, the tournament and even the nature of defeat with 1950 as the backdrop. In its aftermath Brazil mourned as a nation, a collective tragedy felt by all. To this day they remain one of only two world champions never to have won as hosts. A nation with a reputation for colour, over-exuberance and an emotional love of football, Brazil fell into darkness. Nelson Rodrigues the famous Brazilian playwright, author and journalist, described losing the 1950 World Cup Final as Brazil's Hiroshima moment, a collective uniting tragedy.

After that day several new phrases entered the Brazilian lexicon. The game and goal became known as 'fatídico' meaning fateful and the noun 'Maracanãzo' is still used today for any team that beats Brazil at the Maracanã. Such was the impact of the defeat, in a bid to extinguish it from the players minds even the colour of the kit was blamed, the blue shirts, shorts and socks deemed unpatriotic. Eventually this led to a radical change to the yellow and green so steeped in football history today.

To say that this Uruguayan team mattered solely for reasons regarding the opposition is wrong. They had shaken the football world but this was no fluke. They had stuck to a clever, tactically correct game plan instigated by the inspirational Valero. Ghiggia and Schiaffino had shown the greatest attacking team in the world that they weren't the only ones who could frighten with speed and skill. A second World Cup victory was an extraordinary achievement, given the name 'Celeste' it is telling it doesn't only refer to the traditional colour of Uruguay's shirts but also carries heavenly connotations. A small nation in between the footballing giants of Brazil and Argentina, to date Uruguay can boast two Olympic gold medals, two World Cups, and fifteen Copa América titles. This constitutes an unbelievable record for a country with a population of less than four million people.

In 1950 Uruguay changed Brazilian football forever, emerged as World Cup winners against all odds and silenced an entire nation over 90 minutes. For all of these reasons it has to be said that they truly mattered.

Hungary 1950–56

Honours

Runners up at 1954 World Cup in Switzerland

Gold medal winners at 1952 Olympics

25th November, 1953
Wembley Stadium London

England	3 v 6	**Hungary**
Sewell 15		Hidegkuti 1, 20, 56
Mortensen 37		Puskas 22, 29
Ramsey 62 (p)		Bozsik 65

Referee – Leo Horn of Holland

Details of 'The Match of the Century'

On the 25th November 1953, the press eagerly awaited the game they'd hailed as the 'match of the century'. Home team England were regarded as the game's originators and had never been beaten by a continental team on home soil. They were one of football's powerhouses and harboured the suspicion that in reality, they were and always would be the finest exponents of the game. With Stanley Matthews, Billy Wright and Stan Mortensen, whether or not their confidence was misplaced, there was no denying the talent at their disposal. They were buoyed by the press's assertions that the game would be 'easy' and Wright even assumed their opposition didn't have the correct kit when he saw their lightweight boots. Lining up in their trusted 'WM' formation, England assumed it would be a case of how many they would win by as opposed to whether they would even triumph in the first place.

The opposition were somewhat of an unknown quantity but they'd won the most recent Olympic Gold medal. This had been dismissed by much of the world's press as down to the fact that many of the world's best professional footballers didn't compete for their countries, therefore winners Hungary couldn't claim any real superiority. Even though Hungary were ranked number one in the world football standings, England sitting in third place believed that statistics counted for nothing. With a curious and fluid 4-2-4 formation and players with barely pronounceable names like Puskás, Kocsis and Hidegkuti, those involved in the English game waited for their team to steamroller these upstarts and prove that England were the truly the best team in the world.

Pendants were exchanged between Wright and Puskás and Hungary elected to kick-off. A reported 105,000 spectators filled every inch of Wembley's stands and the atmosphere was jovial and expectant. Immediately England's defenders realised something was very different about the Hungarians. Their designated players to mark didn't play in the roles represented by English shirt numbering, they seemed to move amongst themselves making it difficult to know who to follow. Nándor Hidegkuti wore number 9 and for the English defence should have represented a centre forward. When Hidegkuti dropped deep into midfield to pick the ball up in the first minute, his marker English centre-half Harry Johnstone was caught between knowing whether to stick or twist. If he gambled and followed the supposed striker he left a gap for other Hungarian players, notably Ferenc Puskás, to exploit. If he left Hidegkuti he was giving a talented player time and space on the ball.

He elected to sit and with less than a minute on the clock the decision was already exposed as tactically inept. After a series of one touch passes through midfield Hidegkuti found himself on the ball just outside the English penalty area. As Johnstone stood off his man, a quick touch inside to his right foot left the Hungarian with a clear strike at goal. The shot from distance flew past goalkeeper Gil Merrick and a shell-shocked England found themselves a goal behind and faced with a team the likes of which they had never seen before.

However this was England, the self-titled best team in the world and a team who had not lost to a side from outside the British Isles in 52 years of competition. They rallied briefly to equalise with thirteen minutes gone, the Hungarians willingness to attack leaving them exposed after a surge forward broke down on the edge of England's penalty area. The ball worked its way to an unmarked Stan Mortensen who drove goalwards through the centre of Hungary's defence. His pass to an overlapping Jackie Sewell saw the English forward stroke the ball past Hungary's goalkeeper Gyula Grosics and parity was restored. A relieved Wembley relaxed, the Hungarian system that seemed to be pulling the English out of position and leaving defenders hopelessly exposed could be overcome by good old WM. They sat back and awaited the inevitable English pressure that would surely lead to victory.

It was Hungary who were to ram their point home from that moment on. Their frontline's movement was ripping England's defence and midfield to shreds. On twenty minutes Hidegkuti had his second as a scramble in the area saw the ball find him as it would do all game. After coming inside again and onto his right foot, he lashed home from level with the penalty spot for the lead the Magyars deserved.

Just four minutes later it was 3-1 as a moment of genius from Puskás silenced a partisan Wembley in awe. After another one touch passing move the length of the field, the ball eventually found its way to Puskás on the right of the England six-yard box. After a poor first touch Billy Wright had the opportunity to tackle and slid in to win the ball. With a flash of his fabled left foot, Puskás dragged the ball back and watched Wright slide helplessly by. After smashing it in, Merrick completely beaten on his near post, a ripple of applause rang out around Wembley as home support grudgingly began to accept they were witnessing a watershed moment for English football. Never before had the old English ideals of power and pace looked so outdated, so alien when weighed against the wonderful skill and movement of the Hungarians.

On halftime it was 4-2 to Hungary. Puskás had notched a simple second, diverting József Bozsik's free kick in with a reactionary flick. Stan Mortensen had grabbed a goal on the break for England not long before the whistle but the gulf was evident. Two goals behind in the game, in reality England realised they were years behind the way football was being played elsewhere in Europe.

In the second half it took Hungary just five minutes to restore their three-goal cushion. Another sweeping move saw Puskás flash a header against the post and a static England defence fail to clear. From fully twenty-five yards Bozsik seized on the loose ball and hit a screamer into the top left corner. Any lingering ideas of English superiority had now been crushed completely.

Unthinkably it was 6-2 three minutes later. Fittingly to cap a wonderful and revelatory performance, Hidegkuti had his hat trick. Another wonderful flowing move eventually led to Puskás teeing the ball up onto his chest, and then lobbing the ball forward spotting Hidegkuti's run. The number 9 volleyed the ball past Merrick for another brilliantly worked goal. Alf Ramsey's penalty pulled the score back to 6-3 but at the final whistle the applause throughout the stadium was solely for the team in red. England had been outclassed and their football exposed. The Hungarians were technically better and their intelligent movement and captivating attacking style seemed to be from another world. Having now routed the unofficial (and self-proclaimed) world champions, any questions about the Olympic Gold medal had been dismissed.

That game marked the moment Hungary truly became the Magnificent, Marvellous, Magical or Mighty Magyars, depending on whom you read. In reality the seeds had been sown years previously and England was merely one stop on a wonderful run. The Austrian Wunderteam and Austrian football's growth in general had been completely ended by the Second World War but the lessons remained and Jimmy Hogan's time in Budapest had left the same passing and possession football legacy evident in Hungary. If any confirmation were required, coach Gusztáv Sebes cited Hogan as a huge influence and claimed any history of the Hungary's Golden Team should have Jimmy Hogan's name written in 'gold letters'.

Hungary's 4-2-4 had been born from the need to harness the attacking talent of a crop of players almost unrivalled for raw talent until the Brazil squad of 1970. Sebes was a coach who was open to change but also a perfectionist. Each player would be adaptable and able to fit into a raft of positions making them difficult to mark. Each member of the team would be as technically adept as they would be physically fit. Hungarian football was growing in stature domestically and they were as willing as the Austrians had been to embrace new ideas.

Hungarian football's development was concentrated on two teams – Red Banner, the State Protection Authority's team, and the Hungarian army team Budapest Honvéd. Between the two the bulk of the national team was supplied and efforts were made to play in the same style. With everything set to embrace and change Hungarian football, they just required players talented enough to implement Sebes's plans.

From front to back Hungary were blessed. Gyula Grosics in goal was bold and adventurous and often credited as one of the pioneers of a goalkeeper who could use his feet as well as his hands. Grosics would regularly anticipate attacks and race out to clear the ball, common place in the modern game but just one of the many idiosyncrasies of Hungary's impact on football. Defensively Hungary used their midfielders as extra cover when required but in truth, their strength lay in their intertwining and destructive attack.

The triangle at the heart of the Magyars destructive power was Ferenc Puskás, Sándor Kocsis and Nándor Hidegkuti. Hidegkuti's withdrawn role proved to be effective as it allowed Kocsis and Puskás the freedom their talent demanded. All three were outstanding players in their own right but together and on song they could be virtually unplayable. Hidegkuti had spent five years in and around the national side since his debut in 1945. Sometimes employed as a winger, it was the move to what essentially amounts to a playmaker position that really saw his talent emerge. Despite the movement to a deeper position, Hidegkuti remained a goalscorer throughout and scored 39 times in 68 internationals during his career.

Kocsis and Puskás would follow similar career paths. Both finished with outstanding international records – Kocsis scored 75 goals in just 68 internationals, Puskás 83 in 84 appearances – and both men ended up having successful careers in Spanish football after leaving Hungary. To use a cliché their partnership was almost telepathic, fed by Hidegkuti's vision and creation of space. They were both quick and intelligent enough to move between themselves to often devastating effect. Kocsis was a natural finisher but unselfish enough provide service for Puskás and Hidegkuti. Puskás was supremely gifted, wonderfully skilful and his small stature belied real strength on the ball. All three men were equally talented but Puskás was the one who captured the imagination the most. Captain and leader of the Magyars, he was a superstar of his time and quite rightly lauded for his 'beautiful' playing style. Nicknamed the Galloping Major due to his awarded rank on Honved's move to becoming the army's team, Ferenc Puskás rightly remains to this day as one of football's greats.

Surrounding the Magyars attacking triangle, players such as Zoltán Czibor, László Budai and József Bozsik were almost their equals in ability. Czibor was an outside left and possessed the ability to run as fast with the ball at his feet as without. Like the triangle in the middle, Czibor was perfectly happy coming inside and changing roles as and when required, his fluidity and a natural eye for goal meaning he often found himself on the scoresheet. Budai would also play wide like Czibor and also possessed enormous pace and flexibility. Bozsik was the man who made the centre of Hungary's team tick, acknowledged as one of the best midfielders in the world. While he didn't possess the pace of some ahead of him, his ability and vision to pick the right pass was incredible. Often playing deep, the forerunner of the modern phenomenon of a 'quarter-back' type player, he also scored some great goals from distance – as he had in the game against England.

With such a talented collection of individuals and a manager who developed a system that could harness their abilities, Hungary were always going to develop into formidable opposition for any team. After a 5-2 win over Poland on June 4th 1950, they set off on an incredible run that would see them unbeaten up until the 1954 World Cup final. As well as the victory over England they recorded famous and empathic victories over Austria, Italy, Czechoslovakia and Scotland. Olympic Gold was secured in 1952 with a 2-0 win over Yugoslavia with goals from Puskás and Czibor. Even a return game against a now wary England in 1954 played in Budapest was reduced to a non-event by another superb performance. Played on the eve of the upcoming

World Cup in Switzerland, England appeared to have learnt nothing as they were once again put to the sword, this time losing 7-1. As the draw was made for the World Cup pools Hungary were overwhelming favourites to continue their untouchable form and take the trophy.

Ahead of them in Pool 2 lay games against South Korea and West Germany. The unfancied South Koreans were simply no match for the Magyars and promptly lost 9-0. Puskás immediately hit form and scored twice, Kocsis scored his first World Cup hat-trick. The next game against West Germany was to prove pivotal for a variety of reasons.

Sepp Herberger the German coach knew all about the Hungarians power and adjusted his team accordingly. Rather than try to play Hungary on a level playing field, he named very much a reserve side with eight of his strongest eleven rested. Guaranteed a play-off to qualify for the quarterfinals Herberger opted to take the loss. Some claimed in the light of what followed that it was incredible foresight, but in reality it's more likely that with a play-off only three days away it made sense to hedge their bets. Unsurprisingly Hungary were convincing winners, triumphing 8-3 and Kocsis scoring another 4 goals. Puskás and Hidegkuti were also on the scoresheet but the biggest character to emerge from the game was German defender Werner Liebrich. No footage of the challenge exists to say definitively but opinions vary as to whether his tackle on Puskás was just misjudged or something more sinister. It left Puskás with a bad ankle injury and he would have to miss Hungary's next two games. As their influential captain and the tournament's star name was withdrawn, some began to question whether Hungary could continue their impressive form without him.

Those doubts were to prove misplaced as Hungary beat Brazil 4-2 in a quarterfinal that would become known as the 'Battle of Berne'. Two more from Kocsis and one each from Hidegkuti and defender Mihanly Lantos with a penalty were enough to see off the emerging Brazilians, but in reality the football was smallest part of the game's legacy. The match descended into several ongoing battles across the pitch, the first real flashpoint to boil over coming in the 72nd minute when Nilton Santos and József Bozsik traded punches over a tackle. Both men were sent off but the fuse was lit and on and off the ball the violence continued. Brazilian defender Humberto Tozzi was sent off for a bad challenge on Kocsis and then his retaliation. Watching on injured, it was alleged that Puskás hit fullback Pinheiro with a bottle. At the final whistle the game had become all but uncontrollable for English referee Arthur Ellis as both teams continued to trade blows as they left the pitch, and then further in the changing rooms. The highly anticipated game had produced drama of the wrong sort. Even a good performance from Hungary and a stunning goal from

Brazilian Julinho couldn't mask the fact that the game had left a bad taste in the mouth.

The semi-final saw Hungary play World Cup giants Uruguay for the right to play West Germany or Austria in the final. By way of antidote to the Battle of Berne, the game was a spectacular contest between two of the best teams in the world. Hungary led 2-0 going into the last fifteen minutes of the game but over confidence led to Uruguay taking the game to extra time with two late goals from Juan Hohberg. Hungary rose to the challenge and two more goals from Kocsis saw the Magyars through to a final with West Germany, the Germans now having beaten Austria 6-1.

This would be a very different West German side in the final, a full strength team who were as keen as the Magyars to lift their first World Cup. Hungary had been this close before, losing in the 1938 final to Italy in a tournament controversial for political reasons. This now represented their best chance – a golden generation in a World Cup final at the peak of their powers. However, preparations were shambolic as a missed train meant a late night check in to their hotel. To cap the tiredness a row between players over the fitness of Puskás threatened to boil over. While all wanted him to play, it was only with a fit Puskás that most felt they could triumph. The accusations that they would effectively be a man light if he was still struggling were dismissed and Puskas was named in the side to face Germany on the 4th July.

A remarkable first 20 minutes saw the game level at 2-2. Hungary had started well and raced into a 2-0 lead. Any worry over his fitness was dismissed as Puskás scored the first on six minutes and then he played a hand in Czibor's eighth minute strike after a horrific defensive mix-up. Rather than fold, the Germans immediately hit back through Max Morlock's poaching, and then incredibly they were level on 19 minutes thanks to Helmut Rahn. After a corner from the left, Hungarian goalkeeper Grosics uncharacteristically missed his punch. Waiting for just such a mistake was Rahn who tapped in an equaliser.

The match stayed level into the second half but Hungary pushed hard, Hidegkuti and Kocsis hitting the woodwork. Germany also missed chances but with just six minutes left, Rahn took the one that mattered. After cutting inside he dispatched a clinical finish to the bottom left corner. There was still time for Puskás to score an equaliser but much to his disgust the goal was debatably disallowed for offside. The game ended 3-2 meaning West Germany were now the world champions for the first time and Hungary's greatest opportunity to win the World Cup was over. Just as they'd participated in the 'Battle' of Berne, they'd now taken part in a game christened the 'Miracle' of Berne.

After the tournament there had to be the inevitable decline but after two more years of fine results, it was the Hungarian Revolution of October 1956 that actually would end the Golden Team's reign. By chance Honvéd were playing away in the European Cup against Atlético Bilbao as the revolution against Soviet imposed rule began in Budapest. As people took to the streets of Hungary in often violent protest, the home leg against Bilbao was rearranged to take place in Belgium. After the game the uprising continued across the country and Honvéd's players summoned their families to take part in a hastily arranged 'tour'. At the tour's conclusion many of the Honvéd team decided not to return to Hungary and officially became exiles with their families – Puskás, Kocsis and Czibor among the most high profile.

Puskás went on to become a legend at Real Madrid, signing in 1958 after serving a two-year ban for refusing to return to Honvéd. He formed a partnership with Alfredo di Stéfano that would go on to terrorise European football. Kocsis and Czibor moved together to join another Hungarian defector, László Kubala who'd left the country on its move to communism in 1949, at Barcelona. József Bozsik chose to return to Hungary but at 32 years old was entering the twilight of his career. He continued to play until 1962 but never managed to hit the heights of his Mighty Magyars form. Robbed of his team's heart, Sebes resigned and the tenure of Hungary as the greatest team in world football, minus the World Cup trophy to prove it, was officially over.

Between 1950 and 1956, Hungary won 42 games and lost just one – the World Cup final. In the ELO world football rankings at the time of writing, Hungary still hold the highest ever rating achieved after hitting 2166 points in 1954. In the World Cup of that year, Hungary scored 27 goals – still a record for any team to have played in the finals – and Sandor Kocsis's 11 goals in 5 matches gave him an average of 2.2 per game that has also yet to be beaten. During their time they were the first team to defeat Uruguay at the World Cup and the first team outside the British Isles to defeat England at home. Regardless of having only Olympic Gold to mark their time, the Magyars mattered because they were indisputably one of the greatest teams that ever played the game.

It is entirely fitting that in the year that the Hungary team was broken up, Willy Meisl (Hugo's brother) published his self-penned 'Soccer Revolution'. Celebrating the Wunderteam's achievements and their 'Whirl', Hungary had also benefited from Meisl, Hogan and Sindelar's influence, and then taken those ideas to the next level. The freedom from the 'oppression' of overly physical formations and kick and rush football had given birth to a new form of the game, a more attractive and fluid version. Ajax would be the next to truly achieve success playing in a similar fashion as they evolved the Mighty Magyars style into 'total football'.

Wolverhampton Wanderers 1954

Honours

Self-proclaimed Champions of the World

Monday 13th Dec 1954

WOLVERHAMPTON WANDERERS	BUDAPESTI HONVED SE
Williams	Farajo
Stuart	Palicsko
Shorthouse	Kováks
Slater	Bozsik
Wright	Lóránt
Flowers	Banyai
Hancocks	Budai
Broadbent	Kocsis
Swinbourne	Machos
Wilshaw	Puskás
Smith	Czibor

Teams for the infamous 'floodlit friendly' in December 1954

How do you measure who can lay claim to being the 'best' club in the world? The FIFA Club World Cup is perhaps the most obvious yardstick to use but there are those who will claim that any cup competition is not a fair indicator, their argument being that performance should be measured on consistency rather than a series of one-off games. Also football is a sport subject to all the highs and lows associated with any human based endeavour. To put it in a simpler fashion, the greatest sides do not always win the biggest prizes. World Cup history is littered with magnificent teams who fell just short such as 1954's Mighty Magyars from Hungary, or Holland's 'total' footballing side of 1974. By the same token domestic teams do not always earn the very highest honours due to one bad game in the course of a season. For instance can you judge 2010's La Liga winning Barcelona, who collected a record points total of 99 and the Spanish SuperCup in the season, on the basis that they lost the Champions League semi-final to Internazionale?

Whatever your personal take on the subject, any claim to be the 'best' is always going to bring a level of opposition and debate. If you do make the claim you have to be prepared for the view to be challenged. In the case of Wolverhampton Wanderers and their 'Iron Manager' Stan Cullis, while the claim may have been based on a reasonable level of fact, the reaction was such that it would give birth to one of football's greatest competitions.

Cullis was one of football's great disciplinarians, something which endeared him to some and excluded others. His dressing room manner was as uncompromising as it was unapologetic. Cullis believed that football should be direct and played by going forward at every opportunity, but this approach had to be coupled with a greater athleticism than your opponents. As a result his players conditioning and training obsessed him. Above all else though Cullis was a winner, desperate to bring Wolves the success he felt the club was due, an attitude in part forged by his time as a player.

Cullis broke into the Wolves defence as a teenager and quickly became captain. After being spotted playing for his local side Wolves had moved quickly to bring the player to the midlands from his home in Cheshire, well aware of the attentions of Bolton Wanderers and the potential that Cullis represented. Immediately realising his qualities belied his age, he was fast tracked through the youth and reserve teams to the first eleven. By 1936 he was 20 years of age, established as Wolves's first choice centre-half and permanent club captain. Cullis was an elegant and athletic defender but also intelligent enough to do his homework on the opposition he would face from week to week. Eventually his stock rose significantly enough to earn 12 full international caps for England and in what was seen as the ultimate vindication of his attitude, he became his country's youngest ever captain.

World War II curtailed his international career but Cullis still played regularly fro Wolves throughout the conflict as and when games were organised. He also took to guesting for several sides as he sought to keep up his sport in spite of the war. Taking work as a PT instructor Cullis had to sit and wait for the war to end to further his career, briefly brushing past a flirtation with coaching to return to Wolves. An injury then put paid to his career as a professional in 1947 but keen to retain his services, manager Ted Vizard made Cullis his assistant. On Vizard's departure the following year there was only one logical choice to succeed him and Cullis's managerial career had begun in earnest.

The biggest influences that fuelled his desire to become a winner were a series of 'nearlys' throughout his playing career. On breaking into the first team, his initial season in the First Division saw Wolves finish fifth. The following year saw him take his team mates to a second place finish, agonisingly just a point behind winners Arsenal. 1938-39 was to bring heartbreak as yet again Wolves finished as runners-up in the league, having been in pole position until a poor end of season run cost them first place. Salvation could have come from their run to the FA Cup final but they took the disappointing end of season form into the game and lost heavily to Portsmouth, widely considered as underdogs on the day. They had come away with nothing from a season that had at one point promised a potential double. From then on football was regionalised and truncated as the war took hold. Strong in the midlands competitions, Wolves were denied a chance of national honours until its full resumption in 1946.

The 1946-47 season was to be Cullis's last as a player but provide a fitting footnote to his playing career. An exciting race for the title had unfolded with Wolves once again right at the very top throughout. Competing fiercely with them were Liverpool and in almost perfect fashion, the fixtures threw the two together for the final game of the season. With two points for a win the scene was set as the home side Wolves needed just a draw to ensure the title, while Liverpool knew only a win would see them leapfrog into first. The Liverpudlians set about trying to bring the trophy to Anfield and eventually earned themselves the 2-1 victory they needed, but the main talking point of the game emerged from Cullis's refusal to bring down centre-forward Albert Stubbins. As Stubbins ran clean through on goal Cullis chased his man and despite the chance to bring him down illegally, refused to do so allowing Stubbins to score. With a title on the line Cullis attracted the criticism of some but held firm to his belief that he 'didn't want to be known as a man who won a medal by cheating'. With another missed opportunity burning inside him, Cullis's career in management began with him desperate to erase the club's reputation as nearly men.

Cullis's impact was immediate. In his first full season in charge he set about installing the 'kick and rush' style that would become somewhat unfairly his hallmark. While it's true he encouraged the ball to be played long at every opportunity, he looked for the pass to be hit to his wingers rather than just humped forwards without a specific target. The negative connotations we associate with an unattractive 'long ball' style of play were not Cullis's goals when introducing his system. It was a way of capitalising on his teams greater speed and stamina due to his approach to training. The change of style, set-up, and training methods took time to bed in but as the league remained elusive, Cullis did win the FA Cup at the first time of asking in 1949. The cup was the club's first major honour for 41 years and the 3-1 triumph over Leicester City was the perfect way for Cullis to justify his demands on the team.

By 1954 Cullis had taken his team to the peak of the English game by finally delivering the First Division championship everyone involved in the club had so desired. Wolves finished four points clear of local rivals West Bromwich Albion and after a tense 1-0 victory at the Hawthorns had taken them top, never relinquished the position. Cullis had delivered the club the trophy he'd come so close to winning as a player and in his opinion, now managed the best team in the world. His discipline had become legendary, just as the intensity with which he approached and watched the games had, but he'd proved the merit of his system. All he wanted now was a further stage to prove it on.

Cullis had built a fine team – marshalled off the pitch by himself, led on it by the legendary Billy Wright. Wright had played with Cullis but like his manager, had his career protracted by the war. Taking over as club captain after Cullis's playing retirement, Wright had also become England's captain – a position he enjoyed for the rest of his international career. Wright broke several records in his time playing for England, becoming the first player to reach 100 caps for his country and also captaining them for a record 90 times, but his immaculate disciplinary record mirrored his club manager's approach to sportsmanship. Wright was the biggest name in English football of his day, courting then marrying a celebrity – Joy Beverly of the Beverly Sisters – and leading his country into three World Cups. Wright was the leader Cullis needed on the pitch and a figurehead for the club. His 20 years as a player at Wolves would eventually lead to a stand at their home ground Molineux being named in his honour, and a statue gracing the stadium's entrance.

Around Wright a team was built that matched his ability. Cullis's method of passing the ball long to his wingers needed players fast and capable enough to capitalise. Johnny Hancocks and Jimmy Mullen provided the pace and guile required and were Cullis's first choices. Both men also possessed an eye for goal and regularly came inside when the chance presented itself, Hancocks netting an impressive 24 goals in Wolves title winning season of 1954. With Dennis Wilshaw, Peter Broadbent and Roy Swinbourne predominantly forming the triangle of attack through the middle, there was certainly no shortage of goal scorers in the Wolves first choice eleven.

Cullis also built a solid defence based around Wright in a central position. Wolves back line was difficult to break down but able to pick the range of passing required to hit their forwards. Bill Shorthouse in particular had been virtually ever-present in the title-winning year and like Wright, would remain at Wolves for the entirety of his career. With a core of players loyal to himself and his beliefs, Cullis felt his team could take on any side in the world and compete.

As fate would have it, an opportunity presented itself to test that theory. Many clubs such as Herbert Chapman's Arsenal of the 30's had the foresight to install floodlights in their stadiums. While the FA refused to sanction league games played under lights, many clubs across Europe were using the facility to stage prestige friendlies. The nature of being able to play under lights opened up another window of time to best harness a crowd around an average working day. Wolves were quick to realise firstly the potential to host some of the best sides in the world in their new capacity as one of England's biggest clubs, and secondly the revenue such games could generate.

In September 1953 as Wolves were about to embark on their first title-winning season, their own set of floodlights were officially opened with a friendly game against the South African national side. Wolves won comfortably and embarked on a series of games that became known as the 'floodlit friendlies'. Opposition teams were deliberately invited to give the greatest challenge and draw the biggest crowd, the term 'friendly' existing in name only. Immediately Wolves's profile rose across the football world and the games sparked a huge amount of interest. Celtic, Racing Club of Buenos Aires, Maccabi Tel Aviv and Moscow Spartak all arrived at Molineux and were beaten by the English champions elect, Austria's First Vienna struggled to a draw.

By the end of 1954 Wolves were being hailed as the best team in Europe but paradoxically English football's status was at an all time low. Defeat at Wembley to Hungary's Mighty Magyars had cast a shadow over the national team once thought of as comfortably the best in the world. The 3-6 scoreline at Wembley had told only half the story as in reality English football had been light years behind the Hungarians pace, movement and skill. With England 'only' losing by three goals, a return fixture destroyed any doubt there'd been about the nature of the result in November 1953 in Budapest. Hungary once again ran riot and beat the English 7-1. The bulk of that Hungarian national side was playing for one team – Honvéd – and come December 1954 they would be Wolverhampton Wanderers next opposition.

The game was immediately billed as a chance for English football to restore some pride, Wolves taking on the mantle as 'England' for one night only. While it may have only been a suggestion, with national captain Billy Wright leading

Wolves having played in both games against the Magyars and several of his team mates winning full international honours, there was plenty of fire to stoke the pre match hype. Honvéd would play with József Bozsik, László Budai, Zoltán Czibor, Sándor Kocsis and of course the Galloping Major – Ferenc Puskás – in their side, all of who played in 1953's 'match of the century' at Wembley. They were to be feared and Cullis's team were well aware of the danger they posed. On Monday 13th December 1954 a nervous Molineux waited for kick-off in a game that had generated so much interest and it was also being broadcast live on the BBC.

Cullis was taking everything into account and had constructed a plan. The rain had given the match a suitably muddy pitch, something Cullis had been hoping for having seen the Magyars struggle at the summer's World Cup on such a surface. Cullis believed that kick and rush could defeat the Hungarians shorter passing game and a difficult surface would only further his cause. As the game kicked off the pitch immediately began to break up but to Cullis's dismay, Wolves slipped behind to a Kocsis header. Shocked by Honvéd's quick start Wolves attacked and Roy Swinbourne missed a good chance but Honvéd looked to counter at every opportunity. After an attack broke down Honvéd accelerated through the gears and caught Wolves flat again, Machos putting them two ahead. With the score staying 2-0 until halftime despite growing Wolves pressure, the feeling that yet again 'Hungary' were going to defeat 'England' hung in the air.

Sitting with his players at halftime Cullis pointed to their nerves as the reason for the two-goal deficit. Wolves had abandoned their game plan in panic at the scoreline and Cullis told them to return to the style of football that had won them the league. With his team calmed and their focus reset, Wolves set about the second half looking to restore some pride.

The key to turning things around was an early goal and Wolves got their wish when Kovacs struggled to cope with Hancocks' pace. As the forward jinked his way into the area he drew a rash shoulder barge from the Hungarian defender. With a penalty awarded Hancocks picked himself up and took the spot kick himself, hammering the ball in to cut Honvéd's lead in half. Wolves had opened the door and set about trying to kick it through.

Honvéd's defence held firm until the 75th minute when Roy Swinbourne's header drew the teams level. It was no more than the English side deserved after incessant pressure and five minutes later, a flowing move saw the ball rolled into the onrushing Swinbourne's path just inside the penalty area. Without breaking his stride the forward struck it first time and sent Wolves into the lead. The comeback was complete and they now had just ten minutes to hold out. With Honvéd stung into action they turned round the Wolves pressure but couldn't force an equaliser of their own. The final whistle came and Wolves had won 3-2. 'England' had finally beaten 'Hungary', the result lauded as proof positive that the English game still had a place in football.

Billy Wright was delighted, describing the match as 'wonderful' and even earning rare praise from his manager. Cullis was elated, his team had taken on a Honvéd side widely thought of as unofficially the best in Europe, mainly on the back of their players' prominence in the national side, and come back from two goals behind to win. In his post match euphoria he greeted the waiting journalists by pointing to his players and declaring 'There they are, the champions of the world'. Many newspapers ran with the quote and furthermore the angle that Wolves were indeed now the 'best' team in the world.

The reaction to the claim, particularly from French journalist Gabriel Hanot would lead to the snowball that became the European Cup. Cullis would go on to win the '58 and '59 titles and the FA Cup in 1960 before an acrimonious split with Wolves in 1964. After a spell in charge of Birmingham City Cullis retired in 1970 having left his mark on the game and in particular on Wolverhampton Wanderers' history. Mirroring Billy Wright's immortalisation at Molineux, Cullis also has a stand named after him at the stadium and remains their most successful manager to date. Even though he led his team to some reasonable European Cup results they never managed the prestige or the acclaim earned by the 'floodlit friendlies' but Cullis had had his moment and no one could take it away from the man or the club.

Wolves mattered because of the legacy they left in kick-starting a move to full European competition. They also gave football another style in which to be played, a highly athletic form of 'kick and rush' that while it would never earn the plaudits of a 'total' football per say, Cullis used it to turn his club into self proclaimed 'champions of the world'.

Real Madrid C.F. 1955–60

Honours

Primera División Champions 1954-55, 1956-57 & 1957-58

Primera División Runners Up 1958-59 & 1959-60

Copa del Rey Runners Up 1957-58 & 1959-60

European Cup Winners 1955-56, 1956-57, 1957-58, 1958-59 & 1959-60

Latin Cup Winners 1955 & 1957

1956	Real Madrid	4	v	3	Stade De Reims
1957	Real Madrid	2	v	0	Fiorentina
1958	Real Madrid	3	v	2	Milan
1959	Real Madrid	2	v	0	Stade De Reims
1960	Real Madrid	7	v	3	Eintracht Frankfurt

Results of the first five European Cup finals, all won by Real Madrid

In 1954 manager Stan Cullis and most of the British Press proclaimed Wolverhampton Wanderers as 'the best team in the world'. After taking part in a famous series of floodlit friendlies against European opposition, Wolves had triumphed over the Hungarian side Honvéd 3-2 at Molineux having been 0-2 down at half time. That team from Hungary contained many of the 'Magical Magyars', the Hungarian national side that had humbled England at Wembley stadium in 1953 and then followed that with a 7-1 drubbing in Budapest. Televised live on the BBC on a December night in which awful conditions and a muddy pitch prevented the Hungarians more natural passing game, the victory and the dramatic comeback led to hyperbole in the press that reached all corners of the European game.

For Gabriel Hanot the statement was too much. The French journalist, editor, ex-professional footballer and coach was working for L'Équipe, the national newspaper dedicated to sport in France. Already beating the drum for some form of club competition for some time, the misjudged comment caused him to immediately step up his campaign for a European tournament to be played under floodlights throughout the season. Tournaments between teams from different European nations were nothing new – the Mitropa Cup existed and had been relatively successful but limited to Central and Southern European clubs. Also there was the Latin cup between the champions of France, Italy, Spain and Portugal which had produced some great games but Hanot sought to overcome these competition's limitations.

Hanot proposed a European competition between the champions of each nation that were invited to enter. Within four months of his article the competition, now swept along on a landslide of public and official approval, came into being and the European Cup was born. The recently formed Union of European Football Associations (UEFA) wanted a prestigious tournament for Europe's best sides that could act as a showpiece. With the rules drawn up sixteen teams were to be invited into the tournament that would follow a traditional knock out format, with home and away legs to take place until a final played at the Parc des Princes in Paris.

Real Madrid's first taste of success in Europe had just come in the same stadium in the Latin Cup. The competition was first played in 1949 and was currently perceived to be the highest honour available in European club football. Played in a single country at the end of each season, the four-team format meant that a semi-final, third place play-off and final were all played out between the entrants. By 1955 Spain had already produced two wins, Barcelona claiming the trophy in 1949 and 1952, Benfica, Milan and Stade de Reims taking the others between them. After claiming the title in the 1954-55 season Real Madrid had their first entry into the Copa Latino. Madrid beat Portuguese side Belenenses in their semi-final to set up a final against champions of the host nation, Stade de Reims. A 2-0 victory for Los Blancos courtesy of two goals from Argentinean born Héctor Rial set the tone for what would follow for the next five years, the culmination of one man's dream for the club he loved.

In 1943 a lawyer named Santiago Bernabéu became Real Madrid club president and an overhaul of the club from top to bottom began. Having graduated from youth player to first team, he became club captain and a mainstay of Real's squad for fifteen years. Staying with the club on retirement he worked his way through several positions before the Spanish Civil War severed the relationship briefly. On the war's end in 1939 he returned to a broken football club missing most of its key pre-war personnel. Far from looking like the best club in Europe, Real weren't even the best club in Madrid.

Working his way up until taking the presidency after playing a huge part in finding people to rebuild the club, he then put a grand plan into effect. Members of staff were recruited so each level of the football club had people responsible for its success on and off the pitch. More investment was drummed up for a separate training facility built specifically for the club and in 1947 after some tireless campaigning by Bernabéu for funding and permission, a magnificent new stadium was constructed and named the Estadio Chamartín much to the derision of some, who believed it was far too big to just house Real Madrid. After taking their first title under Bernabéu in the 1953-54 season the stadium was extended so it could accommodate 125,000 supporters. On reopening it was renamed after the man who had been involved in every part of its construction and became the Estadio Santiago Bernabéu.

Perhaps the biggest moment in Bernabéu's rebuilding came in 1953 when he and his team convinced Alfredo Di Stéfano to come to Real instead of rivals Barcelona, who believed at the time they had already signed their man. In a protracted transfer saga involving Real, Barca, Millonarios – the Columbian football club to whom Di Stéfano was contracted to at the time – and River Plate who would pick up the player's contract in 1955, Bernabéu used the confusion to convince the 'Saeta Rubia' (blond arrow) to sign with him instead. Barcelona claimed to the authorities that Real Madrid had used government influence to secure the signing and both clubs laid claim to the transfer of Di Stéfano. It was decided he would play alternatively for both clubs for four years, a decision designed to try and overcome the fighting surrounding the transfer. The outrage in Barcelona over the failure to secure the deal and then the indignation of a player switching between the two rivals caused a universal resignation of the club's board. Barcelona's new board and in particular the new President who had been given the position by Real Madrid supporter General Franco himself, decided the best thing to do with Di Stéfano was to sell the transfer rights to Madrid fully and end the circus. Di Stéfano would go on to become one of Real's greatest ever players, scoring 49 goals in European Cup competition alone including scoring in every final between 1956 and 1960. He was as effective with the ball at his feet as he was without, known for outstanding athleticism and a willingness to chase back. Officially classed as a striker by most, the truth was Di Stéfano played where he wanted, just as likely to close down an attacking winger as he would be to latch onto a through ball. With Di Stéfano's signing Bernabéu set the blueprint that would see Real continue to sign the best players in the world, something which subsequent Presidents have tried to continue into the modern day.

The 1953-54 title had been secured ahead of Barcelona in second place. Once again established as a domestic force, Real Madrid had the potential to become the biggest club in European football and Bernabéu knew it. Having not won a title since 1933, Real followed that success by retaining the trophy in the 1954-55 season making them the invited entrants into the proposed European Cup of 1956. After once more beating Barcelona into second place, Atlético Madrid finished in eighth position seventeen points behind their neighbours and Bernabéu's domestic plan had been realised – Real were national champions, signing the best players in the world and ruling the city. Despite strict sanctions by the Spanish Football Association on how many foreigners any side could have in their squad, Real naturalized Di Stéfano and continued to look to sign the finest players in the world. Having seen Barcelona sign László Kubala in 1951 and watched him inspire them to two titles in 1952 and 1953, Real now had their own star signing and their own inspiration to drive them forward.

Bernabéu knew that no stadium, training facility or organization could ever be successful unless the team on the pitch were winners. Di Stéfano was a magnificent player but he was also surrounded by some of the very best in the world as Real built a truly multi-national squad. Argentine Héctor Rial joined Madrid in 1954 and was quickly naturalized to the point where he represented the Spanish national side five times. Di Stéfano himself would claim 31 caps and 23 goals for Spain. Real's attack was completed by Francisco Gento at outside left whose pace was truly outstanding and José Iglesias Fernández (nicknamed Joseíto) at outside right, known for his willingness to chase down lost causes all day long. As the clamour for a European Cup grew in 1955 Bernabéu had been a vocal and prominent supporter, meeting officials in Paris and making sure Real would be involved even before the title was secured. Once invited into the competition Real accepted and would prove themselves the most exciting team, scoring readily and consistently involved in great games.

The first European Cup taking place in the 1955-56 season began with sixteen teams entered. The side that had kick-started the argument was nowhere to be seen, the sceptical English F.A opted not to send Wolves or anyone else into the competition believing it would have a negative effect on any team taking part. Joining Real were teams from all corners of Europe including PSV Eindhoven from Holland, Italian champions A.C Milan,

Hibernian of Scotland and Rot-Weiss Essen from Germany. Real found themselves drawn against Swiss team Servette whom they blew away 7-0 over two legs. Going to Switzerland for the first leg their overall superiority was eventually rewarded by two late goals from club captain Miguel Muñoz and Rial. Back at the Santiago Bernabéu stadium Madrid cut loose and put five past Servette including Di Stéfano's first and second European goals. Into the quarter finals Real faced more of a test in Yugoslavian team Partizan Belgrade but in front of a crowd of more than 100,000, Real's attacking prowess once again proved the difference and they recorded a 4-0 home win on Christmas Day. After a scare in the second leg including a shot that only failed to cross the line due to the mud in the six-yard box, they progressed safely with an aggregate score of 4-3 and now faced a glamorous tie against A.C. Milan.

The Milan side were more of an attacking threat than Real had faced in the competition and in the first leg at home, Rial's early goal was quickly equalised by the great Gunnar Nordahl. A record crowd was gripped as once more Real took the lead and once more Milan equalised. Refusing to get blown away like others before, Milan went in at the break 3-2 down but very much in the tie. Di Stéfano added a fourth in the second half but Real finished with a 4-2 win that left the tie up for grabs in the second leg in Italy. Real played well at the San Siro and even took the lead in the second half, eventually losing 2-1 but securing the aggregate win and a place in the final of the first ever European Cup.

In a repeat of the Latin Cup final their opponents would be French team Stade de Reims who would be on home ground in Paris for the final. In front of a largely French supporting crowd Real took on a team that included Raymond Kopa, a French striker who had agreed to join them the following season. In a wonderfully free flowing game Madrid ran out 4-3 winners despite finding themselves 3-2 behind with twenty-five minutes to go. Two goals from Rial, one from defender Marquitos and another from Di Stéfano saw Madrid crowned champions of Europe. Domestically Real lost their title to Athletic Bilbao, finishing third but they would be back in the European Cup for the following year as holders. Bernabéu had taken his broken football club and stood them on the pinnacle of the world's best with a new trophy to prove it. As he toasted success he knew the competition was going to grow and he was desperate for Real to remain on top.

In the 1957 European Cup there was a new challenge that drew a huge source of publicity, an English team – Manchester United – would take part for the first time and the competition was expanded to twenty-two teams including a preliminary round. The English side embraced the competition and achieved a record 12-0 aggregate victory over Anderlecht, further stoking the publicity machine. As the competition progressed it seemed almost inevitable that Real and United would meet but rather than in the final as some had mooted they were drawn together at the semi-final stage. United had already dealt with Spanish champions Bilbao in the previous round and the tie generated huge interest in both Spain and England. In the first leg in Madrid, Real were wonderful for seventy-five minutes, leading 2-0 until United finally reacted. Hitting Real on the break they managed to pull a goal back in the eighty-second minute through Tommy Taylor who had scored a hat trick in the Anderlecht game. Just two minutes later Enrique Mateos linked with Kopa and scored a third to leave United with a huge task at Old Trafford to win the tie.

Roaring into a two goal lead with Di Stéfano in brilliant form, Real had effectively sealed their final place and the despite a fight back that earned the English side a draw, the 5-3 aggregate win had the English press rethinking their earlier assertions and praising a Madrid side who seemed unstoppable. The final took place in Madrid's home stadium on the 30th May 1957 and Real faced a Fiorentina side that had seen off Red Star Belgrade and Grasshoppers of Zurich on their journey. The Italian side contained Julinho Botelho, one of the stars of the Brazilian 1954 World Cup squad and were known for an aggressive approach. The game laboured to the seventieth minute goalless, tackles and retaliation taking the place of Real's usual flowing style. Eventually Real got the breakthrough with a Di Stéfano penalty after Mateos had been tripped running into the penalty area but angry scenes ensued as the Italians felt he had been offside and the linesman had flagged. A further loss of concentration six minutes later allowed Gento to race clear of the Fiorentina back line and lift the ball over Sarti in the Italians goal. A 2-0 win meant the trophy stayed in Madrid and after being presented the cup by General Franco himself, Real had now established themselves as the dominant force in Europe beyond question.

To further enhance their reputation they once more won the Primera División and took the Latin Cup in the last time the competition would be played. The Latin Cup semi-final finished with Real winning 5-1 against A.C. Milan who were much the same side that had run Madrid so close in Europe the year before. With three trophies now taken in the one season, Real Madrid were legitimately the best team in the world and well on their way to being one of the best club sides ever.

After two La Liga titles and two European Cups manager José Villalonga left Madrid and was replaced by Argentina Luis Carniglia. José Santamaría joined the club to shore up the defence and many still recall him as the best central defender to ever play for Madrid. The 1958 European Cup would be forever remembered for the Munich air disaster, in which eight of Manchester United's improving squad lost their lives in an aircraft crash returning from an away leg against Red Star Belgrade of Yugoslavia. In a muted tournament Real Madrid progressed to the final easily, recording an 8-1 aggregate over Royal Antwerp of Belgium, a 10-2 win including an 8-0 mauling over Seville, and a routine 4-2 semi victory over Hungarian side Vasas. The final renewed rivalry with Milan who took Real to extra-time before losing 3-2 after Gento's winner. Despite the incredible achievement of three European Cups in a row, the eyes of the football world were focussed on Manchester. Real retained the domestic title after a season long tussle with their neighbours Atlético and moving into the 1958-59 season signed Hungarian legend Ferenc Puskás, to further bolster their already world beating squad.

Puskás was another prolific striker in the Di Stéfano mould who continued the tradition of signing the best players in the world. Puskás had refused to return to Hungary after being away with the Honvéd side when the Hungarian Revolution exploded in his homeland. After his family joined him he received a two-year ban from UEFA that prevented him playing in Europe. Once served he was thirty-one and found most clubs unwilling to take a chance on him due to his age. Finally Real signed him and in his first season in La Liga he scored 21 goals in 24 appearances, going on to become a legend in Spain. Following a familiar theme he was naturalized and represented Spain four times in his time in Madrid.

Domestically Real lost their title to Barcelona, coming in second but once more in Europe they proved unstoppable. Defeating Besiktas of Turkey, Austrians Wiener Sport Club and then neighbours Atlético in the semi-final after a play off in which Puskás got the winner, a repeat of the very first European Cup final was set for the Neckarstadion in Stuttgart. This time Real proved far too strong for Stade de Reims, even with Puskás injured they still had the irrepressible Di Stéfano who scored the second in a 2-0 victory.

Now with four consecutive European titles Real were going for a fifth that would see them keep the trophy permanently in tribute to the achievement. In what some believe was the greatest ever Real Madrid side, Puskás, Gento, Santamaría and Di Stéfano remained and were joined by Brazilian winger Canário and midfielder Luis del Sol. As some truly great sides lined up to take Madrid's crown, Real were in no mood to relinquish it without a fight. Sweeping aside Luxembourg's Jeunesse Esch 12-2 in the first round they faced an impressive Nice side in the quarterfinals. Meanwhile hated rivals Barcelona trounced Milan 7-1 on aggregate and then took apart the much feted Wolves 9-2, including scoring five goals at Molineux. Nice succumbed to Real Madrid in the Bernabéu 4-0 after beating them in France and the semi-final the world wanted was set – Barcelona v Real Madrid.

Despite many believing Barcelona would finally end Real's dominance the first leg in Madrid ended with a convincing 3-1 victory for Real. Di Stéfano and Puskás both scored to take some form of revenge for a recent league defeat that had all but ended Real's title hopes. The second leg at the Camp Nou produced a brilliant display from Real who ended with another 3-1 victory to seal a final place against Eintracht Frankfurt. Frankfurt were a strong side but they were unwittingly about to witness one of the greatest performances in European competition of all time.

On the 18th May 1960 at Hampden Park in Glasgow in front of 135,000 fans and live on television to an estimated 70 million viewers, Real reached near attacking perfection. Di Stéfano scored three, Puskás four as Madrid ran out 7-3 winners. A forty-five minute ovation greeted captain José María Zárraga lifting the trophy for a fifth time and that night in Scotland had witnessed a truly great team playing at the height of their powers. For five years Real had reined supreme in Europe and with that performance they had just elevated themselves to the upper echelons of the greatest teams of all time.

The following season Barcelona finally ended Real's European run with a first round aggregate win over Madrid. They would go on to lose the final to Benfica who would then retain the trophy themselves, beating Madrid despite a Puskás hat trick in 1962. Dominant domestically with 14 titles in the twenty years after the triumph in 1960, they would add only one more European Cup in 1966 before the 1998 victory over Juventus.

The Madrid side of those first five European campaigns was almost without compare. In 2003 Di Stéfano was voted the best player in Spain of the last fifty years and in 1995 the IFFHS recognised Puskás as the top scorer of the 20th century. At the head of all of Real Madrid's success was one man, the incomparable Santiago Bernabéu who remained President from 1943 to 1978 and had created one of the greatest clubs in the world game. Real Madrid mattered as they set the standard for achievement, helped the European Cup become the biggest club competition in the world and remain one of the greatest sides to have ever played football.

Liverpool FC 1959–74

Honours

Winners of English Second Division 1961-62

Winners of English First Division 1963-64, 1965-66 & 1972 -73

FA Cup Winners 1965 & 1974

UEFA Cup Winners 1973

'It's there to remind our lads who they're playing for, and to remind the opposition who they're playing against'

Manager Bill Shankly on the famous 'This is Anfield' sign in the players' tunnel at Liverpool's home ground.

In 1977 Liverpool FC took to the field at the Stadio Olimpico in Rome on the brink of fulfilling what many at the club felt was their destiny. Manager Bob Paisley had led his team to the European Cup final for the first time in their history and after several near misses in previous seasons, the club now had a chance to get their hands on the trophy. Ahead of them lay a tough test in Germany's Borussia Mönchengladbach, a team who had wrapped up their third consecutive Bundesliga title just a week previously. Paisley and his players knew there was no reason to be daunted however, they too had just wrapped up a consecutive title win and were now firmly established as the dominant footballing force in England.

After a slow start from both sides Liverpool snatched the lead through midfielder Terry McDermott and held on till halftime. Borussia were proving difficult to break down and dangerous on the break but in the second half the Reds remained patient, continuing to pass and move as was their way. Danish striker Allan Simonsen equalised with a wonderful finish but Liverpool remained compact, refusing to collapse under the mounting pressure.

Goalkeeper Ray Clemence made several good saves as the half progressed and Liverpool eventually wrestled their way back into the lead, defender Tommy Smith powering in a header from a corner with just over an hour gone. As the minutes ticked by and the game stretched through heavy legs and the Germans' need to chase, Liverpool continued to find space and work the ball well. Eventually their patience was rewarded as Kevin Keegan earned a penalty for Phil Neal to convert in the last 10 minutes of the game. The two-goal cushion was enough to take the wind from Borussia's sails completely and the game finished 3-1. With the final whistle came a new name to add to the list of European Cup winners.

That win in Rome sparked an era in which Liverpool would compete in 5 European Cup finals in 9 years, bringing the trophy back to Anfield 4 times. In that same spell they would also win 6 English First Division titles, 4 English League Cups, and before the 80's had ended they would add 2 FA Cups and another 3 league titles. They were now the dominant force in world club football and were now the club that everyone wanted to join and names like Kennedy, Souness, Dalglish, Rush, Barnes, Molby and Beardsley all etched their name in Liverpool's history. The club became a dynasty and an inspiration for their style, while also becoming a huge source of jealousy for others due to their success.

Your immediate thought may be that this is the team that mattered but the simple fact is, Liverpool achieved everything on the back of an era that would both change and define them. Their success through the late 70's and into the 80's under Bob Paisley, Joe Fagan and latterly player-manager Kenny Dalglish, was thanks to the changes the club had made under the leadership of one William 'Bill' Shankly. On arriving in 1959 he found a Second Division club in serious decline, facilities crumbling and staff despondent. On his retirement in 1974 he left behind a powerhouse in the English game ready to make that next step in Europe under Paisley's leadership. In 15 years he completely transformed the club and without him, Liverpool would never have achieved their later success.

Liverpool's history until Shankly's arrival had been one of peaks and troughs. Founded in 1892 after an argument left landlord John Houlding having to form a new club to play at Anfield in the wake of Everton's departure to Goodison Park, they immediately won the Lancashire League and were granted access to the Second Division of the Football League. Their meteoric rise continued as they won the second division without losing a game to gain immediate promotion to the top tier. Life was tougher at the top table and relegation followed as they struggled to adjust but they were shortly promoted once again, and set about trying to establish a foothold in the league. Their first title came in 1901 but they couldn't build on the triumph and fell away over the next three seasons to yet another relegation. Up until the Second World War they had added another three titles but still lurched from one end of the table to another.

Shankly had by now carved himself out a decent career as a player, representing his country several times as a right-half. Born as one of ten children in Glenbuck in Ayrshire, at one point Shankly seemed destined for a life underground. Glenbuck's reasonably remote location gave rise to limited scope career wise and the coal mine remained the main source of employment. Remarkably though, a village with a population of never more than 1200 became a veritable breeding ground for professional footballers. Over 30 years the village produced over 50 professional players before the mine's closure in 1931 caused a decline and eventual abandonment of the area. Shankly himself was one of five footballing brothers and the local team in the area, the Glenbuck Cherrypickers, became a legendary source of footballing talent. Shankly finished a basic education and immediately began working in the mine, all the while playing football and dreaming of an escape through a professional contract.

Growing up in a remote part of Scotland and working in the mine for two years gave Shankly a sense of place and attitude that would never leave him. Knowing the perfect storm of footballing talent that seemed to exist in the area, scouts regularly visited Glenbuck and Shankly was spotted as a young man with some potential. After signing for Carlisle United in 1932 he made his way into the first team and impressed immediately, earning a reputation as a rugged and enthusiastic player with a passion for the game that engulfed his private life. Shankly was only at Carlisle for a year before Preston North End tabled a £500 bid for his services.

Once at Preston he flourished and became a far more complete player. He helped the club gain promotion to the top tier of English football, won an FA Cup winners medal and became a full international for Scotland. His playing career was all but finished by the suspension of the league due to the Second World War, leaving an aging Shankly to consider his future at the conflict's end. His time at Preston North End had been a success and football had become his passion, with little to give as a player beyond a bit part role anymore Shankly moved into coaching and management, taking the first steps in a career that would define his legacy.

Shankly's first break came in 1949 at the club who had taken the chance on giving him a life away from the village, Carlisle United. Despite only having two years in charge Shankly immediately showed signs of a mind a few steps ahead of many of his contemparies. He began a resurgence that he never had the opportunity to finish, parting ways in 1951 after what he saw as a lack of support from his board in terms of bringing players into the club. An uncompromising winner, Shankly saw any doubt in his ability as a personal slight and moved to Grimsby Town to continue his fledgling career. Before taking the position at Grimsby Shankly had interviewed for the Liverpool job and while considered too inexperienced to take the role at Anfield, he left quite an impression and more than enough for the Liverpool board to begin monitoring his career with interest.

In three years at Grimsby Town, Shankly again began to overhaul the club but not get the chance to complete his plan. After stabilising the club's fortunes on the pitch, a point was reached where major investment was needed in the playing staff to take the club to the next level. After another alleged lack of support from his employers Shankly stayed true to himself and once again left a job behind where he had been denied autonomy. A brief spell at Workington again proved that he was a manager who would immediately change fortunes on the pitch and he came to the attention of Huddersfield Town, initially as a member of the coaching staff. Before long Shankly ascended to the manager's chair as had been expected when he first made the move, and once again he began to come into conflict with the club's board.

While he may have never produced real success at the clubs he'd managed, he had developed a reputation as an uncompromising and outspoken manager with an eye for a player. During his three years with Huddersfield Town, Shankly would nurture the career of a young Denis Law and then object publicly to the club's plans to sell the striker. Whilst he had never taken a club to truly outstanding success at this point, he was a noted figure in the game and many observers felt he just needed to find the right home for his ambition.

With his relationship with the Town board beginning to suffer in late 1959, he was approached by Liverpool chairman Tom Williams to take over what he described as 'the best club in the country'. As quick as ever Shankly replied 'Why? Is Matt Busby packing it in?' but leapt at the chance to move to Liverpool, a club who were suitably impressed to trust him to see a long-term plan to fruition. Things at Anfield had deteriorated in every sense of the word and Shankly revelled in making his presence felt at every opportunity.

In a 15-year career it is almost impossible to overstate the effect Shankly had on the club. In the same way Herbert Chapman had 'become' Arsenal in the twenties or Helenio Herrera encapsulated Internazionale in every aspect during the sixties, so Shankly came to embody Liverpool Football Club in his time there. Shankly demanded investment and got the support he'd sought his entire managerial career to date. Although initially the signs of improvement were fleeting, Liverpool were rewarded with a return to the First Division in

1962 after storming to the Second Division title and from that moment on, there was no doubting the merit of Shankly's ways.

Liverpool consolidated their position in the First Division quickly and went on to take the title in 1964 and 1966. The first in '64 had been particularly satisfying as disposing the reigning champions Everton had restored bragging rights to the red half of the city. Shankly's side now included former apprentices like Ian Callaghan and Chris Lawler, as well as astute signings like Ron Yeats (who had become captain), Ian St John and Tommy Smith. The manager had worked hard to create an atmosphere where the team was everything and no one could or would ever be bigger than that philosophy. He leaned towards bringing players in who were hungry for success rather than more established and expensive names. The titles were matched by the club's first ever FA Cup win in 1965 and Shankly had completed the first part of his long term plan – to become the driving force in Liverpool and then in the domestic game as a whole.

Shankly's love of the game was infectious and his connection to the fans served to motivate both. The fans loved his history as a working class lad, ground from Scottish granite and never forgetting his roots. Shankly couldn't help but love them all as he saw himself reflected in every one of them. The stories of his time at Liverpool are littered with tales of match tickets and personally written letters being sent by the manager to all sorts of fans, causes, families and people in the Liverpool area. He had even been known to ring fans the day after a game to discuss the result and aspects of the team's performance. Shankly saw every loss as a slight to their faith and in return, they loved him almost unconditionally for his desire to win.

Shankly also wanted to create a strong sense of belonging within his coaching staff and to that end, the legendary Anfield boot room was born. After designating said room as a meeting place for the coaching staff, hours were spent talking over tactical decisions, recent games, training methods and apprentices who would or would not make the grade. Along with his coaches Reuben Bennett, Bob Paisley and Joe Fagan, Shankly learned that the time spent analysing and often just relaxing in each other's company was invaluable to Liverpool's fortunes. It was from the boot room that the club's next two managers would be chosen – Paisley and Fagan – and in future former players and coaching staff such as Kenny Dalglish, Graeme Souness and Roy Evans would understand the value and reverence a similar approach would command.

It was also from the boot room that 'the Liverpool way' emerged. Over his tenure the now familiar patient passing and constant movement evolved that would become so effective in Paisley, Fagan and Dalglish's hands in the future. Shankly had always favoured an attractive and swashbuckling style knowing not only was it successful, it also satisfied the supporters to see their team try to play in such a way. After learning from a European Cup drubbing in 1966 by a breathtaking Ajax side about to become the 'total' football team that would be so revered, Shankly and his coaches realised that they could play just as attractive football but utilise more patience and possession to even greater success.

After a series of surprising and sometimes naive failures in the European Cup, Shankly would bring Liverpool it's first taste of European success by first reaching the final of the European Cup Winners Cup in 1966. Returning to Scotland for the final at Hampden Park, Shankly took Liverpool to face Borussia Dortmund with a sense that the majority of the crowd would be partisan to their cause, particularly with a Scottish manager and countrymen Tommy Lawrence, Ron Yeats, Willie Stevenson, and Ian St John in the Anfield starting eleven. Liverpool had impressed on route to the final, overcoming Juventus of Italy and Jock Stein's Celtic on the way, but came up short against the Germans. Despite Roger Hunt's equaliser Liverpool were matched stride for stride and after the game moved into extra time, Stan Libuda's wonderful lob sealed a 2-1 victory for Dortmund.

Moving into the seventies and with Liverpool now playing in their own style, another chance at European glory presented itself in 1973. Shankly had overhauled an aging and underperforming team at the start of the decade and a couple of seasons in, the club were now reaping the reward as they once again took the domestic title. The likes of Kevin Keegan and John Toshack represented Liverpool's front line having been spotted playing in the lower leagues, and Steve Heighway had been brought to the club on the back of a non-league career while he completed his education. Defensively Ray Clemence, another player plucked from the lower leagues, was now keeping goal while Larry Lloyd and Emlyn Hughes made up the central partnership ahead of him.

Once again it was German opposition ahead for Liverpool and in an echo of their future, it was Borussia Mönchengladbach who stood in the way of their first European triumph in 1973's UEFA Cup final. A two legged affair, it was Anfield first on the 10th May and Liverpool played brilliantly. Two first half goals from Keegan (who also missed a penalty) and a third on the hour from Lloyd had all but sealed the trophy before the second leg 13 days later. A nervy Liverpool did just enough to see the game out after going in at halftime 2-0 down. With the aggregate score 3-2 Liverpool held on to take the trophy, eternally grateful for a Ray Clemence penalty save in the first leg. Shankly had now achieved his European success. Since coming to the club he had restored them to the top flight, fought their way to the top of the city, become a force in the English game and now won a major European trophy.

A year and another FA Cup triumph later, Shankly made the decision that sent shockwaves through English football and resigned. Saying that he wanted to spend more time with his wife and family, perhaps a reflection of the dedication he had shown Liverpool over the last 15 years, he left the club with a footing for future success. The real tragedy however, was almost instantly he realised he had made the wrong decision. After becoming an increasingly frequent visitor to Liverpool's Melwood training ground and even stepping in to take training at times, Shankly had to be reminded he had chosen to retire. With new manager and former colleague Bob Paisley feeling somewhat undermined he was asked to stop coming to Liverpool unless it was to see a game with the rest of the crowd. His relationship with the club broke down and years of building battles with certain members of the board left some glad to see him finally gone. Shankly moved into media work and as an advisor and friend to many in the game.

Shankly had a huge role in building the club that Liverpool then became. Dominant domestically and in Europe, the team and in particular the structure of the club itself bore his hallmark for years to come. When Dalglish resigned from his role as player-manager in 1991 the true glory days of the era were over but the memories remained. Shankly had given the club what it required to become such a driving force and as that mantel passed to Manchester United to take up in the 1990s, just as they were forever in the shadow and indebted to Sir Matt Busby's service to the club, so forever will Liverpool be with Shankly.

William Shankly passed away in 1981 after a heart attack but Anfield now recognises his contribution to the club's growth after the difficult times following his resignation. He created a football club that mattered to the game for the inspiration they provided across Europe, just as Ajax, Internazionale, Real Madrid, Barcelona and the other great teams would and still do in periods of success. Anfield now bears the Shankly gates, famously inscribed with the name of the club's chosen anthem 'you'll never walk alone', and is also home to a bronze statue of the manager situated by the famous Kop. The statue itself is inscribed with the simplest of sentiments but one that sums up why he mattered to the city of Liverpool itself – 'He made the people happy'.

All photos from and copyrighted by Colorsport unless otherwise stated

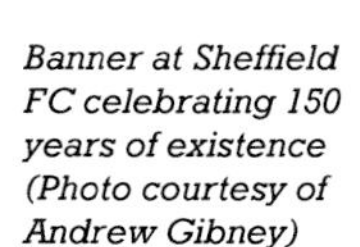

Banner at Sheffield FC celebrating 150 years of existence (Photo courtesy of Andrew Gibney)

Blackburn Olympic's 1883 FA Cup winning side, note the FA Cup trophy itself on the floor (the larger of the two cups on display) later melted down for counterfeit coins having been stolen whilst in Aston Villa's care in 1895

Newspaper cartoon satirising Alf Common's £1,000 move to Middlesbrough, Common warding off the 'ghost' of relegation for his new club

Herbert Chapman's FA Cup winning Arsenal side of 1930, Chapman himself sits far left on the middle row next to David Jack

Hungary's Mighty Magyars line up at Wembley before the 'Match of the Century' in 1953, Ferenc Puskás the closest figure to us on the left of the picture

Luis Del Sol, Alfredo Di Stefano, Ferenc Puskás and Francisco Gento line up for a photo wearing the white of Real Madrid

Gerd Muller leaps to celebrate his goal with captain Franz Beckenbauer in the 1972 European Championship final against Russia

Bill Shankly and Brian Clough sit together before the 1974 Charity Shield between Liverpool and Leeds United

Rinus Michels watches on from the bench during his time as Holland manager

FC Internazionale Milano 1962–67

Honours

Winners of Serie A in 1962/63, 64/65, & 65/66

Winners of European Cup 1964 & 1965

Winners of Intercontinental Cup 1964 &1965

Class + Preparation, Athleticism + Intelligence.
= Scudetto

Slogan placed in Inter dressing room by manager Helenio Herrera

Psychology in football is a difficult subject to pin down conclusively. For a game played out between two teams who on paper often seem almost perfectly matched, it's the game played in the mind that can determine the winner. One of the key aspects of a manager's role is the ability to measure an approach and a system that brings the best from his players regardless of the opposition. The myth of invincibility can become all-important to a team's success, particularly when coupled with a method of playing that enhances the collective abilities of a team. Many managers have implanted a winning mentality throughout a club and also managed to gather a group together who share common motivational traits. In doing so the manager becomes the focal point – the conduit through which success will come, and the man in the role can take on an almost mythical presence within a club.

One such example of a man who had a firm grasp on the impact of attitude and psychology was Helenio Herrera, manager of 'la Grande Inter' and one of the finest exponents of the tactical system that defined Italian football – 'catenaccio'. Herrera led Internazionale to European dominance, left a unique footprint in the game and a lasting attitude towards Italian football. 'His' system has often been derided for its perceived negativity but above all else Herrera was a winner. Once he had moulded catenaccio and Inter to his grand plan no team in the world seemed capable of unlocking them.

Catenaccio is both a system and a mentality to defend as a unit and not concede. The word has no easy translation, cited as 'padlock' by some, a house 'door-chain' by others, and 'door-bolt' or just 'bolt' on its own also. While the meaning is unspecific, the idea created by the name comes through. At its most effective it involved the deployment of a 'libero' (the free one), the modern sweeper position, behind the defensive line to effectively nullify any forward by controlling the space. It became undeniably linked with negativity in the game but this wasn't always the case, as it was simply a way to not concede but at the expense of an extra man in attack. Several managers coupled it with an aggressive attitude to really seal its legacy as a negative force in football but what should never be forgotten, was at its height it became the most feared method of playing in the world game.

In reality catenaccio had existed before Herrera's embracing of the system but that didn't stop him claiming it as his own. The defensive formation has it's origins in Austrian coach Karl Rappan's 'Swiss Bolt' which he used to great effect in a career spent mostly in Switzerland with both domestic clubs and the national team. Several people took note of the difficulty in playing against a defence that moved and worked together to shut out a forward line. As several coaches bastardised their own versions, Italian manager Nereo Rocco was the first to popularise the way of playing in his home country. Using and developing it to achieve surprising results with Triestina, Treviso and Padova, eventually he became manager of AC Milan in 1961. Rocco's Milan were hugely successful with a version of catenaccio that still allowed attacking freedom. His team became the first to Italians to lift the European Cup in 1963, before he moved to Torino and rewarded them with their best form since the mighty Il Grande team of the 40's.

Rocco's system involved using a tight defence to form a springboard for the attack with a win-at-all costs philosophy. Herrera's vision and personal type of catenaccio shared the winning attitude with Rocco, but his priorities were firmly set with the team's defensive responsibilities first. It was the ultimate goal to not concede for Herrera's Inter, the belief being that every win would start with a clean sheet. Once Herrera realised the merit in catenaccio it became almost as big an obsession as winning for the manager, a huge personality even in an age where news travelled slowly compared to new media's instant access. He was a massive figure in the world game for both his record of success and his controversial methods equally.

Herrera was born in Buenos Aires to Spanish parents but travelled throughout his youth, taking in Morocco and France extensively and becoming a professional footballer. In a 15-year career he earned the reputation as a talented and determined player. It was in France at the end of the Second World War that he made the move into coaching and management with Puteaux and Stade Français. After limited success while he learned the role, he moved to Spain to continue his career. In Spain throughout the 50's he really began to grow his standing in the game but refused to settle at one club, moving on from Atlético Madrid even when still in the flushes of success. He repeated the pattern and never truly built a legacy at any one club. Up until 1958 Herrera's career in Spain had taken in Real Valladolid, Málaga, Deportivo de La Coruña, Seville, as well as his time at Atlético and after a spell in Portugal with Belenenses he finally had the chance at a true 'giant' in footballing terms.

Herrera was given the manager's job at Barcelona and immediately realised the power of the mind in regard to performance on the pitch. Real Madrid's legendary side were winning European Cups and the hearts and minds of the world's sporting media – di Stefano, Kopa and Puskás forming the deadliest attack in the game. On paper Herrera knew he had a group of players at Barcelona that could match Los Blancos, the undeniable talent of Hungarians Sándor Kocsis and László Kubala were the foremost available to him, but the inferiority complex Madrid's European triumphs had generated was reflected in the way Barcelona approached any contest with them.

Herrera set about changing attitudes and instilling a huge sense of identity on the club and the players, washing away negativity and getting his team to play in a free flowing fashion that best played to their individual talents. Herrera delivered two consecutive titles and restored Barcelona's domestic standing but after losing a European Cup semi-final to a quite brilliant and revitalised Real in 1960, Herrera was removed from his position of manager amid stories of fall outs with the Barca board and Kubala.

During the 1950s Internazionale of Italy had struggled and needed a similar level of sea change that Herrera had instigated in Catalonia. The manager was now well aware that his short tenure at Barcelona had earned him a reputation and when approached by the Italians and their owner Angelo Moratti to take over, he used this to negotiate a world record salary for a manager and entered the club on a wave of publicity. Promising success and a return to prominence in the city, Herrera now had an abundance of self-confidence and began to restructure the club.

Inter had been founded in 1908 as a breakaway club from what would become AC Milan. After an internal dispute regarding the favouring of Italian players over several Swiss players at the club, a group of officials and players split and formed Football Club Internazionale Milano, the moniker Internazionale meant as a reflection of their desire to see all nationalities play for the team. Taking the now familiar blue, black and gold to contrast the red and black of their former team, the club set about challenging the already established Italian sides and becoming the best team in Milan.

Inter's first title was won in controversial circumstances in 1910, as Pro Vercelli fielded a youth team in a play-off to determine the title winners in protest at what they felt was favouritism towards Inter in the selection of the game's date. As the First World War interrupted Italian football it would be ten years before another national championship was won in 1920, and in an act of remarkable symmetry a third followed in 1930. Brief periods of dominance in the late 30's and early 50's had been followed by long fallow periods and prior to Herrera's arrival, the whole club continued to feel like a giant in waiting rather than a real footballing power.

Across the city AC had also only achieved sporadic early success but in the 50's become a real force – winning domestic titles, appearing in the 1958 European Cup final and also boasting some of the truly great players in world football of the time in Gunnar Nordhal, Nils Liedholm, Gunnar Gren and Juan Alberto Schiaffino. In the shadow cast by AC and Inter's stumbling status in Italian football, Herrera had demanded a blank slate to begin again and recreate the club in his own image and that's what he immediately set about doing.

Throughout his time with the club Herrera created some of the many trademarks of his approach to the role of manager, both good and bad. Autocratic sometimes to extremes, Herrera created a culture where his players every move was monitored and measured. The player's were expected to live and die for the team and any evidence to the contrary meant swift removal from the club. Inter's players had their diet controlled, their sleeping patterns monitored, harsh training routines with no exceptions given for the individual to contend with, and Herrera introduced the 'ritiro' – the practice of taking the players away together before each game in a retreat to eat, sleep, drink, and train for the match. Whilst widely unpopular and divisive to begin with, eventually Herrera had control over a squad of players who accepted his methods and madness. Constantly working on their attitudes through either making them angry enough to seek to prove him wrong, or so reaffirmed by their manager's faith that they played beyond their abilities, the players were bombarded with motivational slogans in their dressing room and around the ground. Herrera was almost despotic in his will to install his own desire to win in every one of his players and sure enough, eventually results turned and Inter began to become Grande.

Herrera's team was incredibly disciplined but also possessed the talent to match their manager's incredible drive. Herrera was a huge personality and needed his team to cede to his wishes but also have the ability to see his vision through. By 1962 Inter had settled defensively into the pattern that would make them notorious. In the libero role was one of its greatest exponents, Armando Picchi, captain, on field leader and sometime challenger of Herrera. Picchi had several run ins with his manager but was a rock behind the defensive line and one of the first sweepers to realise that their role was also to set attacks in motion rather than just snuff out danger. Picchi became a vital part of the Inter machine and it was no coincidence that when Herrera had tired of his attitude and forced him out of the club in 1967, Grande's best days were almost immediately over.

Behind Picchi, goalkeeper Giuliano Sarti joined in 1963 and remained virtually ever present in the Grande side. In front of the sweeper the defensive line also remained fairly consistent. One of most innovative moments of Herrera's career came with the signing of Giacinto Facchetti, a young centre forward from Treviso, who he converted to become a left back to great effect. Facchetti was a superb athlete and was tasked with becoming an extra man in attack for Inter on the break. In the notoriously tight Serie A Facchetti scored with regularity that many forwards would have been jealous of, and his ability to maraud his way through games on Inter's left flank became a huge weapon when they broke. In the centre of defence technically just ahead of Picchi's libero were the aggressive Tarcisio Burgnich and the more elegant Aristide Guarneri, both full internationals and both rugged and determined characters who shared Herrera's vision of a padlock at the heart of the defence. Burgnich was tasked with taking the right side of the opposition attack as Brazilian World Cup winning midfielder Jair had license to roam up and down that flank.

Another layer of defensive cover was added with a deep-lying midfielder, Carlo Tagnin mostly used until 1965 when Gianfranco Bedin took over the role. Just ahead of that position was the quite exceptional Spaniard Luis Suárez, a European Footballer of the Year winner and former Herrera disciple at Barcelona. Suárez moved to Inter for a world record fee and was considered by his manager as a vital part of the puzzle. For a team with such high defensive aspirations it was vital a player of the quality of Suárez was available to turn defence into attack quickly. With Jair and Facchetti running either side Suárez's passing ability became the key to the change of gear Inter required.

Ahead of the midfield in the true attacking forward positions lay Sandro Mazzola and Mario Corso right and left of a central striker. Mazzola was the son of the great Valentino, leader of the Grande Torino team so tragically taken by the Superga disaster. He spent his entire career with Internazionale, playing for over seventeen years mostly as an inside-right and becoming a key member of Italy's national team playing in the 1966, 1970, and 1974 World Cups. Like Picchi, Mazzola became a symbol for Inter and scored some memorable goals for the club, always willing to run with the ball but modest and reserved off the pitch. He became a fan's favourite in Milan and despite a period of poor results when he became a member of the club's backroom staff in later years, his status as a true Inter legend remains undiminished.

Corso played inside-left and was famed for his near complete dependence on his left foot. Often languid and horrifically inconsistent, it was his brushes with genius that retained his place in the side. Herrera publicly derided Corso's work ethic during a game, his laziness was after all the very antithesis of his manager's vision, but he was a favourite of the club's owners and remained untouchable. Many myths arose regarding his playing style but his talent was supreme if inconsistent, often silencing any doubts with a flash of 'God's Left Foot' at a free-kick or with an exquisite pass. Corso may have seemed like a luxury in Herrera's machine but he settled several games and like Mazzola, became an idol for the Inter fans.

Around this core several others orbited, particularly in the central striking position but this was la Grande Inter, Herrera's stalwarts, who brought the club its glory. Players such as Lorenzo Buffon in goal, Aurelio Milani, Joaquín Peiró and in particular Angelo Domenghini in attacking positions also played their part in creating the all-conquering Grande. With a talented team and a focussed manager, they set about bringing in the silverware that led to their indelible mark in football history.

Herrera's team took their first Scudetto in 1963 in typically pragmatic fashion, conceding only 20 goals against across a 34 game competition. They followed this in the next four seasons with two more titles in '65 and '66 and only a lost 'Championship tiebreaker' in 1964 and a last day defeat at mid-table Mantova in 1967 prevented them from making it a clean sweep. Between 1962 and 1967 Inter finished first, joint first, first, first, and second by one point in five seasons. Domestically they were almost untouchable, destructive and solid in defence, quick and deadly on the break. The ultimate 'Inter game' became to steal the lead and then sit knowing they couldn't be broken down.

Inter carried this invincibility into Europe and having watched city rivals AC Milan lift the trophy at Wembley in 1963, went in to the 1964 campaign determined to match the Rossoneri's triumph. Inter barged and bustled their way through games against Everton, Monaco, Partizan Belgrade and Borussia Dortmund to earn slender victories in all and a place in the final. Waiting for them lay an aging but still immensely talented Real Madrid who were defeated 3-1. The decision by Herrera to man mark Puskás and Di Stefano nullified

Real's main threat and drew criticism for the negativity displayed, but two goals from Mazzola and one from Milani had secured the club its first European Cup.

Europe had now seen first hand the stoic Inter defensive mentality and as winners, they now had the chance to play Independiente of Argentina for the Intercontinental Cup, the only competition at that time that could legitimately determine who was the 'best' club in the world. After losing narrowly in Argentina but triumphing at Inter's shared home ground the San Siro, a play-off was held at the Bernabéu Stadium in Madrid to determine the winner. Inter emerged with a 1-0 win and had taken the title to the delight of Herrera. Already firmly in the belief that in reality the star of Inter Milan's successful side was himself, now he had the trophy to prove he managed the best team in the world.

Now riding the crest of a wave, Inter set about trying to retain the trophy in 1965 and go one better than their rivals across the city. Dinamo Bucharest and Glasgow Rangers were swept aside but Liverpool presented a far greater challenge in the semi-final. At Anfield for the first leg, Inter crumbled to a 3-1 defeat to the surprise of many, wilting in the white-hot atmosphere the home crowd managed to generate. For the return leg Herrera had fired his players up by claiming they now had a huge point to prove and a brilliant performance saw the 3-1 scoreline overhauled by virtue of a 3-0 win. Two early goals, one a controversially given but brilliantly taken free-kick from Corso, the other a poacher's effort from Peiró that bought a wave of protest from Liverpool's players as the striker took the ball from goalkeeper Tommy Lawrence, immediately putting a very good Liverpool side on the back foot. As the second half moved past the hour mark, Facchetti cut inside and scored to leave the Englishmen with the almost impossible task of breaking down a determined Inter defence. Another final berth was secured and Benfica, winners in 1961 and 1962, now stood in their way.

With the match venue previously chosen as the San Siro much to Benfica's chagrin, Inter claimed home advantage and edged a tight contest 1-0 thanks to Jair's goal. As soon as they took the lead Inter remained happy to defend, even when Benfica defender Germano had to take over in goal due to injury, the Italians remained camped in their own half. Victory was secured and then the Intercontinental title also retained after another victory over Independiente. La Grande Inter had swept to the top of world football and then stayed there. Herrera felt his approach and ideas were completely vindicated.

By 1967 and after a defeat to Celtic's Lisbon Lions in the European Cup final, the Grande team was breaking up. The following year Herrera left for Roma sensing he'd taken Inter as far as he could and the core of the team split for new horizons, retirement, or Inter's reserves. AC Milan became catenaccio's new guardians but Inter had become a legitimate force in Italian, European and world football. Herrera struggled to hit the heights he achieved with Inter after leaving, in part because he never enjoyed the autonomy he was granted there by then owner Angelo Moratti, but he did win the Coppa Italia with Roma in 1969 and remain a figure in the football world up until his death in 1997.

It is impossible to discuss Herrera's reign without also mentioning the controversy that accompanied it. Persistent rumours circulated that Herrera was alleged to have used performance enhancing 'vitamins' on Inter's first team and similarly during his time in Barcelona. These allegations have been refuted by many of the players but what was undeniable was the culture of absolute control Herrera demanded. Several players voiced their discontent at Herrera's style and were moved on, several club owners and officials also fell foul of his temper. Then there are the completely unsubstantiated allegations of match fixing on Herrera's part, born partly from the man's unshakable desire to win.

Herrera was a controversial figure throughout his career but he courted it readily – he was after all the biggest star at any club he worked for he theorised. While many allegations have been made regarding his tenure in charge, none have ever been proven and the players that have spoken about such things have always denied any such accusation.

La Grande Inter mattered because while Rocco's AC Milan would also show the world catenaccio, it was Inter who used it to sit atop the football pile to such devastating effect. Regardless of any personal feeling or the negativity with which it was tarred, it did become a blueprint for success in the Italian game that is still used today. Herrera was a disciplinarian and power crazy but in today's game a club and manager seeking to have input into a players diet, sleep, psyche and life away from football is completely commonplace. Like Herbert Chapman, he developed the role of a manager at a football club and changed it forever. Whether you believe it was for better or for worse, football's landscape was undeniably changed by Herrera's methods in ways that are still felt today.

AFC Ajax 1965–73

Honours

Eredivisie Winners 1965-66, 1966-67, 1967-68, 1969-70, 1971-72, & 1972-73

Eredivisie Runners-up 1968-69, 1970-71

KNVB Cup Winners 1966-67, 1969-70, 1970-71, & 1971-72

European Cup Winners 1971, 1972, & 1973

European Cup Runners-up 1969

Intercontinental Cup Winners 1972

UEFA Super Cup Winners 1973

'The Inter System Undermined.
Defensive football is Destroyed'

Headline in the wake of Ajax's 2-0 win over Internazionale in the 1972 European Cup Final

Total football is a relatively simple concept. Primarily used by the attacking players in any team, it essentially means that within the structure of the formation any one player can play in every position. This allows players to wander and find where they can be most destructive, it allows midfielders to shield their defenders and drop in when required in attack, and it allows a supremely talented player such as Johan Cruyff the freedom their ability craves.

Despite the simplicity at its heart, total football requires a group of players who are inherently in tune with one another. Ajax not only possessed such a group, they had a manger with the vision to implement such a system and stay true to its principles. With Cruyff on the team sheet as centre forward but playing wherever he felt he could be most effective, Ajax had the system and the player at its head that could dominate Europe.

The concept of total football had started years earlier. Hugo Meisl had worked with English coach Jimmy Hogan and managed the Austrian Wunderteam of the thirties. Using a system in which his forward players would switch and change positions making it difficult for defenders to pick up, the Austrian team went 14 international games unbeaten. The system was dubbed 'the whirl' and would evolve gradually overtime. Matt Busby took some of its principles for his own 'pattern' that brought Manchester United so much success during his reign. The legendary Mighty Magyars, Hungary's national team of the '50's, refined the system and used it for their own ends to become one of the best sides in world football. However it was implemented the basic principals remained the same – create space and work with footballers comfortable in many positions.

Ajax's first brushes with the concept had occurred under the management of Jack Reynolds, an Englishman who took charge of Ajax between 1915 and 1947 almost continuously. Reynolds had enjoyed a relatively undistinguished career as a player and moved into management in 1912. After an agreement to take charge of the German national team was ended by the First World War, Reynolds went to Amsterdam and took charge of Ajax. He went on to pioneer the youth system now so synonymous with the club and repeatedly promoted his young players into the first team. Reynolds also looked to play attacking football with wingers, a new concept to the Dutch and one that would soon be copied by nearly every club in the league. He encouraged his players to play with freedom and move among themselves to wear the defence down, one of the foundations of what would become total football.

As his revolution began to bring success, people took notice of the strange formations and training methods of the Englishman. After making the team the best of his era, Reynolds retirement in the late forties left a legacy of successful, attacking football at the club. This legacy was not lost on a player who had returned from the war to play for the club. While he only worked under Reynolds at the very end of the manager's career, Rinus Michels would go on to write his own page in Ajax's history.

Michels enjoyed a one-club career with Ajax from 1946 to 1958. Never a blindingly skilful player, his hard work and brute strength earned him over 100 goals in his career as a striker. Moving on to a coaching career he eventually took charge of team affairs in 1964 and began to refine his vision of what Reynolds had started.

Dutch football was experiencing the upheaval of a move to professionalism and it was primed for revolution. Working on innovative ideas not seen in Holland before like playing an offside 'trap' or making sure the players were supreme athletes, his attack were all trained to blend seamlessly into one another's roles. The tactic was largely enforced on him by the need to incorporate Johan Cruyff's strengths in the team. Prodigiously talented but liable to wander from his position as striker, Cruyff caused Michels to realise that success for Ajax in the future was dependent on getting the best from his mercurial talisman.

Cruyff had made his debut for the first team in 1965 aged just 17. He had been at Ajax since the age of 12 after his mother, a cleaner at the club, had begged coaching staff to have a look at her boy. After living up to his mother's promises of potential, Cruyff had been through the academy and continued to impress. Coupled to wonderful balance and ball-control, Cruyff had extraordinary vision. When playing in Rinus's system his awareness of his team mates and their movement among positions meant Cruyff became acutely aware of space on the football pitch. If he was being marked tightly at the top he would drop deeper and deeper until a hole had opened in the opposition defence. With his speed either he of one of his team would go on to exploit it with lethal effect. If he struggled to get free through the middle Cruyff would often pull wide and take up the position of a winger, the area of the pitch so exploited by the turn that bears his name. By creating space for himself and others and having the ability to find passes that no one else on the pitch could, Cruyff quickly made himself the lynchpin around whom Michels knew the side had to revolve.

By 1967 Cruyff had made his debut for the national team and was making an impact in the Dutch game. His debut season in 64-65 had been a hugely disappointing one for Ajax who finished thirteenth out of sixteen clubs. With Michels installed as coach and the basic principals of total football emerging, Ajax finished the 65-66 season as champions. The turnaround had been seismic from a club who had lost thirteen times and amassed just 26 points, to losing only 2 games of a 30 game season and finishing seven points clear of rivals Feyenoord in second. Cruyff had been inspirational, scoring 25 goals in 23 appearances.

Ajax would go on to claim the next two titles as well, Michels' system now almost fully realised and Cruyff continuing to be Ajax's and the Eredivisie's exceptional player. He finished as top-scorer in the Ajax's double winning year of'67 and was instrumental in both triumphs. European glory had so far eluded them though, but despite finishing the 68-69 season having been denied three titles in a row by Feyenoord, Ajax found themselves in their first ever European Cup final. In Michels' reign Ajax had achieved some credible results, notably a 5-1 aggregate win over Liverpool, but they now stood on the cusp of an eternal trophy.

Michels' side had now been filtered through four seasons to contain only players who were capable of fitting into the system. Players such as Serbian defender Velibor Vasovic, then a Yugoslavian international, had been bought by Michels because of his ability and comfort on the ball. Vasovic would become captain and play for five years partnering Barry Hulshoff in Ajax's defence before retirement. Henk Groot had been bought back from rivals Feyenoord to play along Ajax's front line and this European Cup final would be his last game.

Some had been retained from the old regime and forced to adapt such as Piet Keizer, a left-winger more than adept at coming inside and making way for Cruyff's adventures on the flanks. Keizer would play for Ajax for 15 years and make over 350 appearances, he and Cruyff would become known as 'the royal pair'. Although reports suggest that their relationship ended in acrimony, on the pitch they had an almost telepathic understanding at times. Keizer was as good as Cruyff at finding space and would drift, hence a magnificent goal return over the course of his career. Joining the royal pair at the cutting edge was 'Mr Ajax', Sjaak Swart. Like Cruyff and Keizer, Swart was a full international and one club man in 1969. After making his debut in 1956 Swart had become a stalwart of the club and a favourite amongst fans.

Now Ajax found themselves playing on their biggest stage so far. On the 28th May 1969, they faced Italian giants AC Milan at the Santiago Bernabéu Stadium in Madrid. Both sides had impressed on route to the final – Milan eliminated 1967 finalists Celtic and 1968 winners Manchester United, whilst Ajax had smashed Germany's Nuremburg and Turkish champions Fenerbahçe, then needed a replay to beat two-time winners and five time finalists Benfica. In their semi-final Ajax held a 3-0 first leg lead over Czech team Spartak Trnava and despite losing the second leg 2-0, safely qualified to be Holland's first ever representatives in the final. Against Milan they simply froze in the spotlight and never showed the form of which they were capable. The game ended with a 4-1 win for the Italians. Led by the controversial but brilliant Gianni Rivera, Pierino Prati's hat trick and a Giovanni Trapattoni inspired midfield left Ajax floundering in their wake to lift the trophy.

Ajax then responded to the disappointment domestically by winning another double. Losing only once over the season, Ajax scored 100 goals and conceded only 23. Despite this the real story was bitter rivals Feyenoord's exploits in Europe. Going one better than Ajax, Feyenoord had become the country's first ever European Cup holders by beating Celtic in the final in Milan. Impressive throughout, even holders and the team who had so comprehensively taken Ajax apart – AC Milan – fell to Feyenoord as they marched to the final. The European campaign undoubtedly cost them in the Eredivisie. Feyenoord only lost one game themselves but drew eleven times to 'gift' Ajax the championship.

Going into the 1970-71 season the battle lines were drawn. Both Feyenoord and Ajax had qualified for the European Cup and both teams had a sprinkling of new faces to aid their push for honours. A hard fought title went to Feyenoord who edged out a chasing Ajax by 4 points. The KNVB Cup came back to Amsterdam though as Ajax retained the trophy, satisfyingly earning a 2-1 away win over Feyenoord in the quarterfinals. It was the European Cup that would once more provide the biggest headlines as both teams created stories for very different reasons.

The Dutch clubs were both drawn against perceived weaker opponents in the first round. Ajax dealt with Albanian champions KF Tirana reasonably trouble free. A 2-2 draw away from home put them in the driving seat, a 2-0 home win at the De Meer Stadium secured their passage. Holders Feyenoord had been drawn against Romania's FCM UTA Arad. The first leg finished in a surprising 1-1 draw but even though the second leg would be in Romania, Feyenoord were still expected to progress. Arad held out for a 0-0 draw and however unlikely it seemed, had knocked out the current champions in the first round.

With substantial bragging rights secured already Ajax then beat Basel of Switzerland 5-1 on aggregate in the second round. Humiliatingly, Feyenoord's conquerors Arad were trounced 6-1 by Red Star Belgrade. Going into the quarterfinals Ajax seemed to be carrying some momentum and easily beat Celtic and then Atlético Madrid in the semi. Once again playing at the pinnacle of European football, a more experienced Ajax faced Greek side Panathinaikos at Wembley.

Still the Cruyff, Keizer, Swart triangle remained and Vasovic still held the captain's armband. Supplementing them were some equally talented players in a true 4-3-3. Dick van Dijk had arrived from FC Twente in 1969 as an out and out striker after impressing in games against his new employers. Michels had moulded van Dijk into a more complete player and he could now function perfectly within the total football philosophy. Also now playing in Amsterdam was the brilliant Johan Neeskens. Employed as a right back in the European Cup final, Neeskens would become adept in central midfield for both club and country. Neeskens would go on to have four very successful seasons at the club.

Better equipped to handle the pressure of playing at this level, van Dijk headed Ajax into a fifth minute lead and they remained comfortable for the rest of the game. Whilst never able to truly cut loose, an Arie Haan goal three minutes from time gave them the two-goal margin they deserved. Ajax had now replaced Feyenoord as champions of Europe and the following season, they would really show the world how successful total football could be.

With 'his' system earning plaudits all around Europe and his stock higher than ever before, Michels was offered a role as manager of Barcelona. Despite being the head coach of the European champions, the offer to manage one of football's biggest names proved too much to turn down. With Michels departure came fears that the great Ajax side was to break up and total football would now only reside at the Camp Nou. Romanian Stefan Kovács was the slightly surprising name chosen to succeed Michels but he would prove to be a very shrewd appointment.

Kovács had a bit of a journeyman career as a footballer but had taken to his coaching career with gusto. As manager of Steaua Bucharest over four seasons he had achieved regular league and cup success. Once appointed Kovács embraced and refined total football even further. If anything Ajax now played with even more freedom. He also recognised Cruyff as the jewel in the crown, particularly as he had now just won his first European Footballer of the Year title. He had already earned a reputation for being opinionated and often abrasive, but handled correctly there were very few players on earth who could cope with Cruyff. He stood out in every sense, even playing under the number 14 at a time where teams were usually strictly 1 to 11. Having started the 70-71 season injured, he had finished fabulously and now sat at the head of Europe's best team as its most talented player.

Kovács first season was to prove extraordinary. Ajax were untouchable in the 71-72 Eredivisie, losing only once and winning 30 out of 34 games. Once again they went past 100 goals and staggeringly, only conceded 20. They had walked their way to another double by winning the KNVB Cup once more, scoring 14 goals in 4 games until the final in which they beat FC Den Haag 3-2. Cruyff scored in that game and finished as top scorer in a season where he had been a defender's nightmare throughout.

It was in Europe where Ajax had played some of their best football. No team had retained the European Cup since the great Internazionale in 1964 and 1965. Ajax set out to achieve that feat with a 2-0 win over Dynamo Dresden in the first round, and then an impressive 6-2 aggregate win over Marseille. Ajax then faced English champions Arsenal and outplayed them comprehensively over two legs. The semi-final proved to be tighter against a disciplined and organised Benfica team. Ajax edged it over two legs and came away with a 1-0 win. The final pitted them against one of the great sides in European football, Internazionale, and provided a wonderful sub text for the impartial fan. Italian football and Inter had become famed for 'catenaccio'. The system meant a defensive approach, usually with the deployment of a 'libero' or sweeper. In contrast to total football, catenaccio required each player to stick rigidly to his task and tactical game plan. It was the most successful attacking football system against the most defensive, positive against negative, ten floating outfield players against ten static.

Horst Blankenburg had replaced the retired Vasovic in defence and Keizer now held the captain's armband for the final. Arie Haan had now taken residence in Ajax's midfield after only appearing as a substitute in the '71 final. Playing at Feyenoord's home ground in Rotterdam Ajax were simply brilliant, their constant movement producing nightmares for Inter's defence. The game is often talked about as the pinnacle of total football and Inter simply had no answer for the breathtaking Dutch. Two second half Cruyff goals gave Ajax a 2-0 win and the trophy once more. His first came after a series of defensive mistakes so uncharacteristic of an Italian defence it had proved how rattled Ajax had them. The second came from Cruyff's head, rising highest amongst three defenders before powering the ball past Bordon into Inter's goal.

In the same year that Ajax had now won the treble, they also took the Intercontinental Cup by beating Argentinean Copa Libertadores winners Independiente, and the UEFA Super Cup by defeating UEFA Cup Winners Cup holders Glasgow Rangers. Total football had conquered all before it.

The following season Ajax retained the European Cup again because there was simply no one who could touch them. Along the way 6 were put past CSKA Sofia, 5 past Bayern Munich and 3 past Real Madrid. The Bayern game had been billed as Cruyff versus Franz Beckenbauer, two of the biggest names in European football head to head. Cruyff and Ajax had come out comprehensively on top.

The final saw another Italian opponent in the Old Lady of Juventus. Again Ajax triumphed and were now the first club to win the trophy three times in a row since the great Real Madrid side of the fifties. Johnny Rep's fourth-minute looping header past Dino Zoff was enough to crown them champions of Europe once again. The treble eluded them as they failed to retain the KNVB Cup after going out on penalties to NAC Breda. The league was won and once again it was Feyenoord in second place.

That European Cup final was the last time the 'Twelve Apostles' of the regular Ajax first team would dominate the European football landscape. Johan Cruyff marked the beginning of the end by moving to Barcelona for a world record fee at the start of 73-74 season. Some claim it was a direct result of his removal as captain after a vote taken by the Ajax first team squad but as ever with Cruyff, his every move seems to have caused rabid speculation. Crowned European Footballer of the Year again, Cruyff's relationship with some of his team mates and Ajax officials was at an all time low. Despite this he left on relatively good terms and after a successful time with Barca, brief spells with teams in NASL and a short-lived move to Levante, he returned to Ajax and won two more titles. In 1983 he was not offered a new contract by Ajax and angry, promptly signed for Feyenoord. In his last season as a player now playing for Ajax's fiercest rivals, he won another league and cup double to cap his incredible career. In recognition for all he did for the club and the success his era had earned, in 2007 Ajax officially retired the number 14 squad number as a mark of respect. As was typical of Cruyff's later years, he disagreed with the decision and said instead it should be given to the club's best player.

1973 saw 'Mr Ajax' Sjaak Swart retire. Johan Neeskens would move and join Cruyff at Barcelona a year later. By 1975 the side had all but completely broken up and the great Gloria Ajax team was over. Their legacy lives on and Ajax continue to turn out talented players through their youth system, all schooled in the total football ethos. Ajax graduates include Ronald and Frank de Boer, Clarence Seedorf, Edwin van der Sar, Dennis Bergkamp, Patrick Kluivert and the great Marco van Basten. Wesley Sneijder, Rafael van der Vaart, John Heitinga, Maarten Stekelenburg, Gregory van der Wiel and Nigel de Jong all played in the 2010 World Cup final and can all thank Ajax's youth programme for their initial development. The club took one more European Cup in 1995, now in the form of the Champions League. Fittingly the majority of their key players had all been at Ajax since their youth.

After 1973 the total football story was far from finished. Mattering because it revolutionised attacking football in Europe, Michels' perfected system was now ready to be applied to his new team. After introducing the Catalan crowd to the fluidity of a 'total' system and then leaving, Michels was now in charge of the Dutch national side. They headed to the 1974 World Cup with high hopes that their way of playing was about to conquer the world, just as it had Europe.

Celtic FC 1966-67

Honours

European Cup Winners

Scottish League Winners

Scottish League Cup Winners

Glasgow Cup Winners

Scottish Cup Winners

'Every time we open a cupboard,
a Celtic supporter falls out.'

British Embassy Official in Lisbon as Scottish fans descended on the city for the 1967 European Cup final

Up until 1967, the European Cup had remained exclusively in the countries that had competed in the Latin Cup – France, Spain, Portugal and Italy. Real Madrid had taken it six times, Benfica of Portugal twice, and the remaining three cups had been shared between Italian clubs Milan and Internazionale. Such was the dominance that only Germany's Eintracht Frankfurt in 1960 and Yugoslavians Partizan Belgrade in 1966 had stopped the final from being an all-Latin Cup affair. In 1967 a club from Scotland was about to storm through the competition and begin a run that would see British, Dutch and German clubs dominate for the next twenty years.

Celtic were formed in Glasgow's East End in 1887 as a way to generate money and growth in one of the poorest parts of the city. The following year they played their first official match – a friendly against local team Rangers – and entered the Scottish League. In 1905 they began to establish themselves as a force by winning the league for the next six successive seasons. Over the next fifty years their fortunes changed as the cyclical nature of football bought other teams to the fore but Celtic earned a huge support and remained relatively successful. By 1965 they had won the Scottish League 20 times, 2 League Cups, and the Scottish Cup 17 times. The majority of their success had come in the early part of the century and as manager Jimmy McGrory stepped down in 1965, city rivals Rangers dominated the landscape of Scottish football. Celtic fans had watched the blue half of their city take the title time and time again throughout the 1920s, 30s, 40s, and 50s and it was time for a manager who could restore their club to their early glories.

Jimmy McGrory had been a hugely popular figure at the club. As a player for Celtic he had become a legend and the club's highest ever-scoring player. In his Scottish football career he had scored over 500 goals, 410 in the Scottish League alone. After moving into management with a brief spell for Kilmarnock, he was appointed Celtic manager in 1945 and held the position for the next twenty years. Although he only ever really achieved limited success, he did manage the team to a famous victory in the 1957 Scottish League Cup final. With even Celtic fans forced to admit that their opponents Rangers were generally accepted as the stronger side, most predicted a close game but Celtic attacked them from the off. 2-0 ahead at half time, instead of the expected Rangers fight back in the second half it was Celtic who pushed on. They lashed another five goals to finish with a 7-1 victory and the League Cup, as well as the bragging rights in the city for some time to come.

With McGrory gone the club looked to another ex-player to try and reignite the club domestically. Jock Stein's playing career had begun with Albion Rovers before a move to full professionalism with a brief stint at Welsh club Llanelli. At Albion he had kept his job as a miner throughout the week but after the move to Wales he turned fully professional. Homesick and unhappy, he signed for Celtic in 1951 as cover for the first team and was glad to be back in Scotland. After taking an opportunity to impress thanks to injuries, he established himself in the centre of Celtic's defence to the extent he became captain. He led the team to a rare league title in 1954, their only one between 1938 and 1965, but injury cut short his career just two years later. While he hadn't been able to truly achieve legend status in the green and white, he was certainly well thought of and had made over a hundred first team appearances. The club gave him a role coaching the reserve and youth teams and his ascent into management began.

In 1960 Dunfermline gave him a chance to become first team manager. In his first year at the club he pulled them from a relegation battle to Scottish Cup winners, a 2-0 victory over Celtic enough to secure the trophy for the first time in the club's history. He developed a reputation for forward thinking and understanding what made player's perform to their best. Hibernian approached in 1964 and he became their manager for less than a season before

McGrory left Celtic and both parties saw a perfect fit. Stein had become an intelligent student of the game and Celtic, without a trophy in eight years, represented the perfect blank canvas.

By the beginning of the 66/67 season, Stein had already turned the club around domestically. He had won the 1965 Scottish Cup shortly after taking over and then landed the prize Celtic fans really wanted in his first full season. The League title of 65/66 had been won by just two points from Rangers but that didn't tell the full story. Celtic had developed under Stein into an excellent attacking unit and had scored 106 goals, 15 more than second place Rangers and 33 more than third place Kilmarnock. They narrowly missed out on a treble after taking the League Cup with a 2-1 win over Rangers in front of over 100,000 fans at Hampden Park. They played Rangers again in the Scottish Cup final but after a goalless draw, they lost the replay four days later 1-0. Hopes were now high under Stein's leadership and Celtic would have a new competition to play in the following year – the European Cup.

Celtic were a huge source of local pride as every member of the first team was born with thirty miles of Glasgow. The side that went on to become known as 'the Lisbon Lions' began with Ronnie Simpson in goal. Glasgow born, he'd moved to Newcastle United and spent a decade there before transferring back to Scotland with Hibernian. He'd been signed by Celtic as cover for their first choice keeper John Fallon but his skill and attitude actually led to him becoming Stein's first choice. In the 1967 European Cup final he took up the goalkeeping position while Fallon looked on from the bench.

Defensively, Stein favoured strength and intelligence but wanted pace from his fullbacks. Captain Billy McNeill took up his position in the centre of defence with John Clark to his left. Clark became know as 'The Brush' for his intelligence and positioning in the sweeper role. McNeill made over 800 appearances for Celtic in his career and was Stein's leader on the pitch in every sense. Right and left back's Jim Craig and Tommy 'Tam' Gemmell were encouraged to get forward and overlap at every available opportunity. They were both pacy and the positions were key to Stein's philosophy. By pushing both on at any given opportunity, the extra men in attack became almost impossible to pick up without leaving gaping holes elsewhere.

In harmony in the centre of midfield were Bobby Murdoch and Bertie Auld. Murdoch was a favourite of Stein's for his intelligence and ability to pick the right pass. Auld dominated opposition and provided the platform for Murdoch to pull the strings. Their manager saw both men as integral to Celtic's ambitions and both played a huge part in the season ahead.

Playing at the centre of Celtic's four-man attack were Stevie Chalmers and Willie 'Wispy' Wallace. Chalmers became one of Celtic's all-time top goal-scorers in twelve years with the club, Wallace was supremely skilful and adept at playing anywhere along the front line. Joe McBride was signed by Stein from Motherwell to play as first choice striker and started the season well, but serious injury left the door open for Wallace to play in his place and he never looked back. On the left Bobby Lennox was given the opportunity to show the acceleration and eye for goal he possessed in spades. Lennox loved to bare down on goal and Stein played to his strengths by using the full backs to provide the width allowing license to move inside. On the right there was a genuine legend, one of the greatest players to ever come out of Celtic or indeed Scotland as a whole – Jimmy 'Jinky' Johnstone. Jinky was quick, fiery and incredibly skilful. He played some of the best football of his career during Celtic's European campaign and while not as prolific as the rest of the attack, it was Johnstone who was providing the assists time and time again.

Celtic possessed a talented squad who had as much commitment for the team's cause as they did individual skill. Every single man in the squad would walk through walls for the club and for Stein himself, and key to their success was their ability to understand their manager's vision on the pitch. Celtic played at pace and passed it short, they moved amongst themselves and pulled defence's out of position for the full ninety minutes. Stein's defence was fluid – McNeill and Clark sitting while Craig and Gemmell enjoyed themselves further up the pitch. The midfield two were a formidable partnership who understood each others strengths and just as importantly their weaknesses and the front four were rampant at times. Celtic didn't win every game, teams rarely do, but when they were on song they'd prove that very few teams in Europe could cope with them.

They would fight on five fronts during the 66/67 season – the Glasgow Cup, the Scottish League, the Scottish League Cup, the Scottish Cup and the European Cup. The least of these was perhaps the Glasgow Cup which had moved down the scale as the League Cup and European competition became more prevalent. Played out between the senior clubs in the Glasgow area, Celtic took the trophy with a 4-0 win over Partick Thistle.

The League Cup joined the Glasgow Cup as Celtic negotiated a trouble free path to a final against Rangers. With the competition split into groups initially, Celtic won six out of six against Hearts, Clyde and St Mirren. Celtic finished those games with a growing reputation for ruthlessness. Clyde had shipped 9 in two games, St Mirren the same. Next came another two high scoring wins over Dunfermline Athletic and then a 2-0 win over Airdrieonians in the semi-final. Rangers had faced slightly more difficult route to the final but had overcome Aberdeen in the semi with the help of a replay. Bobby Lennox scored the decisive goal to give the cup to Celtic and already the attacking football Celtic played was earning plaudits.

The Scottish Cup finished the treble of domestic cup competition on the 29th April. The path had been cleared for Celtic when their closest competition exited immediately. Berwick Rangers had to join the competition in the preliminary rounds to get through to the first round proper. They landed a plum draw at home to giants Rangers and in an extraordinary feat of giant killing, they came away with a famous 1-0 win. The result echoed around Scottish football, not least on the terraces at Parkhead where fans had witnessed Celtic put 4 past Arbroath. While there were still some talented sides left in the competition there was no denying Rangers exit left the path clear. An easy draw gave the Bhoys a 7-0 home win against qualifiers Elgin City and they were then drawn at home again for a 5-3 win over Queen's Park in the quarters. The semi-final took Celtic to a replay to get past Clyde and onto a final against Aberdeen. Two Wispy Wallace goals and a clean sheet gave Celtic Park its third trophy of the season.

Stein had Scottish football beaten. Celtic and their electric front line were outscoring and outpacing all before them. Only Dundee United beat them in domestic games over the season twice in the league, as the Scottish title inevitably came to Celtic for the second year running. Stevie Chalmers finished as top scorer hitting 21 of Celtic's 111 goals. Just as importantly McNeill and Clark were almost peerless at the heart of Celtic's defence, both men contributing a huge amount to the cause over the season's thirty-four games. Celtic dominated their opponents but faced criticism that the level of football they were playing domestically was poorer than that of England or the other major European leagues. Despite winning every competition they had entered in Scotland, it would be the European Cup that would provide the real yardstick – could their all action style conquer abroad as it had at home?

Their campaign began with a first round tie with FC Zürich. Celtic Park buzzed on the 28th September 1966 desperate to see how the team would fare. Goals from Tam Gemmell and Joe McBride gave them a 2-0 win but in truth, it wasn't their best performance. The glare of a home fixture in the biggest competition in Europe had brought some nerves to the surface. The second leg at Letzigrund saw the real Celtic command the game from the kick-off and finish 3-0 winners. A 5-0 aggregate win was impressive for a club taking to a new competition and the form of Gemmell had been the real highlight. The fullback had scored in both legs and marauded his way through his home and away debuts in the European Cup.

The club now faced a trip to France as FC Nantes were drawn as their next opponents. This time they started with the away leg and were clearly beginning to enjoy themselves. McBride, Lennox and Chalmers all scored in France and then both Lennox and Chalmers added another apiece in the home leg. Jinky

Johnstone opened the scoring that night at Celtic Park and the club finished with an extremely impressive 6-2 aggregate win. Europe was starting to take notice.

Then came their first European defeat away in Yugoslavia, and in the return leg their first real test of character. FK Vojvodina had proved stoic at home and sneaked a 1-0 win but now faced an intimidating capacity crowd at Celtic Park. Celtic attacked from the off and found Yugoslavian goalkeeper Pantelic in stubborn form. Moving into the second half they remained calm but continued to build the pressure, Johnstone becoming a huge figure in the game. On the hour Gemmell's sweeping cross was turned in by Chalmers for the equaliser. Green and white shirts now laid siege to the Vojvodina goal. Still Pantelic held firm, saving again and again as Celtic attacked in droves. With ninety minutes on the clock Celtic won a corner and Jinky jogged over to swing it in. Gambling on a quality delivery, Celtic players flooded the area. The towering head of captain McNeill met the cross and his header flew in. Celtic had qualified in the most dramatic fashion, through to the semi-finals at the first time of asking and a final in Lisbon was now only two games away.

Czechoslovakians Dukla Prague now stood in their way. The first leg was at Celtic Park and they started badly. The Czech's passed and moved as the Scots struggled to get in the game, former European Player of the Year Josef Masopust setting the tempo and uncharacteristically allowed time and space. Against the run of play Jinky Johnstone gave Celtic a priceless lead 27 minutes in, finishing a good move through midfield from Wallace and Auld. Now with something to build on, Celtic never looked back. After some promise and an equaliser, Dukla crumbled as Celtic's pace and confidence grew during the second half. Wallace scored twice more, including a crashing twenty-five yard shot for the third, and Celtic had a 3-1 lead to take into the away leg. After a dour 0-0 draw in which the normally attacking Celtic opted to stifle and defend, the Scots had the aggregate win they needed and a European Cup final against Internazionale.

Stein had created a side capable of taking on Europe's best and Internazionale represented just that. Their manager Helenio Herrera had modified and adapted a 5-3-2 formation to birth Catenaccio, the organised and rigid defence that had given the Italians so much success. Renowned for grinding out win after win, the Italians were also recent winners of the European Cup in 1964 and 1965's competitions. Celtic were seen as rank outsiders, a team about to see what European football was really about. With legends like centre forward Sandro Mazzola and captain Armando Picchi at sweeper, the Italians were formidable and experienced. Stein's Celtic had a huge task ahead.

Typically the manager began the mind games early and proclaimed that Celtic were going to attack the Italian Catenaccio like it 'had never attacked before'. The Italian system was seen as impenetrable and all conquering but Stein claimed that Inter's stars would struggle against Celtic as they had players who 'put their club before personal prestige'. Herrera had invited Stein to witness his training methods years earlier to further the coach's career, now the two stood in conflict and Stein busied himself earning a mental edge.

The game started at the Estadio Nacional in Lisbon with Celtic on the attack but within minutes, Internazionale took the lead. Renato Cappellini latched onto a through ball and Jim Craig's tackle in the box was late. Mazzola nonchalantly sent Ronnie Simpson the wrong way with the resulting penalty kick and the Italians had the lead. Content to sit and try and control possession, Inter felt like the game was now in their hands. In reality they had just kicked the hornet's nest as Celtic spent the rest of the game attacking relentlessly, finishing with 42 attempts on goal and forcing an outstanding display from Internazionale goalkeeper Sarti.

Despite holding out until the 62nd minute, Celtic always held the upper hand and the cutting edge to prove it. Tam Gemmell's brilliant European form was rewarded as he smashed in an equaliser from the edge of the area. With Inter unable to break from the lock and key Catenaccio had them under, Celtic roared forward and with five minutes remaining had the winner they deserved. Bobby Murdoch, found by Gemmell's pull back, watched his scuffed shot find the feet of Stevie Chalmers to tap in. Chalmer's finish gave Celtic the lead and ultimately the trophy. The vast numbers of Celtic fans that had made the journey were delirious, a sea of green and white watching captain McNeill lift the trophy and officially give birth to the Lisbon Lions. They, along with the watching football world, were now in awe of the wonderfully attacking Scots and their brilliant manager.

Stein had revitalised the club and taken them to the pinnacle of European football. They'd won every competition they entered in the 66/67 season and become the first British club to win the European Cup. The team is still Celtic's most cherished and in 2002 when fans were asked to vote for Celtic's greatest ever eleven, Ronnie Simpson, Tommy Gemmell, Bobby Murdoch, Bertie Auld, Bobby Lennox, Billy McNeill and Jimmy Johnstone were all voted into the side, McNeill was voted the club's greatest ever captain, Johnstone its greatest player. Stein led Celtic to complete dominance of the Scottish game until he parted from the club in 1978. In just over twelve years at Celtic Park he won 10 Scottish League titles, 8 Scottish Cups, 6 Scottish League Cups, the 1967 European Cup and took the team to another European Cup final in 1970 in which they lost 2-1 to Feyenoord. Stein died whilst in charge of the national side's World Cup qualification campaign in 1985. He suffered a heart attack during a game against Wales and Scottish football was united in mourning the loss of one of its most talented figures.

Stein showed the world that Catenaccio could be broken. His talented team mattered for the best of reasons – as with teams like Il Grande Torino or Gloria Ajax they played attacking and entertaining football and won the trophies that confirmed their philosophy. Celtic's triumphs in 1967 helped enhance the British game's reputation and Manchester United followed the Scots lead and took the European Cup the following year. The Lisbon Lions and their charismatic manager gave birth to many legends and it's testament to their successes that their names still bring such reverence today.

Brazil 1970

Honours

World Cup Winners – Mexico 1970

June 21st
Azteca Stadium, Mexico City

BRAZIL	4 v 1	**ITALY**
Pelé (18)		(37) Boninsegna
Gerson (66)		
Jairzinho (71)		
Carlos Alberto (86)		

HT – 1-1
Att – 107,000
Ref – R. Glöckner (East Germany)

World Cup Final, 1970

If Uruguay's World Cup victory in 1950 had been Brazil's darkest hour, it could be argued that 1970 was their brightest day. Playing with a creative freedom rarely equalled, the Brazil squad of Mexico '70 is one of football's greatest ever. A combination of a solid work ethic helpfully mixed with some of the greatest footballers of all time playing at the height of their form, saw Brazil truly become the entertainers of world football.

Since 1950's watershed Brazil had gone on to win the World Cup twice. In 1954 they had crashed out to Hungary after the 'Battle of Bern' in the quarter-finals. Learning from the outstanding Europeans, Brazil adapted the revolutionary 4-2-4 system to fit their own ambitions and in 1958 triumphed for the first time. Didi, Vavá, and Garrincha emerged as standout performers in the tournament as Brazil played with a swagger and rhythm that would go on to become their trademark.

That World Cup also hosted the debut of a player who at the time was the youngest ever to take part in the tournament. Named Edison Arantes do Nascimento, he would become known the world over by his nickname – Pelé. After two wins and a draw in a group containing the highly fancied England, Brazil qualified to play a quarter-final against Wales. Having made his debut in a group game against the Soviet Union Pelé scored the only goal to put Brazil through. In a crushing semi-final performance Pelé and Brazil outscored the other high-flying team of the tournament France. The game finished 5-2, Pelé with a hat trick took the man of the match award. In the final against hosts Sweden Brazil finished with another 5, Pelé with another 2. For the first time Brazil lifted the trophy the whole nation had been longing for them to win.

By 1962 and the finals in Chile, Pelé was widely acknowledged as the best player in the world. Brazil moved to a loose 4-3-3 after losing their young talisman after only two games to injury. In Pelé's absence Garrincha became their standout player yet again and Brazil went through the tournament relatively untroubled. A 3-1 victory over England in the quarters, then a 4-2 victory over Chile in the semi took Brazil to a final against Czechoslovakia. Having played out a 0-0 draw in the group already, Brazil were not about to let the Czech's have their measure again. Pelé's replacement Amarildo scored an equaliser before Zito and Vavá added a second and third to triumph 3-1. Once again Brazil were champions.

1966 had been an aberration for the aging Brazil side. With many of their real star players past their prime and political pressures dictating some aspects of the squad, Brazil failed to qualify from their group. Pelé was kicked out of their first game against Bulgaria and missed the next against Hungary due to injury. Still struggling but with Brazil needing to beat Portugal to qualify, Pelé was rushed back. The game would be remembered for two goals from perhaps one of the only players in the world who could rival Pelé's talent – Eusébio of Portugal. Brazil lost 3-1 and Pelé left the field bruised and battered once again. After his treatment Pelé vowed never to play at a World Cup again, thankfully for Brazil he would go back on the statement just four years later.

By the time the tournament came to Mexico in 1970 Brazil were blessed with a new generation of great players. Pelé may have been the highest profile member of the squad but those around him were also supremely talented. Captain Carlos Alberto, midfielder Gérson and Pelé himself made up manager Mário Zagallo's inner circle of 'Cobra's'. Zagallo was a World Cup winner in

'58 and '62 as a player and was relatively new to the job as the finals approached. His predecessor João Saldanha left after citing political pressure to pick certain players as unbearable. Zagallo trusted his players to debate and add to his plans for each game and between them they came up with the fluid 5-3-2 formation that could slip into a 3-5-2 easily. Tactically Brazil continued to change and adapt their system throughout the tournament to suit the opposition they were facing. Subtle changes and new roles were made and created to fit the likes of Tostão, Rivelino, Clodoaldo and Jairzinho around Alberto, Pelé, and Gérson. As tactically astute as they were talented on the pitch, the Brazilians became a formidable proposition for anyone drawn to play against them.

Several other factors seemed to be falling in Brazil's favour as the World Cup approached. Played in absolutely blistering heat, some of the European sides would wilt in the sun. Mexico '70 was the first World Cup to be broadcast in colour around the world by satellite and as a result several concessions had to be made. Whilst it may have been the best time to kick games off for European television schedules, starting at midday meant many games were played in over 100 degrees of heat. When you added the temperature to the fact three of the five stadiums were over 7,000ft above sea level making oxygen scarcer than many teams would have ever experienced before, the pace of the games had to slow to reflect the conditions. Brazil's passing game and natural acclimatisation suited the enforced tempo perfectly.

Even the ball seemed to favour the Brazilians. A lighter version – 'the Adidas Telstar' – replaced the older, heavier brown and orange balls. Now made of white hexagon and black pentagon panels stitched together, the ball was easier to see on television and far easier to head.

Mexico '70 was destined to be a tournament of firsts. Perhaps introduced as a reflection of the conditions, the World Cup would play to a new law that allowed two substitutions per team in each game. Also referees were now equipped with both yellow and red cards to deal with serious foul play during a match. With expectation at record levels and the world watching live and in colour, the finals kicked off with sixteen teams spread across four groups. Brazil joined Europeans England, Romania and Czechoslovakia in Group 3. Drawn into the same group by chance, the Brazil versus England game would see the two tournament favourites meet earlier than the final many were predicting.

England beat Romania 1-0 on the 2nd June and then Brazil entered the finals a day later against the Czechs. Surprisingly a goal down after just eleven minutes to Ladislav Petrás's good run and powerful finish, the Brazilians kept passing and built the pressure. Even before the goal Pelé had missed a gilt-edged opportunity and as the minutes ticked on, Brazil gradually began to overwhelm their opponents. In the 24th minute Pelé won a free kick twenty-five yards from goal and in a central position. Roberto Rivelino was a graceful player who seemed to glide over the grass with the ball at his feet but in this situation, he was even deadlier. After thundering the free kick past Ivo Viktor in the Czechoslovakian goal the Mexican crowd nicknamed him 'Patada Atómica' – the atomic kick. Rivelino showed himself throughout the tournament to be the complete player and between him and Jairzinho, the ghost of the great Garrincha that hung over this squad was all but forgotten.

The sides went into half-time still level but the second half was to be all Brazil's. Pelé's clever chest control and volley after Gerson picked him out in the area from forty yards put them into the lead on the hour. Pelé had been shown comments from Czech manager Joseph Marko describing him as a 'spent force' before the game and was now busy proving nothing could be further from the truth. He had already tried to lob the keeper from his own half during the first forty-five minutes, now he had his goal and had made his point.

Two minutes later Jairzinho was set to begin a record-breaking run that would see him score in every game of Brazil's World Cup. Finishing with two, his first goal was at the end of a perfectly timed run. Clean through without a defender in sight Jairzinho lifted the ball over the advancing keeper and finished for 3-1. With ten minutes to go Jairzinho got his second after a brilliant run past three Czech defenders. Picking the ball up just over the halfway line he skipped one challenge, then another and finally when pushed slightly wide still managed to pull his shot from just inside the area across the keeper and in. The game finished 4-1 and Brazil had at times been rampant. They looked every inch the challengers for the trophy they had been widely touted as.

At midday on the 7th June in Guadalajara, England and Brazil faced off for the game most felt would decide the group winners. In a game of iconic moments, the tenth minute saw the first. Pelé rose to meet Jairzinho's cross from the right and powered his header downwards towards England's goal. Gordon Banks dived full length to his right and pushed the ball over the bar one-handed. Often described as the 'Save of the Century', Pelé had turned and shouted 'Golo!' before Banks' wonderful intervention. As the chess game continued England's defence and in particular Bobby Moore kept the Brazilians at bay for the goalless first half.

Into the second half and the balance of play shifted slightly towards the Brazilians. Moore continued to frustrate the wall of yellow he was continually faced with and in particular Jairzinho who after a mazy run, found Moore an immovable object in the area. On the hour Tostão wriggled free on the left of the penalty area and despite three England defenders coming across to cover, managed to scoop the ball to Pelé who was level with the penalty spot. Without looking he simply controlled the ball then shifted it out of his feet to an onrushing yellow shirt to his right. Jairzinho took a simple touch then lashed it past Banks for what would prove to be the winner.

At the game's end Pelé waved away calls for his shirt from England's players to hunt Moore down in the centre circle. As the two men exchanged jerseys smiling and talking between themselves, the world watched the greatest attacking player in the game shake hands with the most complete defender. Pelé would later describe Moore as 'the greatest defender I ever played against' and a fascinating match had ended with a picture that remains symbolic today.

Now in pole position in the group, Brazil ended with a 3-2 victory over final opponents Romania. Brazil raced into a 2-0 lead with a powerful free kick from Pelé and Jairzinho's goal poaching instinct. Florea Dumitrache pulled one back for the Europeans before halftime but Brazil stretched their lead in the sixty-seventh minute. After another cross from Jairzinho, Tostão cleverly flicked the ball into Pelé's path who slid the ball in from six yards. Romania scored another in the closing moments but couldn't mount a serious challenge in the heat to push for an equaliser. Brazil had qualified and their big players were all peaking at exactly the right time.

The group had seen three Brazilian wins, eight goals, three from Pelé, four from Jairzinho and the supposedly weakest link of this Brazilian side – the defence – only concede three. Peru now stood in the way of a semi-final place and Brazil simply swept their opponents aside. Rivelino and Tostão put them two up with only fifteen minutes on the clock and it never looked in doubt from that moment on. Pelé had already hit the post before Rivelino swerved the ball in from the edge of the area in the eleventh minute. Four minutes later Tostão finished from an almost impossible angle after a short corner routine. He would tap another in the second half to make it 3-1, then Jairzinho rounded the keeper with fifteen minutes to go to make it 4-2. Once again Brazil had won and for the third time in four games they had scored three or more. Now they had a semi-final with an extra layer of interest to look forward to.

Their opponents would be Uruguay, the team that broke the nation's heart in 1950. Pelé may have won two World Cups since promising his distraught father he would win one for him after witnessing Uruguay's shock win at the Maracanã but he and his team mates knew they had the chance to truly exorcise the demon of that day once and for all. Brazil started notably tenser than in any match so far in the tournament and at first struggled for the form that had seen them dominate. Uruguay looked to stop the Brazilians physically and mentally, tackles flying in and players talking angrily off the ball almost constantly. Reports suggest that the Uruguayans used the memory of 1950 to try and antagonise the Brazilian players into mistakes. It seemed to be working when in the twentieth minute Uruguayan striker Luis Cubilla benefited from a rare misplaced pass in the Brazilian defence. Seizing his opportunity even though pushed impossibly wide, Brazil's keeper Felix got his positioning wrong and Uruguay were 1-0 up.

Galvanised by adversity, Brazil started to come into the game more and more, Pelé flashed a header wide and Rivelino went close with a clever free kick. Just before halftime midfielder Clodoaldo scored possibly the most important goal of Brazil's World Cup. Taking the initiative in midfield he played a clever one-two with Tostão on Brazil's left. Breaking into the box at speed, Clodoaldo took the return on the half volley first time and crashed the ball home. Brazil had weathered the psychological and physical storm and drawn level at the perfect time.

Uruguay remained difficult to break down and tough in the tackle as the second half began. Pelé had his first attempt in the game at scoring the goal of the tournament early in the half, running from the halfway line evading tackle after tackle before being fouled on the edge of the box. After hopelessly fluffing the free kick, he had his second attempt from a goal kick that fell to him on the volley fifty yards from goal. His shot was on target but goalkeeper Ladislav Mazurkiewicz had recovered enough to gather the ball back safely. Shortly after Pelé went close again as he now seemed to be at war with the Uruguayan defence all by himself. After good work by Jairzinho the ball dropped to the number ten just outside the area. His snapshot flashed just wide of the keepers right post and Uruguay were now clinging on.

With fifteen minutes to go Brazil finally had their breakthrough and it was Jairzinho who gave them the lead their persistence merited. Picking the ball up just outside his own penalty area, he broke and passed to Pelé on the halfway line. His clever flick to Tostão put the ball at the feet of someone clever enough to see that Jairzinho had continued his run. After being picked out perfectly Jairzinho controlled, dummied and then burst past his man to bear down on the keeper. Without breaking stride he put the ball across Mazurkiewicz and Brazil took a deserved lead to the delight of the yellow and green in the crowd.

Uruguay burst back into life and pushed for a goal leaving themselves open to the break. Felix made up for his poor positioning for Uruguay's first half goal with good stop from a Cubilla header. With minutes left Brazil broke and the ball came to Pelé in the area. Calm enough to control the ball and wait, Rivelino burst from midfield and Pelé laid the ball into his run perfectly. Hitting it first time Rivelino put Brazil into an unassailable 3-1 lead and the final beckoned. Still there was time for Pelé to make another goal of the tournament attempt with an audacious dummy past an advancing

Mazurkiewicz at the edge of the box. Despite totally fooling the keeper Pelé couldn't turn the ball in and was denied his goal once more. At the whistle there could be no doubt, Brazil had got to the final by merit and along the way buried one of the darkest chapters of their past on the pitch in Guadalajara.

The final was to be a clash of footballing cultures. Their opponents would be Italy who had just come through an epic semi-final with England's eventual conquerors West Germany. Italy were cautious, resolute and defensively strong – in their group they hadn't conceded a goal. They had overcome Mexico in the second round convincingly and then beaten the West Germans 4-3, five of the seven goals coming in extra time. The final was billed as the attack verses defence, extravagance against efficiency. On the 21st June 107,000 people crowded into the Estadio Azteca in Mexico City hoping for a classic.

Brazil struck first after as they played the game out almost entirely in the Italian half. Good work by Tostão on the left won him a throw in. Taking it quickly he picked out Rivelino's run whose cross was a little behind Pelé. Correcting himself as he jumped Pelé got his head to the ball and powered it past Italian goalkeeper Enrico Albertosi. Now a goal behind the Italians remained cautious and wouldn't allow Brazil the second that would put them out of site. As the minutes ticked by the Azzurri began to probe and threaten themselves, sensing that Brazil's weakness at the back could be exploited.

In the thirty-seventh minute a comedy of errors in the Brazilian defence gifted Italy the equaliser. After Clodoaldo lazily gave the ball away in midfield the Italians seized on the loose ball and pushed towards the edge of the Brazilian area. Felix made a rash decision to come and try and win the ball in spite of Italian striker Roberto Boninsegna's attention. After a collision between Felix, defender Everaldo and the Italian striker, the ball broke to the right and Boninsegna gathered himself enough to play the ball into the empty Brazilian net. With the game poised at 1-1 at half time, the Italians now had a foothold in the game they hadn't been expecting and something to build on.

Brazil returned for the second half determined and with coach Zagallo's words ringing in their ears. Finding another gear they began to dominate an aging Italian defence. Pelé just failed to connect with Jairzinho's ball across the goal mouth and shortly afterwards Rivelino smashed the woodwork from a free kick after Gérson's neat roll back. Gérson was beginning to make the Brazilian midfield tick and it was he who would get the next breakthrough. Quick feet took him past one challenge and taking the shot on just outside the penalty area, the ball flew past the Italian keeper to make it 2-1. The Italians were behind once more and beginning to feel the semi-final's 120 minutes take their energy-sapping toll. Five minutes later Gérson picked out Pelé in the penalty area whose knock down found the run of Jairzinho. After a slight miscontrol he was left with a tap in to make it three and complete his run of scoring in every game. With breathing space the Brazilians simply let the ball do the work now, knocking it effortlessly to one another as weary Italian legs struggled to keep pace.

The fourth Brazilian goal entered history as an example of all that was good about them and indeed, football itself. Tostão, working back and breaking down the Italian threat won the ball in his own half and played a simple ball to central defender Wilson Piazza. Piazza knocked the ball to Clodoaldo who received the ball back after a couple of one touch passes between Pelé and Gérson. Accelerating into blue shirts Clodoaldo effortlessly skipped and danced his way through four Italian challenges. Feeding Rivelino on the left touchline, he looked up and quickly played the ball into Jairzinho's feet. After collecting the ball a little clumsily he cut inside and looked for Pelé who was jogging forward, six yards from the penalty area. Gathering the pass now at walking pace, Pelé played the ball to his right where Carlos Alberto was thundering forward from his wingback position. Without having to break stride the ball was good enough for captain Alberto to strike from just inside the area and score the final brilliant, breathtaking goal.

That moment of the fourth goal had been entirely in keeping with the Brazilians' ethos and talent. Simplistic yet skilful, it was the sort of goal this team was capable of every time they took the pitch. Awarded the Jules Rimet trophy permanently in recognition of winning it for a third time, Brazil's greatest side now had its greatest day.

The best team of all time? The question is open to debate as these issues always are. There is no doubting the cards fell in Brazil's favour for the 1970 World Cup finals. Location, temperature and even the ball were all to the Seleção's liking. What are without debate are the facts. Brazil scored nineteen goals in six games winning all of them along the way. On route to winning the trophy they defeated three former World Cup winners and the then holders England.

Many moments from that Brazilian teams performance at the tournament remain indelibly imprinted on football history forever. The talent at Zagallo's disposal was almost outrageous. An experienced Pelé playing at the top of his game picked out time and time again by the more than gifted Gérson, Clodoaldo and Rivelino in midfield. Tostão's cleverness and Jairzinho's goal scoring form providing real threat and menace from the wide areas. And behind them all, captain Carlos Alberto, one of Zagallo's 'Cobras' marshalling his defence and driving forward at every opportunity to do so.

Some teams matter because they change football for the better or worse, some because they have affected the global game or its rules. Brazil's 1970 vintage mattered for one of the greatest reasons of all; they played the beautiful game at its most beautiful. Whether the debates about being the 'best' of all time are truly relevant or not, it is entirely fitting that any such discussions should and always will contain the Brazil squad of 1970.

New York Cosmos 1971–85

Honours

NASL Outdoor Championship Winners 1972, 1977, 1978, 1980 & 1982

Northern Division Winners 1972

Eastern Division, National Conference Winners 1978, 1979, 1980 & 1981

Eastern Division Winners 1982 & 1983

Trans-Atlantic Cup Championship Winners 1980, 1983 & 1984

'Soccer arrives finally in the USA'

Pelé speaking at the press conference to announce his signing for the New York Cosmos.

America has often been cited as the last great nation to fall in love with the beautiful game. To the bewilderment of the soccer world, Americans have always appeared to prefer their own version of 'football' that bares more in relation to rugby. Many theories have been put forward as to why this appears to be the case, most with an element of truth attached. It's been suggested that there is a historically motivated resistance to a game with its origins in Europe, particularly from a country so obsessed with its national identity. Some believe it's much simpler to explain than that – Americans aren't willing to watch a ninety-minute game without a definite winner. While it may be true that America has failed to fully embrace the sport in the way it has become a national pastime elsewhere, surprisingly the USA has more history with the game than many imagine and what's more, they once had a truly great club.

The game arrived in the United States with 19th century immigrants from European shores. Whilst forms of football had taken place before this point, European rules, traditions and ideas helped formalise the game and start local teams. The first unsuccessful attempts to start professional leagues date back to the 1880's and in 1913 a U.S. FA was formed. Six months after formation the United States of America Football Association (later to change to 'Soccer Association') joined FIFA. By this point many clubs had been established in areas across America, most associated with factories or large businesses.

In 1930 FIFA had their first 'World Cup' in Uruguay and the United States put forward a team that not only competed, they finished joint third after a heavy defeat to Argentina in the semi-finals. Drawn into Pool 4 with Belgium and Paraguay, America defeated both teams 3-0, Bert Patenaude scoring the first World Cup hat-trick against the South Americans. The more established Argentineans proved much tougher opposition and won 6-1 in Montevideo. Four years later in Italy the format of the competition had changed and the USA never got past the first round. They were given the toughest draw possible – hosts, favourites and eventual winners Italy. Unable to cope with the greater athleticism and skill of the Europeans, the USA went down 7-1 and reports alleged that only a wonderful performance from goalkeeper Julius Hjulian prevented the Italians scoring more.

Domestically the game was healthy but only in localised pockets and State leagues. It still failed to grip the country on any combined national level, the public still favouring the 'All-American' sports of baseball, basketball, and of course their own football. Support for the national team was as restrained as support for the game in general. The spectre of war hung over the 1938 World Cup and America was one of many nations who did not compete, but in 1950 they achieved one of the greatest upsets in world football history. The first finals since 1938 due to the war, the USA headed to Brazil given no hope of a win after being drawn against Spain, Chile and joint tournament favourites England. The team was drawn together from amateur players in America's scattered football leagues and most were postmen or miners by day. The qualifying campaign had seen them collect only three points from four games but it was enough to see them in second behind Mexico. The USA had lost both games against the Mexicans heavily but it was a win and a draw against Cuba that had taken them through.

With players drawn from teams like the Chicago Slovaks and St. Louis Simpkins-Ford, as predicted the USA began with a 3-1 defeat to Spain. England opened with a 2-0 win against Chile and were expected to put at least three past America. On the 29th June in Belo Horizonte, Haitian Joe Gaetjens threw himself at Walter Bahr's long-range effort. He managed to deflect it past England goalkeeper Bert Williams and give the USA a 1-0 lead in the thirty-eighth minute. Despite England rallying in the second half, America held on and caused one of the biggest shock results of all time. The final whistle caused a pitch invasion as the Brazilian crowd celebrated one of their own countries great rivals for the cup losing. Gaetjens was carried from the pitch shoulder high. Around the world the game made headlines, some papers in England refusing to believe the result thinking it must be a mistake.

Back home in America, the result caused a ripple of interest but no more than that. Most newspapers devoted a small by-line to the result but none gave it the coverage it deserved. After the USA lost their final game against Chile and England failed to qualify, the team returned to the States to no reception and continued on with their ordinary lives. The American Soccer League (ASL) had already collapsed once in the thirties after some initial success and now only existed on a far smaller scale. Soccer had once again failed to ignite itself in America on any significant level despite the national teams efforts.

After 1950 the USA failed to qualify for the finals in '54, '58 and '66. The 1966 World Cup Final between hosts England and West Germany was broadcast via the BBC to America and viewing figures were surprisingly high. The ASL continued to operate mostly in the North-Eastern United States but still no national league existed that could generate the tribal feelings football thrives on. After a positive response to the World Cup Final even without an American team involved, two new leagues were formed in 1967, both attempting to revive the professional game and both trying to eventually take the competition to a national level.

The FIFA sanctioned United Soccer Association consisted of established European and South American teams transported to franchises in the new league. Stoke City's team became the Cleveland Stokers, Wolverhampton Wanderers the L.A. Wolves. The process had been rushed through to compete with the National Professional Soccer League (NPSL), a rival organisation who had already secured a television contract with CBS. The NPSL had immediately introduced six points for a win, three for a draw, and bonus points for goals scored to encourage attacking. Neither league became a commercial success and after only one season, the two merged to become the North American Soccer League (NASL). The idea was that one national league was far easier to sell and promote to the public, television companies and sponsors. Still the league struggled and despite seventeen teams competing in the 1968 season, twelve would fold in 1969. Just five teams competed in NASL in 1969, six in 1970. Every franchise was struggling to make money and playing in front of a handful of fans. By 1971 new blood was required to generate interest and existing franchises were available for investors to pick up relatively cheaply. Little did the league know that just around the corner a team was coming who would finally fill stadiums and bring that publicity the game was desperate for.

Brothers Nesuhi and Ahmet Ertegun had already entered into a deal with Warner Brothers President Steve Ross to fund and run a soccer franchise, preferably based in New York. All three were dedicated football fans and had enjoyed a World Cup in Mexico in 1970 where Brazil had shown just how beautiful the game could be. The high temperatures had meant a slower tempo to most matches leading to skilful passing displays and some memorable games. Brazil had scored nineteen goals in just six games, Pelé, Jairzinho, Carlos Alberto, Tostão and Rivelino now known the world over for some breathtakingly skilful football. The final had seen the Samba Kings put four past Italy in what remains one of the greatest Brazilian displays of all time.

The real star remained Pelé, four goals in the tournament and a hand in the forth in the final that is often cited as the greatest ever World Cup goal. Even his misses were celebrated, a halfway line effort against Czechoslovakia, a header that brought a truly world class save from Gordon Banks and dummying round a helpless Mazurkiewicz in Uruguay's goal the most notable. Pelé was box office and the Cosmos's owners would return to that thought in later years as their football dream unfolded.

With the potential that a successful franchise based in New York could bring obvious to all involved, investors were secured and the New York Cosmos was born. The name Cosmos was derived from the city's successful baseball team – the New York Mets, Mets being short for Metropolitans. To ape the name the moniker 'Cosmopolitans' was chosen, shortened to Cosmos. Accepted into NASL immediately, the 1971 season was the first for the franchise made up of players largely plucked from New York's amateur leagues. Despite the league's aspirations to be fully professional, in reality many players at this point remained only semi-pro, a result of the lack of generated revenue still blighting the American game. Despite the lack of star players or full professionalism, the Cosmos's first season was a success on the pitch and they qualified for the play-offs. Losing to the Atlanta Chiefs in both legs of the semi-final was disappointing but striker Randy Horton was named Rookie of the Year and hopes were high for the following season.

Several decisions had been taken with a view to long-term success. The team's original colours had been chosen as green and yellow to echo the Brazilian national team. The long-term goal remained to capture the American audience with the sort of football Brazil had graced the recent World Cup with. There was also an underlying dream to one-day see Pelé play for the Cosmos. Clive Toye, an English sportswriter who had been installed as General Manager at the Baltimore Boys previously, was appointed as the Cosmos's General Manager. He in turn appointed English coach Gordon Bradley who had played in American leagues since the early sixties, including nearly thirty games for the original New York football franchise the Generals. Bradley would coach and occasionally play for the Cosmos for the next five seasons. After playing first at Yankee Stadium in front of a sparse crowd, the Cosmos moved to a stadium outside the city at Hofstra University realising that huge grounds with no one inside did nothing for the players or the image of football. To remedy their small crowds huge marketing drives took places with t-shirts, balls, key-chains and just about anything else you could print a Cosmos logo on given away to spectators and the New York public.

In 1972 the Cosmos won the Northern Division and then the National Championship after beating the St Louis Stars in the play-off final. Despite the success and the final being played at Yankee stadium, still crowds were small and exposure desperately limited. The lack of really world-class American footballers or star names in the league in general was hampering its development. Steve Ross however remained in love with 'his' team and could be seen at nearly every home game, rain or shine. On advice from his fellow investors, all stakes in the club were sold to Warner Communications for one dollar, the idea being that clearly no personal risk should be taken and this should come under the company banner to minimise loss.

The Cosmos failed to build on this success in '73, qualifying for the play-offs but losing to the Dallas Tornado in the semi-finals. In 1974 Ross moved the club to a stadium near the prison at Randalls Island in an effort to generate interest by playing closer to the city. The Cosmos responded by finishing bottom of the Northern Division, winning just four games in the process. If the Cosmos were to ever become the behemoth than Ross and Toye still believed they could be, something had to change. That something began with a single player.

The Cosmos had pursued the notion of signing Pelé since their birth. Despite the player's retirement in October 1974, Pelé appeared to be open to a new challenge. Rumoured offers from Real Madrid and Juventus were blown apart by the Cosmos's proposal, backed of course by the Warner Communications Group. Pelé's contract was uniquely structured to include marketing and merchandising rites, future ambassadorial and public relation roles, and three years playing for the Cosmos in NASL. With opposition from the Brazilian government at losing an icon to another country, Pelé put pen to paper and became the highest salaried athlete in the world.

Nine games into the 1975 season the Cosmos sat at the bottom of the table. Pelé's arrival was enough for CBS to broadcast the tenth in front of a packed stadium against Dallas. The largest crowd in the history of the Cosmos watched Pelé play ninety minutes and score the equaliser with a bullet header.

Soccer in America had not only infiltrated the back pages, it was now the lead story across the country. His arrival rallied the Cosmos who eventually finished in third, never able to get back into a position to qualify for the play-offs after their poor start. Record attendances were seen at Cosmos away games. Even when injured Pelé drew a huge crowd in Philadelphia for a game he couldn't play in.

Pelé had now set the blueprint the Cosmos would follow in pursuit of success. By 1976 NASL boasted twenty-two teams across two conferences. The Cosmos now playing in white mirroring Santos in Brazil – Pelé's only other team – had become the biggest club in the league. To cater for the triple-fold increase in support the Cosmos moved into Yankee Stadium. Across the league suddenly other franchises began recruiting star names on big wages to create their own 'Pelé' effect. In the '76 season, George Best played for the Los Angeles Aztecs, Rodney Marsh scored twelve goals for the Tampa Bay Rowdies, Geoff Hurst played in Seattle and the Cosmos signed Italian striker Giorgio Chinaglia from Lazio in the prime of his career.

Chinaglia would have a huge part to play in the Cosmos's future on and off the pitch. Dogged by controversy over his conduct with the national team and his out-spoken nature, the Italian-American community both loved and hated him in equal measure. What was beyond doubt was his talent and he became the leagues all time top goal scorer and played over two hundred times for the Cosmos. Chinaglia would become close friends with Steve Ross whilst managing to alienate nearly everyone else involved with the team. Chinaglia even managed to criticise Pelé on more than one occasion for not passing to him enough or with accuracy. The Cosmos fans turned out to see Pelé and jeer Chinaglia in equal measure and between them they qualified for the '76 play-offs easily. After being knocked out by the Rowdies in the semi-finals, allegations emerged that both were indulging in the high life off the field a little more than the huge wages they commanded on it should have limited it to.

Over the next six seasons the Cosmos would sign players that would make many people's best teams of all time, all on high salaries that the club struggled to support. Franz Beckenbauer signed in time for the 1977 season and spent four years in NASL. Carlos Alberto joined Pelé in New York and played a hundred games in two spells with the club. Johan Neeskens, Dennis Tueart, Romerito and Vladislav Bogicevic would all play in Cosmos colours. Rick Davis would make nearly one hundred and thirty appearances and become the USA national team captain giving the crowd a homegrown hero. In 1977 the Cosmos won the national championship by beating the Seattle Sounders 2-1 in the final. It was Pelé's last season and attendance records were broken time and time again as the Cosmos moved to Giants Stadium in New Jersey and played in front of fifty, then sixty, then seventy thousand people. Television networks paid more for football and showed games at prime time, the Cosmos were the genuine phenomenon that Ross had believed they would become.

More success followed after '77. They finished as Divisional winners every year from 1978 to 1983. The Cosmos won the national championship again in 1978, 1980 and 1982. Life for the players had become one big party, particularly Chinaglia who embraced the fame and fortune lovingly. Press coverage was huge, the league expanded quickly to capitalise on the boom. The Cosmos toured Europe and played some high-profile friendlies, everywhere they went with their huge entourage they brought glamour and interest. The Americanised version of the game was also winning fans with innovations as such as the thirty-five yard line that marked where the offside rule began. So with all the planets aligned for the game to become America's number one sport, where did it all go wrong?

The Cosmos continued to pay huge wages as the league crumbled around them. NASL expanded too quickly and franchises were given to people and in areas that couldn't support them. Resources were spread too thinly to keep up with one team's popularity. Television audiences couldn't take to the game with the network forcing important games to be played at unusual times to suit. The television deals disappeared and the first nails were firmly hammered into NASL's coffin. The failure to land the 1986 World Cup in America left the league with no way to generate interest in the game again after the peaks of 1977-80. The crowd left the game behind and franchises collapsed under the weight of paying aging stars too much to try and compete with the Cosmos. In 1984 the league disbanded after attempts had been made to revive interest to no avail. Indoor and outdoor professional football in the USA had died.

The Cosmos also collapsed. Financially the losses mounted at alarming rates and as times at Warner Brothers got hard, the Cosmos were sold off to a consortium lead by Chinaglia. Years of excess had now come home to roost. Operating at a loss too often for too long, players were sold and Chinaglia installed himself as president of the club. As the league disbanded so did the Cosmos, General Manager Peppe Pinton retaining the great name of the Cosmos and using it to run soccer schools for American children. They had burned so bright for so long they had eventually burnt themselves out leaving behind a legacy of poor decisions and great players. Many had come at the end of their careers, some in their prime, but all had earned more than their fair share of any revenue the Cosmos could possibly generate.

The game in America suffered with such a spectacular failure. After embracing it with open arms football's stock was now lower than ever. The Cosmos had left an imprint on American soccer that is still felt in the game today – a blueprint for debt and failure. Not every team matters for solely positive reasons, never has this sentiment been truer than in regard to the New York Cosmos. They became a metaphor for excess in everything, even playing in a kit designed by Ralph Lauren. Football in America wouldn't die with the Cosmos but it would take a World Cup in 1994, a new league and a transfer that rivalled Pelé for exposure to gain the levels of interest that Steve Ross had briefly achieved with the New York Cosmopolitans once more.

West Germany 1972

Honours

Winners of 1972 European Championships

European Championship Final
June 18th 1972
Stade Heysel, Brussels
West Germany 3 v 0 **Soviet Union**
G. Müller 27, 58
H. Wimmer 52

Ref: F. Marschall (Austria)
Att: 50,000

Details of 1972 European Championship Final between West Germany & the Soviet Union

All of the biggest footballing nations have one side that they can cite as their greatest ever. England can point to a team with a World Cup win as definitive proof of their finest hour in 1966. In a country with multiple World Cup triumphs the subject can cause huge debate as Argentineans will testify, some feeling 1986's side was too dependant on Maradona's brilliance to be described as a truly great 'team', whereas 1978's played more as a unit and achieved the same feat. In the Technicolor age Brazil's 1970 squad is regarded as the greatest ever by many but those with longer memories often point to a Garrincha inspired 1958 vintage as the better team.

The greatest German side in popular opinion was the 1972 European Championship winners from the West. Two years later they too would add a World Cup to their achievements but in difficult circumstances, the team fractured by a disagreement over bonuses and lacking in leadership from their manager. In 1972 however they were united, playing a free-flowing and attractive brand of football the equal of the growing 'total' trend in the game, and had a collection of uniquely talented players whose names are still revered in the game today.

When looking retrospectively at their triumph several names on the West German roster simply can't be ignored. This was a team that could boast Sepp Maier, Franz Beckenbauer, Paul Breitner, Uli Hoeness, Günter Netzer and Gerd Müller at its heart. Beckenbauer and Müller in particular, nicknamed der Kaiser and der Bomber respectively, will feature heavily in any discussion about the greatest players in their position of all time. When together and playing as a unit they bordered on unplayable, as England would find out to their cost at Wembley in April 1972.

The signs that West Germany could be on the verge of success had been at evident at the 1970 World Cup in Mexico. Already able to boast a World Cup win in 1954, that triumph had been tinged with the feeling that despite the records books bearing their name as the winners, the trophy should have belonged to Hungary's Magical Magyars. Having made the final in 1966 in efficient if not spectacular style, a controversial Geoff Hurst goal had given momentum to England in extra time and West Germany had ended up losing 4-2 in the brilliant Wembley sunshine. The defeat in the final had been a bitter pill to swallow, particularly for a young Beckenbauer, and four years later the chance for revenge would present itself in a very real sense.

After walking through qualifying and their opening 1970 World Cup group with a record of 8 wins and 1 draw and having scored 30 goals in those games, the quarter-final drew West Germany with England again. The holders had come through a tough group including a memorable and iconic game against the Brazilians and were made favourites despite the German's form. All the pre-game predictions looked like coming true when England swept into a 2-0 lead in the baking Mexican sun, Alan Mullery and Martin Peters with the goals. With 20 minutes left Beckenbauer strode forward and steered a shot from twenty yards under Peter Bonetti in England's goal to halve the deficit. Bobby Charlton trudged off a minute later as England manager Alf Ramsey reacted to the ease at which England's midfield was being bypassed. Rather than tighten up the middle of the pitch as he'd hoped it actually freed Beckenbauer from his marking duties on England's most influential player and West Germany sensed an equaliser.

Stretching the game England's Geoff Hurst missed the far post with a header by inches but Germany found themselves on top. Müller went close when clean through and then captain Uwe Seeler made the breakthrough with a looping header over Bonetti to level the scores. The game lurched into extra time with England's tired legs suffering against the German's second wind. With 108 minutes on the clock, a flick found its way into England's six-yard box and inevitably Müller was there to finish. The game finished 3-2 to West Germany, a measure of revenge exacted and they moved on to a semi-final against Italy. In another epic contest they found themselves behind again only to equalize but on this occasion, the extra-time was to prove 30 minutes too far as they eventually lost 4-3.

West Germany had impressed throughout and proved unlucky. Two games in four days against two of the strongest teams in the tournament had both required extra-time to settle, and in the oppressive heat the tournament was played in they had acquitted themselves well. They had played attacking football, Beckenbauer had proved himself to be deserving of being grouped among the best players in the world and Müller had taken the golden boot with 10 goals. The next prize on the horizon was the 1972 European Championship – played in a different format to the summer tournament we recognise today – and West Germany were installed as one of the favourites on the back of their World Cup showing.

Manager Helmut Schön would lead his side into qualifying Group 8 and games against Turkey, Albania and Poland. Surprisingly, their campaign began with a draw at home against Turkey, Müller equalising an early goal but unable to add to it as they failed to break down a resilient and determined rear guard action. After their exploits in the World Cup more had been expected and after a tight 1-0 win in Albania in their next qualifier, it was the return fixture away in Turkey that saw them truly regain their form.

With Müller in brilliant international form he added his and West Germany's third and fourth goals of the campaign either side of halftime. With Turkey forced to play a more open game at home, West Germany simply played their way round them and when Horst Köppel added a third with just over fifteen minutes left any thoughts of a potential slump had been forgotten. They went on to win all their remaining games baring their last, a home game against Poland with qualification secure, but a huge test lay ahead over the two legs of the quarter-finals and their greatest rivalry was to be renewed.

On the 29th April 1972 West Germany produced a performance that pushed them even further into the spotlight of the world's press and football purists. They had been drawn to play against England with all of the recent history and ill feeling that any game between the two sides commanded. Played over home and away legs, they would first travel to London and attempt to do what they had never achieved before – win on English soil. Domestically the West German game had been rocked by a scandal that had caught up over two thirds of its Bundesliga clubs in allegations of match fixing, unauthorised win bonuses paid by third parties and individual charges of financial irregularities. With their league's standing at an all time low the national side were now the country's main source of footballing pride.

England were generally assumed as favourites by most, including some in the German camp, particularly at Wembley in the first leg. Their side still contained players who had beaten West Germany in the World Cup final of 1966 at the same ground, the likes of Gordon Banks, Bobby Moore, Alan Ball, Martin Peters and Geoff Hurst all starting for England. Further to that Moore, Ball, Hurst and Peters had all played that hot day in Mexico letting the 2 goal lead slip and were hungry for revenge. Also lining up from that World Cup quarter-final were Franny Lee and the two substitutes bought on to sure up the win only to watch it slip away – Norman Hunter and Colin Bell. England were expected to avenge that defeat in the home leg at least and West Germany would have to be on the top of their game to come away with anything other than a heavy defeat.

However, West Germany also had veterans of both games in their camp and freed of the shackles of the highest of expectations, came to London hopeful of at least a draw. As the game kicked off it became evident that the home side were going to have fight to take anything from the game as the Germans passed around the static English midfield, Beckenbauer and Günter Netzer the main architects. On 27 minutes Uli Hoeness scored the games opening goal with a fierce shot past a wrong-footed Gordon Banks and West Germany had the lead they deserved. Despite Lee's equalizer giving England hope of a draw with just 12 minutes left to play, West Germany went on to record a famous 3-1 victory – Netzer scoring from the penalty spot and Müller adding another in the last minute to make the return leg in Berlin a daunting proposition for the English. Their performance at Wembley had Europe's press purring over the West German's pace, movement and speed of thought. England had been over run in a fashion not seen since Hungary brought the Magical Magyars to the same stadium in 1953. The second leg ended in a goalless draw with West Germany happy to soak up the pressure from an increasingly ragged England as they desperately searched for a way back into the game.

West Germany had won the tie outright and now qualified for the final tournament in Belgium to be played in June. Standing in the way of them lifting the European Championship for the first time in their history was a semi-final against the hosts and a potential final against either Hungary or Russia. After the drama and high profile nature of the quarter final, the semi-final proved to be a slight anti climax as they easily overcame a resilient but not outstanding Belgium side thanks to 2 Gerd Müller goals. A late consolation goal for the Belgians gave the scoreline a far closer look than it deserved and West Germany had safely negotiated their way into a final.

Waiting for them would be Russia who had overcome Hungary 1-0 in a tight game in Brussels. With West Germany now playing near to the very top of the abilities they were faultless in the game, brushing aside Russia's challenge nonchalantly and recording a 3-0 win. The margin of victory remains the highest to date in a European Championship final and in reality, could've have been far more, Müller scoring in each half sandwiching Herbert Wimmer's strike just after half time. West Germany's football was as good as anyone else in the world and they now had a major trophy to put against this remarkable group of player's entries in the history books. With a World Cup on German soil just two years away, they looked almost unstoppable.

In reality 1972's European Championships marked a peak for West German football, all the more remarkable for the fact that they would go on to win the World Cup two years later. By the time 1974's tournament came about the same group of players had become fragmented and divisive. Right up until the eve of the World Cup's opening game a huge row erupted in the camp over bonuses to be paid for winning the competition. Manager Helmut Schön felt marginalised by the player's rebellion, the authorities were struggling to keep all parties satisfied and Beckenbauer had become a leader on and off the pitch. Unhappy about their training camp the bonus row erupted to a level where their whole tournament was in real danger of collapse before it had even begun.

Eventually compromises were reached but a split remained between those in the squad who had back and vocalised a rebellion and those who were more concerned with playing the game over all else. With the authorities heavy involvement and direct dealing with certain members of the squad, Schön felt he had lost elements of his authority and the tight grasp he had tried to keep on the team tactically had gone. West Germany laboured to a 1-0 win over Chile in their first group game with hardly a trace of 1972's verve and energy. A 3-0 win over Australia in their next game gave them a scoreline that flattered their performance on the day, even Beckenbauer not immune to criticism as it became clear something was affecting their mindset.

Going into a final publicity-bating group game against East Germany, defeat was unthinkable both in sporting and political terms. This was cited as the game that they would finally spark them into life, the fission of a country divided now facing each other on any stage would be enough to charge the game but add in West Germany's position as hosts and it was a match they dare not lose. With more rumours circulating of problems within the group regarding Schön's selections and tactics, West Germany played as if the weight of the world rested on their shoulders. The freedom, speed and adaptability that had been the hallmark of their side had gone, replaced by a palpable nervous energy and a lack of creativity. With a sense of inevitability as the minutes ticked down East Germany took the lead thanks to Jürgen Sparwasser taking advantage of hesitation in defence. With just 13 minutes left to play West Germany struggled to rally and at the final whistle, they had suffered the most humiliating and public of defeats.

Ironically, finishing in second place in their group behind East Germany actually gave them a massive advantage in the second round group stages. To qualify for the final they had to top Group B ahead of Poland, Sweden and Yugoslavia. If they had won their first round group they would now be facing Brazil, Argentina and the highly fancied Dutch team and their 'total' football. Despite the favourable draw they still faced huge problems in both resurrecting their morale and form ahead of the upcoming game against Yugoslavia. Schön was a particular worry as he appeared to have lost control completely in the wake of the defeat.

After involvement from the DFB (Deutscher Fußball-Bund – the German FA) concerned about the national side's performance, Beckenbauer was approached and agreed to help an ailing Schön. Stories of his involvement vary wildly from the vastly exaggerated tale that he was now in control of team affairs, to the more probable that he became the link man for the manager to get the respect of his players back. Beckenbauer revelled in the responsibility and subsequently; his leadership and form on the pitch were to prove crucial in the team's fortunes.

One decision that would prove key and deal with one of the squabbles was that Wolfgang Overath would be West Germany's playmaker, not the popular but out of favour Günter Netzer. Netzer had only featured briefly in the game against East Germany as a substitute and despite memories of an outstanding performance at Wembley in 1972 still in the air, it would be Overath who would be tasked with the job of creating chances without fearing for his place. Netzer had signed for Real Madrid in 1973 in defiance of Schön's belief that all his players should ply their trade in the Bundesliga and his repeated omission had been a source of debate.

With his team reworked but the philosophies remaining, Schön's West Germany slowly picked up the form that had made them such an exciting prospect in the first place. A cathartic 2-0 win over the Yugoslavians was followed by an excellent performance and victory against Sweden. A final group game in terrible conditions saw Poland also beaten and despite the problems still bubbling just under the surface, West Germany had made it to the World Cup final. They faced Holland who had cut a dash through the tournament and once again worked together through the various fault lines that ran through the squad to produce a performance.

Working tirelessly to stem the flow of the Dutch attacking ambition, a 2-1 victory was ground out as West Germany used energy to counter flair. Despite falling behind to a penalty conceded before a German player had even touched the ball, the West Germans ceded possession in areas where the Dutch couldn't hurt them and closed them down everywhere else. A Paul Breitner penalty and a typically clinical Müller goal had them 2-1 ahead at half-time and a second half rear guard action saw them home.

The win in 1974 had papered over some considerable cracks but it marked the end of this squad's time together. Gerd Müller, Wolfgang Overath and Jürgen Grabowski all announced their international retirement within days of the tournament's close, Paul Breitner followed shortly after only to return briefly in 1981. Beckenbauer played for West Germany until 1977 when a move to the much-vaunted New York Cosmos breached Schön's still held belief that he should be in the Bundesliga. Der Kaiser's influence in the German game was such that he would eventually become national team manager and lead them to another World Cup win in 1990, becoming only the second man to win the tournament as both player and head coach. Beckenbauer would go on to hold positions within the DFB itself and also head up the successful 2006 World Cup bid for Germany as hosts.

Helmut Schön remained in the role of national team manager in spite of offering his resignation to the DFB. He led West Germany to the European Championship final in 1976 only to be beaten on penalties by Czechoslovakia and then announced he would retire after 1978's World Cup in Argentina. West Germany exited the tournament at the second group stage after a humiliating loss to an already eliminated Austria. In 1972 Schön could lay claim to managing the best side in world football but despite winning the World Cup two years later to prove it, the victory had been laborious and at the price of future success with that band of players.

German football however moved on. After a brief and very relative slump, 1982 and 1986 saw West Germany make the World Cup final again, finishing on both occasions as runners up to Italy then Argentina before reclaiming the trophy in 1990 with a 1-0 win over their conquerors four years previously. To date a now unified Germany have appeared in a further two semi-finals and the 2002 World Cup final, losing this time to Brazil. In European Championship football West Germany won in 1980 before Germany finished as runners up in 1992, winners in 1996 and then runners up again in 2008. The consistency of their performance in tournament football is not open to debate and it has now become almost a cliché to expect any German team to perform well whatever the given circumstances.

1972 was their pinnacle, a team as fluid and attack minded as any to take a major international honour. As with any great team there was of course a liberal sprinkling of truly great players but at their head stood Franz Beckenbauer, a powerhouse of a player, a true leader on and off the pitch and an example for his team mates to follow. Germany are one of the great footballing nations having written their name all over honours lists and record books throughout the game and they are still consistently among the favourites for any given tournament. For that reason 1972's squad and European Championship winners, widely considered their best and most exciting crop of players ever to have collectively played the game, simply have to matter.

Eintracht Braunschweig 1972–73

Honours

Relegated from Bundesliga 72/73

Winners – Regionalliga Nord 73/74

'That's when I realised my idea that German football was a sport rooted only in the lower classes was wrong'

Günter Mast, president of Jägermeister after finding a collection of businessmen huddled around a television watching a game

In 2009 Bayern Munich signed an extension to their sponsorship deal with Deutsche Telekom to keep their names on Bayern's home and away shirts until 2013. The heavily performance related contracts represented one of the largest ever kit sponsorship agreements in football history and according to reports, could earn Bayern €75 million over the length of the agreed contract. Manchester United, Liverpool, Real Madrid and AC Milan have all earned over £50 million in recent history thanks to similarly huge deals.

On top of these kit sponsorship deals Chelsea, Barcelona and Manchester United again have all secured deals with kit manufacturers worth well over £100 million over extended lengths of time. The opportunity to make a kit with your company's signature all over it has proved irresistible to the major sportswear manufacturers, the fact that this leaves a large area for another company to advertise on has proved too tempting to the clubs. These huge revenue streams are now commonplace, in some cases clubs would have simply ceased to exist without them. While Manchester United fans can celebrate a combined total of over

£350m worth of income, few would guess that it took a team struggling in the midst of a bribery scandal in the Bundesliga to bring this money flooding into the game.

Links with advertising and football had already been established, Manchester United extolled the virtues of Wincarnis Tonic Wine as far back as 1909, but club and shirt sponsorship was almost non-existent in the major leagues. Uruguayan team Club Atlético Peñarol were the first team to flirt with kit sponsorship in the 1950's. Capitalising on their domestic success they invited local companies to sponsor them over short periods of time. A decade later the struggling French league embraced the idea and endorsed clubs making short term deals with companies to sponsor teams generally. The deals up until this point were encouraged to involve companies buying kit for the team involved. This would sometimes lead to a small image or note evident in the kit that could be referenced back to the contributor. The leagues of Austria and Denmark, also struggling to raise money and profile, legalised shirt sponsorship in the mid sixties as a way of supporting their largely semi-professional teams. At this moment though the larger and higher profile all-professional leagues of Spain, England, Germany and Italy were strongly against any sort of sponsorship appearing on club shirts, their FA's deciding that the only thing that should be evident on a club's shirt was their chosen badge. The problem they hadn't anticipated was that in that statement, they had just created the loophole.

Eintracht Braunschweig had been one of the sixteen teams to compete in the first season of the newly formed German Fußball-Bundesliga. Situated in the city of Braunschweig in Lower Saxony, the team had been chosen for their success in the Oberliga Nord and the financial stability they had enjoyed in recent years. Their first three years in the new national league had been average, finishing 11th, 9th and 10th respectively but in the 1966-67 season, they were about to make their first big footnote in German football. Built on a solid defence they finished the season as champions, two points ahead of much bigger rivals 1860 Munich. They had come from nowhere to take the title but unfortunately returned back there, unable to build on this success. Another four seasons passed without much of note but unknown to them, a storm cloud was growing on the horizon.

With the 1972-73 season underway, Eintracht Braunschweig found themselves in serious financial trouble for the first time in their history. German football was gripped by a bribery scandal after it emerged that results in the 1970-71 season had been manipulated to help Kickers Offenbach to try and avoid relegation. The resulting fall-out prompted a nationwide investigation and it was discovered that on the 5th June 1971, Braunschweig players had been promised a bonus by a third party if they beat Oberhausen in a home game. Despite the fact that they had been incentivised to win instead of others who had thrown games away for money (and the fact the game ended in 1-1 draw regardless) Eintracht Braunschweig were punished if anything even more harshly than anyone else involved. Team leaders Lothar Ulsaß and Max Lorenz were suspended for the season and another thirteen players as well as the club itself were all heavily fined.

Results inevitably slumped and the fans were staying away. Braunschweig didn't have the resources some of the larger clubs enjoyed but did own their stadium as opposed to most in the league. This was proving to be a dubious honour as it meant they were also responsible for its upkeep and all costs. With attendances slumping their main source of income was slowly disappearing and financially, they suddenly found themselves on the brink.

Günter Mast was a local man who had worked his way through a family business until he was running the company. Their main product was the alcoholic spirit Jägermeister and keen to promote the drink, Mast had already dipped into the waters of sports sponsorship. With no real interest in sport other than self-promotion, after noting the success Martini had had with motor racing Mast decided he wanted that level of exposure for his alcoholic product. In 1972 former world champion Graham Hill drove the first Formula 2 Jägermeister car and a team was born. It would continue to compete at various levels of motor sport right up until the year 2000, by which time some of the very best drivers in the world had raced in the instantly recognisable orange livery of a Jägermeister car. After noticing the interest football was generating Mast had recognised another area to move into but there were several roadblocks to overcome compared to relative ease of buying a motor sports team.

The German Football Association (the DFB) was an amateur body with strict anti-commercialism rules, a format almost universally followed by the major FA's in Europe. There was no way he could buy a football team and get them to a level were the company name was prominent enough to be commercially viable. Similarly there didn't appear to be anyway he could sponsor a team's kit legally. The last club to try – a nearly bankrupt Wormatia Worms – had been roundly rebuked by the DFB for even mooting the idea after being approached by Caterpillar in 1967. The rule remained steadfast, only a clubs badge could be displayed on a team's shirt. However complicated it looked at the outset, it seemed Mast and Braunschweig's destinies were now intertwined.

It is unclear at what point Mast became aware of his local club's financial plight. Club chairman Ernst Fricke never revealed whether he met Mast by luck or design, but a meeting took place and a plan was formed that would shape football finance for years to come. Reports of the figures involved vary from an initial payment of 90,000DM to a deal worth 800,000DM over five years. Whatever the reality was the first long-term shirt sponsorship had been struck, dependant of course on Mast and Fricke's ability to outmanoeuvre the DFB.

An initial approach to the governing body to put Jägermeister on Eintracht Braunschweig's shirts took place in August 1972 and as expected, was immediately refused. Mast and Fricke then called a vote for members of the football club to be taken in January 1973. The motion to be decided upon was the changing of the club's badge to a new design, namely the instantly recognisable Jägermeister deer's head logo. After explanation of the situation and some heavy petitioning by Fricke to the members, the motion was passed by an overwhelming majority to change the badge as had been proposed. On January 27th 1973 it was decided that the new kit complete with new 'badge' would make its debut in a home game against Offenbach and the revolution would begin.

Powerless but annoyed, the German FA began to look at ways they could stop Braunschweig sporting the new company 'inspired' badge. After managing to delay the kit's debut by threatening to call games off if they wore it, the DFB examined all angles of the deal done by Fricke and could only find one point of contention. In a further nod to their new benefactors the club had increased the size of the 'badge' to eighteen centimetres and placed it in the middle of the player's chests. The only thing the authorities could do was demand that the club reduced the size of the crest to a more reasonable fourteen centimetres. Happy to comply and with Mast and Fricke pleased to have exercised the loophole they had found, on March 24th 1973 the kit made its debut after the referee had checked every badge with a tape measure. Within seven months and under the weight of a huge number of requests from clubs to change their badges, the German FA officially sanctioned shirt sponsorship and the rest is history.

The idea and the nature of Fricke and Mast's deal spread throughout Europe. In England the Football Association allowed shirt sponsorship in June 1977 after spending nearly a full year arguing with Kettering Town. Ex-Wolves striker Derek Dougan, now a chief executive at the club, had struck a deal with local company Kettering Tyres and had been going back and forth pushing the boundaries of the laws all season. By 1979 Hibernian, Derby County and Liverpool had all landed deals to play with sponsored shirts in the UK's top divisions and by the mid-eighties, nearly every team in Europe had a sponsor. The television companies had also relented after initial refusal to show teams with businesses names on their shirts and the full potential of sponsoring a football team became evident for all to see.

Sponsorship in football now runs far deeper than just a name on a shirt. Huge companies enjoy close links with major football clubs at all levels of the game – Arsenal and Bolton Wanderers have enjoyed long term sponsorship of their stadiums including naming rights – and most of the bigger clubs in Europe have links with prestige car manufacturers thus ensuring the much-photographed footballers are seen driving their latest models. Sponsorship also led to the explosion of corporate entertainment at football games with boxes and suites available at most grounds for companies willing to pay a premium for the match day experience. While some refuse to play with a sponsor on their shirt this invariably doesn't stretch to other areas of the football club. Barcelona's unique deal with Unicef involved them paying the charity to display their logo on their shirts, but this loss of potential revenue was somewhat tempered by a huge manufacturing deal with sportswear giant Nike.

The river of money that sponsorship provides in the game today continues to grow at odds with any other financial market. Started by two men trying to save a club and circumnavigate the DFB, sponsorship now occupies a huge and growing position in nearly every club in the world's balance sheet. For being the first club in a major league to break the ground and exploit the potential available, Eintracht Braunschweig had written themselves a huge footnote in the game.

Holland 1974

Honours

World Cup Finalists at Germany '74

		P	W	D	L	F	A	Pts
1	Holland	3	3	0	0	8	0	6
2	Brazil	3	2	0	1	3	3	4
3	East Germany	3	0	1	2	1	4	1
4	Argentina	3	0	1	2	2	7	1

Second Round Group A Final Table

In 1974 exposure to global football was limited to coverage of major tournaments. Well before the days of Internet access or designated sports channels, Ajax's European Cup exploits had made them well known but not necessarily well witnessed. With the Dutch national team having now adopted 'total football' themselves and with Rinus Michels – one of its greatest exponents – in charge, Holland's national team headed to Germany in 1974 with a reputation for skilful attacking football that they now had to prove.

The previous World Cup in 1970 had been a riot of colour and noise. Presented live around the world for the first time, audiences had fallen in love with the sunshine and samba football. Mexico '70 had been all about Pelé and his 'Golden Squad'. One of the greatest teams of all time had been involved in some wonderful and unforgettable moments. The expectation had built for 1974 and even though the great Pelé wouldn't be involved, there was a new superstar to look forward to.

Johan Cruyff was now plying his trade in the Camp Nou with Barcelona. He'd been an instant success, helping the Catalans to their first La Liga title after thirteen years of Madrid dominance. Scoring 16 goals along the way, Cruyff had quickly made himself integral to the team's ambitions. The fans took to Cruyff from the off. To their delight he informed the world's press that he'd chosen them over hated rivals Real Madrid due to their links with General Franco. As if to further his cause he chose the Catalan name 'Jordi' for his son when born early in 1974. The greatest player in a team of great players, Cruyff's role in a 5-0 win at the Bernabéu had all but sealed his ascension to sainthood in the eyes of the Barcelona fans.

Rinus Michels had bought his former protégée to the Camp Nou and reaped the benefit of his instant impact. Now in the role of Dutch national manager, he was about to expose Cruyff and total football to an expectant worldwide audience. His teams played in his vision and Ajax and to a lesser extent Barcelona's total football was now Holland's. The Dutch public watched on in hope, knowing full well they had currently the best player in the world playing in the most exciting system. A further sprinkling of world-class talent ran through the length of the squad and there was every hope the country was about to improve on their terrible World Cup record so far.

1974 would be the country's first World Cup campaign since 1938. The national team had been treading water and failing to qualify for World Cups or the European Championship finals, this qualification campaign had been very different from the outset. Ajax had easily one of the best teams in Europe and it was packed with Dutch internationals. Feyenoord remained hot on their heels domestically and also had a largely native squad. On top of a 'golden generation' of talent, a favourable draw placed them in a qualification group with Belgium, Norway and Iceland. Fancied from the start, everyone involved acknowledged this was their best chance to make a finals appearance in over thirty years.

They didn't disappoint. The process began in 1972 with a home game against Norway. Setting the bar for themselves high they routed them 9-0. The Ajax connection of Neeskens and Cruyff scored 5 between them and dominated the game. Their next match was their most difficult – away to Belgium – which they safely negotiated to a goalless draw. After waiting ten months between games, they played the home and away fixtures against Iceland in quick succession. Knowing two wins would draw them level with leaders Belgium, a 5-0 and then an incredible 8-1 victory put them top on goal difference. After Barry Hülshoff's 87th minute goal gave them a 2-1 win in Oslo – set-up by Cruyff's wonderful back heel, the last game against Belgium was set to be winner takes all.

The game was fraught and tense throughout. A linesman's flag wrongly denied Belgium the opener they needed. A game of chess ensued as Belgium had tactically restricted the free flowing but in this instance frightened Dutch. After 90 long minutes the campaign finished with a 0-0 draw between the two strongest teams in the group. Thanks to their vastly superior goal difference, Holland had safely qualified.

Michels job was becoming harder than it looked on the surface. Friction was growing amongst certain members of the squad. The Ajax contingent had issues with their former team mates – Cruyff and Barcelona bound Johan Neeskens. Cruyff captained the squad and yearned for the power he felt his talent deserved, regularly involving himself in team matters. Goalkeeper and PSV Eindhoven player Jan van Beveren was withdrawn from the finals due to an injury many felt it was a metaphor for his relationship with Cruyff and Michels. Both men had already agreed the keeper was no favourite of theirs and may not have been picked anyway. On top of the individual problems, tension existed between the Ajax and Feyenoord factions as a result of their intense rivalry on the pitch.

Michels had to manage the egos but when playing, things just seemed to click. An impressive warm-up game against Argentina finished with a comprehensive 4-1 win, the Albiceleste without an answer for the Dutch movement. With a finalised twenty-two-man squad, the Oranje headed to Germany in confident mood.

If there was ever an example of this team's desire to be different it came with the announcement of their squad numbers. Rather than any conventional 1 to 11 and then the substitutes numbered as you saw fit, the Dutch chose to number themselves alphabetically 1 to 22. As a result starting goalkeeper Jan Jongbloed took number 8 rather than the conventional 1, and defender Wim Suurbier would play in every game as number 20. As ever Cruyff had be different and took the out of sequence 14 he had worn at Ajax. Denied the shirt number at Barcelona, there was no way he wasn't going to wear it for the national side. Cruyff would've been number 1, striker Ruud Geels 14. The swap occurred as the captain was in the habit of getting his own way.

Cruyff's next stand would come over the kit Holland would wear. Realising the possibilities, Adidas had sponsored them and their familiar three black stripes ran down each arm of the orange shirts. Cruyff had his own deal with Puma and refused to play with Adidas's obvious branding on his shirt. After negotiation between Dutch authorities and Adidas officials understandably annoyed the most photographed player in the tournament was taking such a stance, a compromise was reached. Cruyff would play in the same shirt as everyone else but with only two stripes on each arm to show his allegiance to Puma.

With everything now in place surely the team and their mercurial captain could concentrate on their football. Not yet. The week before the tournament disagreements emerged about bonuses and the whole squad threatened to strike. Once again compromises had to be made and eventually with just three days to go before the World Cup began, agreement was struck and trouble averted.

The time for argument and debate was over. In Group 3 Uruguay, Sweden, and Bulgaria awaited and it was time to prove Holland were worth the hype. They opened with a game against the Uruguayans on the 15th June and didn't disappoint. A 2-0 scoreline didn't really tell the full story as the Dutch dominated the game from start to finish. The world watched the constant movement of the orange shirts in awe. On the pitch Uruguay struggled to combat the Dutch rhythm with anything other than some wild challenges. On fifteen minutes the pressure told as Cruyff won the ball and eased past three players before pushing it wide to defender Wim Suurbier. Checking inside onto his left, he picked out Johnny Rep's well timed run between light-blue shirts. Rep's header gave Holland the lead they deserved and their tournament was up and running.

Chance after chance went begging as they struggled to get the second their dominance deserved. Cruyff darted and menaced the aging Uruguay defence constantly, creating openings time and time again and having a goal ruled out for offside. Finally with just four minutes to go, Rep got his and his country's second to seal the game.

After such an impressive performance the next game against Sweden was to prove a disappointment. A 0-0 draw was only really illuminated by the birth of the Cruyff turn as we know it. Cruyff had performed the turn domestically but again, this was the first chance for the world to witness it. After a similar move in a less dangerous area of the pitch against Uruguay, this time Cruyff was just outside the penalty area on the left wing. Hounded by Swedish right-back Janne Olsson, he shaped to cross with his right. With the defender committed a flick pulled the ball back past Cruyff's left leg and away into space, a move copied in every playground the world over the morning after.

Going into the last game all four sides had a chance of qualifying for the second round. Holland would play Bulgaria while Sweden and Uruguay faced off at the same time. Sweden recorded a 3-0 win to secure their second round place, Holland clicked again and put four past the Bulgarians. Neeskens scored two penalties, Johnny Rep a terrific volley and substitute Theo De Jong added a late forth from Cruyff's excellent cross. Holland had qualified for the second round and guaranteed their best ever performance in a World Cup.

The format of the tournament put Holland into Group A of the second round, the winners of which would progress to the World Cup Final. It threw up an intriguing game between the new entertainers of Holland and the old guard of Brazil. Argentina and East Germany would make up the other two teams in the group and the Netherlands set about their new task in the fashion they had just completed their last.

Argentina were up first and Holland were superb. Cruyff had an outstanding game and tied the Argentinean defence in knots with his pace and movement. In the 11th minute Feyenoord midfielder Wille van Hanegem chipped a ball through to Cruyff who took the ball down with his right and touched it past goalkeeper Daniel Carnevali. Faced with a slight angle, Cruyff rolled the ball in with his left to give the Dutch the lead. On twenty-five minutes it was two as defender Ruud Krol lashed in a loose ball from a corner.

In the second half Holland remained on top. Rep added a third with a header from Cruyff's cross and the Argentinean defence looked lost. In the last minute, Cruyff got his second with a brilliant finish from a tight angle. Quite a message had been sent and it'd been brilliant performance. They followed it with a routine victory over East Germany on a greasy pitch. Neeskens swept in the first after some pinball in the penalty area, Rob Rensenbrink – a striker playing with Anderlecht in Belgium – finished neatly for the second. Current holders Brazil had also won both games and although they had a vastly inferior goal difference, the last game in the group between them and the Dutch had effectively become a semi-final. All Holland needed was a draw and they would be in their first ever World Cup Final, Brazil had to win.

On the 3rd July the entertainers currently holding the crown played their natural heirs. Both sides took the pitch in their away kits, Holland white, Brazil blue. Holland were confident – while they'd breezed through their five games, 12 scored and only 1 conceded, Brazil had laboured to this point. After two goalless draws in their group a 3-0 win against Zaire had been enough to see them through on goal difference. Now in the second round it had taken a brilliant Rivelino free kick to beat East Germany and their best performance so far to beat Argentina 2-1. Brazil were well aware of the task facing them in Dortmund and this was not the team of four years ago.

They started in aggressive fashion. The Brazilian way of 1970 had given way to something far more brutal. Cruyff had a shot well saved and then Neeskens drove wide. The Brazilians grew into the game and striker Lima fluffed his lines when presented with a chance. Still the Seleção niggled and bit, referee Kurt Tschenscher struggled to control the game as tackles grew in veracity and yellow cards were proving no deterrent. Incidents began to occur off the ball as Brazil grew more cynical. The halftime whistle after 45 goalless minutes gave both teams the opportunity to calm down and regroup for the second half.

Holland came out fighting in every sense. The Brazilian brutality was now met with Dutch aggression. The difference between the two sides was now apparent as Holland matched Brazil's physicality with their own brand of on or off the ball nastiness. Crucially though, Holland remembered they could also play football. After some neat interplay with Cruyff, Neeskens slid and looped the ball impossibly over a stranded Leao in Brazil's goal. The goal said everything about this Dutch side, an injection of tempo and then the creation of space leading to a clinical strike.

Now ahead and with one foot on the Munich pitch where the final would be played, Holland relaxed and began to enjoy themselves. Cruyff was ruled offside after lobbing Leao from some 30 yards after a quick free kick. Rensenbrink found Krol on the left who sprinted into space, Cruyff had moved central after spending much of the game in wide positions and volleyed in Krol's cross for 2-0. Simple, elegant and devastating, Holland were on their way to the World Cup Final. The game finished with an inevitable Brazilian red card for Luis Pereira and the result over the holders was emphatic.

A nation waited expectantly. They had come so far since the return of professionalism and now they stood on the brink of ruling the world. They had the best footballer in the tournament and played a brand of football that had everyone that mattered talking. All that stood between them and the prize was reining European Championship holders, West Germany.

The West Germans had their own superstar in Franz Beckenbauer. Leader in every sense, Beckenbauer was part of the resurgence of German football. As the heart of the Bayern Munich side that had taken the European Cup from Ajax's grasp, Der Kaiser as he had come to be known was one of the only defensive players in the world to have the intelligence to cope with total football. He had seen Ajax up close in the 1973 European Cup and had been part of a routed Bayern side. He was in no mood to repeat that fate. The Germans also boasted Gerd Müller in their side, one of the greatest strikers in their history and currently sitting on 67 goals in his 66 caps for his country. Müller had an unbelievable scoring record throughout his career and had already scored three times in this tournament.

The German style was based on solid organisation, hard work and rigidity only as and when required. Many felt even as hosts West Germany were facing an uphill task against the cavalier Dutch. The build up was blighted by German headlines alleging a 'naked party' had taken place in the Dutch camp before the Brazil game, Cruyff was said to be particularly affected by the allegation. Despite the headlines and the furore surrounding them, the Dutch pushed it out of their minds and took the pitch at Munich's Olympic stadium knowing they needed to work hard to break the organised German's down.

After a small delay while the missing corner flags were located, Holland kicked off and immediately played the ball to their talisman Cruyff. Loitering in the centre circle Cruyff jogged forward with his man-marker for the day Berti Vogts in pursuit. With a trademark surge of pace Cruyff glided into the area only to be stopped by a lunge from Uli Hoeneß. The tackle was last ditch and Cruyff had already pushed the ball past the defender. Left with no choice, English referee Jack Taylor gave the penalty with just a minute on the clock and no West German having touched the ball. Neeskens dispatched the spot-kick and the Dutch were ahead.

Holland's performance in the final would go on to be a talking point for many years to come but not for the reasons many had hoped. After a blistering start they faded and descended into constant argument with Taylor at every decision. The German's simply stuck to their plan and on twenty-five minutes drew level with a penalty of their own. The Dutch protested fervently that forward Bernd Holzenbein had dived over Wim Jansen's tackle but there was no denying the challenge was mistimed. West German attacking midfielder Paul Breitner, a scorer of some great goals in his career, scored from the spot and Holland seemed to be labouring to get their total football going.

With just two minutes to go before halftime the game had become a tale of two midfields, both struggling to create clear-cut chances in the face of the very different style in opposition. Suddenly West Germany broke down the right with midfielder Rainer Bonhof. Making his way into the box he squared the ball for the lethal Müller. His touch took the ball behind him but thinking quickly and with defender Rudi Krol stranded, he turned and fired in Germany's second. 2-1 up and playing a Holland side struggling for the rhythm that had made them so dangerous, half-time came at the right time for West Germany to plan out their second half.

Holland failed to break down the West German defence marshalled by their captain Beckenbauer. The game became stretched but not enough to create the gaps the Dutch needed. West Germany and Müller had a legitimate goal ruled out for offside; Neeskens flashed an effort wide with the keeper well beaten. Cruyff played deeper than normal but couldn't shake off Vogts or repeat that early burst. Eventually the final whistle bought the curtain down on the Dutch 1974 World Cup dream and the West Germans had won.

It's true that in all sport, the best side doesn't always take the trophy. In 1974 Holland played the brand of football Ajax had used so successfully and exposed it to the world. They mattered because they played their way into the hearts and minds of the football purists and the casual fan a like, they had followed Brazil in 1970 with similarly aesthetic and beautiful football and had become an inspiration, finishing as runners-up somehow only adding to their mystique. Were the West German's better than Holland? On the day – yes, on another? We'll never know. Whatever the reasons for a lack-lustre performance in the final, Holland's 1974 squad had already done enough to write their names into the pages of football history written about the most beautiful to play the game.

A Cruyff-less side would reach the same stage four years later but fall again, this time to hosts Argentina. Cruyff's time at the World Cup had been brief but brilliant, an immense talent coupled with an enormous personality. He would never forget the values of total football and some time later, would take them into management himself.

West Bromwich Albion 1977–78

Honours

FA Cup semi-finalists

6th place in First Division (UEFA Cup Qualification)

'You'll get one of these through your knees if you step on our Wembley turf'

Note accompanied with a bullet sent through the post to Cyrille Regis after he earned his first England call-up.

In 2004 the English national team travelled to Spain for a high profile international friendly at the Bernabéu stadium in Madrid. While Spain eventually emerged with a 1-0 victory the game's headlines had all been written by an element of the home support. During the game black players Ashley Cole and substitute Shaun Wright-Phillips were singled out for the kind of racist abuse now all but eliminated from the English game. On television and radio the 'monkey' chants could clearly be heard and the commentary teams sounded stunned to be confronted with this level of racism once again. The game quickly became bad tempered and Wayne Rooney had to be substituted in the first half to save him from a red card. Ashley Cole picked up a first half booking for a wild challenge on Michel Salgado but could be forgiven as several of his team mates were clearly upset by the abuse.

The incident led to an outcry. England's Under 21 players had also endured similar chants the previous evening and all levels of the English FA were appalled. Some, including chief executive of the Professional Footballers Association Gordon Taylor, were disappointed the England team didn't leave the pitch in protest. The incidents were reported to both UEFA and FIFA but Spain were only punished with a nominal fine. FIFA claimed it had operated to the limit of its powers in response but the storm continued as the English FA called for an inquest into FIFA's own stance on racism – if they'd imposed what they saw as a suitable punishment shouldn't there be a stronger sanction available such as playing games behind closed doors?

The outcry at the very public display of racism inflicted on the England players showed how far English football's attitude had come. It was not so very long ago that football grounds the length of the English league were blighted themselves. In the late 1960s and 70s as more and more black footballers rose to prominence football crowds became a maelstrom of racist abuse and even recruitment for organisations such as the National Front. In turbulent political times football became a focal point for violence and bigotry. Black footballers had to endure a cauldron of abuse, chanting and objects such as bananas thrown towards them every time they took a throw in or a corner. Even though it would've been far easier to sink away from the game, some stood up and let themselves be counted even in the face of such horrific abuse.

The first black professional footballer is widely acknowledged to be Arthur Wharton. Wharton played for Preston North End and Sheffield United amongst others in the late 19th Century as football began to emerge as the national game. He was a specialist goalkeeper in an era when they were few and far between due to the forwards legally being able to 'charge' the 'keeper amongst other such rules in their favour, but he was also talented enough to play outfield when given the opportunity. Wharton was of Ghanaian descent and excelled at several sports, leaving football for running at one point, then turning to cricket after his retirement. Having turned away from a life as a minister for sport, Wharton achieved local fame as he journeyed around the country playing for various clubs. As one of the most talented players of his day many felt he should have represented the country in which he'd made his living but his non-selection was written off as due to his eccentric nature rather than explicitly racial motives. His career came to a close without the official recognition it perhaps deserved and he turned to cricket as his main sporting pursuit. He died in poverty in 1930 but he's now officially recognised for the impact he made in the game and a member of several hall of fames both within the sport and beyond. In 1997 a ceremony was held at his grave in Ellington Cemetery in Doncaster where a memorial stone was placed over his grave recording his achievements.

Over the years several black footballers made an impact in the British game but racial tensions also grew making them targets for abuse. Despite various obstacles in their way several did carve a niche in football history. Walter Tull played at both Tottenham Hotspur and Northampton Town but was taken by the First World War, dying in service of his country at Arras in 1918. Tull had risen to the rank of Second Lieutenant despite army regulations prohibiting 'men of colour' from doing so. Tull was a talented enough footballer to attract the attention of no less than Herbert Chapman, then manager of Northampton who signed Tull for what was described as a 'substantial fee'. It's also recorded he suffered specific racial abuse during his career.

The first black footballer to really become a 'legend' at just one club was Jack Leslie with Plymouth Argyle. He played over 400 times in a 15-year career through the 1920's and 30's with the Devon club, and was only denied an England cap by a withdrawal of a call-up in mysterious circumstances. Leslie suspected that he knew the real reason and it emerged in time that the FA withdrew the offer upon finding out about the colour of his skin. Racial discrimination was not just consigned to the terraces it seems.

As the Second World War came and went and robbed Europe of so many young men, football picked up the pieces and began to put itself together again. Black players still broke through at certain clubs but had to endure the problems the colour of their skin brought from the crowds. Lloyd 'Lindy' Delapenha became a success at Middlesbrough and something of a cult hero in his seven years at the club during the 50s. The 60s saw Albert Johanneson play at the highest levels of the English game with Leeds United, becoming the first black player to play in the FA Cup final in 1965. As ever though every step forward had to be tempered with the abuse reigning in from the terraces and even on the pitch.

There was no condemnation of the attitude, many dismissing it as simple 'name calling'. By 1977 the number of black players in the game was steadily rising but still not one had been seen as good enough to represent the country. The abuse was rarely covered by the media or mentioned by the FA, no task force was ever set up and incidents between the players and the crowd almost never made it into any referee's report. The clubs themselves chose to ignore rather then condemn, fearful of creating any more unrest in what was already a volatile atmosphere in the football crowds of the day. However, First Division West Bromwich Albion were about to help start the change by signing and fielding three black players together in their first team, the so called 'Three Degrees', all of whom became a source of inspiration for the generation to come. All three would give their all for the Albion and the crowd responded by appreciating their talent, rather than just the colour of their skin.

The first of the three to move to the Midlands was the brilliant Laurie Cunningham. Many spoke of Cunningham's ability as being able to live the very best in the world but the consistency needed to join the elite sometimes eluded him before later in his career injury all but stalled him completely. Johnny Giles had played for Leeds United (and had been a team mate of Albert Johanneson's) in a glittering career that in its twilight now saw him at West Brom as manager and some time player. Cunningham was playing at Leyton Orient and creating a bit of a stir on the left wing as a player with the ability to turn a game. He had great pace and the innate ability to run with the ball as fast as he could without, coupling youthful exuberance with enough guile to terrorise full backs across Division Two. He'd come to Orient after an early rejection by Arsenal in 1974, breaking into the first team and quickly establishing himself. Within a year he was identified as one the club's key men.

In 1975 a last minute winner in a game against Millwall saw a knife thrown at Cunningham from the stands. Despite near constant abuse he continued to emerge as a real talent, choosing to ignore the insults and concentrate on the ball during games. By 1977 Giles had identified him as a man who could enhance his West Brom side. The move was made after a fee reported to be in the region of £125,000 had been agreed with Orient, and Cunningham took to life in the First Division well. Despite arriving three quarters of the way through the 1976-77 season he made a big impact, contributing to a seventh place finish and scoring 6 times in just 13 appearances.

His form and rising status also earned him the honour of becoming the first black player to represent England at any level after being called to play for the Under-21s. He would go on to earn England 'B' and full caps but his international career was stunted by the injuries that limited his overall playing career. Going into the 77-78 First Division season Cunningham had rightly been earmarked as a player with a huge future ahead of him but West Brom's prospects were unknown. Having become a good mid-table team under Giles's leadership, the coach had decided to leave the club as he fell out of love with football management. Giles felt the job was pulling him further and further away from the pitch and decided to leave before he became totally disenchanted with the game.

His place was taken by Ronnie Allen, a West Bromwich Albion legend as a player after eleven years service to the club in the 50's. His management curriculum vitae was also impressive having got Wolverhampton Wanderers promoted in his second full season as a manger and then winning the 1969 Spanish Cup while in charge of Athletic Bilbao. After spells in Portugal with Sporting Lisbon and fleetingly back in England with Walsall, he'd jumped at the chance to lead the club with whom he had the greatest affinity.

Joining with the manager was a young striker who'd been playing non-league football up until this point. Allen himself had identified him as perfect for the club and personally funded his £5,000 transfer from Hayes. Cyrille Regis came to the club as the second black player destined for the first team but with very little expectation. To adjust to First Division life after making the huge jump from non-league, Regis was played in the reserves, scoring on his debut and consistently impressing enough to earn an early call up to the first team for a League Cup game. The tie against Rotherham United saw Regis score twice and he retained his place for the following league game against Middlesbrough. Regis scored again and his place in first team affairs was all but sealed from that moment on.

Regis didn't have a classic footballers build. He was a real presence up front, built like a boxer and a nightmare for defenders to try and manhandle. While Regis was never truly prolific he possessed an eye for the spectacular and would go on to win Match of the Day's 'Goal of the Season' competition in 1982 with a typically barnstorming effort against Norwich in the FA Cup. West Brom fans took to his nature as well as his talent, never giving up on a loose ball and never giving an opposition defence a moment's peace. After breaking into the first team in the 1977-78 season, the following year saw Regis win the PFA Young Player of the Year. Like Cunningham he earned full international honours eventually, winning his first cap in 1982 despite death threats and a bullet sent through the post.

By December 1977 both Regis and Cunningham were fixtures in the West Bromwich Albion first team and riding the abuse from the crowds. Ronnie Allen however was gone. Despite a reasonable start Allen felt he didn't have the universal backing of the club in all matters, his funding of the Regis deal being symptomatic of what he felt was a lack of absolute faith in his ability. When the Saudi Arabian FA came in with an offer to make Allen manager of their national side on a far higher wage than he was currently earning, he couldn't say no. He would return to the club as manager in the 80's but his real legacy was already in place by signing Regis.

His replacement was a young manager by the name of 'Big' Ron Atkinson who'd already been successful in the lower leagues with Kettering Town and Cambridge United. At Third Division Cambridge he'd made Brendon Batson his captain and he signed the fullback for £28,000 shortly after joining Albion as manager. Batson was the third of West Brom's three black first team footballers and while he may not have been quite as eye catching as Cunningham on the left, or as strong as Regis through the middle, Batson quietly plied his trade at right back to great success for Albion's stylish first team.

Batson started his career with Arsenal but after failing to break into the first team on a long-term basis, accepted a move to Cambridge to kick-start his career. The move to the First Division with West Brom was not down to any favouritism from his old manager, Batson had developed into a quality footballer and a real leader of the team. He continued to improve and earned England B honours before his career was cut short by knee injuries. Batson spent the rest of the '77-78 season in the first team alongside Cunningham and Regis while Atkinson turned the Midlanders into an exciting attacking team.

Whilst still being subjected to horrific racial abuse on a constant basis, all three became integral to West Brom's success. While Albion's supporters warmed to the trio, away games and fans continued the torrent of vilification. Atkinson commented on all three players excellent attitude to the game even in the light of the abuse, Regis stated in later life how he used to use the anger to enhance his own game. After a visit to the club's ground by the Motown legends of the same name, Ron Atkinson seized on the marketable opportunity and christened his black players 'the Three Degrees' – a nickname that would stick. Atkinson's career was later blighted by accusations of racism after he was heard using a derogatory term whilst commentating for a television network in 2004, but he has always said the use of a racial term was a 'slip'. Whatever the truth of his feelings he made it clear that in signing Batson and playing him with Cunningham and Regis, he'd only been interested in signing the best players available to him rather than making any distinctions based on racial grounds.

West Brom reached the semi-final of the FA Cup in 1978 but lost 3-1 to eventual winners Ipswich Town. They also achieved a sixth place finish in the league and qualified for the following year's UEFA Cup. Under Atkinson they became known for playing with a swagger and flair – Cunningham, Batson and Regis were far from the only talented players at the club capable of turning games. Albion's first team also had Bryan Robson, Derek Statham, Willie Johnston and Tony 'Bomber' Brown to call on. In reality though West Brom's real success came with the generation of footballers they were unknowingly inspiring by ignoring the racists, all three of their black footballers going on to leave a huge mark in the game.

Cunningham became the first Englishman to move to no less than Real Madrid in 1979. Breaking up the trio he became a success at the Bernabéu even in the light of similar levels of abuse from the crowd. The Spanish fans took to Cunningham but dubbed him 'El Negro' and after a good start, his relationship with the club disintegrated after a training ground injury started a long line of absences from the first team. His international career also suffered as injury and Real's refusal to allow him to join up with the England squad kept his caps down to just 6, a paltry return for such a talented player. After leaving Madrid he became a journeyman never quite recapturing his best form, playing in short spells for Sporting Gijón, Manchester United and Wimbledon amongst others. After a good season winning promotion with Rayo Vallecano in 1989, Cunningham was tragically killed in a car crash in Madrid aged just 33.

Cyrille Regis enjoyed a career at West Brom that led him to become a legend, voted as one of the club's greatest ever players in 2004. After leaving in 1984 Regis played for Coventry where he won an FA Cup winners medal in 1987, until a move in 1991 to Aston Villa. After two years with Villa and three seasons spent at Wolves, Wycombe Wanderers and Chester City, Regis called time on his playing career after an injury proved to be one knock too far to recover from. Regis went on to work for various charities and within the game he remains a force for the elimination of racism at all levels of football. In 2008 he was awarded an MBE in recognition for his services to the game and his charitable work, and finally he had a fitting reward for a career that had become about so much more than just football.

Batson's career was cut short due to injury but he became a huge force for change within the game. Always defiant, Batson once picked up a banana thrown at him in a game at West Ham and ate it in front of the group of fans who'd just hurled it in his direction. Batson also eventually earned an MBE – his award coming in 2000 – for his work with the development of the Professional Footballers Association as an organisation and within the game and also becoming a figurehead for both anti-racism and drug awareness campaigns. At one point Batson became Managing Director of West Bromwich Albion, a testament not just to the esteem he was held in by the club but also his standing in regard to the game's administration.

All three men became a huge source of defiant inspiration for a generation of black footballers, paving the way for a greater acceptance of coloured players across the English game. As they came together in early 1978, the summer of the same year saw England's first black full international take the pitch as Viv Anderson of Nottingham Forest took up the position of right back for the national side. The high profile nature of West Bromwich Albion's lack of prejudice began to create the path for an explosion of talented black players to come through, while also marking the beginning of the refusal to accept racism in the English game. Black players such as Ian Wright, Eddie Newton and John Barnes have all acknowledged the debt they owed all three men for their attitude, as well as the way they played the game. It wasn't just the colour of the three's skin that mattered, it was their talent that was easily the equal of any player in the country in their positions.

In the modern English game thanks to the tireless work of the authorities, the clubs themselves and campaigns such as 'Kick It Out', racism is not the problem it once was on the terraces or in the establishment. It remains a constant battle to keep raising the standards of acceptance but if there was ever a marker of how far the game had come, on the 21st June 2002 England faced Brazil in the quarterfinal of the World Cup finals in Japan. In the 79th minute Aston Villa striker Darius Vassell took the pitch in place of Michael Owen meaning for the first time in England's history, there were more black or mixed race players on the pitch than white. In the English game a level has now been reached where the only factor in selecting players for any team is talent and racial abuse in any form is no longer tolerated. While the authorities remain vigilant at continuing to eliminate discrimination, England's game has already come further than once seemed possible.

Taking all that into consideration West Bromwich Albion's team of 1977-78 mattered not for football reasons but something more. As good as the players were, there has perhaps never been another team that have had a bigger impact on society in English football history. In playing 'the Three Degrees' regularly and with such style that they became role models for both black and white children, they had begun to walk a long path to acceptance. All three men endured and then inspired, proving their worth to their team and the game as a whole in time. The saying goes that a journey of a thousand miles has to begin with a single step, West Bromwich Albion were the first to put their foot forward and take it.

Nottingham Forest 1977–80

Honours

European Cup Winners 1979 & 1980

UEFA Super Cup Winners 1979

English First Division Winners 1977-78

League Cup Winners 1978 & 1979

Charity Shield Winners 1978

'I've just been upstairs to give my chairman a vote of confidence'

Brian Clough on then Nottingham Forest Chairman Fred Reacher

When taking over as manager of any team, the man involved has several decisions to make regarding their approach to handling the role. Herbert Chapman and Hugo Meisl used the title to radically overhaul the tactical side of the game. Helenio Herrera became the figure around which the rest of the club had to revolve, making sure the players and in some cases the fans ceded to his wishes. In modern football we see Sir Alex Ferguson at Manchester United using a similar approach but reinforcing the fact that no one is bigger than the club itself, as David Beckham found to his cost when he was moved on due to the 'circus' that surrounded his life. Jose Mourinho is renowned for his attention to detail but he also chooses to fight his player's battles for them, often using the press to criticise and goad opponents and take attention away from anything that could affect his team's mindset.

Various aspects of all of these separate approaches have helped create the 'cult' of the manager. Now as important as the players themselves, a manager is lauded if successful, derided if anything but. They are now the first line of defence for a football club, it's players, it's performances and at times it's owners. While some seek to deflect responsibility if possible and continually focus on the combined effort involved in success, others embrace the importance and can become larger than the players, the club and seemingly life itself.

Step forward one Brian Howard Clough, scourge of football club chairman, firework in the heart of the football establishment and most often cited as the best manager England never had. Clough was box office and made sure those around him knew it. The often used quote about admitting he wouldn't say he was the best manager in the business but he was definitely 'in the top one' was half rooted in the excess of self belief that became his trademark, but also half rooted in truth. Before taking over at Forest, Clough had already established himself as one of the biggest characters in the English game but in taking a previously unheralded team to the top of Europe not once but twice, Clough the mouthpiece became Clough the legend.

The Brian Clough story started in Middlesbrough where he was born and raised. After a happy childhood and a period of national service, Clough set about a career in professional football and proved to be somewhat of a phenomenon. In 274 games with Middlesbrough and Sunderland Clough scored 251 times. He became a noted and free scoring striker, earning full international honours for England twice but his career was tragically cut short by a knee injury. Keen to stay in the game and typically confidant, he became the country's youngest manager at the tender age of just 29 when given the opportunity by Fourth Division Hartlepools United. Clough needed an assistant to work side by side with who understood him and his vision. He settled on enticing former team mate Peter Taylor, an ex-goalkeeper who had been managing non-league Burton Albion and had helped Clough adjust to first team life at 'Boro.

After the pair took on the role at Hartlepools, they spent two years stabilising the club and making steady progress. If there were to be any marker of a future career it would be in the fact that Clough fell out with his chairman in typically bombastic and fatal fashion. There was enough potential to attract Second Division Derby County into employing the pair and it was now that he had his first taste of real success.

Clough overhauled the club from top to bottom, players deemed not good enough shipped out, new blood bought in. With a sprinkling of promising players, some journeymen solid professionals and a few older heads – most notably the great Dave Mackay – Clough clinched promotion to English football's top table in his second season by winning the Second Division title. Their campaign had been emphatic, eventually finishing 7 points clear of Crystal Palace in second place (no small feat with only 2 points still awarded for a win) and Derby had been a class above most they had faced. His first tilt at the First Division in the 1969-70 season could have been deemed just as big an achievement by taking the club to a fourth place position, 2 points ahead of Liverpool in fifth and some 8 points clear of Manchester United in eighth – European Cup winners just two seasons earlier.

After a mid-table finish the following year, 1972 was to prove pivotal in the life of both Clough and Taylor. Now 37 years of age and with his stamp all over the club (much to chairman Sam Longson's dismay at times) Derby were ready for a season long title challenge. In an incredible four-way tussle at that top between Derby, Leeds United, Liverpool and Manchester City, County eventually emerged with the title. Right up until the very last round of games things were very much up for grabs but Derby's consistency and a vital 1-0 win over Liverpool in the latter stages saw them win the First Division for the first time in the club's history.

From the highest moment of his career to date and at a club he loved, Clough then conspired to fall out with chairman and directors alike. His media profile increased with television and newspaper work and some at the club felt Brain Clough believed he was now bigger than Derby County. After failing to defend the title, the media quickly realised that quotes from Clough were headline worthy and a European Cup semi-final defeat to Juventus saw accusations of cheating and bribery coming openly from the manager. Longson had decided as brilliant as his management pair were, Clough was becoming a liability. After recriminations and a feud played out in the halls and walkways of Derby's Baseball Ground as well as on the back pages of several newspapers – both local and national, Clough and Taylor left the club in the October of 1973. Despite repeated calls from fans for both men's reinstatement to the club at the expense of Longson and his board, the divorce was final and both parties came out of the affair the poorer for it.

The nature of both his success and failure had stoked the fires of what was fast becoming a legend surrounding the man. Peter Taylor was known to be disappointed to leave Derby but also loyal to Clough and both men were quickly employed by an ambitious Brighton & Hove Albion of the Third Division. The pair's success at Derby had been rooted in a long-term plan for the team but at Brighton, results failed to come and Clough hankered after a return to the perceived 'big-time'.

In 1974 Don Revie was employed as full time manager of the English national side leaving his beloved Leeds United to take the post. Clough had been openly critical of both Revie and Leeds for their approach to the game, an overly physical and under-handed element he believed tainted everything the Yorkshire club had won. Revie was leaving Leeds as title-holders and had become engrained in the fabric of the club, much as Clough had done at

Derby. Any man coming to replace him would have to have the personality to cope with the comparisons and be willing to try and maintain the expectation the fans now had for the team. Once approached Clough was hooked on the idea and despite Taylor's refusal to join him, he took the job at the biggest club in England believing he could win all Revie had done, but as stated on an interview with local television, he could win it 'better'. With a job to fit his ego, Clough believed he could go one better than he had at Derby and have a run at the European Cup.

To say Clough's tenure at Leeds United was a disaster in football terms is no exaggeration. His 44 days in charge of the club saw him fall out with his players and struggle to make any inroads into what he believed was the lack of discipline on the pitch. At the Charity Shield of 1974 Clough watched his captain Billy Bremner trade blows with Liverpool's Kevin Keegan on Wembley's hallowed turf and knew his senior players were never going to listen to him. After a poor start to their league campaign saw the title-holders wrestling around in the relegation places, Clough left the club with a high-profile failure to his name. Some cited Taylor's absence, others Clough's attitude, and some even argued it was simply a fall from grace for an aging Leeds team that Revie had left before a painful overhaul. Whatever the reasons Clough had struggled, his next move would have to involve rebuilding his reputation a little. An opportunity was about to present itself for a return to the region where he'd made his name with Derby, a reunion with Taylor, and a club who were willing to be rebuilt in his own image for success.

Up until 1975 Nottingham Forest had enjoyed brief flashes but failed to become the club they could potentially have been. Formed in 1865, Forest had won several lower league titles and 2 FA Cups (firstly in 1898, then again in 1959) but never managed a sustained period of success. The club needed a revolution and after parting company with manager Allan Brown in early 1975, Clough arrived to steer them to a mid-table position in his first season and rebuild his claims to be the best manger in the business. If Brian Clough was ever to become the legend he felt he deserved to be, he now had to prove it by returning to his day job and becoming something more than a sound bite.

Clough and Taylor reunited in 1976 after Taylor had successful turned Brighton into a stable club competing at the top of the Third Division. With the pair working together again the Forest revolution began in earnest and by the end of the 76-77 season, they'd won promotion to the First Division courtesy of a snatched third place finish just a point ahead of Bolton Wanderers and Blackpool. Back in England's top tier, Clough and Taylor were about to mastermind a quite incredible ascent to their second title.

Clough had a core of players and added to them cleverly before the 77-78 campaign began, knowing after his time at Derby what it would take to have a successful season in the First Division. Goalkeeper Peter Shilton was signed from Stoke to play behind the likes of Frank Clark, Viv Anderson and Larry Lloyd. Kenny Burns was also signed to the club having been played as a striker by Birmingham City. Clough and Taylor converted Burns to his original position – centre of the defence – and Burns would go on to play well over a hundred times for the club usually in partnership with Lloyd. Burns would take the Football Writers Association Player of the Year for his part in the 77-78 campaign and become a key figure in the future success of the team, scoring some vital goals and working in tandem with Lloyd effortlessly at times.

Clough's captain was midfielder John McGovern, a trusted lieutenant who had played under the manager at Hartlepools, Derby and Leeds. McGovern knew what it took to be successful under Clough and Taylor and eventually moved into management himself. Joining the ranks of Clough and Taylor's 'old boys' were John O'Hare and Archie Gemmill, O'Hare played in midfield and as a striker at various times, Gemmill in an almost playmaker type role. Gemmill's ability on the ball was much admired and as anyone who has seen his goal against Holland at the 1978 World Cup will testify, he had the skill to turn a defence with a change of pace and a dropped shoulder. Clough inherited another midfielder, Ian Bowyer, and in two spells with the club under the manager he would amass over 400 appearances for Forest.

Often played on the right side of midfield another Clough alumni to eventually make that move into management would be midfielder Martin O'Neill, already at the club when Clough arrived but forever changed by his time under him. In later life O'Neill has acknowledged the huge influence Clough had on his career and to date, as a manger he has achieved success with Wycombe Wanderers, Leicester City, Celtic and Aston Villa. On the left wing John Robertson would become one of the finest players ever to play for Forest. Clough and Taylor first turned Robertson into a regular member of the first team and then into an integral part of the Forest attack. Robertson was a skilful winger but his real strength lay in his crossing ability, repeatedly dropping the ball on the head of Forest's strikers with unerring accuracy.

One of those strikers would win individual honours for his part in the 77-78 season. Tony Woodcock impressed during Forest's promotion run and retained his place for the First Division campaign, going on to win the PFA Young Player of the Year for his part in Forest's success. Woodcock's career would take him to Germany, Arsenal and back to Germany in 2 spells with FC Köln and he would also earn 42 caps for England. With a great core to build on, all that remained for Taylor and Clough was to keep adding to a talented squad.

That ability to add to a solid base would serve them well. Over the next three seasons Clough and Taylor would identify players at both ends of the scale. Trevor Francis would become Britain's first £1m footballer in 1979 when signed from Birmingham City. Although Clough had been keen to avoid the label by making the transfer fee £999,999, the reality of the taxes imposed on the deal made it worth well north of the million pound figure. Francis was a striker but he was most often played on the right side of midfield at Forest, never quite justifying the millstone of his fee. Francis lasted only two seasons in Nottingham but is fondly remembered for one goal, a European Cup winning goal no less, and like so many of Clough's former players eventually became a manager with QPR, Sheffield Wednesday, Birmingham City and Crystal Palace.

In contrast to paying a record fee for a player, Garry Birtles came to Forest for just £2,000 in 1976 from the lower reaches of Midlands' non-league football. By 1978 Birtles had forced his way into Forest's frontline and found goal scoring form immediately. In two years in Forest's first team he would score 49 goals before a big money move to Manchester United. After a torrid time at Old Trafford where he struggled with expectation and form, he was reunited with Clough and Forest in 1982 and stayed for a further five seasons with the club. For those initial two years Birtles carried much of Forest's main goal scoring threat with Woodcock, and with quality supply from the likes of Gemmill and Robertson both men profited.

Clough and Taylor took Forest to the top of the English game in their first season in the First Division with the club. Between November 1977 and November 1978, Forest went unbeaten for 42 games in the English First Division, a record only beaten by the Arsenal 'Invincibles' side of 2003-04. Forest walked away with the title and added the League Cup, beating Liverpool 1-0 in a replay thanks to Robertson's second half penalty. Liverpool had chased Forest all season but fallen 7 points short in the league to finish second, consoling themselves with a consecutive European Cup victory. Forest had toppled Liverpool domestically and now Clough and Taylor had another run at the European Cup, fate drawing them together with the Anfield club in the first round of the 78-79 competition. Forest emerged with a 2-0 aggregate win over the holders to win the 'battle of England' and with one of the strongest sides in the tournament already eliminated, the club was on a roll.

While they failed to retain their title, finishing second to a Liverpool with no European distractions, they did take the League Cup for the second year in a row. Garry Birtles scored twice in a man of the match performance as Forest beat Southampton 3-2 to triumph. Only Wolves would stop them taking a third League Cup the following season, defeating them 1-0 in the final. However it was in Europe where they were making the biggest waves, their run in 1979's competition taking them all the way to a final in Munich against Swedish team Malmö FF. Both first time finalists had been outsiders at the competition's beginning but had impressed on route, Forest in particular in overcoming FC Köln at the semi-final stage. At the Olympiastadion both took the field knowing there would be an unfamiliar name on the cup at the game's end.

An injury stricken Malmö opted to sit back and hope that they wouldn't be broken down, a tactic that played to Forest's passing game. With the bulk of the possession and time and space to move the ball about, Forest's pressure told just before halftime when Robertson wriggled free and crossed towards the far post. Meeting the ball with an angled header was Trevor Francis who nodded past a stranded keeper to give Forest the lead. It proved to be the only goal and the small club who just two seasons ago had been playing in England's second tier had taken the biggest prize in European football.

Twelve months later and with a UEFA Super Cup victory over Barcelona also behind them, Forest found themselves dropping to a fifth place league finish but with a chance of retaining the European Cup. Having beaten another Swedish side (Östers IF) in the first round and then Romanian champions Arges Pitesti in the second, Forest beat Dynamo Berlin in a tough tie and then even more impressively, Dutch giants Ajax in the semi-final. Waiting at the Bernabéu stadium in Madrid were Kevin Keegan's Hamburg side who were installed as heavy favourites despite Forest playing as holders. In a tense game it was again one goal that settled it, this time John Robertson's drilled strike from just outside the area in the 21st minute proving enough for Forest to keep the trophy. Any doubts over Clough's ability were no more. He and Taylor had taken a club with very little reputation in their domestic league to the top of European football not once but twice. For all his bravado, bluster, and controversy, Clough now had the proof to back up the talk.

After the high of 1980, Clough remained Forest manager until his retirement in 1993. He managed further success in the League Cup but never held another title or European trophy. The 80's were a tough decade for Clough with the violence on the terraces and the shift in football to something more direct leaving his Forest team looking like an echo of football past at times. Some of the things he had been lauded for demanding of his players in regard to their lifestyle and conduct began to look outdated as money took hold of the game. Clough's last season saw Forest relegated from the new Premier

League, an admission of an alcohol problem and a huge outpouring of thanks from the Forest fans for what he had achieved with the club.

Tragically he had fallen out with Taylor who retired from football in 1982 only to return as Derby manager a short time there after. The decision irked Clough and then the relationship broke down completely when Taylor signed John Robertson, allegedly having never consulted Clough. The transfer all but destroyed their relationship and when Taylor passed away in 1990, a remorseful Clough drank heavily and never really fully recovered in terms of his football career. On the 20th September 2004 he passed away with stomach cancer and football mourned, it had lost one of its true characters.

The 1977 to 1980 Nottingham Forest team mattered because they gave a great man his greatest achievements. A second tier team rising to not only win the European Cup but then retain it is all but unthinkable in the modern game. What 'Cloughie' felt he had started at Derby, he got to finish at Forest. If ever you wanted a measure of the level of respect Clough's achievements have earned you might find it at Forest's City Ground in the renamed Brian Clough Stand. You might also see it in the centre of Nottingham, Albert Park in Middlesbrough or outside Derby's Pride Park Stadium – all locations of statues raised in his honour. Each year any game between Derby County and Nottingham Forest sees the 'Brian Clough Trophy' up for grabs and the main route between the clubs – the A52 – has a section renamed Brian Clough Way to match the street in Middlesbrough that also bares his name. Clough was always quick to point to Taylor's influence in his later years and it should be in no way underestimated the role he played, but Clough became an island within the game itself and did exactly what he set out to do – become a legend.

Brazil 1982

Honours

Qualified for Second Round of 1982 World Cup held in Spain

05.07.1982
Estadio Sarriá, Barcelona

	Brazil	2 v 3	**Italy**
	Peres GK		GK Zoff
	Leandro		Cabrini
	Oscar		Sub (34) Collovati
	Luizinho		Gentile
	Junior		Scirea
	Cerezo		Antognoni
Falcao	G – 68		Oriali
Socrates	G – 12		Sub (75) Tardelli
	Zico		Conti
Serginho	Sub 69		Graziani
	Eder		G – 5, 25, 74 Rossi
	Subs Used		Subs Used
	Paulo Isidoro (69)		Bergomi (34)
			Marini (75)

Details of Second Round Group Game from 1982 World Cup

Brazil's 1970 World Cup triumph created a national stereotype and now at every major tournament, they're expected to deliver. The triumph in Mexico had showed the world style with substance, Brazil not only won they won with a swagger. The first World Cup in colour had seen televisions that had once only offered football in shades of grey get hijacked by a riot of yellow and blue.

Despite 1970 being Brazil's third World Cup win after their performance it was no longer enough to take the trophy, they had to do so in style. While this belief had always existed within the country itself, now the rest of the world watched on too hoping to catch a glimpse of something they would never forget. Brazil became everyone's second team and in the age of colour, they were now football's biggest draw.

In 1974 they failed to live up to their new billing as the entertainers and watched Holland usurp their crown with their 'total' football. In a memorable clash between the two sides, Brazil's aging stars were left wanting by the rising Dutch machine. Instead of the rampaging runs, precision passing and barefaced cheek the world had wanted, Brazil had struggled through the first round after two goalless draws against Yugoslavia and Scotland. A 3-0 win against Zaire had shown the merest hint that there may still be some of 1970's DNA in the squad but in context, the Africans had been beaten 9-0 by Yugoslavia in their previous game. Qualification for the second round bought hope with a laboured win over West Germany and a hard fought 2-1 victory over fiercest rivals Argentina but the game with Holland had exposed the Brazilians who were left in the shadow of Cruyff and his team mates. A 2-0 defeat failed to tell the full story as Holland missed chances and Brazil resorted to cynicism in an attempt to stop them. The 1974 World Cup hadn't diminished Brazil's status in the game, but it had shown that football was changing into a more sophisticated animal and the Seleção needed to evolve.

Four years later and Brazil travelled to Argentina facing the usual expectations but with a squad that was still short of the 1970 vintage. Manager Cláudio Coutinho still looked to an aging and injury hampered Rivelino for inspiration but around him players were either only just beginning to emerge or now past their peak. In a strong group with Austria, Spain and Sweden, Brazil struggled through in wholly unspectacular fashion. After drawing with Sweden and Spain, needing the win Brazil crept past an already qualified Austria 1-0 to make the second round. Now in another qualifying group with Argentina, Poland and Peru, Brazil's form improved but not enough to make the final. After a routine 3-0 victory over Peru, a bad tempered and scrappy game against the hosts ended goal less. Knowing if Argentina bettered their result in the last game they'd be out, Brazil set about beating a robust Poland 3-1 after losing Zico to injury early. It was all to be in vain as Argentina put six past Peru to top the group and Brazil contented themselves with a third place finish after victory in a play-off with Italy. Despite never having lost a game Brazil had fallen short. While they showed their best in patches, they were still to truly sparkle again.

Coming into the tournament in 1982 however, things were a little different. Now managed by Tele Santana the workman like tendencies and the niggling fouls that had crept into the Brazilian game were gone. While it was still only being whispered, there were shades of 1970 about the way the team played. Santana had taken the job in 1980 and been tasked with harnessing the most talented crop of Brazilian players in a decade into something resembling their reputation. As a manager Santana had earned a reputation for his attacking principles and at his disposal he had a wealth of talent. Taking a cue from Mário Zagallo's approach to the embarrassment of riches he faced in 1970, Santana decided that Brazil's best players had to all be on the pitch at the same time. He found a rough 4-2-2-2 formation that allowed his attacking players some license to do what came naturally, and then encouraged them to deal with everything else among themselves.

Brazil's first team began with Valdir Peres in goal. While Brazil had never been famed for producing exceptional goalkeepers, and it's fair to say that Peres was prone to the usual eccentricities that typically came with the role, he proved to be capable if not outstanding. Just ahead of Peres in the centre of the defence Brazil started with Luizinho and Oscar, both experienced and comfortable playing partnering one another. Either side of them and supplying Brazil's only width on paper was full backs Leandro and Júnior. Both were from the long tradition of a full back with attacking ambitions over all else and Júnior in particular loved having a full flank to operate in. While ahead of them Brazil's midfield interchanged and linked, it was both full backs who overlapped and provided the extra men in attack.

The central square of midfielders was testament to the sheer level of talent Santana could call on. With Toninho Cerezo deployed for his work rate just ahead of the defence and doing much of the chasing and harrying, it was then left to Falcão, Zico and Sócrates to create. Falcão took a place in the starting line-up due to injuries and never relinquished it. Based in Europe with AS Roma of Italy, Falcão had a unique insight into a different style of football as every other member of the first team plied his trade in Brazil's domestic league. On paper he joined Cerezo as a defensive midfielder but in reality, as with most of the team it has to be said, he would regularly switch roles and move amongst a fluid midfield. Falcão had a brilliant World Cup campaign and remained in Brazil's first team, eventually making the squad for Mexico '86 four years later although age and injury made him a shadow of the player that graced '82.

Ahead of Cerezo and Falcão (again, on paper if not reality at times) were two of the greatest ever Brazilians to wear the yellow and green. Zico had emerged in Argentina four years earlier but finished the tournament injured and with questions being asked had it been too much too soon. Now comfortable in Brazil's midfield, the player dubbed 'The White Pelé' fitted the stereotype perfectly. A fantastic dribbler, it was Zico who had the ability to move the crowd from their seats with a change of pace, nutmeg or fabulous free kick. Zico also had an exceptional World Cup and like Falcão returned in 1986. Brazil were blessed at his peak with arguably the best player in the world and with a fantastic strike rate for the national side – 52 goals in 72 caps – he seemed to provide them with an extra striker when needed.

Besides Zico in an attacking midfield berth was 'Doctor' Socrates. Socrates style, appearance and ability made him a cult figure in the game, genuinely two-footed and a perfect foil for Zico. Santana made him captain and the responsibility fitted him well, forcing him to lead by example and upping his game in the tournament. Like Zico, Socrates was well aware of his standing in the game and often used it to promote his political beliefs. A staunch drinker and heavy smoker, he gave the impression that the game was passing him by at times. When he did choose to get involved however, he proved that rather than backing away from anything on the pitch he had merely been biding his time, often arriving to make the difference in any move. Lethal from distance, he had every bit as much talent as Zico but his playing style and outspoken nature didn't endear him to everyone within the football world.

With an embarrassment of riches in midfield already, Éder – a wide player by trade – was deployed as a second striker. He proved to be more than capable in the role and used his skills to great effect, fed time and time again by the player's behind him and hitting goal-scoring form early. Next to Éder was Serginho, not considered the finest striker of his generation and unfairly reviewed against the outstanding talent surrounding him. Santana's first choice would have been Careca but injury prevented him from making the finals. Serginho and Éder might have been somewhat of a scratch partnership but both lifted themselves to reflect the company they were in, and in particular Éder would emerge from the tournament with a greatly enhanced reputation.

Qualifying for España '82 was negotiated with ease. Drawn into Group 1 with Bolivia and Venezuela, Brazil won all four games comfortably and showed the moments of creativity that had the football media purring months before they arrived in Spain. As a favorable group stage draw saw them seeded and placed into Group 6 with New Zealand, Scotland, and the USSR, Brazil were rated as one of the favorites immediately.

Opening up against the Soviets, there was a genuine buzz about Brazil entering the tournament. The USSR represented Brazil's toughest game in the group and immediately it proved to be the case. Brazil started brightly, Junior finding Serginho effortlessly with the outside of his right boot only for the striker to volley high and wide. The Soviets worked hard at shutting down their expansive opponents and began to threaten themselves, striker Ramaz Shengelia having his appeals for a penalty denied. On 34 minutes Andriy Bal picked the ball up thirty yards from goal and fired a speculative shot towards Brazil goalkeeper Peres's near post. With much of the shot's sting taken out by a bounce, the 'keeper looked to have it covered easily but contrived to fumble the ball in for a 1-0 lead for the Soviets.

While they had already displayed their ability in flashes, now behind it was time to have a look at Brazil's character. Into the second half and the USSR looked to strike as often as possible, now conscious of the Brazilian's somewhat fragile goalkeeping situation. Brazil kept passing their way through the wall of red in front of them but without carving out a clear cut chance until with a quarter of an hour to go, Socrates decided to take matters into his own hand. Seizing on a failure to clear the ball from a throw in, the ball found it's way to the midfielder's feet who skipped pass one challenge, dummied the shot past another and then unleashed a crashing drive past 'keeper Dassayev for the equalizer. With Brazil now having earned the goal their pressure deserved, they now set about winning the game outright.

After missing several chances the minutes appeared to be against the Brazilians. As the game headed towards the final whistle, it looked like it was going to take something as special to score again. After a series of neat passes with just a minute to go, Falcao's dummy left the ball for an onrushing Éder. Taking the bobbling ball with a flick of his left foot, Éder then checked slightly and volleyed from just outside the area past a stranded Dassayev. They may not have been brilliant for the full ninety minutes but in both goals they had showed that at any one moment, they were just seconds from greatness.

With two brilliant goals behind them their next game against Scotland became the hottest ticket in town. The Scots had a good team with the likes of Graeme Souness, Alan Hansen, Gordon Strachan and Kenny Dalglish but were not expected to be as rigid as the USSR had been. In their first game they'd raced into a 3-0 lead against New Zealand but then showed their frailty in defense by conceding two in the second half. Despite the convincing nature of a 5-2 Scotland win in the end, the Brazilians knew that Scottish ambition would leave them more space to play.

Playing in Seville again, Brazil fell behind to David Narey's snapshot from the edge of the area in the eighteenth minute. Brazil moved through the gears and on the half hour drew level. After drawing a foul 25 yards from goal, Cerezo tossed the ball in Zico's direction for the free kick. Scottish goalkeeper Alan Rough could only watch and admire Zico's perfectly flighted shot sail into the top left hand corner of his goal. With a sense of inevitably beginning to dawn on the Scots, they hung on to the 1-1 until half-time. The second half saw the Brazilians hit top gear and as hard as Scotland fought, they were simply swept aside.

Shortly after half-time Brazil took the lead from an unlikely but very welcome source. A corner was swung towards the near post and then nodded in by defender Oscar for the fourth goal of Brazil's campaign, the first to be scored from inside the penalty area. Just after the hour they moved into a two-goal lead with another wonderful goal, this time Éder chipping Rough from a standing position just inside the area. The goal had been executed beautifully, once again goalkeeper reduced to the role of spectator and with a cushion they continued to push the Scottish defense onto the back foot. With just three minutes left Falcao made it four with a strike from distance and Brazil had the result their performance merited. Two games, two wins, six goals and maximum points, this was looking every inch like a classic Brazil side in the making.

The final game against New Zealand was tackled with consummate ease, Brazil running in four goals, keeping their first clean sheet and playing within themselves throughout. New Zealand were subjected to all manner of flicks and tricks and if Brazil hadn't already been assured of qualification and played to their best, the scoreline could have been even worse for the 'All-Whites'. Zico lit up the first half with two goals, the first a flying volley from Leandro's cross, the second a placed shot after another pass from the full back. In the second half Zico fed Falcao for Brazil's third with just over twenty-five minutes still to play and striker Serginho then added a fourth after tapping in Zico's cross-come-shot.

Brazil had moved into the second round with a perfect record and momentum on their side. Even a tough looking group with Argentina and Italy ahead didn't faze them and after watching the Italians win the first of second round Group C's games, Brazil moved to Barcelona to play their fiercest rivals in world football, Argentina, brimming with confidence. The Argentines had the talents of Ardiles, Maradona and Kempes to call on but never played to their potential in this World Cup. Their game plan involved trying to close the Brazilians down and run stride for stride with them, niggling and fouling to stop any rhythm being built. As early as the eleventh minute they needed to reassess as they already found themselves a goal behind.

Taking a free kick some thirty-five yards from goal, Éder placed so much power, pace and swerve on the ball that Argentine goalkeeper Ubaldo Fillol was completely deceived and could only get fingertips on the strike. Fortunately for the 'keeper Éder's shot crashed against the bar but Fillol had lost the flight of the ball and as he turned to try and claw it away from danger, a lurking Zico tapped it in for the opener. Brazil then began to look imperious,

Falcao grazing the crossbar and Argentina offering little more than some tough tackling. Daniel Passarella's header forced a good save from Peres just before half time but Brazil were well on top and looking to force home their advantage second half.

Maradona had a very good penalty shout waved away but Brazil remained on top, Cerezo going close from distance. Where Argentina were opting for muscle in midfield, they were no match for Brazil's craft. On 66 minutes Brazil edged into the two-goal lead they deserved as Serginho headed in Falcao's cross. On 75 it was three as Junior played a one-two with Zico, completely wrong footing the Argentine defense to run through and score. A late red card for a frustrated Maradona summed up the Argentinean performance who did at least manage a last minute consolation.

With a 3-1 victory over the World Cup holders now behind them, only Italy stood between them and the semi-finals. With both teams having beaten Argentina, goals scored saw Brazil top the group. Anything other than an Italian win would be enough to see them through. The game remains one of the great World Cup matches, both teams playing well and providing the drama football's showpiece tournament thrives on.

Italy started well, taking the game to the Brazilians and getting their reward when Antonio Cabrini's cross found the head of much maligned Italian striker Paolo Rossi. Rossi's header put the Azzurri 1-0 ahead and where some had expected a defensive performance from the Italians, it appeared they had chosen wisely not to invite Brazilian pressure and instead try to turn them round. Brazil rallied and just minutes later Socrates and Zico crafted a superb equalizer, playing a one-two through the Italian defense and then Socrates finishing brilliantly at the near post. A seesaw first half then swung back to the Azzurri when Rossi, energized by his goal, pounced on Cerezo's misplaced pass and ran through for 2-1.

Brazil were shocked but rallied once again, coming out in the second half on the front foot knowing all they needed was a draw to progress. With just over twenty minutes to go they found the leveler they deserved when Falcao's thunderbolt flashed past Zoff in the Italian goal. The strike owed much to Cerezo's overlapping run that took the wary blue shirts ahead out of Falcao's line of sight so he could take the shot on and catch the 'keeper cold.

With Brazil back in control it appeared balance had been restored but with a quarter of an hour to go, Conti's corner found itself at the feet of Italian midfielder Marco Tardelli at the edge of the Brazil area. Tardelli's rather scuffed shot worked its way to Rossi at the edge of the six-yard box who gleefully swept the ball in for his third, and the goal that would prove to be the winner. Italy reverted to type for the remainder of the match and Brazil couldn't fashion the opening they needed. At the final whistle while it would have been wrong to describe the Italian's game as anything approaching ugly, the beauty of the Brazilian game had lost out to something that could be described as a little more efficient.

Italy eventually triumphed over West Germany in the final to take the trophy but the team of the tournament had lost in the Barcelona sunshine in the second round. Four years later in Mexico, Brazil suffered defeat by penalty shoot-out – losing to France at the quarterfinal stage – and the international careers of their biggest players of the generation were over. Zico and Socrates struggled throughout the tournament and looked nothing like the midfielders that rampaged their way through España'82. Both missed penalties – Zico's just after coming on as a substitute during the game, Socrates in the shoot out – and their international careers were destined to end without the World Cup winning moment both deserved.

Brazil's team of 1982 mattered because they thrilled and delighted in equal measure. They were inspirational to watch and represented a world where football was traditionally a thing of beauty just as the 1970 squad had done. In a way that teams before and after have felt almost shackled by the brilliance of the '70 squad, the '82 incarnation reveled in the comparison. With some of the finest players in world football playing together and crafting some wonderful goals, it's no surprise they're regularly voted one of the greatest teams to not lift the World Cup, usually placed with the Mighty Magyars of 1954 and Holland's 'total' football of 1974.

As if any proof were required of the legacy they left in the fans that watched them at that World Cup, a search on YouTube reveals a video entitled 'Brazil 1982 – The 11 Greatest Goals of Brazil 1982's Magic 11'. Uploaded in April of 2009, within eighteen months it received well over one and a half million views.

Tottenham Hotspur 1983

Honours

The first football club to float themselves on the Stock Exchange

'The Directors intend to ensure that the Club remains one of the leading football clubs in the country. They will seek to increase the Group's income by improving the return from existing assets and by establishing new sources of revenue in the leisure field.'

Taken from the 'Future of the Group' section of the prospectus to potential shareholders released in 1983

Football club ownership has produced some memorable characters and stories over the years. Some have adopted differing approaches towards their stewardship of a club, not always successfully. There are as many figures that stand for malpractice as there are for success. Ownership of a football club brings a strange mix of publicity, responsibility, celebration and blame. Every success is an opportunity for confirmation that the people in charge are running things the right way, every failure a chance for supporters to direct blame away from the pitch and back to the boardroom. There is an increasing trend for fans to look further than just the playing staff in their diagnosis of a poor season and the job of chairman in particular has become a thankless task.

Some embrace the power a little differently to others however. When Jesus Gil joined the board of Atlético Madrid in 1981 and then ascended to the presidency in 1987, he was already a controversial figure with a chequered past. Unashamed of his support of General

Franco, in part due to the pardon he was personally granted by the dictator from a five-year prison sentence, his style of leadership was to court publicity and show patience only with immediate success. He remained a volatile figure at the club until 2003 when he resigned due to failing health. His relationship with the fans had veered from popular due to his passion for the role, to dismay as they saw Gil hire and fire sixteen managers and head coaches in his time at the Vicente Calderón. Extraverted to the end, Gil celebrated the club winning a league and cup double in 1996 by parading through the city's streets on his favourite horse. Rather than play the role of owner as a withdrawn catalyst for pushing the club to lasting success, Gil believed he was omnipotent in the running of the club, famously saying that 'I pay the bills and so the coach has to agree with my ideas about the team'. Frequently banned for the forthright views he was so eager to give the waiting press, his list of offences included calling a French referee a homosexual, accusing the Spanish FA of being a 'mafia', claiming his players were less intelligent than his horses and punching another club's director.

Others have embraced the role differently, remembering their desire to own the club originated in a love for the team itself rather then any economic reasons. Jack Walker earned his fortune through steel and once he'd sold the company, he ploughed the money into his boyhood club Blackburn Rovers. After financing several 'star name' players deals at the club before becoming chairman in 1991, he now held the top chair and revitalised Ewood Park and its playing staff, culminating in a Premier League trophy in 1995. While ultimately he failed to bring long-lasting success to the Lancashire club, upon his death after a long battle with cancer in August 2000 it was announced that 'Uncle Jack' had he kept a trust in place to secure Rovers financially for the foreseeable future. Loved by all involved with the club, Walker will forever be remembered as a hero for Blackburn Rovers' fans – not quite the view the majority of Atlético fans hold of Gil.

Even celebrities haven't been able to resist the lure of becoming the figurehead for their chosen team. Elton John famously wept as he took his seat at Wembley to watch his beloved Watford play in the 1984 FA Cup final, eight years after becoming the club's chairman in 1976. He remains involved with the club financially and as 'President' to this day. Famous English chef Delia Smith holds the majority share holding in Norwich City Football Club, Prime Minister of Italy and no stranger to Jesus Gil levels of controversy Silvio Berlusconi owns one of the biggest clubs in the world in AC Milan, and American comedian and actor Drew Carey invested in MLS side Seattle Sounders in 2007.

So history tells us that owners usually fall into two categories – those who see the role as a way to generate money for themselves and to exercise their power and massage their ego, and those who saw the job of owner as one that existed solely to service the interest of the club itself. In 1983 Tottenham Hotspur created a new category, a chairman who existed to serve the needs of the club and its shareholders, as they became the first club to float themselves on the stock exchange.

On the pitch Spurs's recent history had been reasonably successful. Established and steady in England's top division, they had won the 1981 and 1982 FA Cups. The club also enjoyed a successful heritage, 1961 the standout moment when a domestic double of FA Cup and league title had been won. They could also boast the first ever English UEFA Cup win in 1972 and a European Cup Winners Cup title in 1963. While they were struggling to break into the very top tier of English football, due to their large crowds and honours they were considered one of its 'big five' with Liverpool, Manchester United, Everton and Arsenal.

Tottenham's on the field achievements were without question but off the pitch, the situation was a little more confused. Despite outward appearances a brief relegation in the late seventies and vital ground improvements were stifling the club's financial ambitions. Initially interested in possible construction projects at the club's home ground White Hart Lane, entrepreneur and Spurs fan Irving Scholar became aware of the struggling balance sheet and began to look into acquiring a controlling stake. Taken with the idea of involvement in the club he'd supported since he was a boy, Scholar set about buying up various owners' interest in the club for substantial amounts of money. Property developer Paul Bobroff had also been purchasing stakes in the club and after approaching Scholar with a view to selling his share, once the long-term goal of floatation was mooted the pair looked towards a bigger picture. After taking control of the club jointly in 1982 Scholar was to become chairman of Tottenham Hotspur Football Club and Bobroff was to become chairman of the new publicly listed holding company, Tottenham Hotspur plc.

Now in Scholar and Bobroff's control the plan to float the club to generate much-needed funds for the ground and new playing staff moved swiftly. By the end of September 1983, the prospectus for potential shareholders to invest in 'Tottenham Hotspur plc' was published to great interest from the football and financial world. While 'fan-owned' clubs existed in one form or another such as Real Madrid and Barcelona in Spain, this was going to be the first club to fully float on the stock exchange. The plc was identified with Paul Bobroff as chairman, Sheppards and Chase taking the role of stockbrokers and Peat, Marwick, Mitchell & Co as auditors and reporting accountants.

The document cited potential gate receipts from European competition and cup runs in addition to the guaranteed 21 home league games as the current main source of income for the company. The ground redevelopments had increased the potential for revenue from executive boxes and corporate business, and major initiatives were taking place to sell sponsorship in all possible areas. The forecast profits were a bold £850,000 before transfer fess and taxation and reasonable dividends were forecast for all investors. The point of real interest for observers within the football world was Spurs plans for growth – how would they cede to the demands of shareholders not necessarily interested in the fortunes of the club, but in the profit to be made from it.

The key to that demand was turning a football club into a 'leisure group', basically the expansion of the 'brand' Tottenham Hotspur. The plan was that Spurs would be used to launch as many different revenue streams as possible by taking a 'more commercial approach to the Club's affairs'. Scholar and Bobroff believed that by licensing Spurs related product and expanding the existing brand on offer within the club; the revenue would appease both fans desperate for investment on the pitch and shareholders keen to see a return on their stake.

The move was not without its detractors, one of the most notable being club manager Keith Burkinshaw. Burkinshaw was a popular figure at the club and had led Spurs's back into the top division and then to the two recent FA Cup victories. He stayed for the conclusion of the 83/84 season and won the club another UEFA Cup after a victory on penalties against Belgium club Anderlecht. He left amid acrimony with the new regime and was quoted on leaving White Hart Lane that 'there used to be a football club there'. It seemed the move from purely footballing ambitions to an ongoing business concern did not sit comfortably with all.

Ironically Burkinshaw had contributed hugely to the plan's initial success. The share options were sold quickly and in their first year of trading they posted a pre-tax profit of £902,000, a massive increase on the previous years £168,000. The clubs successful UEFA Cup run (including the two-legged final with its second game at a capacity White Hart Lane), the increase in executive hospitality revenue and growing merchandising profits all contributed to the successful return. Suddenly it seemed that Tottenham Hotspur had found the key to increasing the rewards in the ownership and running of a football club, out of nowhere it looked like investing in football might be a quick way to make large profit. Scholar and Bobroff were pleased with the effort, the floatation appeared to be sound and they seemed to have been right to pursue it. As is so often the case with such short-term success, in reality long-term failure was just around the corner and both men had been blinded to the prospect by the current booming balance sheet

Despite the grandiose plans and heady claims made in the prospectus, the business success was dependant on each element turning a profit. Bobroff began to diversify Tottenham's interests as intended but a series of failures meant the promised growth and profit never materialised. Tottenham Hotspur plc became associated with everything from women's clothing lines to boxing promotion. The relationship between the business and the football widened to a point where one couldn't support the other. By the end of the decade the property market had crashed and Scholar's personal fortunes were suffering as much as Spurs. To add to his worries his position had come under intense scrutiny from the clubs fans and shareholders as success and dividends were drying up. Both club and plc were amassing huge debts as they failed to support each other and the clubs financial situation was becoming desperate. Scholar initially courted Robert Maxwell as the man to buy his stake and take over the club but another solution was to present itself. The club and its shareholders would enter a new era with Sir Alan Sugar at the helm.

Sugar, chairman of Amstrad and a Spurs fan, purchased the controlling stake in both the club and the plc in a joint venture with Terry Venables in 1991. Venables was to handle team and club matters, Sugar was look after the plc and deal with the debts and perilous financial precipice Spurs sat at the edge of. The two's relationship would dissolve in a messy legal battle after Venables dismissal as first team manager and his claims to his exact stake in the club. Sugar did bring Spurs back into a financially responsible position over time before selling his stake to leisure group ENIC in 2002. The floatation had peaked early and then taken years to bring out of a deep trough but nineteen years later, Spurs were once again stable and making a small profit.

Other clubs took what Scholar and Bobroff started and achieved greater and lesser degrees of success. The birth of the Premier League and the slew of money that washed into the game on the back of television revenues and greater European rewards caused a rash of floatation's in the nineties. In nearly every case the clubs that have floated themselves successfully have been those that realise while they're now running as a business interest rather than a solely sporting endeavour, it is still success on the pitch that will determine the economic performance of the plc. Manchester United's floatation in 1991 came as no surprise as the club looked to expand its brand. Before they began to diversify too far as Spurs had tried, they ensured through providing money for Alex Ferguson to constantly improve his title winning squads that the gate receipts, executive revenue, interest and merchandising would swell naturally as the club's trophy cabinet grew in size.

As football evolves clubs are now seeing a return to private ownership as sporting conglomerates and enormously wealthy individuals seek to add a football club to their portfolios. For all Manchester United's success as a plc, Malcolm Glazer's takeover in 2005 took the club away from the thousands of shareholders and distanced some that felt the debt loaded onto the club by Glazer was unacceptable. Their neighbours Manchester City ran as a plc until 2007 when it moved into private hands again, culminating in the Abu Dhabi United Group Investment and Development Limited's takeover in September 2008. London club Chelsea also watched their expectations change overnight in the wake of an overnight takeover by Russian billionaire Roman Abramovich in 2003.

Whether the trend continues or not will depend on the clubs financial performances compared to the realistic expectations of its owners. It remains a source of concern for some who see the gap widening between clubs whose owners can keep pouring money into a club for as long as it retains their interest, and those who run a fiscally responsible operation and never gamble future income against immediate success. Current UEFA President Michel Platini has been particularly vocal in voicing the need to strike a balance for all.

The nature of football club ownership has changed greatly as teams have generated legitimate sources of revenue. It is a matter of personal opinion the effect the supporters feel this has had on the game and the teams they love. Spurs mattered because they were the first team to really acknowledge the financial potential that could be harnessed from the option to float on the stock exchange. They made the first move to take a football club and turn it away from the just the sporting aspect and realise the importance of its brand. Although they never achieved the success that others who took the same route have acquired, for better or worse they did provide the blueprint and the impetus that others would use to make the same move.

Argentina 1986

Honours

World Cup Winners at Mexico'86

'...a little with the head of Maradona and a little with the hand of God...'

Maradona speaking about his controversial opener in the quarterfinal

Football, in its very essence, is a team game – eleven men working together to achieve one result. Having said that, occasionally there are exceptions to the rule. Every now and then, a player puts in a performance where he seems to be playing on his own, tying up a whole defence almost single-handedly. Most of these games are one-offs, some are just a reflection of their team mates' poor form. In the case of Argentina's Diego Maradona at the Mexican World Cup in 1986, however, it was simply because he was better than anyone else at the tournament.

Born in 1960 in Buenos Aires, the young Maradona takes to football immediately. At age ten he entertains the half-time crowd at the Argentinos Juniors Stadium with his already unbelievable ball-juggling skills. Five years later he makes his debut for their first team ten days before his sixteenth birthday. As talented as he clearly is, he doesn't look like the average footballer with his squat 5ft 5in frame. It becomes clear though that Maradona is deceptively strong, quick and, importantly, can run with the ball just as fast as without. Over the next four years, Maradona's reputation grows and in 1978 he becomes the Metropolitano Championship's youngest ever top-scorer. He repeats this feat in 1979 and 1980, the latter also being the year when Maradona drives Argentinos Juniors into a second place finish just behind River Plate, their best ever league position to date.

By the time that Boca Juniors purchase Maradona for £1m in 1980, he has already had his first brush with controversy. The £1m fee was a world record at the time for a teenager but he's already an established international footballer. Maradona made his debut for the La Albiceleste in 1977 just four months into his professional football career. Playing in a friendly against Hungary as a 16-year-old, the crowd immediately recognises the potential he represents. Coach César Luis Menotti faces a choice for the 1978 World Cup – Maradona or Mario Kempes, potential or experience? When he opts for Kempes and cuts Maradona from his 25-man squad when announcing his final 22, there's huge national debate. Maradona himself falls out with Menotti at his exclusion and becomes a polarising figure for the Argentine football public.

As Argentina win the World Cup and Kempes himself takes the Golden Boot, Menotti's choice has been vindicated. Maradona, smarting from missing the chance to play for his beloved Argentina in a World Cup on home soil, takes his frustrations out on the pitch. The following year he travels to Japan for the 1979 FIFA World Youth Championship and is exceptional. Voted unanimously as Player of the Tournament, Maradona scores in all but one of Argentina's six games. The young Argentines leave with the trophy and an outstanding record – played six, won six, scored twenty, and conceded two. Captain Maradona has been the star, pulling the strings when dropping deep and deadly up front. He saves his best performance for the final against the Soviet Union, a 3-1 win where he bags the third goal with a wonderful free kick.

When Boca Juniors sign Maradona it seems to be a marriage made in heaven. Maradona loves Boca and Boca loves him, the local boy who was a childhood fan now being compared to Pelé in terms of his potential. He leads them to a title and is consistently brilliant. The biggest clubs in Europe are now circling, eager to pick him up before the World Cup in Spain where it's felt Maradona is destined to be the star of the tournament. Internationally Diego is now established in the full side and all acrimony with Menotti has been forgotten as, in attacking terms, the game plan very much revolves around him. After scoring his first goal against Scotland in 1979 and then his World Youth Championship heroics, he has become the main source of the national team's inspiration.

Spain '82 doesn't go to plan for Argentina or Maradona. Playing every minute for their first group games, he can't prevent the holders losing to Belgium in their opener. Picking their form up, Argentina thrash Hungary

4-1 in the second game, Maradona plays well and scores twice. A final win over El Salvador secures qualification into a second group stage where Argentina face Italy and Brazil. Despite his best efforts in the face of some overly physical attention, Italy beat them 2-1 and then old rivals Brazil offer a final ignominy. 3-0 down and with Argentina facing elimination from the tournament, the 85th minute sees Maradona lunge at Brazilian substitute Joao Batista clumsily. Despite protests from his team mates, Maradona receives a red card and leaves the tournament in controversy. The holders are out and Maradona has never really sparkled consistently like many were predicting.

Despite the World Cup's trials and tribulations Maradona's mind is immediately elsewhere – he has a new challenge ahead. Boca Juniors have reluctantly agreed to sell their star player while his price is at a premium and that premium is a world record £3,000,000. Spanish giants Barcelona, now managed by Menotti, win the race for the little man's signature. Club president Jose Luis Nunez has been instrumental in bringing the best prospect in the world to his club.

Maradona struggles at first but finds his feet in a strong Barca side. In 1983 however he suffers a huge blow when the 'Butcher of Bilbao' – Athletics' defender Andoni Goikoetxea Olaskoaga – shatters his left ankle in a horror challenge. Out for four months, on his return he continues to suffer from rough treatment and injury throughout the rest of his time at Barcelona. By 1984 a move away suits both club and Maradona; his form has been patchy and he's unhappy in the city and with the club's directors. Juventus are interested but their president rejects the idea of buying Maradona on the grounds he's too short to cope with the physical Italian league.

Napoli have no such fears. Barcelona are happy to sell to a club who they don't class as European trophy rivals. Maradona holds talks with the club and is immediately keen on the move and agrees to sign. Another world record fee is brokered, Napoli pay £5,000,000 for el Diego's services and sell thousands of season tickets on the back of the transfer. Happier domestically and adored by his Italian public, Maradona starts a revolution and Napoli rise to third in Serie A.

1986 brings a happier Maradona another chance to play at a World Cup. Expectation is at record levels and coach Carlos Bilardo has made Maradona captain and fulcrum of the national side. Qualification has seen Argentina top their group and average two goals a game; they are placed amongst the favourites for the tournament from the outset. Like Brazil in 1970, Argentina are naturally acclimatised and ready for the tournament. Originally given to Columbia, the finals were awarded to Mexico after fears about security and resources came to light in 1982. Once again some games will be played at midday and the heat is ferocious. Argentina are drawn into Group A with the holders Italy, Bulgaria and South Korea. With two teams guaranteed to qualify from each group, a third if they are one of the best third-placed finishers, Argentina are expected to progress relatively easily.

The Argentinean plan for Mexico '86 is all about Diego Maradona. Coach Bilardo has got him relishing in both the responsibility of being captain and his role in the system. Argentina are playing with a loose 3-5-2 that allows Maradona the freedom to play how he likes to play. The freer role lets him come deep and control the game or burst forward to score when the opportunity arises. Their first game approaches and Argentina face South Korea. Italy and Bulgaria have already played out a 1-1 draw so the chance is there for Argentina to take the early initiative.

Maradona is immediately singled out for rough treatment but he has grown stronger than he was in 1982. Argentina now play in a new fashion and predominantly through Maradona – old captain and former talisman Daniel Passarella is not involved due to illness, leaving no spectre of '78 over the team. Six minutes in, Maradona is fouled by midfielder Huh Jung-Moo; he collapses clutching his left knee but recovers to take the free kick. As his effort fails to beat the wall, he cleverly heads it forward towards Real Madrid striker Jorge Valdano. Valdano cushions the ball and strikes the opener; Maradona is already having a decisive influence.

Twenty minutes in and Argentina are well on top. Jorge Burruchaga has hit the post from distance and Argentina have another free kick with Maradona over the ball. His cross is headed in by defender Oscar Ruggeri and Argentina have a two-goal cushion. It stays that way until the 46th minute when Maradona explodes onto a loose header out wide on the right. Taking on two men he barrels past them and crosses to the far post. Missed by defender and goalkeeper alike, Valdano lurks and taps in his second. Argentina eventually run out 3-1 winners, Maradona has had a hand in all three and it's clear he's trying to stamp his authority on the tournament already.

Argentina now face the holders and Maradona's new adopted country Italy. The Italians are well organised and passionately supported, Maradona is man marked and picked up every time he finds a little space. Behind to a sixth-minute penalty, he begins to move more expansively to find room, desperate not to lose to a side that beat them in '82. With his influence on the game growing by the minute, in the 34th minute he slips his marker and breaks into the box. Valdano has flighted a ball his way and having to take it high with both feet off the ground, Maradona conjures a finish that leaves Italian keeper Giovanni Galli rooted to the spot. With the scores now level, Argentina continue to knock on the door, Italy remain dangerous and tempers flare.

A series of bad challenges from both sides mar the rest of the game. Italy hit the post in the second half but neither side scores again. With a 1-1 draw, Argentina have three points, Maradona one goal and three assists.

All but assured of qualification, barring a goal difference catastrophe in their last game, Argentina face Bulgaria relatively pressure free. Valdano heads them into an early lead and Maradona lights up the first half with a breathtaking run past the entire Bulgarian defence. His shot flashes just wide but it's a sign of things to come. With ten minutes to go, Maradona breaks down the left wing, collects the ball and crosses for Burruchaga to nod in a second. Argentina have walked through their group and qualify top; Maradona is now beginning to hit peak form.

Now in the knockout phase, Argentina are drawn to face Uruguay. Despite never really getting into top gear, Argentina win 1-0. Once again Maradona is effervescent, hitting the crossbar with a brilliant free kick from some thirty yards and then having a goal correctly ruled out in the second half. Argentina's strike comes just before half-time, Maradona involved early on in the move that ends with striker Pedro Pasculli sweeping the ball home. Now through to the quarterfinals, Argentina face England in the game that will make Maradona as infamous as he is famous in football history. With the Falklands conflict between the two countries still fresh in the memory, the game seemed to get the world's attention focused on the Estadio Azteca on the 22 June.

England have made a slow start in the competition but just brushed aside Paraguay in their second round game. Form says Argentina should win but England are well organised and particularly dangerous upfront. Terry Fenwick and Steve Hodge of England both give away fouls by hacking a dribbling Maradona down early. A free kick whistles by Shilton's post but the first half passes, despite the intense heat, without really catching fire. Maradona is just about to change that going into the second half.

Fifty-one minutes on the clock and Valdano and Hodge clash on the edge of England's penalty area. Hodge hooks the ball skywards towards his keeper, hoping Shilton will claim the ball safely. Maradona spots his opportunity and ghosts in under the ball. One of the smallest players in the tournament jumps with Shilton and clearly punches the ball in with his left hand. The England players immediately raise their arm for the handball. Surely the ref saw Maradona punch the ball – could the Argentinean number ten get a booking for the deliberate infringement? Unbelievably as Maradona wheels away celebrating, the referee gives the goal and is running to the halfway line for the restart. Maradona has just cheated on the biggest stage and what's more, he has got away with it.

England are rattled by the injustice, Maradona is now bubbling. Just three minutes later he picks the ball up in his own half and spins, leaving Peter Reid and Peter Beardsley for dead. That deceptive pace kicks in as he bursts past the attentions of Fenwick again and Terry Butcher who misses his tackle. Maradona's balance, as he dummies and feints, is outstanding as he finds himself bearing down on Shilton again. Despite Shilton's best efforts and Terry Butcher's last-ditch tackle, Diego rounds the keeper and passes into the empty net for one of the outstanding goals in World Cup history.

And there we have the enigma of Maradona summed up in just three minutes. Flagrant cheating to give Argentina the lead, sheer brilliance to extend it. England fight back and score through Gary Lineker but it's not enough. An agonising last minute cross by John Barnes misses Lineker's head by millimetres and the final whistle sounds to the disbelief of the English crowd. A villain to some, a hero to more, Maradona and the hand of God are now everywhere.

The semi-final against Belgium gives Maradona another man of the match award. He forces panic in the Belgium area in the first half and hits the crossbar. Valdano follows in and finishes, but this time the officials see his handball and disallow the goal. Belgium start the second half on the attack but six minutes in, Maradona bursts into the area and collects Burruchaga's clever though ball. Taking it first time, he lifts it over Jean-Marie Pfaff in Belgium's goal and Argentina have the lead. Twelve minutes later, the tie is all but over as Maradona scores another brilliant goal.

Collecting the ball from Jose Cuciuffo's break from the back, Maradona finds himself central with four Belgium players between him and the goal. Isolating one man in the pack, Stéphane Demol, he forces him to attempt a tackle. Maradona easily skips past and drives centrally through two more Belgium defenders. Jinking to his left Maradona leaves himself with just Eric Gerets to beat. Pushing the ball away from the defender he simply strikes the ball across Pfaff and claims his second of the match. Belgium continue to struggle with Maradona who comes within inches of scoring an almost identical third. His break and clever pull back gave Valdano an open goal to aim at but the striker fluffs his lines. At the final whistle the Stadio Azteca rises to Maradona who's been as close to unplayable as it's possible to be.

So to the final. How can opponents West Germany cope with Maradona at his best? Franz Beckenbauer sets Lothar Matthäus the task of chasing Maradona for the day. The German proves to be up to the job, Maradona struggling to shake the midfielder and once again coming in for heavy tackles early on. Despite their captain's shackling, the rest of the Argentina side rally and build a two-goal lead. Maradona is felled by Matthäus wide on the right in the twenty-third minute. The free kick is swung in and powered home via the head of defender Jose Brown for 1-0. Into the second half and Maradona plays the link man in a move which ultimately sees the ball at the feet of Valdano, thirty yards from goal and without a defender in sight. As the Germans scramble back, the tall striker remains calm and slips in Argentina's second. Maradona looks like becoming a World Cup winning captain.

Argentina briefly collapse under the weight of expectation. Defensive lapses see first Karl-Heinz Rummenigge and then Rudi Völler profit to draw the Germans level with ten minutes to go. Frustrated by the unprofessional way in which they'd conceded, Maradona rallies his troops once more. With eighty-three minutes on the clock, he wriggles free of Mattäus's attention and plays the perfect through ball to Burruchaga. With no sign of nerves, Burruchaga races clear and scores the goal that gives the Argentines the trophy Maradona's performances have merited.

It can be argued that after 29th June 1986, Maradona went on to enjoy the best years of his footballing life. After lifting the World Cup and being carried from the field by team-mates and fans alike, Maradona was truly at the peak of his game. He would return to Napoli and perform miracles with them over the next four years, bringing the club their first ever league titles, domestic cup success and a UEFA Cup. His Italian public took him as a messiah-like figure and Maradona repaid them on the pitch. In what was arguably the toughest league in the world at the time, he was the standout player, time and time again proving the form of Mexico '86 was no flash in the pan. Maradona became the best player in the world outright and then kept the title over his time at Napoli.

Italia '90 marked a watershed in the life of Diego Maradona. Struggling with injury, weight and expectation, Maradona and Argentina flattered to deceive despite making the final. A West Germany side on a revenge mission robbed them of the chance of retaining their crown. Along the way Maradona had alienated himself from his adoring public in Napoli by claiming that the locals should support Argentina rather their opponents in the semi-final – Italy. When they booed through the national anthem to show Maradona how they felt about his statement, Diego could be seen mouthing 'sons of bitches' repeatedly.

For someone who had climbed so high, the downfall was always going to be spectacular. In spring '91 Maradona was banned from the game after failing a drug test. His 15-month ban from Italian football was extended to world football and the story was huge. The most talented player in the world was now banned from playing at any level. Arrests for cocaine possession followed, along with unsuccessful comebacks in Spain with Seville and then his native Argentina with Newells Old Boys. Against all odds he made the squad for the

'94 World Cup in America and scored in a rout against Greece. Regrettably after the game he was subjected to another drug test and failed. Expelled from the game once more for another 15 months, Maradona's life descended into farce.

Officially retiring in 1997 aged 37, it was now the world watched its once greatest player battle drugs, journalists (often literally) and all sorts of demons that turned his life into a circus. Stomach stapling operations, a stint as a talk-show host, infidelity allegations, Italian tax-evasion, drug addiction and regular mud-slinging with football officials and greats in the game all served to taint El Diego's legacy.

However in 2008, Maradona took the reigns of the Argentinean national side in preparation for the 2010 World Cup. Swept into the job on a tidal wave of public opinion, Maradona struggled to get a supremely talented side to click. Once again he managed to receive a ban but this time there were no drugs involved, just his conduct – a tirade against journalists deemed overly offensive by FIFA. After securing qualification there were glimpses in South Africa of what Argentina could be under Maradona, a 4-1 destruction of South Korea and a terrific second round performance against Mexico being the most notable. It was not to be though; old nemesis Germany routing Argentina 4-0 in the quarterfinals in a display that highlighted a tactical naivety on Maradona's behalf. He parted company with the role in the wake of Argentina's failure and another very public chapter of the man's life came to an end.

It is impossible to say Argentina were a one-man side at Mexico '86. Maradona was a surrounded by the very talented likes of Valdano, Burruchaga, Ruggeri, Pumpido and Guisti to name but a few. However, what should be said is that never has one man mattered so much to a side over the course of a full tournament. Maradona was peerless in Mexico, even if his moral code was questionable. While England fans all remember the 'hand of God', too few remember the moment of genius that followed. The controversy should not outweigh the talent but unfortunately, headlines regarding Maradona seem to have less and less to do with football once more. Maradona will always polarise opinion but what is without doubt is that for thirty days in Mexico, he took on the world and won.

A.C. Milan 1987–96

Honours

Winners of Serie A 1987/88, 91/92, 92/93, 93/94, & 95/96

Winners of European Cup 1989, 1990, & 1994

Winners of UEFA Super Cup 1989, 1990, & 1994

Winners of Intercontinental Cup 1989 & 1990

Winners of Italian Super Cup 1988, 1992, 1993, & 1994

Player	Apps for Milan
Franco Baresi	719
Alessandro Costacurta	662
Paolo Maldini	902
Mauro Tassotti	583

Appearances for Milan of each of the 'Inseparable' back four

Italian football and in particular the Milanese teams are familiar with occupying a position at the head of European football. Helenio Herrera's 'Grande' Inter and Nereo Rocco's Milan had taken the European Cup four times between them in the 60s, and both had played a huge part in the fearsome and unloved reputation 'catenaccio' had developed. However the 70s had belonged to a new breed starting with the Brazilian World Cup winning side. What the Seleção had shown was a lethal way of playing attacking football carried on by Ajax and Holland's 'total' philosophies that had achieved both great success and huge popularity. At face value, Italian football needed to evolve – it's one thing to be successful if unpopular, it's another to be unloved and left behind.

The early 80s saw a sway towards the English clubs but a World Cup win for Italy at España '82 saw them begin to reassert themselves. The national side didn't employ quite the 'pure' form of 1960's catenaccio but defensive football was still very much the bedrock of their success. The Italian win, and in particular a monumental triumph over a quite brilliant and expansive Brazilian side in the second round, was seen as a triumph for defence over attack. The Italians had forced their way through the early stages, stumbling all the way, but the Brazil game had lit the touch paper and given them belief.

Having not occupied a final berth in the European Cup for ten years, 1983 saw Juventus represent their country but lose to Hamburg. A year later it was AS Roma's turn to finish with losers' medals after failing to win a penalty shoot out against Liverpool. Finally in 1985 the cup was once again on Italian soil but Juventus's 1-0 win over Liverpool was completely overshadowed by the crowd violence and subsequent death of 39 people at Heysel Stadium. Italian football was going through a difficult metamorphosis and needed a club to lead the way with a manager who could couple a more incisive form of attack without compromising the defensive principles they so valued.

In March 1986 Silvio Berlusconi became Associazione Calcio Milan's new president. Milan had fallen from their 60s grace quite spectacularly; starting the 80s in Serie B and watching manager after manager come to the club and fail. Berlusconi set about bringing players to the club to chase former glories but by the end of 86-87 season, it was clear that current manger and club legend Nils Liedholm was not the man to lead the revolution. Berlusconi approached an up and coming manager by the name of Arrigo Sacchi to take over at Milan, a man who had revitalised Parma and impressed the president immensely by beating Milan twice in the Coppa Italia. Sacchi accepted, despite criticism about his lack of playing credentials, and between him, Fabio Capello and Berlusconi, he would bring about the greatest era in Milan's history.

Sacchi would be at Milan for four seasons until departing to manage the national side in 1991. In his first year he took the team to their first Scudetto since 1979. It was the season that Alessandro 'Billy' Costacurta would make his debut before becoming part of the 'inseparable' defence. Costacurta would continue to play for Milan until his retirement in 2007, amassing 662 games for the Rossoneri and 59 caps for the Italian national side. Also part of the four was Mauro Tassotti – 'the professor' – vice captain and most played at right back. Tassotti was often the starting point for all attacks down his flank and was a considered a quiet man, playing until his retirement in 1997 at the age of 37. Tassotti stayed with Milan post-retirement, eventually becoming Carlo Ancelotti's assistant manager and remains a popular figure in the club today.

Usually on the left of the four was the great Paolo Maldini. Having made his debut as a 16-year-old Maldini remained at Milan for the entirety of his career. As well as playing over 900 times for his club, Maldini also became Italy's most capped player of all time with 126 appearances for the Azzurri over 16 years (now surpassed by Fabio Cannavaro) with 74 of them coming as captain. A cultured player blessed with an imposing natural physicality, the Maldini name had been associated with Milan through his father Cesare. Maldini Senior was also a defender, playing centrally with most success and captain of Milan in the 60s. After a successful and European Cup winning career, Cesare moved into coaching with the club and eventually managed Milan. After short stays at various Italian clubs as coach he moved into the national set up, becoming the Italian U21 manager and handing his son several caps at that level. Maldini Junior's career with both Milan and Italy surpassed his father's and upon his retirement from Milan, retired his number 3 shirt, only to be used again if one of his sons makes it into Milan's first team squad. On retiring in 2009 he'd won 7 Scudettos, 5 European Cups, 5 Supercoppe Italiane, 1 Coppa Italia, 2 Intercontinental Cups, 1 FIFA Club World Cup, 5 UEFA European Super Cups and countless other individual awards and honours.

With Costacurta, Tassotti, and Maldini in place, it's hard to believe that the remaining member of the back four could surpass all of them in terms of the fans affections. In his last game at the San Siro for Milan, an ungrateful faction of the home support greeted Maldini with a banner that simply read 'There is only one captain' with a huge (and again retired) shirt number 6 emblazoned on it. As harsh as that was after a career giving fantastic service to one club, in the hearts of many of the Milan faithful no one can ever surpass Sacchi's captain, Franco Baresi.

Baresi was also a one-club man who not only became a true footballing great, he defined the position of 'libero' in the modern Italian game. Beginning as a true sweeper, his role changed as things moved towards a flatter back four. Baresi glided across the turf, just as adept at carrying the ball forward as playing on the back foot and defending. He is often cited as one of the finest defenders the game has ever seen by professionals and pundits alike, but his career could have taken a different turn if Internazionale had not rejected him at an early age. Determined to make his way in the game, Baresi trialed at Milan and was offered a contract. After making his way into the first team in 1977 he would spend 20 years there, through the darker times of Milan's struggle in the late 70s and early 80s, surviving Berlusconi's ascent and mini cull of the playing staff, and then becoming the talisman for the club on the pitch and the supporters in the stands. Internationally he won 81 caps for Italy, taking a World Cup winner's medal as part of the 1982 squad although he didn't feature on the pitch, and then missing a penalty in the shoot out 12 years later at the 1994 World Cup final against Brazil. Baresi was recovering from an injury but was outstanding in final, completely eliminating the threat of Golden Ball winner Romário and his tears in defeat became one of the iconic images of USA '94.

That four-man defence is often cited as football's greatest ever. Baresi mentored Maldini and led the unit to move together and play zonally, a system that requires an intense level of understanding between team mates. The unity came from hours spent on the training pitch and as the team became successful, that success bred desire for more. Sacchi demanded his defence press and harry, mindful of their position in relation to each other and keeping a high line to spring the offside trap at any given opportunity. With this foundation to build on, it only remained to make sure Milan were as potent in attack as they were resolute in defence.

For Sacchi's first season in charge, new recruits arrived from Holland in the form of Marco Van Basten and Ruud Gullit. Van Basten came on the back of a quite exceptional scoring record in the Dutch league with Ajax, and despite his career being cut tragically short by persistent knee problems, he remains one of the finest strikers European football has ever produced. Capable of scoring all sorts of goals, Van Basten was also happy chasing down defenders as Sacchi demanded every player on his team press when not in possession of the ball. When forced into retirement at the age of 30 by a persistent ankle injury in 1995, the striker could look back on a career that had seen him become FIFA World Footballer of the Year in 1992 and European Footballer of the Year in 1988, 1989, and 1992. He had also become a European Championship winner with the Dutch national side of 1988, setting the tournament alight and emerging as by far the most talented player on view. Van Basten was truly exceptional and his 124 goals in 201 appearances for Milan have ensured he remains second only to Franco Baresi and the legendary Gianni Rivera in Milan fans affections.

Similarly Gullit had performed exceptionally in Holland with several clubs before his move to Italy. He had started his career as a classic sweeper but been converted to attack and remained versatile throughout his career, spending much of his time at Milan playing just behind Van Basten as an attacking midfielder-cum-striker. They would line up as a classic 4-4-2 but Gullit spent as much of his time in midfield and 'in the hole' as he did as an out and out forward. He arrived at Milan with a world record price tag and a huge reputation as current FIFA Ballon D'Or holder and proved a success until falling out with the management regime in 1993. Gullit was an imposing player, tall and strong in the air, deceptively quick and like so many of his Dutch counterparts, blessed with the vision to pick the right pass. Van Basten's injuries limited his involvement in his first season with the club but Gullit was a huge influence in both attitude and form from the off.

Sacchi led Milan to the Scudetto playing to both their strengths in defence and attack. They finished three points clear of a Diego Maradona-inspired

Napoli and while their rivals had proved to be more free scoring, Maradona and Brazilian striker Careca scoring 28 goals between them, Milan had only conceded 14 goals in 30 games. The standout result had been a 3-2 victory in Naples with just three games of the season left, 2 goals from striker Pietro Paolo Virdis and a third from Marco Van Basten proving enough to take a vital and decisive lead in the title race. Berlusconi and Sacchi had delivered on their first promises to return Milan to the top of the domestic game, now Europe was in their sights.

During the summer a third Dutchman came to the club to play in Milan's midfield alongside Carlo Ancelotti, Roberto Donadoni and Angelo Colombo. Frank Rijkaard was strong and combative, coming to the club via a farcical transfer to Sporting CP in Portugal too late to be eligible for competition for the club after falling out with then Ajax manager John Cruyff. He had been loaned from Portugal to Spain immediately and played for Real Zaragoza before being taken by Milan in 1988, Sacchi converting him from a central defender into a midfielder. Where as some making the same move would always retain their defensive principles above all else, Rijkaard became a huge influence in Milan's attack, vital for winning possession and driving the team forward. He played for Milan for five years, making 201 appearances in total and moved into management after retirement, taking Barcelona to a Champions League triumph in 2006.

Many saw Rijkaard as the final piece of Sacchi's puzzle and the following year, a 'complete' Milan won the European Cup for the third time in their history. The run to the final had been a little bit stumbling but the team clicked in the second leg of the semis and crushed Real Madrid 5-0 at the San Siro, all three of the Dutchmen on the scoresheet along with Italian internationals Ancelotti and Donadoni. In the final, Milan were just too strong for Romanians Steaua Bucharest, thrashing them 4-0 with a brace apiece from Gullit and Van Basten and, in truth, unlucky not to have added heavily to the score line. Van Basten had been imperious throughout the season building on his European Championship international form, and the team added the European Super Cup and the Intercontinental Cup to complete the sweep.

As well as the marquee players, Milan had a fine supporting cast throughout. The likes of Diego Fuser, Daniele Massaro, Alberigo Evni and Marco Simone were either signed or developed by the club and proved reliable when called. Milan had arguably the best first eleven in world football at the time but also one of the finest squads. With long-term success they continued their goal to promote from within and recruit players that fitted with the club's philosophy and playing style.

Milan retained the European Cup in 1990 with a 1-0 victory over Benfica thanks to Rijkaard's goal, but Sacchi's team had peaked. Every truly great team evolves and the 1990-91 season marked the moment for Milan. Sacchi fell out with Van Basten whilst all the time being courted by the Italian federation for the job of national team manager. The club failed to defend the European Cup and found themselves hit with a one year ban from European competition after refusing to return to the field after a floodlight failure whilst behind to Marseille of France. As expected Sacchi left to coach Italy and his glorious time with Gli Immortali (the Immortals) was over.

After the immortals, it was time for Gli Invincibli (the Invincibles). The man to replace Sacchi was Fabio Capello, a former Italian international who had played for Milan in the twilight of his career. He had briefly managed the club before Sacchi had been chosen to take over and in recent history had been working alongside the manager. Having an intimate knowledge of the players and their motivations, he kept the much-feted 4-4-2 of the immortals, but whereas they had a certain amount of freedom to create, Capello favoured a more rigid approach. Still with the Tassotti, Costacurta, Baresi, Maldini back line to rely on for the bulk of his tenure until leaving in 1996, Capello certainly had the base to build on. A noted disciplinarian, he fell out with several players during his management who were moved on and Gullit, Van Basten and Rijkaard's time all passed, but he kept the standards as high as Sacchi had, if in slightly more defensive fashion.

During his time, Milan's midfield shifted to include several players. Marcel Desailly became the holding midfielder having moved from Marseille in 1993 and proved to be equally adept at playing in the heart of the Milan defence if required. From the youth system Demetrio Albertini was promoted and became a vital link between defence and attack in the Rossoneri midfield. Roberto Donadoni remained on the flanks until 1996 and Croatian Zvonimir Boban often joined him on the opposite side of the attack. Boban drifted behind the strikers in a more classic 'playmaker' role and outlasted Capello to stay with the club until 2001.

The strikers included a more prominent place for Daniele Massaro who had moved from a strictly supporting role under Sacchi, often in midfield, to an out and out centre forward under Capello. Joining him was Dejan Savicevic, signed from Red Star Belgrade who could play as a withdrawn striker or on the wing. While he initially struggled to settle in he eventually became a first team regular and a goal in European Cup final would leave him with one of the lasting memories of Capello's time at the club.

Berlusconi also supported Capello by flexing his financial muscle when required. Jean-Pierre Papin was signed for a world record fee but lasted only two seasons after struggling to settle into to both the team and Italian football in general. He laboured with injuries and was eventually sold to Bayern Munich in 1994. Another world record fee was paid, somewhat surprisingly this time, for winger Gianluigi Lentini from Torino who never achieved the stellar career a £13m fee should have commanded. His career at Milan was perhaps mostly noted for a horrific car crash in which he nearly lost his life, spending two days in a coma in 1993. He made a full recovery but after being sold to Atalanta in 1996, he became a nomadic player making his way through several Italian clubs and disappearing down the leagues.

Capello's Invincibles were crowned as such, thanks to an unbeaten season and Scudetto win in 1991-92. A rejuvenated Van Basten finished as Serie A top scorer with 25 in his last full season not decimated by injury. The run eventually stretched to 58 games and that title was followed by three more in the next four years. Milan were the dominant force in Italian football, Capello the most successful manager. Still he remained stoic and committed to his defensive principles, still he wouldn't tolerate a player's rebellion as Paolo Di Canio found out in 1996 when he was swiftly moved on from the club. The 93-94 season is often seen as the definitive 'Capello's Milan' campaign, finishing three points ahead of Juventus to take the title despite only scoring 36 goals in 34 games. The bedrock yet again was the Milan back line, conceding only 15 times and managing 19 clean sheets, goalkeeper Sebastiano Rossi setting a record by going 928 minutes without conceding.

Milan also returned to the top of the European game, competing in three consecutive European Cup finals, losing to Marseille and Ajax in '93 and '95 but gloriously beating Barcelona in 1994. Johan Cruyff's 'Dream Team' lined up against Milan in what was billed as the ultimate game of defence versus attack. The Spaniards started with a front two of Brazilian Romário and the legendary Hristo Stoichkov but were absolutely outplayed by Milan. A 4-0 victory was illuminated by Savicevic effortlessly lobbing Barcelona 'keeper Andoni Zubizarreta from the right wing in the 47th minute. As a message about Capello's methods when weighed against a more attacking philosophy, it was conclusive.

Capello left the club in 1996 having delivered another Scudetto to take up the reins at Real Madrid. The Invincibles time was over and Milan faded as others rose to the pinnacle of both domestic and European football. The inseparable defence was officially broken apart in 1997 and an era had ended. Berlusconi had revitalised the club, Sacchi had perfected it, and then Capello had successfully evolved it into a quintessentially successful Italian team. Both the 'Immortals' and the 'Invincibles' are often cited among the greatest teams of all time, together as a period of success there are few that have matched them.

Football and, in reality, all sport is ultimately about success and on those terms, Milan have to matter. Sacchi presided over a team who were the ultimate contradiction – resolutely firm yet fluid in attack. Capello's incarnation may have not been the spine-tingling force of a total footballing Ajax in the 70s, but any questions can simply be answered by pointing to the trophy cabinet. Presiding over both was captain Baresi's back line, a watershed moment in the standards a defence could achieve and standing alone as the greatest back four of all time.

Cameroon 1990

Honours

World Cup Quarter Finalists at Italia'90

'I'd always been an intelligent player, so I knew if I got fit I had a chance. My first aim was to get fit, and then it was up to the coach to decide whether I was good enough'

Roger Milla speaking in May 2010 about his unexpected call-up to the 1990 Cameroon squad

In 1982 Cameroon's national football team left the FIFA World Cup Finals in Spain with an unbeaten record but no trophy. After qualifying for the first time in the country's history, they joined Algeria as Africa's representatives in the showpiece tournament. Both teams acquitted themselves well but failed to qualify through the first group stages on goal difference. Cameroon left the tournament with their heads held high but also a sense of injustice at a poor refereeing decision that cost them a place in the second round.

Drawn into Group One with Poland, Peru and Italy they always had a mountain to climb to qualify. After watching the two favourites for the group, Italy and Poland, play out a goalless draw a day earlier, they faced Peru and matched that result with a 0-0 of their own. The game's legacy was one of controversy, in particular a Roger Milla goal disallowed wrongly when judged offside. Replays showed Milla had been a yard onside when the ball was played – had it been allowed to stand they would've headed the group and eventually qualified into a second group stage in round two. Following that disappointment they faced an excellent and experienced Poland side and once more earned a credible goalless draw. Going into the final game against footballing giant Italy, they now knew only a win would take them through. They day before the game, Poland had thrashed Peru 5-1 to ensure their qualification and by virtue of Italy having scored once in their first two drawn games, Cameroon knew only a victory would be good enough. After Italy took the lead in the 60th minute through Francesco Graziani's looping header, the Africans equalised immediately, Grégoire Mbida stabbing home from six yards out to give them a real chance to go on and win. After half an hour of stifling midfield dominance from Italy and a lack of experience from Cameroon, the game finished 1-1 and the men in green were out.

Coming through the group with three draws was no small matter when placed in the context of what transpired once Cameroon had been eliminated. Poland went on to claim third place in the tournament, Italy became the eventual winners after defeating West Germany in the final. The impressive performance and ability of both African teams sent a message to the football world – the continent's football was on the rise. Maybe Walter Winterbottom's assertion that an African team would win the World Cup before the end of the century was closer to the truth than ever before.

In the eight years that followed, Cameroon tasted success in the African Cup of Nations twice. The first title in 1984 came courtesy of 3-1 victory over Nigeria in the final, followed by a loss at the same stage in 1986 on penalties to Egypt. Qualification for the world cup in Mexico in the same year hadn't gone well, hammered 5-2 on aggregate by Zambia in the second round and denied the chance to improve on that unbeaten record. After another Cup of Nations title in 1988, Italia'90 loomed large in the horizon and they were in no mood to make the same mistakes again. After topping their group they sealed their passage to Italy with 3-0 aggregate win over Tunisia and prepared for one of the most extraordinary appearances by any team in the history of the tournament.

After retiring from the national side in 1987, Roger Milla had watched his national team qualify from afar, now living happily on Reunion Island in the Indian Ocean. Playing sporadically for semi-professional local side JS Saint-Pierroise, he received a phone call from Cameroon president Paul Biya that would change the course of the rest of his career. After falling out with the Cameroon Soccer Federation because he believed they had failed to look after his dying mother while he played away in Saudi Arabia for the national team, and despite now being 38 years old, the President asked him to come out of retirement and join up with the squad for the trip to Italy. Despite opposition in Cameroon and within the Soccer Federation, Milla agreed and travelled to Italy with one of the most talented squads ever assembled from an African nation.

Built on a strong defensive platform, Cameroon boasted the luxury of one of the best goalkeepers in the world going into the tournament. Thomas Nkono played in Spain's top leagues for over a decade after earning a move to Espanyol for his performance in the 1982 World Cup in the same country. Known for his athleticism and bravery, Nkono rarely missed a game in nearly a decade for the club and played every minute of the campaign in 1990.

Cameroon also had the likes of midfielder Cyril Makanaky who played successfully in France and Spain for over a decade, the talented defender Emmanuel Kundé who would score in the quarter final against England and not forgetting the striker whose name would become known around the world after the first match of the tournament – François Omam-Biyik. Add to that names like Louis-Paul Mfédé, Thomas Libiih and Jean-Claude Pagal amongst others and although unknown to most, it would become clear the squad was not short of quality.

Cameroon arrived in Milan on the 8th June 1990 with the world watching and nothing to lose. Drawn into group B with Romania, the Soviet Union and reigning champions Argentina, they would take centre stage straight away playing the first match of the tournament against the holders. In an expectant San Siro, the pre-match build up focused on one man, Diego Armando Maradona. After bursting onto the international scene at Spain in 1982 before a red card against Brazil, Mexico'86 had been Maradona's tournament and his confirmation as the best player in the world. Now playing his football in Italy at Napoli, he had lifted the Southern Italian side from mid-table mediocrity to a Serie A winners. He had brought them their second title in the season before the World Cup and had now reached an almost godlike status in the South of the host nation. Now thirty years old and playing domestically at the peak of his powers, the iconic Argentinean captain was surrounded by fellow Mexico '86 winners Nery Pumpido who had played in goal every minute in Mexico, legendary defender Oscar Ruggeri who would eventually take the captaincy of the national side from Maradona in 1994 and Jorge Burruchaga, the clever attacking midfielder who had scored the winning goal in the final in 1986. Coupled with this experience was the emergence of new talents like exciting blonde haired striker Claudio Caniggia and midfielder Pedro Troglio who like Maradona, was also plying his trade in Italy.

Cameroon's team was not only unknown but also expected to take a back seat to the Maradona show. Lining up against the familiar light blue and white stripes of the Argentine team, Cameroon's colourful and unfamiliar kit of green shirts, red shorts, and yellow socks mirrored the Argentine approach in taking the colours of the national flag. Russian manager Valeri Nepomniachi (via an interpreter) set the Cameroon team out as conservatively as their natural instincts allowed. His back four was to stay rigid and unadventurous, tellingly Maradona was to be man marked by Benjamin Massing throughout and if possible, doubled up as much as the Cameroon midfield could allow. The San Siro, renamed the Stadio Giuseppe Meazza days before the tournament, buzzed with anticipation as the game started and the Argentineans took a strangle hold straight away. Good chances fell to Balbo and Fabbri but Cameroon weathered the storm and grew into the game. Repeatedly frustrating their opponents they also began to pose a threat at the other end, Makanaky failing to capitalise on their best chance. Maradona had been quiet and the rest of the Argentina side couldn't call on his inspiration for once. After going in level at the break belief was growing that Cameroon could get something from the game.

The pattern continued into the second half but in the sixty-first minute naivety and disaster struck. André Kana-Biyik, François Omam's older brother, was sent off for a crude tangle of legs with Claudio Caniggia who threw himself forward at the touch. The straight red looked harsh and it was feared that Argentina now had the advantage their overall play hadn't earned. Five minutes later the unfazed Africans moved the ball forward and worked it out to the left wing where Makanaky went over Lorenzo's challenge winning the African's a free kick. Cautiously, Cameroon only pushed two players into the box – Makanaky on the front post, Omam-Biyik around the penalty spot. The Argentinean back four watched the waist-high free kick fall to Makanaky who could only flick it on hopefully behind him. Taking an age to fall from the sky, Omam-Biyik rose almost impossibly high above a static Sensini and headed the ball goalwards. Nery Pumpido in the Argentinean goal had it covered comfortably but conspired to let the ball squirm under and away from him. Against the odds Cameroon were 1-0 ahead. Of the 78,000 people in the San Siro, anyone not supporting the team in blue and white erupted. With twenty-five minutes left to play Cameroon stood on the brink of one of the most remarkable results of all time.

As Argentina poured forward they struggled to turn pressure into chances, their talisman Maradona still nullified by his markers. As time crept down Cameroon went down to nine men, Benjamin Massing crudely taking out a stumbling Claudio Caniggia with his shoulder in the eighty-ninth minute. Despite the disadvantage Cameroon held on for a 1-0 win and exploded onto the conscious of a watching public always keen to cherish an underdog.

Even in the light of such a remarkable result, Cameroon still had to play a talented Romania and workmanlike Soviet Union to qualify from the group.

Moving to Bari six days later for the game against Romania, suddenly the world was watching to see if that success could be repeated. It looked as though the magic might all have been used up as they struggled through a dull first half to go in at 0-0 at the break. On the hour, Roger Milla was called from the sub's bench to replace the ineffective Emmanuel Maboang. In the seventy-sixth minute the wily 38-year-old latched on to a bouncing clearance the Romanian defence was hesitating to deal with. After winning the ball and controlling it with his chest, he kept his balance before lifting the ball over the advancing Silviu Lung in Romania's goal. Cameroon were ahead with less than fifteen minutes to go. As soon as the ball crossed the line Milla became the oldest goalscorer in World Cup history, a record he would then break in the eighty-sixth minute with his second. An age-defying burst of pace took him past a Romanian defender to latch onto his own knock on. In space on the right of the box but at an angle, he lashed the ball high into the top corner and Cameroon had a two-goal cushion. A late Balint goal for Romania proved no more than a consolation and Cameroon had already qualified for the next round.

The Romania game gave the world three things – Roger Milla's dancing celebration that would be copied in playgrounds the world over, proof that the Argentina game was no flash in the pan and confirmation that this Cameroon side coupled hard work with genuine technical ability.

Their final group game was a blip, a lazy 4-0 defeat to the Soviet Union who had still had an outside chance of qualification on goal difference. Omam-Biyik later admitted that Cameroon had been celebrating qualification a little too much and been 'drunk, drunk, drunk' for much of the time rather than preparing. Argentina and Romania's draw in their game meant that Cameroon topped the group with 4 points, Romania finished second by virtue of more goals scored than Argentina, who also came through the group as one of the best third placed teams. Next up for The Indomitable Lions was last sixteen match against a Columbian side, pushed as the best for some time in the country's history. Containing flamboyant goalkeeper René Higuita, brilliant attacking midfielder Carlos Valderrama and striker Freddy Rincón, once more Cameroon found themselves in the position of underdogs.

After opening the tournament Cameroon now played the first of the second round games. This time they found themselves in the heat of a Naples afternoon and a largely forgettable ninety minutes passed into extra time with both sides goalless.

Columbia's dominance in a clustered midfield had yet to turn into a goal and their over elaboration was costing them dearly. The largely Italian fans whistled as the game went on, most had bought tickets in anticipation of

Maradona's Argentina making it through their group and playing at this second round venue – his home stadium for Napoli. Little did they know they were about to be treated to the Roger Milla show once more.

In the second period of extra time, following a simple one-two with Omam-Biyik, a brilliant turn and shuffle took Milla into Columbia's penalty area with only Higuita left to beat. After a slight bobble, Milla side-footed the ball high past the stricken keeper into the top left hand corner of the net. As he once again danced his way to the corner flag the stadium turned and cheers rang out for the men in green. Three minutes later Milla was at it again, this time seizing upon Higuita's decision to try and dribble the ball past him some forty yards from goal. Milla's well-timed challenge led to him running the ball in as the despairing goalkeeper lunged at him from behind. Now just eleven minutes from becoming the African continents first World Cup Quarter Finalists, Cameroon found themselves on the back foot as Columbia changed styles to be more direct. On 116 minutes Bernardo Redín pulled one back for the Columbians but Cameroon held firm and had now officially cemented their place in African football history.

Belief now flowed through the Cameroon camp, they knew it was no fluke they had come this far and their tight defensive work, neat passing and incisive counter attacks put them on a par with anyone left in the tournament. On the 26th June David Platt swivelled and volleyed in Paul Gascoigne's free kick to beat Belgium and Cameroon knew it was England who now stood in front of them and a semi-final place. In a tournament low on genuine quality and high scoring games, Cameroon had become the neutrals team of choice. Robbed of Argentina and Maradona until at least the semi-finals, Naples was again to be the venue for Cameroon's next game and the local crowd were now firmly behind the men in green.

England's team contained one of the stars of the tournament so far – Paul Gascoigne. He was well supported by the likes of previous World Cup Golden Boot winner Gary Lineker and talented wingers Chris Waddle and John Barnes. Undaunted Cameroon attacked them from the off and veteran keeper Peter Shilton saved brilliantly from Omam-Biyik after Mfédé's wonderful chipped-through ball. Gradually England came more into the game and on twenty-five minutes, left-back Stuart Pearce crossed and David Platt nodded in England's first attempt on target. Now behind for only the second time in the tournament, the first being the capitulation against the Soviet Union, all eyes were on how Cameroon would react. Would naivety and emotion cause a similar collapse?

The rest of the first half was played out mostly in midfield. Cameroon's passing remained neat and concise but they struggled to breach the England back line. Libiih completely fluffed his lines when faced with a free header in the England penalty area and half-time came with Shilton untroubled again. Going into the second half, both teams went on the attack, one looking to save the game, one to seal it. As ever Cameroon looked to Milla for inspiration and he latched onto a through ball and drew a trip from Gascoigne in the penalty area. With no hesitation at all referee Edgardo Codesal pointed to the spot and Emmanuel Kundé lashed in the penalty to equalise (to be consistent with p.2?). Sensing the need to press home their territory advantage, Cameroon upped their tempo and kept at England. Makanaky saw a deflected shot whistle over and England were in danger of losing their footing in the game. In the sixty-fifth minute Eugène Ekéké danced through a static England midfield and exchanged passes with the effervescent Milla. After he lifted the ball over Shilton, Cameroon found themselves in a deserved 2-1 lead. The stadium erupted and unbelievably the little team from Africa who weren't even supposed to qualify from their group, were on the brink of a World Cup semi-final.

England manager Bobby Robson admitted after the game they had underestimated Cameroon's ability but his decision to switch and play largely through the middle would change the game. Platt and Lineker looked to latch onto Gascoigne's through balls and after a couple of near misses, in the eighty-first minute England got it right. A floated free-kick was cleared but eventually the ball found its way back to Lineker in the box. As he took the ball down Benjamin Massing challenged clumsily and after a dramatic fall, a penalty had to be given. Lineker dispatched the spot kick and Cameroon now went into extra time having been much the better side for most of the game.

The first period began with Makanaky again running the English defence ragged and Shilton grateful for some nervy finishing from the Africans. With just a minute to go before the end of the first period Gascoigne latched onto a loose ball and sent Lineker racing clear. As the striker closed down on goal he chose to go round Nkono who could do nothing but bring him down. The calmest man on the pitch, Lineker drove the penalty straight down the middle of goal to score and England now had fifteen more minutes to soak up Cameroon's pressure without conceding. Rather than hanging on, England attacked the now tired legs of the Africans who had given everything in the second half. Lineker was within a whisker of another World Cup hat trick after brilliant work from Gascoigne. Unable to make any real impact in the second period, extra time finished and Cameroon had been eliminated from Italia'90 after what was widely acknowledged as the best game of the tournament.

If Mexico'86 was Maradona's tournament, Italia'90 was Cameroon's. Ask football fans worldwide what they remember about the tournament and most will mention the Lions overachievements in the most glowing terms.

Cameroon would go on to qualify for USA'94 where Milla would break his oldest goalscorer record at the age of 42, but fail to qualify out of their group. Further qualification would come in 1998 and 2002 but again Cameroon failed to get through the group stages never coming close to repeating the dizzying success of 1990. In that breathless campaign lasting just five games, Cameroon gave the playgrounds new names and celebrations to copy and most importantly, played with an infectious smile on their faces that inspired and illuminated the whole tournament.

England 1990

Honours

Losing World Cup Semi-finalists at Italia'90

Manager – Bobby Robson

No.	Position	Player
1	GK	Peter Shilton
2	DF	Gary Stevens
3	DF	Stuart Pearce
4	MF	Neil Webb
5	DF	Des Walker
6	DF	Terry Butcher
7	MF	Bryan Robson
8	MF	Chris Waddle
9	FW	Peter Beardsley
10	FW	Gary Lineker
11	MF	John Barnes
12	DF	Paul Parker
13	GK	Chris Woods
14	DF	Mark Wright
15	DF	Tony Dorigo
16	MF	Steve McMahon
17	MF	David Platt
18	MF	Steve Hodge
19	MF	Paul Gascoigne
20	MF	Trevor Steven
21	FW	Steve Bull
22	⋆ GK	Dave Beasant

⋆ – Beasant called up in place of injured David Seaman

England World Cup Squad 1990

Just as David Beckham carried the hopes of a nation going into major tournaments in the twenty-first century, after 1990 the responsibility laid with Paul Gascoigne. Immensely talented and media friendly thanks to a mix of humour and controversy,'Gazza' found life in the spotlight after Italia'90 almost too much to bear. Whilst in Italy, Gazza had been England's brightest star in their best tournament since 1966, a performance that also led to a revolution in the English game. England's campaign – including a heart-breaking defeat to an old enemy – helped to turn an increasingly anti-football media and make a nation fall in love with the game again.

English football in the 1980s had been touched with tragedy and violence throughout. Early European successes by first division clubs Liverpool, Ipswich, Tottenham Hotspur, Aston Villa and Nottingham Forest had all been overshadowed by the Heysel Stadium disaster in 1985. After several flashpoints with English hooligans abroad in previous campaigns, the tragic events of the 1985 European Cup Final between Liverpool and Juventus led to UEFA launching an indefinite ban from all European competition for English clubs.

Domestically the 'English disease' of hooliganism was rife on the terraces of virtually every club. In 1985 after a riot between Luton and Millwall fans, Prime Minister Margaret Thatcher was forced to act on football violence. The Popplewell Committee was tasked with investigating the problem and looking for solutions. One of its earliest findings in 1986 was that 'football may not be able to continue in its present form much longer'. The game found itself on the front pages for all the wrong reasons – an ID card scheme was proposed and excluding all away fans was seriously considered. On top of the problems with violence, in 1989 after a horrific incident at an FA Cup semi final between Liverpool and Nottingham Forest, ninety-six people lost their lives. Policing at games and the stadiums themselves was now called into question. In response to the issue of violence many clubs had fitted high steel fences on the terraces to ensure that fans couldn't invade the pitch or throw missiles. This resulted in 'pens' on the stands and the overcrowding on that day resulted in scenes football would do its utmost never to repeat. The decade also saw a fire at Bradford City in 1985 kill fifty-six people and injure over two hundred and fifty more, as well as many other deaths attributed directly to football, its fans or its organisation.

On the pitch it was also evident that English football was suffering. The ban left some of the league's most talented players leaving to seek European competition. In 1986 World Cup Golden Boot winner Gary Lineker left Everton to join Spanish giants Barcelona, where he would go on to make over a hundred appearances. Welsh international Mark Hughes followed him to Barcelona to link up there with English manager Terry Venables. Another high profile Welsh international left for foreign shores when Ian Rush joined Juventus in 1987, after over two-hundred games and nearly one-hundred and fifty goals for Liverpool.

The second half of the decade also saw Clive Allen, Glenn Hoddle and Chris Waddle all leave to play in France for Bordeaux, AS Monaco and Marseille respectively. Attendances were falling, the standard was getting poorer and the leagues of Italy, Spain and Germany were all making more money and providing better entertainment in what was perceived as a 'safer' environment. In 1988 the first rumours of a breakaway 'super league' surfaced but an enhanced television deal and some serious negotiation stopped the leading contenders pursuing it.

Internationally there had been little to lift the English game either. Second round failure at the World Cup in Spain in 1982 was followed by the 'hand of God' exit to Argentina in '86. While '82 had been put down to injuries to key players, '86 led to cries of injustice and whispers of conspirators bringing the English game down. The other major tournaments – the European Championships – had also been a source of little joy. After qualifying in 1980, England were fancied to reach the semi-finals but failed to get through a tough group. A 1-0 loss to hosts Italy cost England despite victory over a strong Spanish side and a draw with Belgium. Failure to qualify in 1984 was almost as disappointing the performance in 1988.

Travelling to Germany, England had been drawn with the Netherlands, the Republic of Ireland and the Soviet Union. Strongly tipped to qualify easily, England first slumped to a 1-0 loss to the inspired Republic. A 3-1 defeat to the eventual champions Holland was deemed slightly easier to take thanks to a brilliant hat trick from one of the best players in the world, Marco Van Basten. With qualification gone, England travelled to Frankfurt to play the Soviet Union, still expected to win. Another 3-1 loss condemned them to leave Germany pointless and with a goal difference of minus five.

Returning home to a media outrage, manager Bobby Robson was determined to stay despite a barrage of abuse from the tabloid press. Poor performance at Euro'88 and then the humiliation of a goalless draw against Saudi Arabia in November led to an outcry from the back pages for Robson to go before qualifying for Italia'90 began. Drawn into group 2 with the fancied Sweden and Poland, as well as the relatively unknown Albania, qualification was far from guaranteed. Robson's cause was further decried when the campaign began with a goalless draw at home to Sweden. Seven goals without reply in the next two games against Albania were dismissed as no more than England fans could expect and still the calls for Robson to leave kept coming. A good home result against the Poles and goalless draws in the last two away games saw England qualify in second place. Despite the relative ease with which they had negotiated the group it had never been spectacular and still the press rounded on Robson and his 'ineffective' team.

Despite the alleged state of the national side, the 1989-90 season had shown some encouraging signs that things could be changing in the English game. The European ban had been lifted for the following season thanks in part to the dedication being shown to deal with the widespread problems in the game. Striker Gary Lineker had returned to the first division with Tottenham Hotspur and finished top goal scorer with twenty-four. Over eighty more goals had been scored in the top division than the previous year and as if to confirm that there was a push to make the game more entertaining, both FA Cup semi-finals provided sensational games. Oldham forced a three-all draw with eventual winners Manchester United and on the same day, Crystal Palace beat league winners Liverpool in a thrilling game that ended 4-3 after extra-time.

The policing of football and stadium conditions had also begun to significantly change, reducing the incidents of violence and increasing safety. The Taylor Report had been published in January 1990 and several recommendations had already begun to take effect. One of the most significant was that all first division clubs should have all-seater stadiums by 1994, every other league club by 1999. With football beginning to make positive strides towards dealing with its problems on and off the pitch, it was also agreed to expand the first division to twenty-two clubs for the 91-92 season. It was now down to the national side to try and continue the positive trend with a strong showing at Italia'90.

Still vilified in the press, Robson picked his squad and headed to Italy trying to create a siege mentality around the players. Placed with the top seeds largely because of the hooligan problems, England went into Group F with all their group games to be played in the Stadio Comunale Sant'Elia on the island of Sardinia. Although Spain had more of a claim to the preferential seeding, FIFA wanted the England fans contained and seeded them into Group F to ensure the best chance of keeping a lid on any potential flare-ups. Robson would have the chance to exorcise some of the demons of Euro'88 as once more they face a group with the Republic of Ireland in game one, and then the Netherlands in game two. Finishing with a game against Egypt on the 21st June, the tabloid press wrote England off before a ball had been kicked.

England's squad was deceptively strong. Veteran Peter Shilton would play every minute in England's goal in the tournament. Dave Beasant had been drafted into the squad due to David Seaman's broken finger in the run-up and Robson later admitted, if he had named Beasant among the substitutes for the Germany game he would have brought him on for the penalty shoot-out as he was considered a specialist. In defence England boasted the lightening quick Des Walker as well as Terry Butcher and Mark Wright. In the tournament's later stages England would play a sweeper system with both Wright and Butcher filling the role. Robson's wrestling with whether to play a traditional 4-4-2 or the 3-5-2 with a sweeper became a feature of the criticism and praise that arose from the tournament. To Robson's credit the change between systems did provide turning points in the games against Holland and Cameroon.

England were also strong at fullback with Stuart Pearce and Paul Parker the preferred choices, Gary Stevens playing just the first game against Ireland on the right. The midfield was rich with attacking quality, Waddle and Gascoigne joined by John Barnes and David Platt in providing much of its creativity. Captain Bryan Robson whose involvement was limited due to injury provided the bite, Steve McMahon deputising against Egypt and Belgium. Joining the experienced Lineker up front was Peter Beardsley and the partnership was already a proven success. Back up came in the form of Steve Bull who could provide a more direct threat than Beardsley if required. Going into the opening game against the Irish with the press's words ringing in their ears, England's players were determined to qualify for the later stages.

Against an Ireland side fired up by recent history, England took an early lead through Lineker's bundled control that took him past keeper Bonner and onto an open net. Despite leading for most of the game, England never really threatened to add the second that would have put the game out of Ireland's reach. Substitute McMahon's mis-control on the edge of the area in the seventy-third minute cost England dear as Kevin Sheedy rifled in an equaliser. The draw inevitably drew heavy criticism from the press but England were quietly happy to have negotiated a tricky opening game after the defeat of two years ago. Five days later they faced the Netherlands who had just drawn disappointingly themselves against Egypt in their opener.

The current European Champions, Holland, could still boast one of the best attacks in the world with Van Basten and the brilliant Ruud Gullit, as well as defensively having Frank Rijkaard and Ronald Koeman to call on. England played with a sweeper from the off but still took the game to the Dutch. The 0-0 England earned on the night might have seemed a good result before kick-off but there was no denying that they could have won the game. With Gascoigne putting in a man of the match performance, an audacious Cruyff turn a highlight for the England fans to purr over, he was one of two England players to see goals ruled out on the night. Lineker handled after Van Breukelen blocked his shot and Gascoigne's indirect free kick flew in without a touch. The performance managed to appease some of England's fiercest critics momentarily and with 'World in Motion' – the official England World Cup song – at number one, the public was now behind the team. A battling performance against Egypt, who had drawn with Ireland and Holland in their first two games, saw England grind out a 1-0 win thanks to Mark Wright's header and they had qualified in first place. Drawn against Belgium in the last sixteen, the England team were starting to believe they could go all the way.

Back home, record-viewing figures were recorded. Belgium dominated the game and hit the post but couldn't find a way past England's defence. As extra time crept towards penalties, England won a last minute free kick thanks to a surging Paul Gascoigne. Gazza himself shaped to shoot some forty yards from goal but opted instead to loft the ball into the area. Dropping over his right shoulder, David Platt swivelled and volleyed England into a quarter final against neutrals favourites Cameroon. The dramatic nature of the winner and the match-up against the surprise package of the tournament in the next round only increased attention back in England. With a record in the charts to match the performance on the pitch, suddenly football seemed 'cool' again.

A seesaw quarterfinal took England to extra time for the second time in the tournament. Cameroon's exuberance and a tactical shift by Robson contributed to a 3-2 win courtesy of David Platt's header and two Gary Lineker penalties. Undoubtedly one the best games in a dour tournament, England admitted they had underestimated the Africans' technical ability. After taking a first half lead England had been 2-1 behind at one point but with an expectant public watching, they had triumphed and set themselves up a media friendly semi-final against West Germany. Once again Gascoigne had been brilliant and involved in much of England's best work and he now found himself the focus of the country's hopes.

England had World Cup history with West Germany. Stretching back to 1966 and England's only World Cup triumph, there was a rivalry on and off the pitch between the two countries. At Mexico'70 England looked to repeat their success over West Germany, this time at the quarterfinal stage. 2-0 up by half-time the Germans fought their way back into the game and eventually beat the joint favourites 3-2 to progress. Two years later they met in the European Championship second round and once again West Germany emerged as winners. This would be the highest profile meeting of the teams since and the nation's press turned to almost reluctant encouragement.

On the 4th July 1990 at the Stadio delle Alpi in Turin, a crowd of nearly sixty-three thousand waited expectantly for a classic to unfold. The first half failed to live up to expectations but England, widely regarded as underdogs for the game, more than held their own against the perceived might of a German side who had scored thirteen goals in the tournament so far. On fifty-eight minutes the game burst into life.

Left-back Stuart Pearce lunged at German midfielder Thomas Häßler and a free kick was given just outside of England penalty area. Choosing to roll the ball back to Andreas Brehme gave England full back Paul Parker time to close the shot down but the ball deflected skywards from his shin. Shilton had come a yard off his line and the deflection was enough to carry it over his despairing dive to give the Germans a 1-0 lead. Refusing to capitulate, England pushed for an equaliser, sweeper Terry Butcher making way for Trevor Steven and 4-4-2. Redeeming himself for his previous intervention, Parker moved into the German half on eighty minutes. After checking inside and then back over onto his favoured right foot, he swept the ball into the German area where Lineker lurked hopefully. After German defender Juergen Kohler found himself the wrong side of the ball he could only flick it towards the England striker who controlled the ball on his right thigh and then rolled it across keeper Bodo Illgner. The England support in Italy and at home went wild as this was certainly no fluke, England deserved their equaliser and for the third time in the tournament they were heading for extra time.

The extra time would be remembered for one thing from the England fans point of view. Despite Chris Waddle's brilliant effort striking the woodwork and tired England legs trying to stop the game going to penalties, it would be Gascoigne who provided the enduring image. Booked in the ninety-ninth minute, Gazza realised the yellow card would prevent him playing in the final if England qualified. His tears as a reported twenty-five million people watched the game back in England seemed to encapsulate what English football now meant to the greater public. After Gary Lineker signalled to the bench to 'have a word with him', Gazza wiped away the tears and continued to push just as hard for a winner as he had done before. The goal wouldn't come and the game crept into the dreaded penalty shoot-out that would bare no regard for which team had played better.

Electing to take first, Lineker, Beardsley and Platt all scored the first three penalties for England. Germany also scored their first three despite Peter Shilton going the right way for every one. After Karl-Heinz Riedle scored Germany's third, Stuart Pearce stepped up and elected to emulate Lineker's style by hitting it hard and straight. Illgner, diving to his right, threw his legs out and deflected the penalty away giving West Germany the advantage. Guessing right again Shilton couldn't keep out Olaf Thon's penalty and it fell to Chris Waddle, brilliant on the night, to keep the English dream alive. Like Pearce he opted for power and the ball flew high over the bar breaking English hearts.

Three days later, a tired England lost a third place play-off to the hosts Italy. With no Gascoigne and no World Cup final, there seemed to no point. It is impossible to say whether England would have gone on to beat Argentina in the final as West Germany did, but there were several reasons why some believed that they would have had a chance. With no Gascoigne to wind up the Argentinean midfielders would have had to cope with an unflappable England midfield all playing at the top of their game. Several England players played in the '86 quarterfinal and the injustice of Maradona's handball still burned within. This, along with Gary Lineker playing at the top of his game and a defence that had proved they were up to coping with the world's best, all led to strong arguments that England could have triumphed.

What was without debate was that England had become interested and involved in what happened on the pitch at a football game once more. Despite horrific press criticism and pressure going into the tournament, Bobby Robson and his England team had surpassed all expectations and produced the best tournament performance from an England side since 1966. Robson and the FA had already agreed that he would leave his post after the tournament and he went on to Holland to manage PSV Eindhoven successfully. Eventually he returned to English football with Newcastle in 1999 after managing in Portugal, Barcelona and PSV once more. Hindsight afforded him the recognition he deserved for the tournaments success. Gascoigne became a national treasure overnight, launching everything from a best selling t-shirt bearing his crying image from that night in Turin, to a pop career that saw him reach number two in 1990 with 'Fog on the Tyne'.

English football was re-ignited by the team's performance. Two years later the break away dream was realised and the Premier League was formed. The top level of English football suddenly found itself richer and better supported than ever before. Violence still existed but the new resources, stadiums and general desire to return to the game to the pitch rather than the terraces began to show positive results. Within years the league was competing with the other European powerhouses for the best players and the major European competitions.

Despite England not losing a game at Italia'90, they had missed out on the greatest prize in international football. In reality, by uniting a nation behind a football team again and returning the game to the fans rather than the hooligans, they had actually won the prize that really mattered.

Colo-Colo 1991

Honours

Winners of 1991 Copa Libertadores

June 5th 1991
Copa Libertadores Final 2nd Leg
Att: 64,000

Colo-Colo	3 v 0	**Olimpia**
L.Perez 13 & 15		
Herrera 84		
		*Gonzalez S/O 26

Ref: J.Wright

Second Leg of 1991 Copa Libertadores won by Chilean club Colo-Colo

South America is often talked about as attacking football's home. As well as the obvious success Uruguay, Brazil and Argentina have earned internationally, there is also a rich history of some truly great club teams across the continent. Santos of Brazil took on the world in the 60s led by Pelé's brilliance and won, taking two Copa Libertadores and two FIFA Club World Cups. River Plate of Argentina enjoyed a team in the 40s whose attacking line up was so feared it earned the nickname La Máquina (the Machine). The stories go on – Boca Juniors became Maradona's 'spiritual home', Millonarios of Colombia became the original Gálacticos, Peñarol of Uruguay won the first two Copa Libertadores and took the World Club Cup twice, even Paraguay can boast

Club Olimpia – three-time Copa Libertadores winners from a country with a reported population of under 7 million people.

Add to that list the name of Chile's 'Club Social y Deportivo Colo-Colo', the team who united a nation in a desire to win Chile its first ever Copa Libertadores in 1991. As they took to the pitch for the second leg of the final, the whole nation stopped to watch and held its collective breath. A nationwide street party lay in wait in the case of an unlikely win. While their noisier neighbours had been quick to ridicule Chilean football and its lack of intercontinental success, a series of 'nearly' moments had done nothing to silence the claims that Chile couldn't produce a team capable of winning the continent's premier competition. In 1973 Colo-Colo had made the Copa final but lost in a play-off to Argentina's Independiente. Up until 1991, Chile had provided finalists in three more Copa's without ever being able to boast a winner. On June 5th 1991, Colo-Colo represented Chile's fifth attempt to bring the Libertadores to the country, and ninety minutes stood between them and greatness.

Colo-Colo's story began with a rebellion. Players from Santiago-based football club Magallanes broke away from the club in 1925 after becoming disenchanted with a resistance to change. Having witnessed the Argentinean and Uruguayan national sides superior methods of preparation, conditioning and tactical awareness, members of the playing squad had sought to bring these ideas to Magallanes. The club, already being slowly pulled apart internally by wrangles over power and a move to professionalism, wouldn't acknowledge the importance of a new direction. After a bitter split, a group of players led by forward David Arellano formed a new team, also to be based in Santiago and who would look to move forward in line with the rest of South American football.

The club took the name, a term for wildcat, from a Mapuche Indian chief that was famed for his courage in battle and wisdom, repeatedly repelling Spanish attacks and protecting his people. The name was to symbolise a new era for Chilean football and reflect their desire to grow. White shirts were chosen with black shorts and the club's crest was designed to reflect the nation's flag. In their first season in the Santiago based Campeonato Liga Central de Football they not only stormed to the title, they did so without defeat. Quickly establishing themselves as hugely popular in the city and beyond, in a game still played at a mostly amateur level Colo-Colo were operating with professional discipline and paying wages to their staff.

Always wishing to appear at the forefront of any development, just two years after formation they sent a team to tour Spain and Portugal. Exposure to the European form of the game could only be of benefit to the team and they set off confident to win, lose or draw. The trip would prove to be worthwhile, although during a game against Real Valladolid, Arellano collided with an opposition player and suffered a blow that led to peritonitis. Shortly after the game despite medical attention, Arellano died and Colo-Colo had lost their club captain and the main reason they came into being.

The loss was huge and immediately a black band was installed on the club's shirt that still survives to this day, now taking residence just above the badge. After a small period of unrest the club continued to be successful and their reputation grew. By the time a national professional league was established in 1933, Colo-Colo were at the head of the queue of clubs willing to join. Four years later they won their first title having been forced to watch Magallanes take three in a row and they set about creating the reputation that now accompanies them as Chile's biggest team. From that first triumph onwards, Colo-Colo rarely dropped from the top three, winning 18 titles up until the 1991 Copa Libertadores campaign. Entering into that tournament they were on the verge of winning three consecutive Primera Divisións. Still the status of Chilean football had never really risen in stock, despite Colo-Colo's massive popularity, and the four losing Copa finals involving Chilean teams had done little to further their cause.

Colo-Colo had been heavily involved in the formation of a continental championship for domestic clubs as early as 1948. After becoming the biggest team in Chile, Colo-Colo were chosen to host a new tournament – the South American Championship of Champions. The idea had been floating around some of the biggest clubs in South America since the 30s and Colo-Colo's board were among the loudest supporters. As the pieces fell into place Chile seemed a natural destination and six national champions travelled to join Colo-Colo in a league format for the title. The competition was the first continent wide tournament in the history of football and Brazilian's Vasco da Gama took the title, finishing a point ahead of River Plate. The Chileans represented themselves well against the 'bigger' opposition provided by clubs from footballing giants Uruguay, Argentina and the emerging Brazilians. Despite the relative success of the tournament, logistically it had been problematic and the ideas needed refinement.

As issues of gate receipts, organisation and prize money became arguments, the tournament died as quickly as it had been birthed. It wasn't until the late 50s when the idea of a continent wide tournament was mooted once more, particularly in the light of the hugely successful European Cup now taking place. With a chance to play the European Cup winners for what would become the Intercontinental Cup (now the FIFA World Club Cup) in 1960 the Copa Libertadores came into being to be immediately and predictably dominated by Uruguayan, Brazilian and Argentinean clubs. It wasn't until 1979 when Paraguay's Olimpia beat Boca Juniors that a team from outside those three countries tasted Copa final success. After Colo-Colo's close call in 1973, the club never troubled the competition seriously since.

By the time 1991's tournament came round with Colo-Colo installed as Chile's current champions, there was little evidence to suggest they were about to embark on a run all the way to the final. The format of the competition had now changed from a straight knock out to a similar system to Europe's Champions League. Twenty teams made up five groups of four teams, fifteen of them qualifying for the next round of sixteen. The previous years champions – Olimpia of Paraguay, took the outstanding berth.

Colo-Colo's last two Copa performances had been disappointing for contrasting reasons. In 1989 they'd finished bottom of their group in the first round in controversial circumstances. With the last round of games played simultaneously, Colo-Colo fought out a 2-2 draw with countrymen Cobreloa. The result meant the two remaining teams in the group, Paraguay's Sol de America and Olimpia, needed just a draw to progress but with the game taking pace at the same time had no way of knowing it. In the first half of the Paraguayan's game floodlight failure meant the game was forced to be abandoned. Now playing a day later and knowing a point would be enough for both, the teams played out a 4-4 draw, a result and performance which saw them fined by CONMEBOL but was allowed to stand, nevertheless meaning Colo-Colo were eliminated.

In 1990 they had used the pain to put in an impressive qualifying campaign and topped their group. After losing their first game they'd remained undefeated and looked strong going into the second round and a tough game with Vasco da Gama. After home and away draws, it was penalties that split the teams with Colo-Colo suffering the pain of defeat. After two difficult campaigns 1991 was being approached with a mixture of excitement and fear as to what may unfold.

Croatian Mirko Jozic now managed Colo-Colo. Jozic had visited Chile with his Yugoslavian team for the FIFA World Youth Championship in 1987 and they'd won the tournament in breathtaking fashion. Two years later and now not working in the midst of Yugoslavia's growing political problems, Colo-Colo had approached him and given him a route to full management his ambition desired. Working with a talented and hard-working squad, he'd achieved domestic success and Copa disappointment so far. With the team drawn into Group 2 with countrymen Club de Deportes Concepción and Ecuador's Liga Deportiva Universitaria de Quito (LDU) and Barcelona

Sporting Club, Jozic was confident of getting his team through the group and possibly beyond.

Colo-Colo dominated their group, finishing unbeaten with three wins and three draws. Not only had they topped the group, they had only conceded 3 goals across the six games and scored 10. While not being blessed with superstars, Jozic had a collection of solid professionals to pick from, who were all willing to give everything for the team. Defensively, internationals Javier Margas, Eduardo Vilches, and Lizardo Garrido gave the team a mixture of pace and experience. In midfield Jaime Pizarro provided industry and would earn over fifty caps for his country. Providing the bulk of the goals were Ricardo Dabrowski and Argentine Marcelo Barticciotto. Both men played well throughout the Copa campaign but Barticciotto in particular was on his way to becoming a club legend. His semi-final performance underlined the outstanding contribution he made to the team's success. Around them was a further collection of good players but no one individual was bigger than the team ethic and all played their part.

The round of 16 saw Colo-Colo matched against Universitario of Peru. The draw had been favourable as Flamengo, Corinthians, Olimpia and Boca Juniors had all been avoided. With all ties now played over two legs, in a pattern that was to repeat Colo-Colo's home form was pivotal. After a goalless draw in Peru they won 2-1 at home a week later to progress. The quarter-final pitted them against Uruguay's vastly experienced and three time Copa winners Nacional. A brilliant attacking performance in the home first leg saw Chile's champions beat Uruguay's 4-0 and all but seal a passage to the semi-finals. Despite losing 2-0 in the second leg, Colo-Colo were now one game away from their first Libertadores final since 1973.

The only problem was that the game in their way was against Boca Juniors, one of the strongest teams in the continent and current employers of brilliant striker Gabriel Batistuta. With many not giving Colo-Colo any chance of progression, a 1-0 defeat in Buenos Aires was seen as a good result by most involved. With nothing to lose in the return in Santiago and after a goalless first half, it seemed the dream was inevitably about to die. Forty-five minutes later and largely thanks to two Barticciotto goals, Colo-Colo had recorded a 3-1 victory and snatched a final berth in face of elimination. The performance had been exhilarating, Colo-Colo moving into a 2-0 lead before Latorre's header gave Boca a window back to the final. Boca's players openly provoked their opponents but Colo-Colo reacted by snatching a third to give them the win. A well-worked move ended with Barticciotto benefiting from a one-two to clip in his second. The stadium erupted at the final whistle in the face of a performance up there with any a football team from Chile had ever produced. They now faced Paraguay's Olimpia in the final still in the position of underdogs but deliriously happy to have made it and on the back of a huge confidence boost from the Boca win.

On the 29th May Colo-Colo forced a goalless draw from a bad-tempered game in Paraguay. Both teams finished a man light but the scene was now set – the return in Santiago was winner takes all. Just a week later on June 5th both teams took the field at the Estadio Monumental David Arellano, the Colo-Colo home ground that had become a fortress in the competition. They would now play out the Copa Libertadores final in front of 64,000 fans packed into every inch of the ground. Any trace of nerves had to be dismissed as both sides sat on the brink of greatness. Colo-Colo would become immortal in their home country if they managed to bring it its first Copa Libertadores; Olimpia were on the brink of retaining the trophy and taking their third Copa overall.

The game started in barnstorming fashion. Just 13 minutes in, a rampant Colo-Colo took the lead through Luis Peréz's simple finish after a good move. Peréz had been a surprise inclusion in the starting line up and further justified the position with a second shortly after. After a defensive slip Peréz found himself with the chance to control and strike for goal from just past the penalty spot. After lashing in Colo-Colo's second, the adrenaline-filled stadium erupted knowing their team was already on the brink with just fifteen minutes on the clock. By the time substitute Leonel Herrera tapped in a late third, Olimpia were down to ten men and out of the game. Colo-Colo had achieved what had seemed all but impossible – they had won the Copa Libertadores. If they'd never earned one of several nicknames El Eterno Campeóns (the eternal champions) before, they had earned it that night.

The whole country joined in the party and wild celebrations took place both organised and impromptu. Lizardo Garrido dedicated the win to simply 'the people', a sign this was a victory for all of Chile and not just Colo-Colo's fans. They had taken the trophy and done it with style, beating teams when written off and winning every home tie from the group stages to the final. At the time of writing, Chile are yet to provide another winner and with each passing year, the scale of Colo-Colo's achievements becomes a little clearer.

Colo-Colo are still the biggest club in Chile but have since suffered a rollercoaster ride of financial problems and bankruptcy since their triumph in 1991. Domestic success continued and a new era under new ownership has seen them dominate the Primera División but so far further Copa success has been elusive. For a fantastic run and one electric night they mattered for all the right reasons – success, enthralling football, but most of all, for delivering a trophy that united and stood for the whole country.

A tearful Pelé speaks to the crowd at his final game in 1977, an exhibition match between his two club sides – the New York Cosmos and Santos of Brazil

Laurie Cunningham, one of West Bromwich Albion's 'Three Degrees', playing for Real Madrid in a game against Barcelona in 1980

Zico's free-kick curls in for Brazil's first goal against Scotland at the 1982 World Cup in Spain

The exceptional Diego Maradona steals between two Bulgarian defenders during a group game at the 1986 World Cup in Mexico

England's Paul Gascoigne typically wrestling his way through Cameroon's midfield during the epic Italia 90 quarter-final clash between the two sides

Johan Cruyff on the bench before the 1991 European Cup Winner's Cup final between his Barcelona 'dream team' and Manchester United

Pep Guardiola, mainstay of Barcelona's dream team throughout Cruyff's reign, takes the ball from Manchester United's Lee Sharpe. He would later manage the club to its most successful ever year in 2009

Mia Hamm playing for the USA's national side during the 2004 Women's Football Final at the Athens Olympics

Entrance to the Goldsdown Ground, Enfield Town's home whilst forced to share with Brimsdown Rovers as the break-away club looked for a permanent home back in Enfield (Photo courtesy of Stuart Fuller)

Banner held up as David Beckham was paraded for the first time as a Los Angeles Galaxy player at the Home Depot Center in 2007

Futbol Club Barcelona 1990–94

Honours

Primera División Champions 1990-91, 1991-92, 1992-93, 1993-94

Copa del Rey Winners 1989-90

UEFA European Cup Winners 1991-92

UEFA European Cup Runner-up 1993-94

Supercopa de España Winners 1991, 1992 & 1994

UEFA Super Cup Winners 1992

UEFA Cup Winners Cup Runner-up 1991

European Cup Final
20/5/92

FC Barcelona 1 v 0 **Sampdoria**
Koeman (111)

Wembley Stadium, London
Att – 70,827

Barcelona's first European Cup win in their history under the management of Johan Cruyff

Once Johan Cruyff's playing days had ended, he was far from finished with the game he'd all but mastered. A last hurrah at Feyenoord for the 83/84 season had provided another Dutch league and cup double, as well as giving the burgeoning talent of Ruud Gullit the chance to play with one of his heroes. After indicating he wanted to move into management and publicly courting the job at his first club AFC Ajax, he was swept into the position on a wave of fan support in 1985. Any controversies surrounding Cruyff's lack of the necessary qualifications were conveniently quashed and old tensions with board members and officials were swiftly forgotten. Cruyff immediately set about trying to return Ajax to the top of the Dutch game.

Blessed with the emerging attacking talents of the brilliant Marco Van Basten and a teenage Dennis Bergkamp,

Cruyff proved to be a success overall. Ajax won two KNVB Cups and another European title in the 1987 Cup Winners Cup Final under his stewardship. Van Basten in particular would profit from his time under Cruyff's management by scoring 37 league goals in just 26 league games in 85-86 and then 31 more in the 86-87 season. He became a fulcrum for a side that began to break goal-scoring records but couldn't overhaul Guus Hiddink's PSV Eindhoven at the top of the Eredivisie. Van Basten moved to AC Milan and continued his rise after scoring Ajax's winner in European final, and his natural successor Bergkamp began to blossom into the outstanding player he would become.

Typically it hadn't all been plain sailing under Cruyff's leadership. Frank Rijkaard was in the process of conversion from a rugged central defender to various positions within the midfield under Cruyff. After a training ground argument the pair fell out spectacularly, eventually forcing Rijkaard's exit from the club. Cruyff had also grown frustrated at Ajax's and its board's limitations. After cutting his teeth in the Dutch league with a club he was outgrowing, he was now ready for a bigger challenge.

FC Barcelona were struggling to make the leap into greatness their history demanded. Formed in 1899 by a group of Swiss, English and Spanish men, the Catalonian club enjoyed success in the regional competitions they played in until the national Liga's formation in 1929. Thanks to their strong local record, Barcelona were invited to play in the new league and accepted immediately. They continued to play in the Catalan Championship at the same time and quickly became one of the strongest teams in both.

After winning the first ever league Barça then went on to win five Catalan Championships until the Spanish Civil War halted competitive football. On its resumption Barça initially struggled to regain their success after losing players, officials and momentum to the war. They were now trying to compete with Athletic Aviación Club from Madrid (now known as Atlético Madrid) who proved to be the early front-runners in the Primera División. Barcelona found themselves the subject of the increasing political factions growing within the league, their Catalan roots denied by the removal of their flag from their badge and the elimination of 'non-Spanish' names. As time passed the club's success and various stands taken in the face of adversity gained them fans across the globe.

A great Barcelona side grew in the forties and continued into the fifties, picking up seven La Liga titles and six Copa Del Reys in some style. The team contained players who would become club legends like the Hungarians László Kubala and Sándor Kocsis, goalkeeper Antoni Ramallets, Brazilian striker Evaristo and defender and 'Great Captain' of the 'Barcelona of five trophies' Joan Segarra, who played for the club over 500 times. After their glorious run of success ended into the sixties and disappeared under Real Madrid's domestic dominance, subsequent Barça teams struggled to live up to their history.

Up until 1988 Barça had added just two more La Liga titles to their honours list while witnessing bitter rivals Real Madrid take seventeen. Los Blancos lauded their success over their Catalan rivals, particularly their accomplishments in the prize Barcelona coveted the most – the European Cup. Barça's European success had been confined to early Latin and Fairs Cup victories, and two Cup Winners Cups in 1979 and 1982. Real Madrid had to date taken six European cups, admittedly all in the early days of its conception. Barcelona remained one of the biggest clubs in Europe but without the continent's highest prize to show for their history.

The European Cup had become a dream that turned into a nightmare in the 1986 final in Seville. After a single cup final appearance in 1961 in which they lost to a great Benfica side, Barcelona's 1985-86 run to only their second final had been hugely anticipated. Under the leadership of future England manager Terry Venables, they had overcome Sparta Prague, Porto, Juventus and IFK Gothenburg. They now faced FC Steaua Bucharest of Romania in the final and were installed as heavy favourites to win Europe's biggest prize for the first time in their history. After a dull game passed its way through 120 goalless minutes, penalties would now have to decide the winners. Steaua keeper Helmuth Duckadam became the 'Hero of Seville' after saving all four of Barça's spot-kicks. The Romanian's captain Stefan Iovan lifted the famous trophy and Catalonia went into mourning, now feeling further away than ever from the honour of being crowned Europe's best club.

Barcelona needed a sea change from within to re-establish themselves as first the dominant force in Spain, then as champions of Europe. One thing they still had in their favour was that even in the light of so many false dawns, the Catalan support remained passionate and adoring. This pride was in part due to the pride of supporting a 'Catalan' club in the 'Spanish' league, and in part down to a tradition of attacking and entertaining football.

Barça still had no problem attracting some of the biggest names in world football to join them at the Camp Nou. In recent history the fans had been blessed with Mexico 86's brightest light Diego Maradona and it's Golden Boot winner Gary Lineker. Despite his reputation as a difficult character German midfielder Bernd Schuster played for Barcelona for eight years in the eighties and was recognised as amongst the best in the world in his position. Before this the seventies had brought Barça fans Dutch legend Johan Neeskens, Austrian striker Hans Krankl and of course Johan Cruyff.

Despite his performance on the pitch fading towards the end of his time in Catalonia, Cruyff remained a fan favourite as much for his full embracement of Catalan culture as his swashbuckling playing style. He'd provided the fans with some memorable images in his time there including the title in 1974, a celebrated 5-0 win over Real Madrid in the Bernabéu and an 'impossible' goal against Atlético Madrid to name just three. Now in 1988 the club needed a revolution and manager Luis Aragonés was proving he wasn't the architect of such that Barça required. With promises of a new era to come, Cruyff was installed as manager to face the permanent expectation that the club sat on the cusp of greatness.

Cruyff's appointment had been partly from a necessity due to a wide-scale and high profile rebellion in the club. In a shock move the playing staff had met in the Hotel Hesperia and decided to demand the resignation of the board, then led by president Josep Lluís Núñez. Backed by Aragonés, the players called a press conference and stated their case. While various accusations were made it was clear there could only be one winner from the conflict either way. Núñez stayed firm and it was the players who bore the brunt of the punishment from club and fans alike. As Cruyff arrived at the club to change its philosophy, he also needed to re-establish the playing squad as only nine of the full squad survived an end of season cull.

Never known for a lack of confidence, Cruyff was well up for the challenge. He began to shape a squad that could play in a fashion rooted in the ideals of total football. By the beginning of the 1990-91 season he had his team playing his way. Cruyff's philosophy was to play the game 'simply' by encouraging triangles of players to retain possession and create space. This was best achieved through the use of fluid formations and players capable of switching between positions quickly – the very ethos of the football he had so enjoyed under Rinus Michels's management. Although he had inherited some exceptional players at Ajax, Cruyff now had the opportunity to raise a side and pick players he could mould into 'his' team. By the start of the 1990-91 season Cruyff had already won the Cup Winners Cup in 1989 with a 2-0 win over Italians Sampdoria in the final, and the Copa Del Rey in the 89-90 season with a win over Real Madrid. This was to be the season that he would begin the reign of the 'Dream Team'.

Cruyff worked to have individuals that complemented the system as a whole. Spanish international goalkeeper Andoni Zubizarreta survived the Hesperia Mutiny and was almost ever-present over the Dream Team's four years of glory. In front of him Cruyff had recruited fellow countryman Ronald Koeman in 1989 and he was to prove to be a pivotal figure in Barcelona's imminent success. Joining Koeman in Barça's defence, usually as a full back, Catalan Albert Ferrer was successfully promoted to the first team in 1990 and stayed there for eight years. Joining him was fellow academy graduate Guillero

Amor who would eventually play 550 times for the first team. In the centre of defence Barça also played captain José Ramón Alexanko, a veteran whose transfer had been instrumental in the opening of the door to Basque players. Cruyff's defence was prone to leak goals on occasion and could often look brittle but in truth, his real strength and priorities lay in the attacking areas.

In midfield Cruyff achieved something approaching the perfect mix of skill, speed and invention. Josep 'Pep' Guardiola allayed any fears the Catalan crowd might have had of a move away from their geographical routes. As Cruyff bought in foreign players and Basques to satisfy his needs, Guardiola became the lynch pin around which all others would move. Born and raised in Barcelona he signed for the club's youth system at the age of 13. He was moved into the senior side for the 90-91 season and quickly became an integral part of the machine at the tender age of 20. He possessed a wonderful range of passing as well as a natural ability to move into space to receive the ball and ease the pressure on his team mates. The fans loved him as he remained fiercely loyal to his Catalan roots throughout his time at Barça, proud of the flag, the people and even the language which he used in several post match interviews.

Around Guardiola's holding midfield position, Cruyff surrounded him with players who would benefit from his defensive instincts. Michael Laudrup was an immensely talented Danish midfielder who revelled in the pass and move philosophy of the club. Joining him regularly in Barça's midfield were Basques José Mari Bakero and Txiki Begiristain – two early recruits to Cruyff's master plan, both from Real Sociedad. Joining them were fellow Basque Andoni Goikoetxea who had been purchased in 1988 but loaned out for two years to Real Sociedad. He would establish himself on the right of midfield over Barça's Dream Team years and his return in 1990 was part of the inspiration they found to take their play to the next level.

Another huge part of that inspiration came in the purchase of Bulgarian striker Hristo Stoichkov. Striker Julio Salinas had moved to Barcelona in 1988 and started successfully but ultimately proved to be limited. While he remained a part of the first team a new striker was required to bring the tempo and aggression up front that the midfield was generating. The constant movement and invention needed an equal talent in tandem to really dominate other teams. Identifying Stoichkov as the answer, his reputation preceded him as a volatile character not afraid to lash out in anger. Able to play wide or through the middle, Stoichkov had been in equal parts brilliant and controversial throughout his career. Regularly suspended the striker now had no choice but to move from CSKA Sofia after reacting angrily to losing the 1990 Bulgarian Cup Final. The previous year CSKA had played and lost to Barça in the Cup Winners Cup. Noting his talent Cruyff remembered the Bulgarian and signed him when presented with the opportunity in 1990. He would become a favourite for the fans, still controversial but often sensational and winner of European Footballer of the Year in 1994.

After finishing third the previous season, Barça finished the 90-91 La Liga season in first place and 10 points clear of second place Atlético Madrid. Rivals Real sat in third and had witnessed the beginning of something special first hand. Barça played with freedom and the bravery to back themselves to beat any opponent. Further glory had just eluded them in the Cup Winners Cup final after former player Mark Hughes fired Manchester United to a 2-1 victory. Barça had to cope with the loss of Stoichkov for that final and a large chunk of the season thanks to a suspension for stamping on a referee's foot and various injuries. Amor and Zubizarreta also missed the final through suspension and in truth, Barça never found their rhythm until they were 2-0 down.

The following year Catalonia's dreams finally became reality. While the city geared itself up to host the summer Olympic games, their football team was producing some of the best attacking football ever seen in the country. Another Liga trophy was secured on the last day of the season in dramatic fashion. Real Madrid were in pole position going into the last game and needed just to win to take the title. 2-0 up away to Tenerife, a club that had been involved in the relegation scramble for much of the season, Real Madrid fell apart in the second half and lost 3-2. Barcelona's final day win over Athletic Bilbao handed them another title. Stoichkov scored 17 goals, Koeman 16 – a wonderful return for a defender. However, despite the domestic success the real story of the season came with Koeman's most important goal at Wembley Stadium on the 20th May 1992.

Barcelona's European campaign had progressed steadily throughout the season after a second round scare in Germany. After dispensing of Hansa Rostock in their first round game – Laudrup scoring twice in the home leg and producing a man of the match performance – Barça were drawn against another German side FC Kaiserslauten. After a routine 2-0 win in the Camp Nou, they travelled to Germany and contrived to lose 3 goals over 90 minutes. With Barça heading for the exit, a last minute Bakero header secured an away goals victory from the jaws of desperate defeat.

The eight remaining teams were now drawn into two groups in a change of format for the competition; a precursor to the Champions League rebranding that would take place the following year. The winner of each would then play in the final in London. Barcelona safely negotiated their group, losing only once away to Sparta Prague. Their home form was imperious, winning all three games and outscoring their opponents 8 to 3, the 3-0 home win over Dynamo Kiev particularly one-sided. The final would see them play Italians

Sampdoria, the team they had beaten in the Cup Winners Cup final as recently as 1989.

Despite remaining goalless the game was still entertaining as it moved into extra-time. Sampdoria coped well with the Catalans movement but Barça's midfield sparkled in patches. The Italians had their own threat up front with 'the goal twins' – captain Roberto Mancini and the brilliant Gianluca Vialli. The game ebbed and flowed, both teams probed and threatened but couldn't break though. Koeman's 111th minute free kick eventually sealed the game for Barça and Catalonia exploded in celebration. Veteran captain Alexanko, substituted on for Guardiola with seven minutes left to see out the game, lifted the trophy that Barcelona had craved for so long. Rivals Real had cited their European Cup triumphs as evidence of superiority over the Catalans but had not lifted the prize since 1966. Barcelona now had their hands on the trophy in the modern era and what's more, were making headlines for the style of their football as much as the success. After the Olympic games saw the American basketball team dubbed the 'Dream Team', the Catalan press were swift to name their own dream team and the moniker stuck.

92/93 saw another league title in the same incredible circumstances they'd gained the previous one. Real Madrid travelled to Tenerife again knowing a win would bring them the title that would break Barcelona's domestic dominance. They struggled and laboured for ninety minutes, eventually losing 2-0 to the Islanders who were playing for a UEFA Cup place after a much-improved season. Barcelona beat Real Sociedad and once again had taken the title on the last day of the season. Although it had taken a final game swing to put Barcelona into first place, they had won more games and scored 12 more goals than Real.

In the European Cup they had slumped to a disappointing 4-3 aggregate defeat to CSKA Moscow in the second round, losing 3-2 in the Camp Nou when they looked set to progress after a drawn first leg. As holders though they contested the European Super Cup with Werder Bremen and won 3-2 over two legs to take the trophy for the first time in their history. Despite another league win and Stoichkov playing at his brilliant best, Cruyff needed another element to freshen up the squad and push for the major honours once more.

Brazilian Romário arrived in time for the 93-94 season – the last hurrah of the Dream Team – and finished as winner of the Pichichi trophy for the league's top goals-scorer. He continued his incredible goal scoring record earned at previous club PSV Eindhoven and while Stoichkov would finish as European Footballer of the Year in 1994, Romário was voted FIFA World Player of the Year. Barça took their forth-consecutive La Liga title, this time on goal difference, once again in dramatic circumstances. Their rivals had been Deportivo de La Coruña for much of the season who finished with a home game against mid-table Valencia. Deportivo failed to score against the Los Che, even missing a last minute penalty. Characteristically Barcelona had chased them all year and weren't about to let them off the hook, smashing 5 past Seville to take the trophy again.

Barça were also European Cup finalists once more. Progress had been spectacular at times, the Catalans scoring 5 over two legs against Dynamo Kiev in the first round and 5 more against Austria Vienna in the second. They then sailed through Group A, scoring 13 times and only conceding three in six games against Monaco, Spartak Moscow and Galatasaray. The semi-final had been similarly routine with a 3-0 win over Portuguese champions FC Porto. They faced Italians AC Milan in the final in Athens and were immediately installed as favourites due to the Rossoneri's personnel problems. Cruyff's protégée Marco van Basten was injured and would miss the final for Milan, as would the world's most expensive footballer – Gianluigi Lentini. The Italian's defence was also decimated by the loss to suspension of the legendary Franco Baresi and Alessandro Costacurta, and the non-national rule in European competition decreed that each team could only field three foreign players in their side. This meant Milan would also be without Jean-Pierre Papin to compensate for the loss of Van Basten.

Things didn't go to plan as Barça found themselves in a game with opponents who were tactically far more astute than them. AC Milan had studied Barça intensely and knew all about their defensive weaknesses. Missing so many key players, Barcelona were humbled 4-0 by an Italian side who goalkeeper Zubizarreta admitted were 'perfect'. The Catalans were never allowed to build the pressure from midfield to set their own tempo in the game, Milan pressed and harried them all over the pitch. By the time Marcel Desailly rifled in Milan's fourth on the hour, the game was long gone as Barcelona failed to gain the possession their football demanded.

That game marked the beginning of the end for this 'Dream Team'. Romário struggled the following season and moved on. Stoichkov also moved in 1995 to Parma before returning to the club in 1996 despite being unable to recapture his very best. Koeman also moved back to Holland with Feyenoord, Laudrup made the controversial move to Real Madrid after allegedly falling out with Cruyff in '94. Cruyff left his post in 1996 after becoming Barcelona's longest serving and most successful manager ever. After '94 he had struggled to create a team who could match the Dream Team's intensity or skill. Typically he left amid rumours of a fall out with President Núñez and the Barça board. He remains a huge figure at the club to this day, often seen as a spokesman for the fans for and against Barça's board. Still typically outspoken, Cruyff took the position as Catalonia national manager in 2009 and remains unafraid of the controversy his views can raise.

The Dream Team restored Barcelona's position as a power to match Real Madrid in the Spanish game. They're still lauded by the Catalan public for all they achieved and the names of Stoichkov and Cruyff are still sung today. They mattered because they gave one of Europe's great clubs its biggest prize for the first time, but memorably they also did it in style and amidst the sort of high drama that football can generate. Another truly great Barça team would rise again in 2009 and Cruyff's Dream Team and love of fluid football would cast a huge shadow of influence over their success.

Denmark 1992

Honours

Winners of 1992 European Championships in Sweden

		P	W	D	L	F	A	GD	Pts
1	Yugoslavia	8	7	0	1	24	4	20	14
2	Denmark	8	6	1	1	18	7	11	13
3	Northern Ireland	8	2	3	3	11	11	0	7
4	Austria	8	1	1	6	6	14	-8	3
5	Faroe Islands	8	1	1	6	3	26	-23	3

1992 European Championship Qualifying Group 4

All sport needs its truly memorable moments. Among many cricket has 2005's Ashes, widely acknowledged as the greatest test series ever. Boxing has James 'Buster' Douglas knocking down Mike Tyson and Mohammed Ali's rope-a-dope to name but two. The truth is every time we watch any sport we do so hoping to see something truly memorable. Football has had more than its fair share of the fantastic but in 1992, it would be entirely fitting that the country that gave the world Hans Christian Andersen would give football one of its biggest fairy tales.

Denmark embraced football early; their FA (the Dansk Boldspil-Union – DBU) was formed in 1889 and was the first to be created outside of England's borders. Their leagues had always been well supported but struggled with funding, hence a move to full professionalism not occurring until the late seventies. The move created a stronger national side and 1986 saw the team qualify for their first ever World Cup finals. The team topped Group E and produced one of the standout performances of the whole tournament by thrashing Uruguay 6-1. They went on to a second round exit at the hands of Spain but had left a lasting impression as a team of talented individuals lacking experience on the biggest stage.

The European Championships had seen slightly more success, semi-final appearances in 1964 and 1984 in particular had showed promise. At Euro '88 Denmark failed badly in West Germany – a tight qualification group was safely negotiated but once there a tough draw placed them in Group 1 with the hosts, Italy and Spain. Denmark's team still contained the core of the Mexico '86 side that had impressed, including the supremely talented Michael Laudrup, but the Danes struggled and left the tournament without a point and having scored only two goals in three games.

Having failed to qualify for the World Cup of 1990 in Italy despite being drawn in a weak qualification group with Romania, Greece and Bulgaria, hopes for the campaign to reach the European Championships of 1992 were low. Placed in a group of five with only the winners reaching the finals in Sweden, Northern Ireland, Austria and the Faroe Islands represented less of a challenge then the final team in their path – favourites Yugoslavia. Hopes dipped even further when Laudrup and his brother Brian, as well as midfielder and sometime fullback Jan Bartram retired prematurely from the national team due to differences with manager Richard Moller-Nielsen early in the qualification campaign. After starting with a routine 4-1 home win over the Faroes in which Michael Laudrup scored twice, Denmark drew in Northern Ireland and then lost at home to Yugoslavia prompting disagreement with the manager's tactics and the three players withdrawal.

Results picked up but not enough to top the group. Despite a brilliant away victory in Belgrade, Denmark finished a point behind Yugoslavia and the summer of 1992 looked like a long holiday for all had been involved in the failed qualification campaign. As the season wound down and those that had qualified for the tournament began preparations with their national squads, manager Nielsen busied himself by preparing to decorate his kitchen. With most of his squad away on holiday, it looked like he would be one of the millions watching the tournament unfold on television.

Elsewhere politics were conspiring to give the Danes another chance. Yugoslavia was plunged into the midst of a civil war and the country was breaking into claimed states and republics. With little choice as doubts surfaced as to the increasing validity of a 'Yugoslavian' team and what that would constitute, UEFA sought advice as to the country's position. On hearing the United Nations were to impose heavy sanctions after exposing various war crimes and horrific fighting between ethnic groups, UEFA banned Yugoslavia from major competition for the foreseeable future and immediately expelled them from Euro '92.

Rather than construct some sort of play off system or draw into the tournament, the place was given to Denmark for several reasons. Not only did the Danes finish as runners up in Yugoslavia's group, they were also easily the best second place team – two points ahead of the next best (Portugal from Group 6). With just two weeks to go before the tournament began, the DBU were informed of the situation and invited to enter the Championships. After a scramble the squad was pulled together with just ten days to prepare.

Denmark's current squad had to live with constant comparison to the 1984 and '86 tournament teams. The Euro '84 semi-final had been all about the thrilling side of Soren Lerby, Frank Arnesen, Jesper Olsen and Jan Molby. Mexico '86 had seen the brilliant striking combination of Michael Laudrup and Preben Elkjaer. The hastily assembled squad for 1992 relied on hard work and organisation more than outright flair. Their most gifted attacking player was undoubtedly Brian Laudrup, back in the fold despite his brother's continued refusal to join the squad. They were defensively sound and unspectacular, but that's not to say they lacked talent.

Peter Schmeichel was on his way to becoming the best goalkeeper in the world with Manchester United and in front of him, John Sivebaek, Kent Nielsen, captain Lars Olsen and Kim Christofte provided ample and experienced cover (to the tune of nearly 200 caps between them). Christofte was seen as something of a gamble before the tournament but would play in all five of Denmark's games. In midfield John Jensen and Henrik Andersen provided industry, Kim Vilfort, Flemming Povlsen and Henrik Larsen produced much of the attacking thrust. Laudrup was there to give something extra and was perhaps the team's one truly exceptional player but where they might lack outstanding individuals, the team as a whole was capable of drawing the very best from one another.

Denmark faced three difficult group games ahead but rather then feel any great fear, they were just glad now to be taking part. They embarked on a mission to prove they weren't only there to make up the numbers despite their last minute draft, the manner of their entrance to the Championships meant no time for expectations to really build but going into the first game against England in Malmo, they were widely expected to lose. Both teams started nervously, England struggling with the usual weight of expectation and a dull first half ended goalless and virtually incident free. In the second half the game never sparked into life in truth, Denmark worked hard to shut down England's attacking options and nearly scored themselves when Jensen hit the post. At the final whistle of a dour 0-0, the Danes were happy to have earned a point against a team who had reached the World Cup semi-finals just two years previously. Despite early nerves from Schmeichel in particular, they had emerged unscathed and with something to build on.

Next up was fellow Scandinavians and hosts Sweden. Every team in the competition feared the Swedish attacking talent of Thomas Brolin, Martin Dahlin and Anders Limpar. A fascinating game ensued with Denmark countering Swedish pressure as the match ebbed and flowed. Another goalless half from the Danes didn't tell the whole story as the tempo and excitement had been a direct contrast to the chess match with the English. The nerves seemed to have dried up as John Jensen admitted 'there was no pressure on us at all, we could relax and just go out and play'. The second half continued to be played at a terrific pace but Denmark would ultimately finish as losers. On the hour Brolin worked his way loose in the area to finish a flowing move for the game's only goal.

While they didn't get the result they deserved Denmark's performance was confident and exciting. They faced the last game against France bottom of the group with no real expectations but crucially, they still had a chance to progress. Sweden sat top of the group with three points knowing a draw against final opponents England would see them through. France and England sat level having both drawn their first games and then played out an ill-tempered 0-0 between themselves. If Denmark beat France and bettered England's result, they'd be through to the semi-finals. Both group games kicked off at the same time and all Denmark could do was win.

In Solna at the Rasunda Stadium, England started well as David Platt's fourth minute volley flew past Swedish goalkeeper Thomas Ravelli. Unaware they were facing elimination Denmark also scored early through Henrik Larsen, the Dane's first goal of the tournament. The French were blessed with genuinely world-class talent but struggled to maintain their discipline. The hard working Danish couldn't compete man for man with the likes of Eric Cantona, Didier Deschamps and Jean-Pierre Papin but as had been their game plan throughout, closed down the opposition and harried them all over the pitch.

Both games ended the first forty-five minutes 1-0 and as things stood, Sweden and England were going through.

Into the second half and Sweden worked themselves the equaliser their pressure undoubtedly had earned. They were doing the Danes a huge favour by continuing to take the game to England despite the point being enough for their own aspirations. Just nine minutes later Papin's precise finish equalised for France and the pendulum had swung again, this time France and England back in the running and Denmark needing both games to swing in their favour. With twelve minutes left the Danes worked an excellent winner, substitute Lars Elstrup side-footing in Povlsen's cross for a 2-1 victory. They had done all that had been asked and fortune favoured their bravery as Sweden's Thomas Brolin worked another excellent goal between himself and Martin Dahlin to give Sweden a 2-1 win.

From nowhere Denmark had equalled 1984's performance. They may not have swept the group aside but they'd grown from that first performance against England. The games against Sweden and France had seen confidence swell and a team emerge who were difficult to beat with a cutting edge on the counter-attack. They would have to wait until the following night to learn their semi-final opponents from the other group but either way, they looked like they would be underdogs once more.

Group B had run to form with Germany and Holland rising to the top. Facing off against each other to basically see who finished top of the group, there was a chance that the losers could be eliminated if the CIS (formerly the USSR) could beat Scotland. Holland cruised to a 3-1 win and Germany took second place by virtue of a 3-0 win for Scotland. That meant Denmark would face the reigning European champions Holland in the semi and if they got through that game they either faced a Sweden side that had already beaten them in the group or Germany – the current World Cup holders.

Sweden and Germany played first and served up an entertaining game with late drama. Germany controlled the game from the off after Thomas Häßler's early free kick gave them the lead. Karl-Heinz Riedle extended that lead in the second half before Brolin's penalty gave Sweden hopes of a comeback. On eighty-eight minutes Riedle ran through to restore the two-goal lead only for Kennet Andersson to immediately reply for 3-2. A tense final few minutes saw Germany take the win and await the winners of the Denmark vrs Holland game.

The Dutch side walked tall as holders and contained some of the best players in the world. The names of Ronald Koeman, Frank Rijkaard, Ruud Gullit, Frank de Boer, Marco Van Basten and Dennis Bergkamp were rightly feared throughout the game. They had eased through their group without hitting top gear and were expected to brush Denmark aside to set up another huge Holland vrs Germany game in a major tournament.

Against the script though Denmark controlled the game in the first half and deservedly led 2-1 at halftime. Henrik Larsen's header had given them the lead in the fifth minute before Bergkamp replied with a deft finish for the Dutch. Rather than shrink into their shells after their good work, Denmark looked for another and Larsen again provided a finish after the Dutch failed to clear a long ball into the box. The ball bobbled and bounced its way towards Larsen on the edge of the penalty area who with time to measure his finish, lashed home Denmark's second. The second half saw Holland turn up the pressure but Schmeichel was now at his very best, denying Gullit brilliantly at the near post as they struggled to turn possession into chances. Laudrup was working hard up front pulling the Dutch defence out of position with clever movement at every opportunity. As the minutes ticked by it looked for all the world like Denmark could actually be about to beat the holders. With just five minutes left a corner found its way to the feet of Rijkaard just outside the six-yard box and he couldn't fail to score. It had been snatched from the Dane's grasp at the death and extra-time and more Dutch pressure loomed ahead.

The extra half an hour passed without either side getting the vital breakthrough. Holland probed and teased, Denmark stayed firm but struggled to support their strikers. The semi-final moved to a penalty shoot-out and Schmeichel had an opportunity to shine. While he couldn't keep out Koeman's first penalty, he dived to his left and pushed Van Basten's effort away to give Denmark the edge. Danish nerve stayed firm as they converted all five of their penalties and incredibly and somewhat improbably, Denmark were through to the 1992 European Championship final.

That victory was still not enough for the majority to give them a glimmer of hope against the world champions Germany. Moller-Nielson's team had now developed a winning mentality to match their endeavour, they now feared no one but had to respect the challenge the Germans represented. On the 26th June at the Ullevi Stadium in Gothenburg, captain Lars Olsen led out his team to face some of the best players in world football, names like Illgner, Brehme, Sammer, Effenberg, Häßler, Klinsmann and Riedle. At the end of the ninety minutes it would be the names of his team mates that were on the lips of the football world as they were about produce one more great performance.

The Germans started confidently and Schmeichel immediately set his stall for the game by making good saves from Riedle, Stefan Rueter and Guido Buchwald. Against the run of play Denmark broke clear and Povlsen found himself approaching the German penalty area with a mass of white shirts descending on him. He pulled the ball back to the edge of the area where uncharacteristically, John Jensen was running on from midfield. Not known for his goal scoring (he would play at Arsenal 132 times and score 1 goal) Jensen lashed the ball goalwards past the stumbling Effenberg and over Illgner's dive for 1-0. Rattled by the goal Germany fought back into the game but found Schmeichel in absolutely magnificent form, Klinsmann forcing the best of the goalkeeper's first half work.

Still people struggled with the notion of anything other than a German fight back in the second half. Denmark broke early and Laudrup's great work rolled the ball into Kim Vilfort's path. Taking the ball into the area he pushed the ball agonisingly past the post knowing he could have killed the game. The Germans kept up their first half assault and after a neat spin from Klinsmann, Kent Nielson found himself hooking the ball away from underneath his own crossbar to keep the Danish ahead. Klinsmann then watched Schmeichel's fingertips push his powerful header onto the bar and surely an equaliser was just moments away.

Still the Danish backline and in particular Schmeichel held firm. With twelve minutes to go the unthinkable happened as the ball broke to Kim Vilfort after some head tennis in midfield. With a suspicion of handball, Vilfort brought the ball down and worked the space to shoot from just outside the area. The shot flew past Illgner to his left and went in via the post giving Denmark the second goal that all but sealed the win. At the final whistle the team ran to celebrate with Schmeichel – their saviour throughout the game – and their crowd was delirious with excitement. The Danes had won a competition they'd gate crashed, beaten the European and world champions along the way and undoubtedly deserved to lift the trophy. On their return to Denmark over a million fans flooded onto the streets of Copenhagen to welcome them home, a huge celebration to mark an incredible achievement.

The most improbable of winners, Denmark now had its first major football trophy. Not since Sweden took gold at the 1948 Olympic Games had Scandinavia held one of the big footballing honours, their last real moment of glory coming with Sweden's hosting of the 1958 World Cup and appearance in the final. Denmark may have blindsided their way into the semi-finals but then they trod the hardest path possible to win. In an expanded European Championships in 1996 they failed to qualify from their group, soundly beaten by Croatia and labouring to a draw with Portugal. Their time as holders was over.

Football needs fairy tales. In an increasingly cynical and business driven sport, it's important that players in a team like Denmark can still work together to become more than the sum of their parts. In 2004 Greece won the European Championships in Portugal along similar lines but their style of play didn't capture imaginations or hearts as the Danes had managed. Denmark mattered because of the story they gave football history in 1992 and for proving if nothing else, an exceptional team can beat teams of exceptional individuals.

Colombia 1994

Honours

Qualifiers for 1994 World Cup in America

'See you soon, because life goes on'

Last sentence of Andres Escobar's last newspaper column in the Bogotá daily 'El Tiempo' discussing Colombia's World Cup campaign

Colombia's story from their 1994 World Cup campaign was a sobering dose of reality for the entire football world. A fantastic team tipped for success by no less than Pelé himself, a disappointing tournament was ultimately overshadowed by a terrible tragedy. After a blazing qualifying campaign and a sensational result in Argentina, the murder of Andres Escobar as a direct result of his actions on the pitch was a terrifying reminder that there are those who see football as more than just a game. For a team's performance to have such final and tragic consequences showed the world that events on the pitch could transcend football and take on new and tragic meaning.

Colombia's national team up until 1994 had a relatively unremarkable history on the pitch. Consigned to the position of sporadically brilliant losers, Colombia's highest point in international football was a second round appearance at the 1990 World Cup. After battling through their group they had became a victim of the Cameroon bandwagon and lost 2-1. Perhaps the most enduring image of Colombia's football from Italia'90 was erratic goalkeeper René Higuita losing the ball to

Cameroon's Roger Milla to concede a deflating second goal. The Colombian team had been touted before Italia'90 as potentially one to watch due a sprinkling of eccentric characters but in truth they'd never played at their best.

Fast-forward four years and the Colombian team was now littered with highly skilled individuals and came into the World Cup in America on the crest of a wave. Their main strengths lay in attack where Faustino Asprilla and Adolfo Valencia provided the threat, Freddy Rincón and Carlos Valderrama the guile. Valderrama was in breathtaking form throughout Colombia's qualifying campaign and with a hairstyle that made him instantly recognisable around the footballing world, he was Colombia's one superstar capable of living up to the billing. Backing up their attack there was also quality, in particular with Leonel Álvarez in midfield and with popular defender Andres Escobar.

Escobar was an elegant player who had attracted the attention of some of Europe's biggest clubs. His performances at USA'94 were being scrutinised by among others AC Milan, who had identified the Colombian as their potential new 'libero'. Equally adept at playing as either sweeper or a true central defender, he developed a reputation and a nickname for being a gentleman. This was in part due to his playing style and in part due to a relatively privileged upbringing, a rarity in Colombian football. Escobar was a huge talent, capable of the rough and the smooth in defence and known for his strength in the air. After making his debut for hometown club Atlético Nacional in 1985 he quickly established himself in the first team and after a brief European adventure with BSC Young Boys of Switzerland, he returned to Nacional and played out what would tragically be the rest of his short career with the club. Escobar's debut for the national side had come in 1988 and just as he had at club level, he'd become a regular and vital member of the first team.

Colombia's South American qualifying group saw them drawn with 1990's World Cup finalists Argentina. Joining them were Paraguay and Peru making the group a tough prospect, particularly with Colombia's last game coming away in Buenos Aires. Their campaign started with a whimper as a goalless draw at home with Paraguay seemed to suggest nothing of what was to come. A battling and credible away win in Peru thanks to Rincón's solitary goal led them into the first game against Argentina, a team on the back of a 33 game unbeaten run, and the moment their campaign really sparked into life.

In front of a packed Estadio Metropolitano, Colombia put in a great performance and came away with a 2-1 win. Goals from Iván Valenciano and Adolfo Valencia and an outstanding performance from Valderrama gave the Colombians the highly prized scalp. Another good performance in Paraguay should have earned more than a draw but they were rewarded for being bold by a 4-0 win over Peru. Five games gone, Colombia now faced Argentina away from home knowing their results meant just a draw would see them through to the finals in America.

As the game kicked off both sides immediately set themselves out to attack, Argentina needing to win to qualify edged the early exchanges and Colombia's goalkeeper Oscar Cordoba was called upon to make several good saves. As the minutes ticked by without Argentina breaking the deadlock, so Colombia's belief and in particular Valderrama's influence grew. In the 41st minute the ball broke to him and his control and touch took him away from his three Argentinean markers. After laying the ball off and into his team mate's run, Freddy Rincón's first touch was heavy but enough to put him one on one with Goycochea in Argentina's goal. A slight dummy and touch round the Albiceleste's 'keeper gave him an open goal and after scoring, he had given Colombia a huge advantage in the race to qualify.

Now 1-0 up at halftime and brimming with confidence, Colombia's second half performance was extraordinary. Just four minutes in, Asprilla added a second after some clever control and a measured finish. Cordoba then survived a mini siege on his goal as Argentina looked for a quick way back into the game but things took a turn for the unbelievable in the 62nd minute when Rincón plundered his second and Colombia's third after a classic counter attack.

On 64 minutes any hopes Argentina had in the game disappeared as Asprilla seized on the ball after a mix-up in defence and went on to lob Goycochea quite brilliantly. The goal was a thing of beauty and Colombia were now ripping the Argentine midfield apart. They played the ball amongst themselves at will enjoying the silenced stadium's despair, Valderrama continuing to find himself on the ball with time and space. With just six minutes left Adolfo Valencia tapped in a fifth after another counter attack and the rout was complete. Colombia received a standing ovation from the home crowd and Los Cafeteros (the coffee growers) had made the World Cup in style.

On returning to Colombia the team were mobbed by fans delighted by undoubtedly the greatest performance in their national team's history. Colombia's football now represented the free flowing and attacking South American style so lauded in others. As they received the plaudits their qualifying performance had earned including Pelé's label as potential World Cup winners, they could look forward to a tournament in America in a climate they were used to with a team thought to be the equal of just about anyone else there.

Colombian football was now making headlines for the right reasons but historically this hadn't always been the case. From the domestic league's Dimayor rebellion in the 50's to persistent rumours of bribery and outside influence affecting the sport, the real nadir of the country's game to date came in 1989. Linesman Alvaro Ortega was shot and killed amongst rumours he had refused to be bribed by an infamous crime syndicate before a big game. The league was temporarily suspended but the horrific crime was never solved, prompting more scandal and unrest at the levels of corruption possibly operating within Colombian football. Even as the national team prepared for the upcoming World Cup in 1994 with such a talented side, still the spectre of organised crime hung over the preparations.

Placed into Group A with very winnable games against Romania, the USA and Switzerland, Colombia's squad travelled to America carrying a weight of expectation never felt by a national team from the country before. Immediately the rumours of betting syndicates and crime cartels threatening players and officials within the party began to circulate. Whatever the reasons, what is without doubt is that the Colombia team that took the field against Romania on June 18th looked a shadow of the side so rampant in Buenos Aires.

The swash buckling style had gone and been replaced by frustrated and impatient possession. Although they flickered with brilliance at times, Romania took the lead against the run of play and then added another before halftime. Although Adolfo Valencia gave them a glimmer of hope with a header, despite several good chances and plenty of possession Colombia couldn't force an equaliser. As is so often inevitable in football, it was Romania who broke and scored again consigning one of the most highly fancied teams in the tournament to an opening defeat.

Next came the match against the USA that would become infamous the world over. Before the game had even begun manager Francisco Maturana and defender Gabriel Gómez allegedly received death threats delivered to the team hotel. The threats to the player and his family caused him to remove himself from selection after playing in the first game, and outside influences were now having a direct say in performances on the pitch. The game began with the Colombians taking the same slightly cautious approach and their minds clearly affected by the negative air now surrounding their campaign. Again they made the running without ever finding the cutting edge so prominent in their usual play.

On 35 minutes the moment came that would prove fatal for Escobar after Colombia's exit from the tournament. America's John Harkes crossed the ball hopefully towards Earnie Stewart in the box. Reading the danger Escobar stepped across and stretched to divert the ball wide with his left foot. Unfortunately the ball spun straight past a stranded Cordoba for an own goal and an American lead. Struggling for form and urgency, Stewart scored a second for the USA shortly after halftime and Colombia had a mountain to climb. Again they enjoyed the greater possession and carved out decent opportunities but a goal couldn't be found until the last minute from Valencia. Celebrations were muted and after the final whistle and another defeat, Colombia needed a miracle to survive.

Their only hope to qualify was to beat Switzerland in their last game and hope goal difference and a Romanian defeat would see them into third and they could become one of the four best third place finishers that would progress. The allegations of match fixing and influence wouldn't go away but Colombia did put in their best performance against the already qualified Swiss. A goal in the first half from the head of Hernán Gaviria thanks to Swiss goalkeeper Marco Pascolo's error and a last minute Lozano run and shot gave them a 2-0 win but it wasn't enough. Romania beat the USA and Colombia had finished rock bottom of Group A. For a team touted as having a good chance to go all the way, the tournament had descended into poor performances, death threats and persistent and troubling rumours involving gambling cartels.

The events following the Colombian's departure from the tournament went on to stun the sporting world. After returning to his home country, on the night of the 2nd of July with the World Cup now into its second round, Escobar headed out with some friends for a night out at the 'El Indio' bar in Medellin. After a few hours drinking and dancing, Escobar headed to the car park where he found himself in an altercation with three men and a woman who angrily shouted at him about his own goal against the Americans. Drawn into the argument Escobar suddenly found himself faced down by a loaded gun. After being shot twelve times, each bullet allegedly accompanied with a shout of 'Goal!' from the shooter, Escobar died shortly after being taken to hospital. Humberto Muñoz Castro, a man with links to an infamous Colombian cartel and a driver for a wealthy gambler who had lost a huge amount of money on the team's World Cup performance, was convicted of Escobar's killing in the June of 1995.

The murder shocked the football world still gathered for the tournament in America. Escobar had used his last regular column for a Colombian newspaper to call for the country to move on from the disappointment and still respect the achievements in qualification. It seemed the message had been lost on some. 120,000 people lined the streets to attend Escobar's funeral and many more visited the grave in the days after the service. A nation lay in mourning for such a high profile victim of a violent society. To this day fans still attend Nacional games with pictures and banners bearing Escobar's image or name and his grave has become a shrine of memento's and messages.

Colombia's team of 1994 and in particular Andres Escobar mattered because they gave football something it's often accused of lacking – perspective – even if it was in the absolute worst way possible. There is a popular Bill Shankly quote that gets used in jest to explain a supposed 'devotee's' approach to football. It goes '…some people think football is a matter of life and death, I assure you, it's much more serious than that…'. Whilst some claim they subscribe to the same view, if football was ever to be more important than a purely sporting endeavour there must also be consequences. Colombia's players learnt that when their World Cup campaign came to mean something more than national pride or sporting achievement. Andres Escobar paid the ultimate price.

Nigeria 1996

Honours

Winners of Gold medal at 1996 Summer Olympic games of Atlanta

Group D Results				
Nigeria	1	v	0	Hungary
Nigeria	2	v	0	Japan
Brazil	1	v	0	Nigeria
Quarter-finals				
Mexico	0	v	2	Nigeria
Semi-final				
Nigeria	4	v	3	Brazil
Final				
Nigeria	3	v	2	Argentina

Nigeria's results in their Gold Medal winning run.

Once Cameroon had showed the world that African football's star was rising in 1990, it would then be Nigeria who proved that raw talent could be turned into success. The West Africans would go to the Atlanta '96 Olympics on a wave of optimism and emerge with a huge amount of respect for both their talented squad and the African game as a whole. Once viewed from afar as something exuberant, exciting but ultimately naive, Nigeria would take the first steps towards African football being taken just as seriously as any other continent's in the world.

Football has been a part of all but two of the modern Olympic games. Dominated by European nations up until 1996, only Canada and Uruguay (twice) had managed to take the gold medal away from the continent in 20 meetings. Whilst FIFA fail to acknowledge the competitions during the games in Paris in 1900 and St Louis in 1904, Great Britain and Canada were awarded gold medals for winning the three-team tournaments. Officially entering the Olympic canon in 1908, the competition was strictly for amateurs to reflect the rest of the game's ethos. Up until the first World Cup in 1930 the Olympics remained the only major international football tournament.

By the time the games came to Atlanta in '96 the competition's rules reflected the change in the nature of the sport. Now open to all professionals, the tournament took an Under-23 format with the stipulation that three 'over-age' players were allowed per squad. It was hoped the inclusion of three 'star' names would boost the profile of the tournament. Much to FIFA's disgust none of the games would actually take place in Atlanta but then, they had always enjoyed a fractious relationship with the Olympic committee.

With sixteen national teams present, the quality involved gave the tournament the potential to be the best ever. From South America came two qualifiers, Brazil and Argentina. Coached by Mário Zagallo (a Brazilian World Cup winner as a player in '58 and '62 and as a manager in 1970) the crop of youngsters making up the Brazilian squad contained names that would go on to light up the next decade of world football. Dida in goal would have an unhappy tournament but go on to be Brazil's number one for over a decade despite Zagallo bringing Cláudio Taffarel back for the '98 World Cup. Striker Ronaldo would become one of the top scorers in World Cup history and play for Barcelona, Real Madrid, Internazionale and AC Milan before retirement in 2011. Also in the squad were Roberto Carlos, Flávio Conceição, Juninho and Rivaldo, all of whom would become key members of future Brazilian World Cup squads. Taking established defender Aldair and striker Bebeto who had so impressed in the World Cup two years previously as over-age players also built on an already formidable air.

Argentina had their own World Cup winner in charge. Daniel Passarella had captained the team that won the 1978 World Cup on home soil. Choosing to use his overage players to build a solid spine, he called left-back Jóse Chamot and central defender Roberto Sensini into the squad along with defensive midfielder Diego Simeone, a player who would be in Argentina's full side for over decade and through three World Cups. Added to that experience Passarella could call on Ariel Ortega (a player mooted at one point to be Diego Maradona's natural heir), Roberto Ayala, Javier Zanetti and two strikers who would have extremely successful careers ahead of them – Hernán Crespo and Claudio López.

Amongst the other qualifiers the trend went on. 1994 World Cup finalists Italy were coached by Cesare Maldini and brought names that would go on to become legends – goalkeeping back up Gianluigi Buffon and Under-21 defender Fabio Cannavaro – as well as players who would carve out successful international careers such as Marco Delvecchio, Damiano Tommasi and Alessandro Nesta. Raymond Domenech's France boasted future World Cup winners Patrick Vieira and Robert Pires, as well as future Real Madrid and Chelsea player Claude Makélélé and Arsenal 'Invincible' Sylvain Wiltord. Europe were also represented by Javier Clemente's Spain whose squad included Fernando Morientes, Gaizka Mendieta and Raúl, and an emerging Portugal side with striker Nuno Gomes and defenders Beto and Rui Jorge who would amass over 150 caps for the full team between them.

The task facing African qualifiers Nigeria looked daunting from the outset. Drawn into Group D with giants Brazil, three-time Gold medallists Hungary and relatively unknown quantity Japan, the top two would qualify so it looked like Brazil and one other. Determined to make themselves the other, Nigeria faced Hungary in their first game, Japan in their next and then their hardest opponents Brazil. While the rest of the football world looked past Nigeria at the more established talent on show, in reality this tournament was the culmination of just over a decade of success for the Super Eagles.

Eleven years earlier at the first FIFA Under-17 World Cup (then an Under-16 tournament) in China, Nigeria had shone and won outright. On route to the trophy they beat the Italy, Hungary and Germany – all 'bigger' European teams with long established professional leagues and youth systems. To prove it was no fluke they finished as runners up in the next tournament in 1987, taking eventual winners the Soviet Union all the way to extra-time. As players grew both literally and in football terms, the Under-20 side then got in on the act and finished runners-up themselves in their World Cup in 1989, losing 2-0 in the final to Portugal. With strong players coming through in the youth teams, it was inevitable that success would graduate into the full side.

The first signs of this came in the 1988 and 1990 African Cup of Nations tournaments. Having only won the competition once in their history (1980) Nigeria would finish runners up in consecutive tournaments thanks to narrow 1-0 losses to Cameroon and Algeria. Qualification for the 1990 World Cup became the next priority and despite being favourites in their group, Cameroon took top spot by two points and the rest is history.

Whilst they missed out on Italia '90, Nigeria's emergence was confirmed by qualification for the 1994 World Cup in America. Nigeria had raced to the top of their World Cup qualifying group and remained unbeaten. Africa had been granted three berths into the main tournament so Nigeria now had to qualify from a smaller group of three to get to the States. Drawn with Algeria and the Ivory Coast, Nigeria qualified on goal difference and a strong showing at USA '94 further showed progress but this time they were going toe to toe with the best sides in the world. Topping Group D on goal difference ahead of Bulgaria and Argentina, Nigeria left the tournament after a heartbreaking second round game with Italy. 1-0 up thanks to Emmanuel Amunike's first half goal and one man up thanks to Gianfranco Zola's harsh red card, Nigeria looked set to qualify for the quarter-finals just as Cameroon had four years earlier. However, player of the tournament Roberto Baggio scored a last minute equaliser for the Azzurri and then in extra time dispatched the penalty that knocked the Super Eagles out.

Despite winning the African Cup of Nations in the same year, the World Cup elimination hurt, even if it had been at the hand of eventual finalists. Impressive at home and now making waves on the biggest stage, the Olympics meant a chance to push on and win Africa's first major international honour. As the most densely populated country on the continent, many felt that Nigeria did indeed represent the Confederation of African Football's best chance for glory.

The squad picked by Dutch coach Jo Bonfrere was not short of quality even when held in comparison with the South American and European sides. Full back Celestine Babayaro graduated from the 1993 Under-17 champions and would eventually make the team of the tournament in this Olympic games. Already playing in Europe he would go on to spend eleven years in England's Premier League with Chelsea and Newcastle. Joining him in defence were the uncompromising Taribo West and Uche Okechukwu who gave Nigeria's attacking players the freedom they required to flourish.

It was in attack where Nigeria's true strength lay. Daniel Amokachi was a frighteningly strong striker plying his trade in England with Everton. An FA Cup winner in 1995, Amokachi would transfer to Turkish side Besiktas in the summer of '96. Feeding Amokachi was the supremely talented Jay-Jay Okocha who would enjoy success at a variety of clubs around Europe and winger Emmanuel Amuneke who would go on to play for Barcelona. Nigeria could also call on the gifted Sunday Oliseh and winger Tijani Babangida, both of who would arguably play their best football in extended spells with Ajax.

The jewel in the crown was striker and captain Nwankwo Kanu. By the '96 games Kanu was already established in an Ajax side that had provided him a Champions League winners medal in 1995. He was sold in 1996 as African Footballer of the Year to Internazionale for £4.7m. To date Kanu has become the most decorated African footballer of all time, going on to win two Premiership and two FA Cup winners medals with Arsenal, another FA Cup winners medal with Portsmouth and another African Footballer of the Year title in 1999. He was also part of the Ajax squad that won three Eredivisie titles between 1994 and 1996 and the Internazionale squad that won the UEFA Cup in 1998. A tall rangy player, Kanu possessed brilliant close control and an eye for a spectacular goal. In these Olympic games he was to play a pivotal part in Nigeria's campaign.

Group D began with a genuinely shocking result. Japan beat Brazil 1-0 and suddenly every team faced a new challenge. The result meant that instead of the group falling as Brazil and one other, with Japan on three points and having played the favourites already they looked to be in poll position to qualify.

At the same time Nigeria kicked off against Hungary in Orlando's Citrus Bowl. An edgy game saw Nigeria triumph 1-0 thanks to Kanu's well-worked first half finish. Two days later the top two faced off and with eight minutes to go, found themselves locked at 0-0. Whilst Nigeria had most of the play Japan were proving to be stubborn opposition. A Japan own goal gave the Africans the breakthrough they deserved and then Okocha's last minute penalty was to prove decisive. Sitting top with six points going into the final group game with Brazil, Nigeria couldn't rest easy as both their opponents and Japan could still catch them. Japan would play out a dramatic 3-2 win over Hungary, a fine result considering they had been 2-1 down with ninety minutes on the clock. Nigeria lost another nervy game 1-0 but had safely qualified along with the Brazilians courtesy of a two-goal better goal difference than Japan.

Moving into the quarter-finals Nigeria were to play a dangerous Mexican side. Despite keeper Jorge Campos's best efforts, a fine display saw Nigeria triumph 2-0 thanks to Okocha and then Babayaro's second half goal. Standing in their way in the semi-final was the team who'd just beaten them in the group – Brazil. Beyond that a final against either Portugal or Argentina awaited the winners. Although they didn't know it, Nigeria were just about to take part in two of the greatest games in Olympic football history.

The semi-final started badly for the Africans. Conceição's first minute free kick deflected past keeper Joseph Dosu to give Brazil the lead. Rallying Nigeria created half chances and took the game to the Brazilians. In the twentieth minute they had their reward as Roberto Carlos sliced Jay-Jay Okocha's cross into his own net for 1-1. Despite the foothold in the game over the next twenty minutes everything went wrong. The Nigerians looked to have lost their chance of Olympic gold as Brazil bullied their way into a 3-1 lead, first through Bebeto, and then Conceição's second of the game after a brilliant lay-off from Juninho.

An extraordinary second half then unfolded as Nigeria gradually fought their way back into the game. Brazil remained as dangerous as ever, one goal ruled out for offside and another chance fired into the side netting by Ronaldo. At the other end Nigeria suddenly won and then missed a penalty. All things being equal it really looked as though this was not to be the Super Eagles day. With twelve minutes left a long ball from midfield saw the ball break to the left. Striker Victor Ikpeba bore down on the bounce twenty-five yards from goal. Side-footing in an accomplished finish, Ikpeba gave Nigeria hope at 3-2.

In the final minute of the game a long throw caused chaos in Brazil's penalty area. With his back to goal, the ball found Kanu in the six-yard box. With brilliant presence of mind he flicked the ball up as he turned and left keeper Dida stranded. Tapping in an equalizer meant that Nigeria had taken the Brazilians to extra-time having been dead and buried in the game. In the first half of extra-time the ball broke to Kanu somewhat fortuitously just outside the penalty area. After moving the ball past two yellow shirts effortlessly, Kanu rifled in the winner from just inside the box. After a famous 4-3 victory the Nigerians were into an Olympic final and now guaranteed a medal to show for their campaign.

In the other semi-final Argentina had dispatched Portugal with far fewer fireworks. Two Hernán Crespo goals had secured the win and the final was set for August 3rd at the Sanford Stadium in Athens, Georgia. With referee Pierluigi Collina in charge and 86,000 fans in place, the gold medal was there for the taking for both sides in an electric atmosphere.

Yet again Nigeria gave their opponents an early head start, Claudio López stooped to head home for a 1-0 lead in the third minute. The game ebbed and flowed with Argentina content to retain the ball and Nigeria happy to pressure at any given opportunity. A hole in Argentina's defence opened for the first time in the game but Amokachi could only hit the post with the chance. On the half hour pressure told as a short corner caught Argentina sleeping and allowed Babayaro to head an equalizer. With their tails up Nigeria ended the first half much the better team but unable to get another to nudge into the lead.

The second half started with another blow to the Nigerian 'Dream Team's' ambitions. Taribo West was harshly judged to have tripped Ortega and a penalty was awarded. An inconsolable West could only watch as Crespo drilled the penalty in for 2-1. With confidence that they could once again come from behind, Nigeria attacked and themselves were denied a clear penalty for handball. The injustice was building and the Nigerians were using it to find new energy and vigour.

An equalizer began to feel inevitable and with 16 minutes to go, Amokachi's clever lob brought the Nigerians level. With the tide firmly turned and with no desire to go to extra time again, in the fashion to which they had now become accustomed, they conjured up a last minute winner from Amunike. After winning a free kick wide on the left himself, Amunike took up a position level with the penalty spot waiting for the set piece. The Argentinean defence tried to catch their opposition cold by quickly moving out to leave the Nigerian attackers offside. Slightly mistiming their charge, the ball fell to Amunike on the volley without a defender within six yards of him. After a smart finish Nigeria had their gold.

As midfielder Sunday Oliseh remarked, Nigeria felt the victory was for all African countries. It had rubber stamped their emergence as a genuine force in football .The Nigerian team of '96 was talented, disciplined, tactically astute and never going to give up in a game whatever the circumstances. They mattered because they marked the emergence of a genuine contender in world football from a continent where the game itself represented hope.

African football had its second gold in 2000 through Cameroon. Nigeria would again make the final in 2008 and again play Argentina, this time at the wrong end of a 1-0 scoreline. In the 1998 World Cup in France, Africa would have a record five representatives in recognition of their growth and Nigeria again topped a group containing strong European and South American opposition. The culmination of Africa's new prominence in the football world came in May 2004 when the continent was given its first ever World Cup as hosts, to be held in 2010 in South Africa. The tournament was a success and Ghana joined Cameroon in 1990 and Senegal in 2002 on the list of African World Cup quarter-finalists. Represented by six teams, only UEFA could boast more entrants than the Confederation of African Football.

African footballers now play at the very top level of international football across the globe. The Ivory Coast's Didier Drogba and Ghana's Michael Essien are among the best in the world in their position and have achieved major success with Chelsea in England. Mali's Mahamadou Diarra and Seydou Keita have patrolled the midfield of Real Madrid and Barcelona respectively. Add to those names players like Cameroon's Samuel Eto'o – winner of three Champions league winners medals for Barcelona and Internazionale respectively, Emmanuel Adebayor of Togo, Frédéric Kanouté of Mali, Sammy Kuffour of Ghana and George Weah of Liberia to name but a few of the very highest profile.

African football is now rightly thought of among the best of the world for producing talent. After Cameroon's energy and trail blazing in 1990, Nigeria turned potential into trophy winning reality in 1996. Walter Winterbottom may have been wrong about an African team winning a World Cup before the year 2000 but few now would back against an African winner before the turn of the next century as the continent's football continues to go from strength to strength.

Manchester United 1998-99

Honours

Premier League Winners

Champions League Winners

FA Cup Winners

"Football eh…bloody hell!"

Alex Ferguson, 26th May 1999

On March 1st 1998, Manchester United stood on the brink of a real challenge for the one trophy that manager Alex Ferguson craved above all others. Now draped in the Champions League guise it had taken since 1992, the European Cup had become the greatest club competition in the world. Out of both domestic cup competitions to Ipswich and Barnsley respectively, the much talked about issue of fixture congestion was no longer a problem for United. Currently they sat a comfortable eleven points clear at the top of the Premier League table after an edgy 1-0 victory at Stamford Bridge on the last day of February. F.A Cup holders Chelsea had held them to a draw earlier in the season at Old Trafford but a rare Phil Neville goal had earned an away win and placed United firmly in the box seat for the title. Arsenal lay in wait as their main challengers with three games in hand but on March 14th, they would come to Old Trafford and a win would all but seal the title before April. With the week in, week out strain of the Premier League run-in potentially dealt with, United would never have a better chance for a clear run at the Champions League latter stages.

Already impressive in Europe, United had qualified through a tough Champions League group in first place with an outstanding record – played six, won five, lost one. The solitary loss had come in the final group away game at Juventus when qualification and first place had already been secured. The real icing on the cake for Ferguson was the draw against the French Champions Monaco in the next round and then a potential rematch in the semi-final against Juventus who they had already beaten when it mattered in this campaign. United would be heavy favourites for the quarter-final and a Champions League final place was once again within reach after going out of the previous season's competition at the semi-final stage to Borussia Dortmund.

On Wednesday March 4th 1998, the red half of Manchester travelled to the Stade Louis II and watched a dull 0-0 draw that furthered United's cause. Even without the advantage of an away goal, Ferguson still knew that a home win against one of the least fancied teams left in the competition was all that was needed to progress.

Fast forward to May 20th of the same year and the Amsterdam Arena in Holland. The Champions League final has just finished and rather than delighting in club captain Roy Keane lifting a European Champion Club's Cup swathed in red and white ribbon high above his head, Ferguson is watching as Real Madrid Captain Manuel Sanchis accepts the trophy for the Spanish club's seventh European title. David Trezeguet's single away goal in the 1-1 with Monaco at Old Trafford had ended United's promising Champions League campaign at the quarter-final stage. To compound matters further, in Arsene Wenger's first full season in charge of Arsenal he had led them on an incredible run including a 1-0 victory at Old Trafford that had helped to overhaul the eleven-point gap and taken the title from Ferguson's grasp. Arsenal had completed the double with a 2-0 win over Newcastle United in the F.A. Cup final leaving Manchester United firmly in second place domestically and facing a qualification round for entrance to the Champions League for the following season.

Throughout the summer in preparation for the 1998-99 season Ferguson knew he needed to improve his squad. Rather than the previous year's addition of a couple of players to develop into key personnel in time, United needed to sign players who could go straight into the first team. Brian McClair and Gary Pallister, two of the longest serving playing staff were allowed to leave and a bid from Tottenham Hotspur was accepted for Ole Gunnar Solskjaer. Solskjaer couldn't agree terms on a contract with the Londoners and stated his determination to stay at Old Trafford, a turning for point for player and club neither would regret. Several fringe players were allowed to leave and thoughts now turned to recruitment.

The tabloid rumour mill was cranked up to maximum in the wake of the previous season's perceived failures. United were linked to Argentine's Gabriel Batistuta and Aerial Ortega, allegedly offering big money for both after Argentina's fairly unimpressive World Cup campaign. John Hartson was touted as a possible replacement for Teddy Sheringham who in turn would be pushed out of the club. Patrick Kluivert, the exceptional Dutch striker famed for his attitude as much as his ability was also allegedly a target. Coupled with the rumoured incomings was more reported interest in Solskjaer from abroad, Spanish giants Barcelona sniffing around David Beckham and even a resurrection of the Ryan Giggs to Inter Milan stories that seemed to surface every year.

Despite the various names being thrown around in relation to Old Trafford the first signing was relatively low-key in all but fee. On July 1st Jaap Stam became the most expensive defender in the world when he agreed terms on a £10.75 million pound transfer from Eredivisie runners up PSV Eindhoven. His elegantly aggressive playing style, driving attitude and partnerships with David May, Ronny Johnsen and to a lesser extent (only due to injury) Henning Berg in the centre of United's defence would become the bedrock the season was built on. Next to sign was Jesper Blomqvist, a Swedish winger comfortable on either wing who would deputise for Ryan Giggs and David Beckham at various points throughout the season. Arriving from Italian club Parma for £4.4 million, he had been on United's radar since an impressive performance against them for IFK Gothenburg some four years earlier.

He would be shortly joined by what was perhaps the key signing of United's season. Dwight Yorke was an enigmatic Aston Villa striker who had yet to quite live up to the potential he so clearly displayed in performances like a brilliant hat trick against Newcastle in a pulsating away game. After United had made it clear they were interested in the possibility of signing Yorke, Aston Villa manager John Gregory made it equally as clear he was going nowhere. Undeterred, a clumsily handled negotiation process began and the beginning of the end came with Yorke telling Gregory he wanted to go. Famously the Villa manager said he would have shot Yorke if he had a gun in his office. The drawn-out signing was eventually completed on the 28th of August for £12.6 million pounds taking United's outlay to over £27 million for the season. His partnership with Cole would yield 53 goals between them and a near telepathic partnership that would live to prove the difference for United several times over a long season.

Tactically Alex Ferguson now had his foundation in place. An aggressive spine was formed with the formidable Peter Schmeichel in goal, Stam and Gary Neville both playing over fifty games in the season in front of him in defence and then the driving force of Roy Keane in midfield. This was built upon with the dependability of players like Denis Irwin, Ronny Johnsen and Nicky Butt, the creativity of David Beckham, Paul Scholes and Ryan Giggs, and the luxury of four internationally capped strikers to rotate.

Cole and Yorke were ably deputised throughout by Sheringham and Solskjaer who contributed another 23 goals to the cause between them despite both being heavily linked with moves away pre-season. Adopting an attacking 4-4-2 system United could afford to be slightly more defensive in midfield in Europe knowing their strikers were always capable of getting goals home or away. Although they consistently conceded in the Champions League they had an attack that few sides could contain and the four strikers, all with unique playing styles, would profit time and again.

The season began disappointingly with a 3-0 defeat to Arsenal in a one sided Charity Shield notable from United's point of view only for Stam's full debut and Roy Keane's return. The powerhouse midfielder had missed almost a full year's worth of football due to an infamous knee cruciate ligament injury sustained in a challenge with Alfe-Inge Haland of Leeds United. Many critics and Ferguson agreed that there was basically two reasons for the implosion the previous season – an injury to Schmeichel and a lack of leadership on the pitch in Keane's absence. He had taken the captains' armband from the retired Eric Cantona at the beginning of the 1997-98 season and lasted only nine Premier League games before the injury. Despite his return and the new signings efforts to gel quickly, the poor start continued with a home draw against Leicester City on the opening day of the season.

Finding themselves 2-0 down with eleven minutes to play, Teddy Sheringham's deflected first touch halved the deficit. It then took a last minute David Beckham free kick to rescue a point. Beckham would have a huge say throughout the season, weighing in with nine goals in spite of vicious abuse from away fans owing to a petulant sending off in the 1998 World Cup second round game against Argentina. Pre-season the talk had been of Beckham moving abroad to escape the vilification of the English crowds stoked by a tabloid campaign that had done little to dampen the emotion. He would stay, buoyed by an adoring Old Trafford who responded to the attack on one of their own by cheering him every time he touched the ball. The Leicester game in particular had seen banner after banner around Old Trafford proclaiming their love for their number 7.

Sandwiched around this fixture and another draw (this time away at West Ham United) Champions League Group Stage qualification was negotiated with a 2-0 aggregate win over Polish champions LKS Lodz. The first leg at home ended with advantage to United thanks to Andy Cole heading a second late on after Ryan Giggs first half strike. Away from home United nullified the Polish champions and saw out a goalless draw to safely see them through to the draw for the group stages.

Throughout September and October Premier League form improved and was only marred by another 3-0 loss to Arsenal in which Nicky Butt saw red for a trip on Patrick Vieira. Even though they remained sporadic, there were flashes of the form in which they would end the season. Yorke found his scoring touch immediately and stand out wins against Charlton Athletic, Liverpool and Wimbledon saw them vying for top spot with front runners Arsenal, Chelsea and Aston Villa.

Off the field matters were dominated by Rupert Murdoch's BSkyB Corporation's bid to buy the club. Support was split with demonstrations carried out against what some fans feared as one man gaining control of the club to use for no more and no less than a way to make money, whilst others were simply excited about the prospect of becoming financially the biggest football club in the world. Eventually the Monopolies and Mergers Committee would throw out the bid but the undercurrent of boardroom unrest would simmer along all season.

An incredibly difficult Champions League group stage draw saw them placed with Spanish giants Barcelona who in the 1994-95 group stages had given them a footballing lesson in the Camp Nou. Also in the group were German Champions Bayern Munich. German football had provided a Champions League finalist in the 1996-97 season – Borussia Dortmund – who had beaten United home and away at the semi-final stage of the competition. The European campaign began with a seesaw 3-3 draw at home to Barcelona, David Beckham providing the first two goals for Giggs and Scholes and then scoring a typically spectacular free kick in the second half.

A controversial 2-2 draw in Munich followed – the Germans' first goal was offside, United's first came courtesy of Oliver Kahn's mistake. United then took the lead through Paul Scholes although he appeared to handle the ball when controlling it, then Peter Schmeichel's late error allowed the Germans to equalize in the last minute through a Teddy Sheringham own goal. The fourth team in the group was Danish side Brondby who were dispatched 6-2 and 5-0 in match days three and four with the minimum of effort.

The campaign continued somewhat improbably with another six-goal draw with Barcelona in a match that provided a breath-taking goal from Andy Cole in the 53rd minute that showed the extent of his developing partnership with Yorke. A dummy from Yorke and then a one-two allowed Cole to control the ball on the edge of the Spaniards penalty box before rifling it home through an outclassed Barcelona defence. After the humiliation of a 4-0 drubbing in his last visit to the Camp Nou, Ferguson now knew he had a team more than capable of playing the attacking football needed to compete at this level. Qualification in second place was complete with an uneventful 1-1 draw at home to Bayern Munich in December and Internazionale awaited them in the quarter-finals.

Meanwhile the league campaign continued at pace into the New Year. After elimination from the Worthington Cup at the hands of eventual winners Tottenham, a series of three draws and then a third defeat of the season (their first at home) to Middlesbrough in December marked a turning point for United who then remained undefeated. On Sunday 16th May, the final day of the Premier League season, a home victory against Spurs would guarantee the title and the first part of a potentially historic treble. Despite going 1-0 down to Les Ferdinand's first half strike, David Beckham's angled finish and Andy Cole's lob ensured a 2-1 victory and a first place finish, one point ahead of Arsenal in second. The title race had been tight all season but Manchester United had produced the headline grabbing performances when then needed to – four points from two games against Liverpool, a home draw against Arsenal to keep them top in February, four goals against West Ham, Everton and Charlton, five against Wimbledon, six against Leicester City and an incredible eight away from home against Nottingham Forest. Although it had gone to the last day, when United went top of the Premier League on the 31st January 1999 they would remain there going into all but three of their remaining fifteen league games.

The second leg of the potential treble ahead – the FA Cup, was secured with a 2-0 win over Newcastle the following Saturday afternoon. United's path to the final had been anything but clear cut. The third round victory over Middlesbrough was followed by a home game against Liverpool. 1-0 down with two minutes left to play, elimination from the competition was on the cards. Dwight Yorke's equalizer and then Solskjaer's coolly place last minute winner took them through to an unlikely fifth round tie with Fulham. After an unremarkable 1-0 win at Old Trafford, United faced Fulham's West London neighbours after the draw paired them with fellow Premier League contenders Chelsea. A stormy draw at Old Trafford saw red cards for Paul Scholes and Roberto Di Matteo of Chelsea. In the replay at Stamford Bridge, two more Dwight Yorke goals saw United through to an epic semi-final against Arsenal, a team they had played three times already in the season and currently held the uninspiring record of lost two, drawn one. Villa Park played host to a drab 0-0 draw, the only real event of note a debatably disallowed Roy Keane goal and a replay was set for three days later with United still unable to beat Arsenal outright.

The replay became an FA Cup classic, a game that to use a cliché contained everything. David Beckham's early long-range strike was equalised by the brilliant Dennis Bergkamp whose shot deflected in off a stranded Jaap Stam. Roy Keane then walked after receiving his second yellow card on the hour to leave United a man down and looking at a mountain to climb. In second half injury time with both sides still pushing for the win, Phil Neville's clumsy challenge on Ray Parlour gave Bergkamp the chance to win the tie from the penalty spot. Bergkamp went to Schmeichel's left but placed the kick at a good height for the keeper who saved and then thumped the air as the ball was hacked to safety.

Now with their tails up, the ten men from Manchester went into extra time looking for an unlikely breakaway winner. A tired pass on the halfway line from Patrick Vieira in the 109th minute was intercepted by Ryan Giggs and after a slaloming dribble, his shot from a tight angle passed David Seaman and flew into the roof of the net to give Man United a cup final date with Newcastle. After the bluster and bravado of the replay the final could never live up that game, goals from early substitute Teddy Sheringham and then Paul Scholes in the second half took the trophy to Manchester and a Champions League final waited for them at the Camp Nou four days later.

Following a 3-1 aggregate victory over Internazionale in the quarter-finals Manchester United had returned to Italy for the semi-final against Juventus. A 1-1 draw at Old Trafford in the first leg had come courtesy of a last minute Ryan Giggs goal after a desperate scramble in the six-yard box. In what many would describe as his finest performance, Roy Keane overcame an early booking that would see him miss the final to lead United to a 3-2 win in the Stadio Olimpico di Torino.

Missing their talismatic captain as well as the also suspended Paul Scholes, Manchester United lined up with Nicky Butt and David Beckham in the centre of midfield. The final against fellow Group qualifiers Bayern Munich was then won in the style of much the season – late drama. After being behind to Mario Basler's sixth minute free kick for most of the game, United equalized in the 91st minute through substitute Teddy Sheringham's instinctive finish to Ryan Giggs's scuffed volley. Less than a minute after the restart Manchester United forced another corner which Beckham swept towards Sheringham at the near post. The England striker's glancing header across goal found the outstretched right foot of Solskjaer who flicked in from three yards to win the game. As United lifted the trophy for the second time in the club's history, they became the first English team to win the European Cup in the Champions League format and the first English team to lift the treble of Premier League, FA Cup and European Cup in one season.

The finish to that one game brought Ferguson the trophy he so desired. It was also the culmination of a run that since December had seen United remain unbeaten for thirty-three games in all competitions. England now had its first European Cup winners since Liverpool in 1984 and the ultimate aim of the creation of the Premier League –to improve the standard of football in England at the highest level – was complete. They had ridden their luck for sure but having an English team win Europe's biggest trophy again confirmed that England's clubs were back at Europe's top table for good. Over the following decade the Premier League would prove the point by being represented in the final five times, Liverpool and Manchester United again taking the trophy once apiece. Fergie's treble winners kicked the door down, England's top clubs made sure it remained open.

USA 1999

Honours

Winners of FIFA Women's World Cup

10th July 1999
Los Angeles Rose Bowl

USA	V	CHINA
1. Briana Scurry (GK)		18. Gao Hong (GK)
4. Carla Overbeck		2. Wang Liping
6. Brandi Chastain		3. Fan Yunjie
9. Mia Hamm		6. Zhao Lihong
10. Michelle Aker		8. Jin Yan
11. Julie Foudy		9. Sun Wen
12. Cindy Parlow		10. Liu Ailing
13. Kristine Lilly		11. Pu Wei
14. Joy Fawcett		12. Wen Lirong
16. Tiffeny Milbrett		13. Liu Ying
20. Kate Markgraf		14. Bai Jie

Referee: N. Petignat (SUI)

Starting Line-ups for 1999 Women's World Cup Final

The history of women's football is littered with misfires and false dawns. Many countries have tried and failed to sustain female leagues, in some cases the notion of women's football has courted controversy. However, currently the game is experiencing worldwide growth, particularly at youth level, which hints at a brighter future ahead. In part this success is due to the 1999 FIFA

Women's World Cup where the game broke onto the wider conscience and achieved levels of popularity some thought never possible – particularly in a host nation where football has historically struggled before.

The earliest recorded games between women date from the late 19th Century in England and Scotland, with the first international taking place in 1920 between an English and French XI. The English team was made up of largely 'Dick, Kerr's Ladies', a team based in Preston who drew huge crowds for charity games in the extended absence of high-level men's football due to the war. The game was enjoying an Indian summer but in 1921, despite a recent game at Goodison Park attracting 53,000 supporters, the English F.A saw fit to ban women from playing on football league grounds. They stated that the game was 'unsuitable' for women and 'ought not to be encouraged' in spite of its apparent popularity. At a time when England was still seen as football's 'home' despite well-known problems with FIFA, the ban was a huge blow to the game's long-term success.

Around the world women's football progressed at a snail's pace as many football associations took a similar stance to the English FA's. While interest remained in a female form of the game, there was no real way to raise awareness to the sort of levels needed to boom. By the late sixties the tide was slowly turning and in England a Women's Football Association (the WFA) was formed with 44 clubs signing the initial charter. In 1971 the ban forbidding women playing on league grounds was officially lifted and the biggest barriers standing in the games way were falling one by one. A year earlier Italy had broken new ground by allowing women to become part-time professionals and interest in the game was beginning to be rekindled on a larger scale globally.

As the game picked up at domestic levels, so national teams began to be formed. Around the world continental championships both unofficial and sanctioned came into being to cater for the game's growing status. While some such as an unofficial 'Women's World Cup' in Mexico in 1971 called the exploitative nature of women playing football and its appeal to a male audience to the fore, others such as the formation of The UEFA European Women's Championship in 1984 were genuine sporting endeavours. Eventually and after several invitational tournaments, FIFA established a Women's World Championship to take place in the People's Republic of China in 1991. The tournament allowed a team to officially become the 'best' in the world and the game now had a level of legitimacy, if not yet the popularity to match.

In America the game had struggled with the same shackles of sexism and limited exposure that had blighted the world's overall view. Women's football existed in small pockets and mainly limited to gym class in the first half of the 20th Century. It would be a groundswell of interest at college level that would encourage development of the game in the seventies. Women's soccer became part of the physical education syllabus and moved backwards from college to high school. As many girls played the game throughout school and then into college, the sport as a recreational activity beyond the education system demanded the formation of women's teams and leagues.

In 1972 the 'Educational Amendments' to 1965's Education Act demanded equal access and equal spending on athletic programs at college institutions. Within months a huge varsity program between colleges existed and females had a new way to access both the sport and higher education. By the mid-eighties a vast number of clubs existed outside of the educational spectrum to cope with the growing interest at all levels. The sport experienced rapid growth at youth level and by 1990 the figures for girls playing football at high school level had grown tenfold on figures taken at the turn of the 80's. America had taken to the game and with the formation of a national team in 1984 after some early organisational problems, they headed to the first Women's World Cup keen to prove that they were not only a good side, but they were now leading the charge of the women's game worldwide.

Part of FIFA's reasoning to organise the Women's Championship was to mark the growth of the game, but also to specifically mark the USA's newfound love for 'soccer'. With the men's World Cup heading for the country in 1994 and a commitment in place to restart the professional game for men, the emerging women's game was also an opportunity for the sport to gain a real foothold in a historically resistant area. As if playing along with the plan, the USA duly won the first World Cup in China in impressive fashion.

Twelve teams made up the competitors for the inaugural tournament. The USA were drawn into a competitive looking Group B with Sweden, Brazil and Japan. Their superiority showed immediately as all three games were won comfortably. A quarter final against Chinese Taipei was dealt with as ruthlessly, the USA putting 7 past the rank outsiders. The Germans also proved to be no opposition for the USA in the semi to set up a final with Norway – perhaps the only team in the world who could go stride for stride with the Americans. Two Michelle Akers goals either side of halftime proved to be enough for the USA to take the trophy and the Women's World Cup had arrived on the football calendar for good.

As big an advance as the tournament and the USA's triumph had been, the competition received very little coverage worldwide. The second women's World Cup in Sweden and Norway's eventual triumph still made few inroads into the levels of publicity the male game could generate. The second tournament provided a means to qualify for the competition at the 1996 Summer Olympics, the first time the women's tournament would be played in the games history and importantly, the first time a major women's soccer event would take place in the USA.

Both male and female competitions were a huge success at the '96 Olympics. The men's competition served up an African winner and some truly wonderful games. The women gave the USA a Gold Medal as hosts. While the women's game had undoubtedly grown, it had struggled to really generate public interest until now. Suddenly the USA women national team's games were well supported and finally captured the imagination that any sport needed to thrive. The USA men's team failed disappointingly but the women excelled in a very competitive field. The two teams considered the best in the world – China and the USA – played out an entertaining final with America winning 2-1 to take the Gold Medal. One of the most significant statistics to emerge from the win was the attendance – the men's final had attracted just over 86,000 fans to the Sanford Stadium, the women had been watched by over 76,000 at the same venue, an incredible crowd for women's football at the time. If the first World Cup had proved America was taking the game seriously, the Olympics had now proved there was a growing market and profitability in the game.

American women's soccer was crossing slowly over into the greater conscience. Not only did the Americans have the successful team to drive publicity in a hugely nationalistic country, but they also had a superstar. A 19-year-old Mia Hamm had starred in the 1991 World Cup triumph and a year later had been signed by Nike in recognition of her newfound marketability. Hamm had quickly become one of the women's games megastars but also had the talent to back up her exposure. Despite losing in the semi-finals Hamm played well throughout the 1995 World Cup and increased her profile again. With the television coverage at the Olympics in 1996 she had become a poster girl for the game, an all American soccer player with a number 9 shirt that was far out selling any of her male counterparts merchandise. By the time the next World Cup was to be played Hamm had become spiritual leader of women's football in the USA and now globally. She was now also an inspiring sportswoman in her own right and had the marketing contracts to prove it.

The USA had been awarded the 1999 Women's World Cup as FIFA wanted the tournament to continue playing in areas traditionally supportive of the women's game, just as China and Sweden had historically been. When then FIFA President João Havelange had conceived an official world championship for women the idea was the game would expand on the back of a prestige tournament. 1999's World Cup would prove to be a watershed moment, producing moments that became iconic across the sport and even managing to cross the gender divide.

The tournament was bigger than ever. 67 teams spanning 6 continents attempted to make the 1999 World Cup finals. Eventually 16 teams qualified in what represented the largest ever field for the tournament. For the first time there would be four groups of four and the standard was higher than ever. The USA were now accomplished hosts, enjoying not only the 1996 Olympics but two years previously the huge men's World Cup of 1994. The games would be played in vast sport stadiums rather than the lower league football grounds of previous years and the press coverage across the world and particularly in the host country was on a scale rivalling the men's event. The United States put on an incredible show, now the sport itself had to live up to it.

The Group draw threw up some intriguing games. The USA's Group A had been fairly routine, the hosts and Nigeria were expected to progress and did just that. The USA were in imperious form and won all three games handsomely. Denmark were first put to the sword, beaten 3-0 in front of nearly 79,000 fans in New York. In a fairytale start Hamm had scored the country's first goal of the tournament. Julie Foudy and Kristine Lilly adding second half goals to seal the win. As the home side moved to Soldier Field in Chicago for their next game against Nigeria, they really settled into the tournament and thrashed the Africans 7-1, scoring six first half goals to captivate another full stadium. Hamm was on picture book form, veteran of 1991's World Cup final Michelle Akers scored and the team was doing all that was asked by the watching public. American television coverage was providing the country with live games and the host nation were building up a head of steam. Safely qualified, their last game against Korea gave the opportunity to rest some of the first team and entertain another 50,000 fans in Boston. Everything had so far gone to plan for both FIFA and the USA.

Group B was a far closer contest. Second place in the group would see a quarterfinal against the American juggernaut and Germany, Brazil (who'd become one of the most progressive teams in world football of either gender), Italy and Mexico were all keen to avoid the match-up. Brazil started brilliantly and their electric forward line of Sissi and Pretinha both scored hat-tricks in a 7-1 win over Mexico. Germany laboured to a 1-1 draw with the impressive Italy but then put six past Mexico. Brazil beat Italy and now played out a final group game with Germany to decide who topped the group. In a terrific match, the lead seesawed between the teams before midfielder Maycon grabbed a last minute equaliser to give the Brazilians the draw they required to finish first. Germany would face a daunting game against the USA and Brazil felt they had the easier ride against Nigeria.

Groups C and D were slightly less competitive and largely went as expected. In Group C Norway and Russia qualified easily, while Group D saw the powerful China and equally dangerous Sweden emerge. All four groups had enjoyed large attendances for all games and the standard of the football had entertained those at the stadiums and the watching television audience alike.

The glamour tie of the quarterfinals went the way of the USA as they twice came from behind to eventually beat Germany 3-2. Nigeria gave Brazil a real scare by fighting back from 3-0 down to take the game to extra time. Sissi's 104th minute golden goal saw them progress and in the double header of games on the 1st July in Washington DC's Jack Kent Cook Stadium, the USA, Germany, Brazil and Nigeria had provided 12 goals and two hugely entertaining matches.

On the other side of the draw Norway and China once again progressed without the headlines of the other quarterfinals. This set up a very one sided semi-final which China marched through 5-0, the aging Norwegian team struggling with the Chinese athleticism and demands of their fifth game in fourteen days. The USA versus Brazil game wasn't quite the meeting of attacking styles it could've been but it did provide the 73,000 watching with the result they craved – a 2-0 win for the host nation.

The USA and China would contest the World Cup final just as they had played for the gold medal at the 1996 Olympics. A world record attendance for a women's sporting event packed into Pasadena's Rose Bowl – 90,185 spectators in total – and viewing figures suggested over 40m American televisions were tuned to the game. It had captivated the nation enough to leave a legacy regardless of the game's result but a United States win would all but seal the sports ascent in a nation so resistant to 'soccer' previously. With such a build-up, the pressure on both teams was immense. A nervy ninety minutes remained goalless and briefly threatened to boil over late in the game as the knife-edge between victory and defeat sharpened in the closing stages. Extra-time also ebbed by goalless and it would need a penalty shoot-out to decide the 1999 World Cup winners. After a slightly disappointing game, the watching audience would have the most dramatic and unpredictable finish possible.

China would take their penalties first and Xie Huilin and Qiu Haiyan converted their first two with the minimum of fuss. Carla Overbeck and Joy Fawcett responded with successful spot kicks for the USA and the spotlight now fell on Chinese midfielder Liu Ailing. Ailing struck the ball low to goalkeeper Briana Scurry's left who managed to push the ball away and save the penalty. Kristine Lilly then scored to give the USA a vital advantage. Zhang Ouying and Sun Wen both scored for China's next two, Mia Hamm had also put away her penalty to leave the USA with the definitive kick. Defender Brandi Chastian scored to give the trophy to the Americans and gave the football world a truly enduring image as she removed her top to reveal a black sports bra while sinking to her knees in triumph. The USA had won the biggest tournament in women's football history in front of the sport's largest ever audience. The game had truly arrived in the country and now had new and unprecedented levels of exposure worldwide.

The women's game has continued to grow if not quite at the same pace it enjoyed shortly after that World Cup. Current figures suggest there are now 7m registered female footballers in the USA alone and many leagues worldwide have gone semi or fully professional. The 2007 World Cup saw prize money awarded to the winners for the first time and new competitions at club level are increasing the rewards and standards in the game universally. Internationally there are now fully-fledged Under 17 and Under 20 World Cups as well as youth tournaments in nearly every continent worldwide. Domestically UEFA has now established it's own Women's Champions League European Cup competition and CONMEBOL of South America held the first women's Copa Libertadores in 2009. The winners of both faced off in the FIFA Women's Club World Cup and never has there been more focus on the sport's development at all levels.

Mia Hamm retired in 2004 after seventeen years of international football with the United States. She finished with the outstanding record of 158 goals and 144 assists in 275 internationals. Such had been her impact on the American sporting conscious; she had achieved everything from gracing the cover of Sports Illustrated to winning FIFA Women's World Player of the Year in 2001 and 2002. Phil Knight, then chairman of Nike, compared Mia's achievements to that of Michael Jordan in basketball and Tiger Woods in golf and she remains the top international goalscorer of all time in male or female soccer. Football continues to thrive in the US despite the collapse of a national women's league and at youth level it remains one of the biggest sports in the country.

Women's football may never have the impact the male form of the game has globally but there is no denying that the standard and exposure it's currently enjoying can only be of benefit in the long run. The United States not only hosted a fantastic World Cup in 1999, its national team provided the sport with an explosion of profile that has benefited all countries who embraced the women's game before or after. While Germany have become the new powerhouse of the women's game, the USA remain strong contenders for the major honours and continue to break through barriers the male game has sometimes struggled with in the country.

Leeds United AFC 1999–2004

Honours

Champions League Semi-Finalists 00/01

UEFA Cup Semi-Finalists 99/00

3rd in Premier League 99/00

4th in Premier League 00/01

5th in Premier League 01/02

15th in Premier League 02/03

19th in Premier League 03/04

'When I saw the figures I could hardly believe it, I calculated then that they were going to need to find £40m to keep trading. In fact I was wrong: they needed £50m'

Bill Gerrard, an economist at Leeds Business Scholl and consultant to Leeds United speaking to The Observer in March 2004

In recent history the back pages of our newspapers have carried almost as many stories regarding clubs balance sheets as they have their performances on the pitch. Money has never flowed through football as freely as it does in the modern era. Sponsorship, television royalties, corporate hospitality and merchandise all provide profitable revenue streams that the clubs have fine-tuned to maximise their worth. It's somewhat of a paradox then that as football becomes a higher profit enterprise than ever before, more and more clubs are experiencing financial difficulties, administration and in some cases complete collapse.

This is because success in football is still dictated by what a team can achieve on the pitch – the balancing act is deciding just how much any one club can invest to obtain its goals. While many chairmen and club officials set themselves strict limits to operate within, sometimes much to the chagrin of the club's fans it has to be said, some are a little more cavalier in their approach. Some are willing to gamble debt against potential and in Leeds United's case, they became the highest profile casualty of just such a wager that the board didn't win.

Leeds United were originally born from the ashes of the disbanded and disgraced Leeds City, a club forced to fold amid stories of financial irregularities and accusations of illegal payments. Their early years remained unspectacular, John Charles' time in the first team and his record transfer to Juventus providing their most notable early moments. When Don Revie arrived as manager in 1961 he was faced with a team flirting with relegation to the third division and a club struggling financially. If Revie couldn't turn things around there was a serious prospect that Leeds United could go out of existence.

Revie didn't just turn things round, he created one of the best teams in England. After earning promotion to the top flight in 1964 as champions of the Second Division, it took Revie just five seasons to win the First Division for the first time in the club's history. Leeds remained in the top four every season until Revie left the club in 1974 with another First Division title to their name. Revie went to take the job as England manager at the request of the FA. In his time he had turned Leeds United from a troubled side languishing in the lower end of English football to a team with two First Division titles, a League Cup in 1968, an FA Cup win in 1972 and two European Fairs Cup wins in 1968 and 1971. His team was rugged and brutal, they thrived on a reputation for being difficult to beat and tough in the tackle. Players like captain Billy Bremner, Johnny Giles and Norman 'Bites Yer Legs' Hunter did little to dispel the myth and the crowd loved them for their commitment to the badge. In the midst of it all remained Revie, a tactician, a perfectionist and superstitious to the very end.

After such as period of success decline was inevitable as age caught up with a Leeds United first team that had relied on a spine of the same players for nearly a decade. A succession of nearly moments ensued and as a consequence various managers came and went through the Elland Road doors. Eventually in 1988 Howard Wilkinson was appointed after ex-captain Bremner had failed to get Leeds back into the First Division after relegation in 1982. Wilkinson brought the title back to Leeds in 1992 but couldn't sustain the standard in the light of an emerging Premier League and Manchester United's rebirth. By 1998 Leeds United were managed by David O'Leary and there was a feeling they could be on the brink of success again.

O'Leary had been at Leeds as previous manager George Graham's assistant. Having made his name as a player at Arsenal where he played over 700 times for the club, O'Leary had developed a reputation as a cultured and intelligent defender. Leeds United initially moved for Martin O'Neill but when no deal could be struck, O'Leary accepted the offer to become first team manager.

Initial success promoted optimism and the Leeds board backed him as he set about trying to create a side that could challenge Arsenal and Manchester United at the top level of English football.

Executive Chairman Peter Ridsdale led that board. A local man and life-long supporter, Ridsdale had risen to the post in 1997 and had been influential in the decision to chase O'Neill and then promote O'Leary. The two shared the same vision for Leeds United's future and after a successful first full season in charge, Leeds United had finished fourth earning entry into the UEFA Cup. The balance sheet also showed increases in television money, merchandising and gate receipts.

The 99/00 season was to be the moment that Ridsdale and O'Leary wanted Leeds fans to talk about as the catalyst for real success. It would be a turning point but not for the reasons either had hoped. While they had been blessed with a talented input of home-grown players, many of them blooded in the first team by O'Leary himself, both men wanted to add to the squad to make the leap to the next level.

Joining youth-team graduates such as Jonathon Woodgate, Alan Smith, Ian Harte and Stephen McPhail came the high profile signings of Danny Mills, Michael Duberry, Michael Bridges and a little known Norwegian player by the name of Eirik Bakke. Just over £15m had been spent on four players who O'Leary felt were key to continued progress. While all four players did impact the first team, in reality it was in these deals that the financial problems began due to the way they were structured.

Ridsdale knew he couldn't borrow the money from the bank to purchase the players as very few would deal with such an outlay and not expect their money back in a timescale unrealistic for a football club. Any given football club's revenue is dependant on it's success over a season when you are talking about the sorts of figures Leeds United currently required. Now faced with the prospect of a huge overdraft and a bank requiring payment much quicker than the club could generate it, Ridsdale took advice and began to reduce that risk by borrowing transfer fees from other financial institutions. The exact fee would be borrowed and paid back at agreed rates over the length of player's contract to the lender. If the club failed to maintain it's repayments the player would be sold and the proceeds used to write off the remaining debt. If there remained a difference between the sale amount that left money still owing, an insurance policy would cover the difference. Ridsdale used this system to purchase players as it allowed the overdraft to remain at a comfortable level, the cost of the transfer was spread over years and the initial expensive outlay on the insurance policy seemed like sound business practice.

There in its essence was the gamble that Leeds United would lose over the next two years. While transfer deals had been structured this way successfully by some clubs, O'Leary's desire for new players and Risdale's willingness to provide them meant this new way of financing the deals, coupled with the belief that future Champions League qualifications would cover the outlay, proved misplaced and ultimately brought the club to the very brink of collapse.

The 99/00 season seemed to prove O'Leary and Ridsdale's approach initially to be right. Leeds United made the UEFA Cup semi-finals, Michael Bridges scored an impressive 19 goals and most importantly the club reached the promised land of Champions League qualification. The competition had become the land of milk and honey for clubs who made the group stages, the revenue from television alone could be anywhere in the region of £15m. Further strengthening of the squad was required in O'Leary's eyes and Ridsdale and his board agreed – not only would it give them an opportunity to have a run at the European Cup, it should also guarantee further qualification by improving their Premier League results. The club had everything to look forward to once again and felt invincible, they'd even weathered a PR storm when players Lee Bowyer and Jonathon Woodgate faced charges over an incident at a Leeds nightclub. It was still felt investment in players was key to the plan's success and the process began again by spending nearly £18m on Dominic Matteo, Oliver Dacourt and Mark Viduka.

As the season progressed Leeds stunned the football world by launching a huge bid for West Ham United defender Rio Ferdinand. A fee of £18m was agreed and after some scrambling behind the scenes, further finance deals were agreed to cope with the outlay. The money was found after assurances were made that another Champions League qualification was inevitable, Leeds United had entered English football's top three and had no intention of leaving any time soon.

But there in lay the problem. The club enjoyed a successful Champions League campaign and were making a real stir in European football. Having qualified for the group stages Leeds had been placed into a series of gate receipt spinning games with AC Milan and Barcelona. Leeds had not only given a good account of themselves but had qualified in second place a point clear of Barça. The club enjoyed famous draws against at home to Barcelona and away in Milan and again, the huge investment seemed to be paying off on the pitch. A further group stage gave them trips to Anderlecht, Lazio and Real Madrid, and once again Leeds qualified in second place for the next round. After a victory over Deportivo La Coruña in the quarterfinals thanks to an exceptional 3-0 home win in front of a full Elland Road, Leeds were two games away from a possible final appearance in Milan. A goalless draw at home set up the second leg against a strong Valencia as winner-takes-all. Leeds fell short and were beaten 3-0 to end their first run in the Champions League as losing semi-finalists.

So far so good but the European adventures took their toll in the league. The rigours of eighteen additional high tempo games to the normal league season heaped pressure on the squad. Behind the scenes loans and finances had been secured on the strength of Champions League football for at least the following season and hopefully beyond. To ease the pressure and allow further investment, the transfer deals were restructured so that repayments were halved to leave one last payment of half the outstanding transfer fee borrowed. As well as this financial reshuffling another deal was brokered to secure further loans, this time against the future revenue generated by ticket sales and corporate hospitality, in particular that secured by Champions League match days. Ridsdale and Leeds United had become incredibly good at securing financing, the problem was the risk involved was out of their hands, it was down to what the team could achieve on the pitch.

The first real sign that there could be trouble ahead came as despite their fantastic European run, Leeds United could only finish fourth after a tight run in behind Liverpool. Fourth was not a disaster but it did mean the moderately profitable UEFA Cup instead of the much-needed bounty of the Champions League. O'Leary identified a lack of depth of squad as the root cause and asked for more players, Ridsdale gambled again and during the 01/02 season in came Robbie Keane, Robbie Fowler and Seth Johnsen at a combined cost of £29m. On top of the outlay on players money was committed to improving training facilities but as UEFA had now increased Champions League qualification in England to the top four, all Leeds had to do was match their previous seasons performance to start earning the money they owed back.

The season was a disaster. Woodgate and Bowyer's court case dragged on and was finally settled in December of 2001, not before it had clearly affected both players form. O'Leary hadn't helped with the release of his book 'Leeds United On Trial' which players and in particular Ridsdale took exception to. The dressing room became divided, O'Leary was now seen as the enemy and the team suffered a humiliating F.A. Cup exit to Division 2 side Cardiff City. The League Cup had gone thanks to a 2-0 home loss to Chelsea, the UEFA Cup went after a 1-0 aggregate defeat by PSV Eindhoven. All that was left to lift the club was a Champions League berth and after leading the table for much of the early part of the season, the inevitable happened and Leeds's form plummeted. They finished in fifth and stories had already broken in various papers that Leeds United finances were tenuous and several players would be sold in the summer. The missed Champions League qualification was disastrous and the meltdown began in earnest.

The summer of 2002 bought the first very public signs of what was to come. The loans secured on the revenue the Champions League returns would create and the interest on the clubs huge debt was slowly crippling the club. Captain Rio Ferdinand was sold to hated rivals Manchester United for a fee believed to be about £30m amid outcry amongst the Leeds fans. Ridsdale defended the deal as it was too good to turn down but after four years of progress and ambition, the supporters had come to expect more from their club. O'Leary was sacked after openly criticising the move but tension between him and Ridsdale ran deeper than just the Ferdinand transfer. Terry Venables came to the club and started the 02/03 season with assurances that the clubs finances were not as bad as speculated and his key players wouldn't be sold.

As well as huge overdraft and loan repayments, Leeds United were saddled with a completely unsustainable wage bill. Venables watched the inevitable fire sale occur and many of his first team left the club without his say. Some were shipped out initially on loan to reduce the weekly stress of paying their wages, Olivier Dacourt moved to Roma for 6 months before the move was made permanent for a below market value €5m. Robbie Fowler moved to Manchester City for an initial £3m but so desperate for the income, Leeds had to structure a deal where they continued to pay the proportion of the strikers wages.

The deal that pushed Venables too far was the sale of Woodgate to Newcastle United. Ridsdale had promised that in the light of Ferdinand's departure Woodgate would remain at the club to provide the stability their defence required. In reality the £9m deal was necessary due to the amount of debt spiralling to an almost uncontrollable level. Venables fell out with his chairman and board and in reality, everyone involved had to go. Peter Reid was bought in to try and turn around a season that had already become a relegation battle. The full extent of the financial turmoil at the club was now widely known and Peter Ridsdale had no option but to step down when faced with the facts and the fans protests. Reid just kept the club in the Premier League but with a reported debt of £127.5m, it was merely delaying the inevitable.

Professor John McKensie took over the impossible position as Leeds United chairman and courted any possible investment he could. Reid left and Eddie Gray was given the job of keeping Leeds in the Premier League but ultimately failed. He was dealing with the bare bones of O'Leary's squad with no money for investment or improvement. Leeds United finished the 03/04 season in 19th position and were relegated to the Championship. The club had now been sold to a consortium led by businessman Gerald Krasner who had negotiated a lifeline to sell their training ground and Elland Road with deals to lease the stadium back.

Since 2004 the ship has been steadied but not before more heart break and relegation. Unable to build a side, any remaining talent was sold and the club turned to loan deals and youth players. Some respectable results in the Championship and investment from new 50% stakeholder Ken Bates looked to suggest a brighter future but the fact was, the club could only ever really exist to service the debt. In 2007 they entered the administration that represented their only way out. The club was sold to a company part owned by Bates but not before a long drawn out process of offer and appeal. All the while the club faced calls to be removed from the Football League for financial mismanagement. Leeds United suffered points deductions and relegation to the third tier of English football, their lowest level since acceptance into the Football League.

Ridsdale has remained relatively unrepentant and evasive on the subject of attributing blame to Leeds United's problems. Returning to football with roles at Barnsley, Cardiff City and Plymouth Argyle, he faced the same accusations after his time in Wales of gambling Cardiff City's future to achieve success today. He parted company with Cardiff in May 2010 after finding investment for the club and then stepping aside for the new Malaysian owners. He wrote his own book, published in 2007 and titled 'United We Fall', making accusations about agent's fees and illicit payments during his time with Leeds. He also claimed that O'Leary lost the dressing room and had forced his hand as the players threatened mutiny at the thought of O'Leary remaining manager after the 01/02 season. O'Leary returned to football unsuccessfully with Aston Villa in 2003, leaving in 2006 still without a trophy in management.

The Leeds United story has become the ultimate cautionary tale for football club owners faced with the prospect of weighing success against safety. They're far from the only club to have financially imploded but they are the most high profile. In 2010 Portsmouth F.C became the first Premier League club to go into administration and they will now look to Leeds as an example of a how far they must fall, to one day rise again. As I have stated before not every team matters for solely footballing reasons, some have to serve as examples of failure even if that has been born in the boardroom rather than on the pitch. Now stable again after finding themselves in the centre of an uncontrollable financial storm, Leeds United have a long way to go before they can eat at football's top table again. As difficult as that fact is to take, their fans can take some consolation in the stark reality that at least their club still exists.

Enfield Town FC 2001--02

Honours

Essex Senior League Runners Up

Cherry Red Books Trophy Winners

Essex Senior League Cup Winners

Middlesex Charity Cup Winners

'Enfield Town FC was formed on 23rd June 2001, when the members of the Enfield Supporters' Trust voted overwhelmingly to break away from the Isthmian League Club and start afresh.'

Excerpt from the 'History' section on Enfield Town's website.

Not all teams matter because of their performance on the pitch. Undoubtedly in the 2001-02 season Enfield Town Football Club could lay claim to a very successful year. Winners of three separate cup competitions and runners up in the Essex Senior League, Enfield Town could also boast the league's top goalscorer in Daniel Clarke who hit 46 goals in all competitions. Even though they finished second in the Essex Senior League to Leyton, they had also broken the leagues all time scoring record by one and finished some sixteen points ahead of third placed Burnham Ramblers.

The real story of Enfield Town's year lay in events off the pitch however. The 2001-02 season was in reality Enfield Town's first ever, the club formed officially on the 23rd June 2001. Their conception was unique; the first club to be formed by a breakaway supporter's trust and begin again in the face of financial and personal problems with the running of the original club still in existence – Enfield FC. The disharmony really began in 1999 and after two years of poor treatment and an owner unwilling to listen, a group of fans decided they'd had enough.

Enfield Football Club has a history and level of recognition many non-league and amateur clubs would die for. Formed in 1893 as Enfield Spartans they enjoyed success throughout their time in the lower leagues. Winners of the F.A. Amateur Cup in 1967 and 1970, F.A. Trophy winners in 1982 and 1988, amateur league winners twelve times and regular local cup competition winners - the club was legitimately one of the biggest non-league clubs in existence. In 1999 the decision was taken to sell the Southbury Road stadium they had been located at since 1936. It was this act that would eventually mark the downfall of one club and ultimately the formation of two new ones.

The sale left Enfield FC homeless. After sharing grounds with several local clubs the lack of stability was telling so a long-term option was taken up in Borehamwood. Ten miles away from the borough of Enfield, the move brought about an immediate decline on and off the pitch. Supporters were unwilling to travel outside of the area to watch their 'local' team and they dropped down the table almost as fast as their match-day revenue figures. As details of the ground share and its long-term nature emerged, there was genuine concern that Enfield would be left without a football club in its borough.

Unhappy with the running of the club and the performance on the pitch, a group of concerned supporters rallied and began work to ensure a more successful future for Enfield. The main purpose of forming the group would be to return the club to the borough of Enfield by finding it a new home. Working jointly with the council three possible locations within the borough of Enfield were identified. Despite this the chairman and hierarchy wouldn't act upon them. Undeterred the group formalised themselves and became The Enfield Supporters Trust, this time hoping to gain control of the club for themselves. Despite tabling a deal to take over the club that would have left Enfield debt free and in the hands of the fans, the chairman was still unwilling to act decisively.

Feeling they were left with no option and working closely with the newly formed Supporters Direct organisation, the decision was taken to break away from Enfield Football Club and form their own team based in the borough. Working their own ground share deal with local team Brimsdown Rovers at the Goldsdown Road stadium and now elected into the Essex Senior League, Enfield Town Football Club was officially born. Taking a reasonable support with them, the success in 2001-02 was testament to a group of fans unwilling to accept what they saw as mismanagement of the club they loved.

Enfield Football Club continued to decline on the pitch in the wake of the split. Relegated in 2003 and then again in 2004, the club moved to Wodson Park in Ware and tried to regain some of its former glory. The chairman and board parted ways with Enfield FC and an F.A. hearing decreed the club were owed a reasonable sum of money from the sale of Southbury Road by the outgoing management. At the end of the 2006-07 season Enfield chose to resign from the Isthmian League Division One North to remove the unrealistic debts created by the previous management. Reformed and renamed as Enfield 1893 Football Club, the club entered the Essex Senior League themselves and from the ashes of one club, two were now trying to flourish in the local area.

Following their lead groups of supporters would react in 2002 to moving Wimbledon Football Club to Milton Keynes by forming AFC Wimbledon in the local area. Once more it showed how fans could have their say in what has to be considered the ultimate protest. By creating a team in spite of the original's existence the fans had had the ultimate say. In 2005 following the Glazer's acquisition of Manchester United, the blueprint was once again followed and Football Club United of Manchester (F.C. United) were born.

These three clubs are by no means the only examples of 'breakaway' teams but Enfield Town and their work with Supporters Direct undoubtedly laid the foundations and blueprints that others have followed. Currently football is reacting to financial constraints worldwide and 'phoenix' clubs are rising from the remains of dissolved clubs such as Chester City and Scarborough. In nearly every case they are working on the supporters trust/fan controlled model established by Enfield Town whether their club still exists or not.

There has been some talk of a merger between the two clubs now based in Enfield but established with their own identities, both clubs seem keen to move forward independently. Importantly, both clubs are now playing in the borough of Enfield. Enfield Town had been playing at the Goldsdown Road ground but secured permission to use and redevelop the nearby Queen Elizabeth Athletics Stadium. Officially opened on November 16th 2011 with a friendly against Tottenham Hotspur, Enfield Town now have their permanent home at the QE2 athletics stadium in the borough a mere stroll away from the site of their old Southbury Road ground.

Meanwhile Enfield 1893 were forced to ground share with Broxbourne Borough V & E for a spell and having had their own bid for the QE2 stadium denied, they now occupy the Goldsdown Road stadium themselves. The club merged with Brimsdown Rovers in 2010 and now have a permanent residence in the borough just like Enfield Town and again, they are only a short walk from the original Southbury Road Stadium. The merger and finding themselves a permanent home had an immediate impact as they took the Essex Senior League title in 2011 but failed to gain promotion to the Isthmian League due to improvements needed to the ground. With time the work will be done and both clubs will continue to climb the non-league ladder as high as fortune takes them.

The creation of Enfield Town is proof of a football club's links to its locale and that the supporters can make a difference. Their legacy has culminated in the formation of admittedly higher profile teams, AFC Wimbledon becoming the first supporter's trust model club to achieve full league status in 2011 with promotion to League Two via a play-off. Taking that in to consideration it should never be forgotten that the fans of Enfield Football Club were the first to say 'no' to their owners in the modern era in the most spectacular way possible and succeed.

Korea Republic 2002

Honours

Semi-finalist at 2002 World Cup held jointly between Japan & South Korea

Date					
		Group D			
04.06.02	South Korea	2	v	0	Poland
10.06.02	South Korea	1	v	1	USA
14.06.02	Portugal	0	v	1	South Korea
		Second Round			
18.06.02	South Korea	2	v	1	Italy
		Quarter-Final			
22.06.02	Spain	0	v	0	South Korea (P)
		Semi-Final			
25.06.02	Germany	1	v	0	South Korea
		Third Place Play-Off			
29.06.02	South Korea	2	v	3	Turkey

South Korea's results in full from 2002 World Cup

Every World Cup leaves a legacy in the hosting country. The 2010 tournament in South Africa was so much more than just a football competition for the hosts. It was confirmation of their growth as a country in both sporting and political terms. While some World Cup hosts are chosen because of their country's affinity and support for the game such as England or Italy, others are chosen because it gives the game the chance to make a real impact in a relatively new area. The USA benefited enormously from this approach after hosting the 1994 World Cup, now boasting a competitive national side and a thriving professional league. In awarding the 2002 tournament to a joint bid from Japan and South Korea

FIFA were not quite dealing with American levels of apathy to the game, but they were looking to develop football in a continent that still had untapped potential.

As FIFA's decision in awarding the tournament loomed in 1996, Asia emerged as the continent with the strongest chance of hosting 2002's World Cup. South Korea, Japan and China all prepared bids that surpassed their South American rivals, promising vast amounts of money and new facilities to cater for FIFA's prestige event. Eventually, after persuading an eager South Korea and Japan to re-launch a bid to each co-host, FIFA's delegates had a relatively easy decision to make in awarding them the competition jointly. The decision was met with huge enthusiasm across Asia as they now had the chance to stage a truly global sporting event. Having enjoyed individual cities holding the Olympic Games and several world youth tournaments, the continent now had a chance to impress on a bigger scale than ever before.

Football in Asia was only really being fully embraced and professionalized in the latter stages of the 20th Century. Asian football operates under the banner of the AFC (Asian Football Confederation) and has enjoyed some notable footnotes in World Cup history but little true success. In 1966 North Korea stunned the world by qualifying from their group and beating the mighty Italy along the way at the finals in England. Despite the huge upset, their naivety came to the fore as they then cruised into a 3-0 lead in the quarter final against Portugal, only to go on and lose 5-3. Saudi Arabia also represented the confederation at the finals in 1994 and reached the second round but their main entry into football folklore was an incredible goal scored by Saeed Al-Owairan. In a tight group game against Belgium, Owairan picked up the ball with only five minutes gone midway in his own half. He then dribbled the length of the pitch beating five men along the way before lifting the ball over Michel Preud'homme for a sensational solo effort.

Internationally speaking the World Cup had given little more than experience to Asia's teams, the Asian Cup representing their best chance of winning a tournament. Held every four years since the inaugural competition in 1956, the Cup took over from the Asian Games as the continent's premier championship. Up until 2002 the competition had been dominated by South Korea, Iran, Saudi Arabia and Japan. Only Israel and Kuwait had taken the trophy away from the four more established countries. With a distinct lack of any real success globally and arguably a lack of competition from within, even as hosts there was very little expected from Japan or South Korea or Asia's other representatives at the 2002 tournament – Saudi Arabia and China.

Both the host countries had taken huge strides to develop the professional game in their recent footballing history. Japan's J-League had been launched as the country's first fully professional men's league in 1993, providing major competition with sumo for the population's sporting affection. Another one of the biggest sporting obsessions in Japan was baseball and it was this passionate support and drama that football immediately made inroads into. After the expected initial explosion and blaze of publicity, the league had settled and managed to maintain healthy crowds and keep standards improving on the pitch.

The move to full professionalism was also benefiting the Japanese national side as a steady stream of talented players emerged, some then moving into European football to further their experience. Hidetoshi Nakata had success in Italy with Perugia, Roma and Parma, and after the 2002 tournament also played for Fiorentina and Bolton Wanderers. Junichi Inamoto played in England with Arsenal and Fulham and midfielder Shinji Ono became an established member of Feyenoord's Eredivisie squad. More experienced than ever before and buoyed by the rampant home crowd at the 2002 World Cup, Japan qualified impressively though Group H – beating Russia and Tunisia and gaining a very credible draw with Belgium. Despite a huge ground swell of support they fell short in the second round and went out after a 1-0 loss to Turkey.

South Korea had a footballing head start on their co-hosts. Officially recognised as the Korea Republic by FIFA, they could boast a far more successful international history than the Japanese who were playing in only their second World Cup. South Korea's first appearance had been as far back as 1954 where they had the ignominious honour of conceding 16 goals in just two games – a World Cup record. It had then taken 32 years to qualify for their next tournament, 1986's World Cup in Mexico. Since then they had managed to qualify for every subsequent World Cup up until their own in 2002. Even in the face of a poor record – 14 games, 0 wins, 4 points across 5 tournaments – South Korea were well placed to make a bigger mark in 2002.

Domestically the professional game had arrived with the five team K-League in 1983. By 2002 the league had expanded to ten and following the national team had become an obsession for the supporters club – 'the Red Devils'. With a talented pool of players to pick from a strong K-League, it was inevitable as had happened with Japan that some would move abroad to further their careers. With players making inroads in the leagues of Holland, Italy and Japan, South Korea now had a team to try to match the huge levels of expectation raised by the World Cup. With so many elements seemingly in their favour to improve on their previous World Cup results, they now needed a manager with the talent to draw the very best from the team.

With no qualification campaign to overcome as hosts, Dutchman Guus Hiddink was selected and appointed as the man to lead South Korea into the World Cup. Hiddink had served his managerial apprenticeship with PSV, eventually leading them to European Cup glory in 1988 and cementing his growing reputation as one of the best coaches in Europe. After spells in Turkey and Spain, Hiddink took over the Dutch national team and led them to defeat against France on penalties in the quarterfinals of Euro'96. Still in charge at the 1998 World Cup in France, he led his talented Holland side through Group E – including a 5-0 rout of South Korea – and to another heartbreaking penalty shootout, this time at the semi-final stage to Brazil. Hiddink's teams attacked but coupled invention with high work rate, traits which took him from the national job to Real Madrid. After an unhappy time with Los Blancos and then Real Betis, by late 2000 he was without a job. With South Korean manager Huh Jung-Moo attracting criticism for his team selection and Asian Cup failure, plans were made and Hiddink was approached to take over the position. On January 1st 2001 Guus Hiddink's contract as full coach of the South Korean national side began, a tenure that would last 18 months and end with a stadium named in his honour.

As the nation geared up for the upcoming World Cup, Hiddink's reign began to attract criticism for an apparent lack of commitment. With little competitive football available, South Korea's performance in friendlies was disappointing. After the 2001 Confederations Cup the reality of the task was plain to see. Despite edging Mexico and Australia in their group, a 5-0 hammering by France saw their goal difference plummet and no progression. To compound matters, Japan had beaten Cameroon and Canada convincingly in their group and forced a goalless draw with Brazil to end their campaign at the top. After a semi-final victory over Australia, France only just shaded the Japanese 1-0 to take the cup. Hiddink's team were seen as having the far greater potential but were just not living up to it.

After accepting an invitation into the 2002 CONCACAF Gold Cup to give the squad a further chance of tournament football, Hiddink and his team needed to improve to justify the growing support South Korea were gathering. The Gold Cup was held in America and having been invited from outside the CONCACAF federation along with Ecuador, the Koreans finished in fourth place. Although the standard of competition was nothing like they had faced in the Confederations Cup, they'd been unlucky to lose to a last minute goal to the hosts, but emerged from the opening defeat to show glimpses of potential. They continued to improve gradually in a series of friendlies leading up to the tournament, including a convincing wins over Finland and Scotland, and good draws against Turkey and England.

With the domestic schedule cleared by the Korean FA to allow Hiddink as much time as possible to work with his players, the squad was selected and given time to become comfortable with each other. South Korea couldn't lay claim to football superstars but that's not to say they lacked talent as a collective. Guus Hiddink worked closely with his assistant Pim Verbeek to mould the squad into the hardest working team at the tournament. Any perceived inadequacies they had were more than outweighed by their industry. Using Hiddink's instructions and the adrenaline created by the atmosphere, South Korea's athleticism became the key feature of their tournament and made them consistently more dangerous then any opposition gave them credit for.

The World Cup draw saw South Korea seeded into a challenging Group D with Poland, Portugal and the United States. By the day of their first game on the 4th June against Poland, the whole country had come to standstill to watch. An estimated five million people took to the streets to watch the game on specially constructed big screens in city centres and fan parks. With merchandise emblazoned with the motto 'Be the Reds!' filling every corner of shops and stalls in the cities, the country became a sea of crimson as kick off approached. With everything in place for the tournament to be a huge success as a whole, all that was left was team to live up to expectations and qualify from the group.

As the game started in front of a bouncing Busan Asiad Stadium, Poland took the early initiative. Midfielder Jacek Krzynowek and striker Emmanuel Olisadebe both went close to the breakthrough. Unable to score despite enjoying the greater possession, Poland began to realise they were up against a team who would chase every loose ball down. The longer the game stayed goalless, the more South Korea grew in confidence. On 26 minutes the country erupted as they scored their first goal of the tournament and took the lead. After breaking down the left, a one-two found winger Lee Eul-Yong with space to pick a cross towards the waiting Hwang Sun-Hong. The striker took the opportunity first time and cushioned a volley inside Jerzy Dudek's near post. The atmosphere in the stadium exploded and Poland looked visibly shaken by the noise now coursing through the arena.

Into the second half Poland struggled to make inroads into a now confident and flowing South Korean midfield. Park Ji-Sung would emerge from this tournament with a huge reputation, further enhanced by moves to first PSV Eindhoven and then Manchester United. He was proving to be thorn in Poland's side and drew a magnificent save from Dudek early in the second half. With each passing minute South Korea looked more in control and on 53 minutes had the second their pressure deserved. Central midfielder Yoo Sang-Chul pounced on a loose ball twenty-five yards from goal and fired a hopeful shot towards the Polish goal. After several good saves in the game, Dudek misjudged the flight of the ball and only succeeded in helping it on its way in. If a 1-0 lead had caused bedlam, 2-0 caused near pandemonium in and around the stadium.

As the game played out South Korea were unlucky not to have added to the score. A combination of poor finishing and Dudek atoning for his mistake just about kept them out. At the final whistle Hiddink had succeeded in making his team believe what their fans did – they could win. South Korea had their first ever victory in the World Cup finals. The next game against the USA couldn't come quick enough for a baying public and the team were now on the crest of a wave.

Six days later the party moved to Daegu and over 60,000 supporters turned the brand new stadium into a bright red cauldron for the USA. With a fever pitch level of excitement the Koreans started brightly but froze and fell behind. American full back Frankie Hejduk's clever ball found Clint Mathis, whose control was excellent, his finish clinical. With drums beating and nearly every voice in unison the pressure grew on both teams for very different reasons. Finishing the first half still 1-0 behind, South Korea had contrived to carve out chances and miss a penalty as they searched for the equaliser. Having been beaten in the Gold Cup by the Americans the tension increased in the second half as the game dripped towards the host's first defeat.

Goalkeeper Brad Friedel was in excellent form to deny a growingly anxious South Korea. With 12 minutes left Lee Eul-Yong floated a free kick into the penalty area hopefully. Substitute Ahn Jung-Hwan rose and met the cross with a glancing header. The touch was just enough to divert the ball past Friedel and an ecstatic and relieved crowd rejoiced. Earning the point turned Ahn Jung-Hwan into a hero and it was going to prove to be an eventful World Cup for the striker. Going into the last game South Korea sat proudly atop Group D knowing just a point would be enough to secure passage to the second round. Standing in their way were Portugal's so called 'Golden Generation' who had just put 4 past Poland. The Portuguese knew only a win would guarantee their own passage and despite another full and intimidating stadium at Incheon, the odds favoured the Europeans.

South Korea played brilliantly for the first 70 minutes and completely frustrated their more accomplished opponents. In the 26th minute Portugal's exasperation boiled over and João Pinto received a straight red for a horrible lunge at Park Ji-Sung. Despite remaining goalless South Korea were very much in the ascendancy and went close several times. In the 66th minute Portugal's task began to look impossible as they lost another man, fullback Beto who received his second yellow card. Just 4 minutes later Park Ji-Sung scored an excellent goal to all but seal their passage to the next round. Despite having to weather a nine-man Portuguese storm for the last 20 minutes, South Korea survived and topped the group with seven points. They had matched their country's enthusiasm with results. Ahead of them lay a tough fixture with European giants Italy.

The Italians weathered a frenetic start and another missed South Korean penalty to take a 1-0 lead. Christian Vieri's near post header looked to have given them a mountain to climb. The Italians reverted to type looking to retain possession and defend but they were becoming increasingly frustrated at a series of refereeing decisions they felt went against them. On the hour striker Alessandro Del Piero was substituted for defensive midfielder Gennaro Gattuso and it seemed Italy were now only intent on seeing the 1-0 win through. As desperately as the Koreans continued to attack, the Italian back line under the watchful eye of captain Paulo Maldini held firm.

With just 2 minutes to go the unthinkable happened. As a hopeful ball dropped comfortably to Christian Panucci in the Italian penalty area, the normally faultless defender inexplicably mis-controlled and presented it to Seol Ki-Hyeon. The midfielder's snap shot went through Panucci's despairing tumble and in for a vital equaliser. The stadium erupted into ecstasy as the drama of extra-time with a possible golden goal loomed. Suddenly the Italians realised they were up against it as Vieri missed an open goal, Francesco Totti picked up an extremely harsh second yellow card for diving and finally a perfectly good Italian goal was ruled out for offside. The rising atmosphere was clearly affecting them and their discipline was gone. With 3 minutes left Lee Young-Pyo's deep cross found Ahn Jung-Hwan for the golden goal that took South Korea through to the quarter-finals.

The nation erupted into a mass street party. Over a 1.5 million people descended on Seoul and turned the city red. The Italians left in acrimony, citing conspiracy and even telling goalscorer Jung-Hwan he wouldn't be welcome back at the Italian club that employed him – Perugia. No one in South Korea cared about any of that at the moment, Hiddink's men had done the impossible and everyone was invited to the party.

If the Italy game had seen lady luck favour South Korea, the quarter-final against Spain saw her fall in love with them. As a dour 0-0 moved into extra time, the decisions falling in the Koreans favour mounted up. By full time and with a penalty shoot out ahead Spain had seen several offsides wrongly given, a Fernando Morientes header incorrectly ruled out and an own goal disallowed for a foul seen only by the referee. With the crowd creating an intense atmosphere for the Spanish penalty takers, man of the match Joaquin missed and Hong Myung-Bo scored to take South Korea to the semi-finals. With another European side leaving in controversial circumstances the Red Devils carried the party on nationwide, the sky filled with fireworks and a semi final with Germany in Seoul lay ahead.

South Korea's final two games in the competition felt like a let down compared to the drama that had preceded them. Germany proved to be up to the task of the onslaught on the pitch and from the stands. In the white-hot atmosphere they defended well throughout, silenced the crowd and their big players used their experience well. As Korea chased and harried, Germany gently probed and passed their way into the game. After taking the sting out of the match they moved through the gears in the second half to eventually lead in the 75th minute, their playmaker Michael Ballack following up his own shot and scoring a decisive goal. From that moment on Germany stayed professional and retained the ball well, the final whistle meaning a nation had been denied its dream.

The crowd reacted with an incredible ovation for their heroes. Even another defeat in the third place play-off against Turkey couldn't tarnish their fantastic campaign. Each and every member of the team had carved their place in the country's football history and were hailed as national idols for achieving what had been seen as impossible. They had surpassed all expectations and delivered the passionate crowd more than it had dared to dream for. The World Cup stadium in Gwangju where Spain had been beaten in that dramatic shoot-out was renamed the Guus Hiddink Stadium but the enigmatic manager was leaving a country that had now fallen in love with him. He had seen his stock rise worldwide and tellingly, among his first signings when back at PSV were Park Ji-Sung and Lee Young-Pyo.

Rarely has a team so captivated a nation and for that fact alone they matter. Football in Asia boomed once again on the back of hosting a World Cup but it had been South Korea's performance that had showed what could be possible. In 2006 South Korea qualified for the finals in Germany but failed to get through their group, 2010's tournament meant the nation had qualified for their seventh straight finals. Both Japan and South Korea qualified for the second round of the tournament before narrow defeats. Asian football is now considered alongside the rest of the world as more than competitive where once it had been thought of as no threat at all. South Korea had rode their luck but earned their crowd's support tenfold. In an age when people often make comments regarding how long it will be before we see an African World Cup winner, perhaps the same question should now be levelled towards the continent of Asia.

FC Porto
2002–04

Honours

Portuguese Liga
Winners 02/03 & 03/04

Cup of Portugal
Winners 02/03

Portuguese
SuperCup Winners
2003 & 2004

UEFA Cup Winners
02/03

UEFA Champions
League Winners
03/04

'Please don't call me arrogant, but I'm European champion and I think I'm a special one,'

José Mourinho speaking at his first press conference as Chelsea Manager

The name José Mourinho will conjure up different emotions across a range of football fans. For some he is the antithesis of the game – arrogant, only interested in self-promotion and never willing to shoulder the blame for defeat. For others he is a genius, a tactical mastermind with the Midas touch and the trophies to back up his claims. As with most polarising issues the truth probably lays somewhere in between but what is without doubt, is that Mourinho can never be discussed as anything other than a proven winner.

Before taking the reigns at Porto in 2002 he had already enjoyed a colourful career. His father José Manuel Félix had been a goalkeeper at Vitória F.C. and Belenenses, earning one cap for Portugal during his playing days. It was obvious early on though that José Junior was never going to follow his dad and play at the highest level. Realising shortly into his playing career that the second division in Portugal was as high as his skills were ever going to take him, he studied Sports Science and Physical Education at a university level. Then whilst working as a P.E. teacher in Lisbon, he earned his coaching badges and worked his way back into football. After youth team positions and an assistant coaching role in and around Portugal's lower leagues, he came onto Bobby Robson's radar as a translator employed to work with the Englishman at Sporting CP.

Robson realised early that Mourinho had the potential for more than just translation and after moving to F.C Porto in 1992, brought him across as part of his backroom team. Between them they won the Cup of Portugal in 1994 and then the Portuguese Liga in 94/95 and 95/96. Robson's stock had now risen considerably, producing attacking and free-flowing teams complimented by the emerging Mourinho's defensive work. In the summer of '96 Robson was appointed manager of Barcelona and as part of the deal 'el tradutor' (the translator) came with him. Now working closely with the team and heavily involved in coaching, Mourinho outlasted Robson who left after two years with the club. Despite an offer in 1999 to follow his former mentor to Newcastle United, the partnership had run its course for José who was busy carving his own reputation for fastidious attention to tactical detail. After three years in Catalonia as a number two to Robson and Louis van Gaal, Mourinho was ready to become a number one and that desire would take him back to Portugal.

Shortly after taking charge at Benfica Mourinho had his first brush with controversy. After a change of club president and an ultimatum, Mourinho left after only eleven games in management. Already showing signs he was unwilling to beat someone else's drum, he had a new job within weeks as manager at União de Leiria. After a successful end to the season in which he guided the club to their highest ever league finish, he entered 2002 as the leading candidate to replace the departing Octávio Machado at FC Porto. Fondly remembered from his time under Robson, he took over half way through the 01/02 season and pushed Porto into finishing third and qualifying for the UEFA Cup. 2002/03 was to be his first full season in charge of a leading club and Mourinho was about to make his biggest impact yet.

With a modest budget to shape his team, new players were bought into the squad that fitted the team ethos. Built on a pressing game that forced every player to close the ball down from front to back, Mourinho was only interested in players who could fit his system. After promising Porto's fans he would make them champions, he published training reports on the club website to show both the teams progress and his intensely detailed approach to preparation. His squad already boasted Portuguese international goalkeeper Vítor Baía along with talented centre-backs Ricardo Carvalho and Jorge Costa, who was recalled from a loan spell at Charlton Athletic. Mourinho also inherited defensive midfielder Costinha, another international who would play the best football of his career over the next two years.

Going forward Mourinho knew he had one real crown jewel in Brazilian midfielder Deco. Given the job of playmaker, the midfielder revelled in the role and even repatriated himself to play in the same position for Portugal in 2003. At the head of Porto's attack sat a new recruit, Brazilian striker Derlei who Mourinho took from his former club UD Leiria along with full back Nuno Valente, joining Portuguese U21-international Hélder Postiga in trying to provide the goals. Also midfielder Maniche moved to Porto after problems at Benfica and fullback Paulo Ferreira joined from Vitória ready for the new season to begin.

The 2002-03 season was a phenomenal success for Porto. Warming up for the year with a SuperCup success over UD Leiria, the league was then won with ease. Porto only lost two games over the season, recorded the highest ever points total in the league's history and finished eleven points clear of Benfica – the club who let Mourinho go. They also completed a double by beating UD Leiria again, this time in the final of the Cup of Portugal. Their cup run had been as dominant as their league form, twelve goals scored and only one conceded in four games. Domestically they had been without compare but it was in Europe where they were set to make the biggest headlines. After a rousing 4-1 aggregate win over Italians Lazio in the semi, Porto had made their first ever UEFA Cup final.

FC Porto's fans travelled to Seville for the game against Celtic dwarfed by an enormous Scottish contingent that had made the trip regardless of the small matter of a ticket. Porto had plenty to be weary of from the Scottish champions, in particular Swedish striker Henrik Larsson. A slow first half ended with Derlei scoring on the stroke of half time to give Porto the lead but a flurry of goals in the first fifteen minutes of the second half saw the scores level at 2-2. Larsson's two headers for Celtic and Russian international Dmitri Alenichev's tap in remained the only goals of the second half and the tie moved into extra time. With Celtic down to ten after Bobo Baldé's red card, Derlei's second goal with just five minutes to go gave Porto a 3-2 victory and Portugal's first ever UEFA Cup winners.

Porto's success and their charismatic coach had not gone unnoticed. The manager and several of his players were now linked to Europe's top clubs but Mourinho had no intention of going yet. He kept the spine of his team together and looked to improve in certain areas before and during the season. South African striker Benni McCarthy had a successful loan spell at Porto in Mourinho's first half season in charge in 2002, after selling Postiga to English club Tottenham Hotspur the fee was used to buy McCarthy outright from Celta Vigo. Carlos Alberto was signed from Fluminense and Pedro Mendes from Vitória to add to Deco's guile in attack. José Bosingwa also moved from Boavista as cover at full back.

After another SuperCup victory, the 03/04 league was retained with the same ease it had been won the year before. Once more it was Benfica in second place and once more Porto only lost two league games over the season. Such had been their dominance that the league had been secured with five weeks left to play. McCarthy took the league's top scorer with twenty goals in just twenty-three games and Deco became the player of the year. They just missed out on another double by losing to Benfica in the Cup of Portugal final but by that point they were going for another prize, an unprecedented European double after their UEFA Cup in Seville.

In the Champions League Mourinho had his chance to mix with the very best of Europe. Delighting in the opportunity he quickly gained a reputation as an astute tactician with a very talented squad. Drawn into a Group F with Real Madrid, Marseille and Partizan, many expected Porto to exit the competition before troubling the knock out stages. After a draw away to Partizan, Madrid came to Portugal and left with a 3-1 victory that proved to be a turning point for both Mourinho and his players. Winning their next three group games, including an away win in Marseille, Porto earned qualification from the group and ended with a draw in the Bernabéu. Their second place finish earned them a tie with Manchester United and a chance for Mourinho to go head to head with one of the best managers in the world, Sir Alex Ferguson. The game would also bring Mourinho to England where Chelsea were already casting admiring glances his way despite current manager Claudio Ranieri's position at the club.

At home in Estádio do Dragão for the first leg, Porto played well and contained United to earn a 2-1 win thanks to McCarthy's two goals. Still expected to lose in the away leg at Old Trafford, things were looking tough when a Paul Scholes header gave Man United a thirty-second minute lead. United also had a first half goal ruled out when replays suggested Scholes had been two yards onside. Despite the pressure United's second goal never came and both teams entered second half injury time knowing a goal either way ended the tie. United's one away goal put them in the box seat but if Porto scored United had to score again with no time left to force extra time. With the tie on a knife-edge Phil Neville brought down Edgar Jankauskas to gift Porto a free kick thirty yards from goal with just a minute left. United goalkeeper Tim Howard parried McCarthy's strike but Costinha swept in the loose ball to give Porto the aggregate lead. Mourinho sprinted down the Old Trafford touchline and joined his players in the corner, celebrating a famous victory over a genuine European giant and placing himself firmly in the Premier League's shop window.

Now in the quarterfinals and brimming with confidence, Porto swept past Lyon into the last four. A 2-0 home win in the first leg and two goals from Maniche in France gave Porto a 4-2 aggregate victory. Playing at the top of their game they'd never fallen behind in one hundred and eighty minutes of football. In a year of Champions League upsets the familiar names tumbled from the competition just as Manchester United had. AS Monaco beat Real Madrid, AC Milan went out despite leading Deportivo La Coruña 4-1 from the first leg and the new money at Chelsea knocked out the unbeaten in the league Arsenal in the all-English quarterfinal. Suddenly FC Porto found themselves one of the form sides in Europe and still left in the competition.

Still rumours mentioning Mourinho and Chelsea in the same sentence surfaced in spite of a possible Champions League final meeting between the two. Porto edged an incredibly tight semi-final against Deportivo La Coruña after a goal less draw at home in the first leg. Having learned the lesson not to concede the killer away goal, the second leg in Spain was another defensive affair until Cesar's clumsy challenge on Deco in the second half. Derlei's fifty-seventh minute penalty effectively gave Porto a two-goal lead. For the rest of the game the team that had just beaten AC Milan 4-0 couldn't break down a resolute Porto defence. Mourinho had now taken his side to a second European final in two years.

In the other semi AS Monaco put five past Chelsea over two legs to all but seal Ranieri's fate. Whilst Monaco provided Porto the perceived weaker opponents in the final, Chelsea's exit ramped up their interest in Mourinho. Whilst the story had run for weeks on the back pages citing Chelsea's interest if Ranieri failed to meet their expectations, Liverpool, Real Madrid and several other clubs were also investigating Mourinho's position. Although he admitted that he would be interested in managing a club 'like' Liverpool, Chelsea had a shortlist of one and a position that afforded Mourinho a bottomless pit to build his own side. The Champions League exit and some strange tactical decisions had given the Chelsea board the impetus to remove Ranieri despite being well on the way to their best ever Premier League finish, in short the Italian's days were numbered. Stories of Chelsea Chief Executive Peter Kenyon and Abramovich himself flying to Europe for one to one meetings with Mourinho emerged and as the days dragged on, it appeared more and more likely that Chelsea were not going to take no for an answer.

On the 26th May 2004, Gelsenkirchen in Germany buzzed with fans of FC Porto and Monaco as Europe braced itself for a final with an unfamiliar feel. Monaco had their fair share of talented players, Spanish striker Fernando

Morientes was currently top scorer in the tournament with nine, while strike partner Dado Prso sat just behind with seven. Both strikers had benefited from the brilliance of captain Ludovic Giuly who along with Jérôme Rothen played on Monaco's flanks. For the final Monaco sought to match Porto's 4-3-3 with of their own but while Porto's front three consisted of two strikers and Deco playing just behind, Monaco left Prso on the bench with Morientes to be supported from a wider positions by Giuly and Rothen. Both sides played out a cagey opening, neither willing to over commit in the early stages. Monaco had been high scoring throughout the tournament but they were finding Porto's defence difficult to break down under the spotlights in the Arena AufSchalke.

On twenty-two minutes Monaco captain Giuly limped off with a groin injury. With the Frenchmen now shorn of their talisman Porto took control and then the lead. After the ball ricocheted in the penalty area to Carlos Alberto his snapshot flew past Flavio Roma in the Monaco goal to give Porto a half-time lead. The only non-Portuguese national in Porto's staring line-up, his inclusion as Derlei's strike partner over McCarthy had now been justified. Into the second half Monaco tried to force themselves back into the game. As they pushed for the equaliser Porto looked to counter attack. As another attack broke down in Porto's half the ball found its way to Deco who fed Alenichev. As he looked to pull the ball back Deco dropped off into in space and the Russian nudged it across to the playmaker. Deco controlled and then passed the ball into the goal for 2-0. Deco now had a fitting reward for another man of the match performance. Just four minutes later in the seventy-fifth minute the game was effectively over. Another counter attack found Derlei and Alenichev with the freedom of Germany to operate in. Derlei's deflected pass found Alenichev who finished emphatically.

At the final whistle Mourinho was never pictured celebrating with his team. After months of speculation and rumour, Mourinho admitted in television interviews that he wanted to leave Porto now he had brought them to the pinnacle of European football. The day after the game came the first public admission that he wanted to manage Chelsea and negotiations officially began. Kenyon met with Porto directors and agreed compensation for taking their manager, Mourinho and his agent Jorge Mendes negotiated the terms of his contract with Chelsea. On June 2nd, exactly one week after leading Porto to Champions League victory, Chelsea confirmed they had appointed Mourinho and made him the highest paid football manager in the world. He would go on to bring them two league titles, two League Cups and an FA Cup before leaving in 2007 amidst rumours of a collapse in his relationship with Abramovich. From Chelsea he would move to Internazionale where he enjoyed a further Champions League trophy in 2010, taken as part of a treble with the Serie A title and the Coppa Italia.

Mourinho's FC Porto side had gone from a group of hard-working professionals to a team of world-class players in his two and a half years at the club. Deco would also leave in the summer of 2004 for Barcelona after becoming one of the hottest properties in world football. Despite an offer to join his former manager in London, he chose Spain and would go on to win the Champions League again in 2006. Full back Ferreira and centre back Carvalho did go with Mourinho to Chelsea, both establishing themselves in the first team. Pedro Mendes also arrived in London but with Spurs as his employers and popular Russian Alenichev returned to Moscow to play for Spartak. The golden era under 'the special one' had ended. Mourinho returned to Porto the following year after Chelsea were drawn into the same Champions League group as the holders. After defeat at Stamford Bridge, Porto won the home game against Chelsea to qualify from the group in second place. They were then knocked out in the last sixteen by Internazionale of Italy and their fantastic European run was over.

Mourinho continues to divide opinion but in the time he spent at FC Porto he created something nobody expected. The team he inherited in 2002 had no idea that their new manager was about to change the course of their careers. Egotistical and outspoken, he brought the club seven trophies in two glorious seasons and took them to the very top of European football from a position of also-rans. Now with hindsight it has become a little clearer that when he proclaimed himself the 'special one' upon joining Chelsea, he may just have been on to something.

Arsenal FC 2003--04

Honours

Premier League Champions

	Pld	W	D	L	GF	GA	GD	Pts
1. Arsenal	38	26	12	0	73	26	47	90

Arsenal's league record at the end of the 2003/04 season

Until the 15th May 2004, only one team could lay claim to having been truly invincible in the English league. In the first season of the newly formed Football League (1888-89), Preston North End earned the title after going a full season without losing a game. The term Invincibles had originally been a sarcastic jibe at the amount of 'non-English' players Preston had brought to play football at the club. With a large number of Scottish professionals in their ranks, Preston mauled a 12-team league to finish eleven points clear of Aston Villa. Scoring 74 goals in the process they were almost unplayable when attacking at their best but a defensive record of less than a goal a game conceded shows the gulf at either end of the pitch between them and everyone else. Added to this new League trophy they won the F.A. Cup without conceding a goal, beating Wolverhampton Wanderers 3-0 in a final played at the Kennington Oval in London. They would continue to dominate the domestic football landscape for the next five years, retaining their title in 1890 and finishing runners-up for the following three seasons but never able to repeat the feat of remaining undefeated.

In reality no team could match the feat across the Football League right up until it's evolution into the structure it now inhabits. The top division had grown from twelve teams to twenty two and in the 1992-93 inaugural Premier League season, Preston North End were relegated from what had become Division Two to the lowest tier of English football. At the other end of the scale the increased television revenues and restructure of England's top division brought an influx of money into the country's top teams. Manchester United and Aston Villa battled it out for the title, United eventually triumphing and Arsenal after a mediocre league season finished 10th.

Outside of the indifferent league campaign had been a very different story for this Arsenal team though. Lead by George Graham the teams efficient style had brought major success in the form of a double of both domestic trophies. A squad containing the likes of David Seaman, Ian Wright, Tony Adams, Paul Merson and David O'Leary won the Coca-Cola Cup in April and then followed it up with an FA Cup in May. Both finals had been against Sheffield Wednesday, the Coca-Cola Cup sealed with a 2-1 victory courtesy of a Steve Morrow winner. The FA Cup had been a little harder fought, Arsenal taken to a replay and then into extra time before a last minute winner from Andy Linighan gave them the cup double. The following year brought a far better League finish, 4th place, and a European trophy. The European Cup Winners Cup was won with a 1-0 victory in Copenhagen over holders and huge favourites Parma. Now regarded as cup specialists, Arsenal went into the 1994-95 season full of optimism and hopeful of pushing further up the league.

By November things had begun to unravel. Playmaker Paul Merson admitted himself into rehab for extensive addiction problems. The following February manager George Graham was sacked in the midst of allegations of financial-misdealing and Arsenal's season was in danger of total collapse. After steadying the ship in his caretaker position, Steward Houston guided Arsenal to another Cup Winners Cup final appearance that ended in disappointment after a 2-1 defeat by Real Zaragoza. At the season's close Bruce Rioch was appointed as Arsenal's new manager and once more league form had tailed off to a limp 12th place finish.

Now the rebuilding process began. England Captain David Platt was signed from Sampdoria for a record fee and shortly joined by enigmatic Dutchman Dennis Bergkamp. Bergkamp had just endured a torrid two years at Inter Milan and his reputation as a world-class player was in tatters. Arsenal performed better in the League and finished 5th qualifying for the UEFA Cup in the process. Bergkamp had a difficult start but his partnership with Ian Wright grew over the season and his 16 goals were a sign of things to come. Wright himself hadn't had the happiest of times, played out of position by Rioch with whom he then had a very public falling out. Rioch even talked about Arsenal playing better when Wright wasn't involved. Dropped from the side he handed in a transfer request that was initially refused.

After the nationwide euphoria of Euro'96 Arsenal optimistically looked forward to the 96-97 season hoping for stability and improvement. On the eve the opening day Rioch parted company with the club after a dispute over control of transfer funds and the refusal to employ the backroom staff he recommended. Suddenly Arsenal were in turmoil again and disillusionment grew amongst the Highbury faithful. By September they had their new man but he had a huge task ahead. Surprisingly, and to the derision of some, they had gone for a relative unknown whose main successes had just come in the Japanese J-League. The name of Arsène Wenger had been completely off the radar of most Arsenal fans and this softly spoken Frenchman would have some work to do to win them over in the light of recent upheavals.

Little known at the time, over the next six seasons Wenger would bring the Arsenal fans success and a brand of football they daren't hope for at the time of his appointment. Guiding them to third in the season he arrived part way through, the following year he brought the club a Premier League and FA Cup double, finally breaking Manchester United's stranglehold on domestic success. Clever signings, tactical intelligence and a loosening of the reigns for Arsenal's attacking players had brought immediate results. In the treble winning season of 98-99, Manchester United could only beat Arsenal once in five games between the sides. Arsenal missed retaining the league by one point and then missed retaining the FA Cup due to a Ryan Giggs wonder goal in the semi-final replay.

Off the pitch Wenger had revolutionised the club. Any trace of the infamous drinking culture at Arsenal had been removed, training facilities had been improved and Arsenal's players found themselves under inspection from nutritionists, psychologists and sports scientists. The nickname 'Professor' had been earned as much for his looks as his approach. Another two 'nearly' seasons included two cup final defeats caused Wenger to rethink and carry out a minor overhaul of his squad. The Arsenal's board's transfer outlay was rewarded with another double winning season in 2001-02.

Going into the 02-03 season Arsenal stood on the brink of dominating English football for some time to come. Pundits and critics alike were universal in their praise for exciting brand of attacking football that Arsenal employed regardless of the opposition. Going into the season, Wenger signed a new four-year contract and hopes were high – there was even talk of another treble winning side in the offing. Despite setting records for consecutive Premiership wins and dominating the first half of the season they couldn't shake off a resilient Manchester United side who whilst nowhere near as breathtaking as Arsenal in full flight, continued to clock up point after point. Despite sitting eight points clear in March, Arsenal's run-in exposed a flaw – an alleged soft underbelly, which saw Manchester United finish as champions, five points ahead of Arsenal. Despite retaining the FA Cup after another disappointing Champions League campaign which saw them go out to Valencia – perhaps the only side in Europe who could go stride for stride with Arsenal when it came to attacking football – the season felt anti-climatic. After promising so much it felt like an FA Cup was scant reward for the expectations everyone involved with the club had held.

Wenger believed in his squad and more importantly, his philosophy. David Seaman had kept goal for Arsenal in over 400 games but despite some brilliant performances in the FA Cup campaign, there was no doubting some of his mobility had been lost to age. Rather than an undignified end to his Highbury playing days, his contract was simply not renewed and he was allowed to leave with his head held high and hero status intact. Arsenal moved in eccentric German keeper Jens Lehmann to become their number one and he would play every minute of Arsenal's Premier League campaign. Several fringe players were allowed to leave either permanently or on long-term loans and every other player signed was considered one for the future. The names of Senderos, Clichy and in particular Fábregas, would all figure in Arsenal's first team eventually but this season was considered a little early for all to break through.

Entering the first day of the 2003-04 season, Wenger's side remained much the team of the last two years highs and lows. Defensively Sol Campbell remained the rock and the leader the rest of the defence was built around. Partnering him would be Kolo Touré, an Ivorian singed by Arsenal as a midfielder and full back. His pace and understanding with Campbell would be a revelation as the season progressed. Both first choice fullbacks Ashley Cole and Lauren would partner the aggression in the centre of defence admirably but also show their attacking flair on more than one occasion. Cover was provided in the centre by Pascal Cygan and veteran Martin Keown, Gael Clichy came in at left back when required and Touré moved to right back if needed. Even with ample cover Arsenal's first choice back four all made over thirty appearances in Arsenals thirty-eight game Premier League season.

With that foundation to build on Arsenal's midfield was allowed to cut loose and at times attack at will. Club captain Patrick Vieira had been the driving force behind so much of Arsenal's success since arriving from Milan's reserves in 1996. His raw aggression and fantastic close control had made him a legend to the Arsenal faithful long before the start of this campaign. Allowed to attack by the defensive work of Brazilian Gilberto, Vieira could be a devastating force and a key supply line to Arsenal's flair players. Robert Pirés on the left and Freddie Ljungberg on the right of midfield contributed twenty-nine goals between them, in part because of the protection afforded them by opposition midfield's trying to play central to keep Vieira's influence to a minimum. At times throughout the season Ray Parlour, Edu, and Sylvain Wiltord would cover and Edu and Wiltord would contribute a further eleven goals from a prosperous midfield.

Profiting from this supply line was striker Thierry Henry who would finish as Europe's top goalscorer, the PFA Players' Player of the Year, the Football Writers' Footballer of the Year and runner-up for the 2004 FIFA World Player of the Year. With Dennis Bergkamp playing just behind Henry the French striker was the cutting edge to Arsenal's midfield blade. Scoring thirty-nine times over the season, Henry was capable of getting all sorts of goals. Exceptional pace and an ability to move out to the left wing and then come back inside made him incredibly difficult for defences to pick up.

With a squad of players he was satisfied with and an attacking style Wenger believed could blow away most opposition, the 2003-04 campaign began with Arsenal once more earning the critic's praise for their performance. In their first home game of the season on the opening day, Everton were dispatched 2-1 despite Sol Campbell's red card for a desperate lunge at Thomas Gravesen in the 25th minute. Even though they had been down to ten the performance forced Everton manager David Moyes to admit that 'Henry occupies all the players at the back on his own'. Middlesbrough were put to the sword at The Riverside eight days later and conceded three in the first twenty-five minutes to an Arsenal side already approaching top gear. At the end of August Arsenal had played four Premier League games and already topped the league having won every one, scoring ten goals in the process.

September provided three games of real significance to Arsenal's season. On the 13th Portsmouth came to Highbury and took the game to the home team. Behind on twenty-six minutes to Teddy Sheringham's header, Arsenal were for once struggling to come up with the fluid passing that had become their reputation. Despite equalizing through a Henry penalty before half time, the lasting memory would be Pires allegedly diving to win it. Pires appeared to deliberately go over Stefanovic's outstretched leg when he could have easily evaded the challenge. Arsenal couldn't go on and win it from there and Pompey left with a deserved point. A disappointing week continued with a 3-0 defeat to Inter Milan in the Champions League and on the 21st Arsenal travelled to Old Trafford with the critics making Manchester United heavy favourites to win.

The match would be forever remembered for the scenes that greeted Ruud Van Nistelrooy's stoppage time penalty miss. In a tense and fractious game both sides sought to cancel out each other's attacking threat. Arsenal had the better of the chances but in the last minute of the game Keown, playing in Campbell's absence whose father had just died, bundled Forlan to the ground in the penalty area. Van Nistelrooy stepped up having missed his last three penalties, including one in the Charity shield against Arsenal. Despite hitting the ball true enough, it struck the bar and Arsenal survived. The vision of Arsenal players then surrounding Van Nistelrooy, particularly Keown, would become one of the iconic images of the season. In a game of seven yellow and one red card (for Patrick Vieira) and dramatic scenes in the final moments, Arsenal left Old Trafford still unbeaten and with a vital point earned. Seeing the month out with a 3-2 victory at home to Newcastle after coming from behind, Arsenal retained top spot going into October.

Now playing at close to their best, Arsenal safely negotiated October, November and December. Liverpool were beaten at Anfield, the cash rich boys from Stamford Bridge didn't have enough to stop Arsenal beating Chelsea and local rivals Tottenham were dispatched 2-1. In the league Arsenal recorded four draws and eight wins over the three months and by the turn of the year had gone a full half season without defeat. Their Champions League group had seen Arsenal qualify in first place including a 5-1 victory in the San Siro over Internazionale that had shown Europe Arsenal's breakaway football at its best.

On January 18th a 2-0 win at Villa Park saw Arsenal regain top spot from Manchester United after two Thierry Henry goals. Arsenal wouldn't relinquish the position again all season. Keen to capitalise on the first half of the season's good work, Wenger signed José Antonio Reyes in the transfer window from Seville. A left-winger who could also play as a striker, Reyes was a pacy and intelligent player in the mould of Arsenal's attacking ethos. Making his debut in the home victory against Manchester City on February 2nd, he would go on to score some important goals for Arsenal in the latter stages of the season.

Arsenal eased through February and to the end of March still unbeaten. Another victory over Chelsea along the way provided them with a wealth of confidence going into a two-legged Champions League quarterfinal against the same opponents. Arsenal now faced a series of games that could make or break their season. In between the Chelsea cup-ties lay a waiting Manchester United twice, once in the league and then again in the FA Cup semi-final. The FA Cup campaign had been relatively event free, two 4-1 wins against Leeds United and Middlesbrough, a home win against Chelsea in the fifth round and then a 5-1 romp at Fratton Park against Portsmouth. Already losing semi-finalists thanks to a Carling Cup exit to eventual winners Middlesbrough, Arsenal wanted to retain the FA Cup for a third time.

The first of these four games fell Arsenal's way. A one all draw in the first leg of the Champions League at Chelsea gave Arsenal the much sought after away goal to take into the second leg. Manchester United then arrived for a league game which Arsenal let slip through their fingers. 1-0 up with four minutes left to play, Manchester United's January signing Louis Saha found himself unmarked in the penalty area to tap in Solskjaer's low cross. Arsenal had contrived to snatch a draw from the jaws of victory. The momentum shifted to Manchester for the semi-final and United progressed thanks to Paul Scholes first half strike. Despite outplaying them for long periods in the game Arsenal couldn't conjure an equaliser.

Going into the second league of the Champions League games with Chelsea, Arsenal were tiring. Despite taking the lead through Reyes's goal right on half time, Jens Lehmann's failure to deal with Claude Makelele's half volley pushed the ball into Frank Lampard's path who levelled the tie overall. Struggling to cope with Chelsea's pressurising five-man midfield, eventually Arsenal conceded an eighty-seventh minute goal to Wayne Bridge's low shot after a fine passing move. Chelsea's tempo and the tactical decision to stifle Arsenal's full backs had, if nothing else, left Arsenal with a clear run now to finish the Premier League season with no more distractions. Still jealously guarding the league form, they knew that even though the disappointment of cup exits was fresh, to do the unthinkable and go a full season unbeaten would be an achievement that would write them into football history.

Wounded Arsenal went into a home game with Liverpool in which Thierry Henry produced one of his best displays in a red shirt, scoring three of Arsenal's goals in a 4-2 win. Behind twice in the game, Henry had been doubtful to start after going off injured with ten minutes to go in the Chelsea game. His surge past Liverpool's defence in the 50th minute banished all thoughts of disappointment and Arsenal were very much focused on finishing this historic season at their very best again.

A draw against Newcastle was followed by a rousing 5-0 win over Leeds United in which the irrepressible Henry scored four. On the 25th April the title was secured with a 2-2 draw at White Hart Lane against derby rivals Tottenham. The trophy itself was almost a sideshow, the real circus still involved the feat of Arsenal staying unbeaten for the four remaining games. Two draws against Birmingham City and Portsmouth, the latter courtesy of Reyes's equaliser brought the achievement within sight and all that remained was an away trip to Fulham and a home game against Leicester City.

After beating Fulham thanks to Reyes's solitary goal, Leicester City came to Highbury in the position of potential party poopers. After an early scare when Paul Dickov headed City into the lead, Henry's second half penalty eased the worries and then Patrick Vieira's winner wrote Arsenal's name into the history books. Finishing top of league, eleven points clear of Chelsea in second and fifteen points clear of pre-season favourites Manchester United in third, Arsene Wenger joined his team on the Highbury pitch to celebrate a memorable season.

The fact that Arsene Wenger had always harboured an ambition to go unbeaten for a full season came as no surprise for a man renowned for seeing the larger picture. As commentators and plaudits rushed to congratulate the record breakers, the scale of the achievement seemed to grow in hindsight. No team before or since had managed to go through a 38 game season unbeaten and although it wouldn't lead to the sustained dominance the football world was predicting, the Arsenal side of 2003-04 were truly invincible.

Los Angeles Galaxy 2007

Honours

North America Superliga finalists

5th in Western Conference

$250,000,000 or £128,000,000
(roughly £25.6m Per Year of Contract)

Alleged value of David Beckham's 5-year contact with the MLS and the LA Galaxy

On July 4th 1988, the United States of America was offered another chance to truly embrace football. After the demise of NASL (the North American Soccer League) and the failure to push the sport as more than a passing fad, US Soccer had made the decision that the only way to reignite interest was to bid for the 1994 World Cup. After receiving over half the votes, America was chosen over strong bids from Brazil and in particular Morocco. Amongst the usual requirements regarding capability and updating of facilities, a very important condition had been set dependant on awarding the tournament to the USA. A commitment had been made to re-establish a nationwide professional outdoor soccer league, to begin as soon as possible after the conclusion of the World Cup.

In December 1993, World Cup USA chairman Alan I. Rothenberg announced the proposal that would keep that promise. Plans were revealed for Major League Soccer's launch and by October 1995, ten teams had successfully gained entry into America's new professional football league. The inaugural season began in March of the following year with the teams split into an Eastern and Western Conference, each comprised of five sides. The MLS was sold to the masses as a revolution in American sport and as the season began, fingers were crossed that the public would take to it as they had the World Cup. USA '94 had been watched by a record number of fans in World Cup history – the average attendance for each game was 69,000, total attendance was over 3.5 million – and the tournament had become the highest attended single-sport event ever in United States history. Believing they were riding the coat tails of the World Cup's popularity perfectly, expectations were high that the MLS was the perfect vehicle to cash in.

The Los Angeles Galaxy had already achieved a coup by becoming one of the ten clubs chosen for the MLS out of the twenty-two who applied. A second triumph had come in the signing of Cobi Jones, one of the most recognisable members of the United States national team still so fresh in the public's mind. Blessed with pace and natural flair, the midfielder had been with Coventry City of the English Premier League and most recently Vasco da Gama of Brazil. He'd played for the national side since 1992 and had been a standout performer for the host nation in the recent World Cup.

One relatively high-profile player was then joined by another – Jorge Campos, a Mexican goalkeeper who had also made his mark at USA'94. As famous for his garish kit as his ability to play as a striker if required, Campos was considered a world-class goalkeeper at the time. His signing was significant not just for his role on the pitch, it also represented a financially intelligent attempt to capitalise on the strong Latin American fan base in the Los Angeles area. He was joined by Eduardo Hurtado, an Ecuadorian striker with proven ability, and Mauricio Cienfuegos, a gifted Salvadoran midfielder who would go on to play for the Galaxy for the next eight years. With strong local support and gifted players on the pitch, LA Galaxy were immediately installed as one of the favourites to take the first ever MLS Championship.

The bookmakers were proved right when LA won the Western Conference, finishing a full eight points clear of the Dallas Burn in second. Despite this a Bruce Arena managed D.C. United took the ultimate prize – the MLS Cup, by beating Galaxy 3-2 in the final. Undoubtedly though the first season in the Galaxy's history had been a success. Hurtado had scored twenty-goals and was named in the MLS best XI for the '96 season. He was joined in that side by team mates Robin Fraser and Cienfuegos. The league had also been a relative success, well supported and attracting a sprinkling of star names. Carlos Valderrama played brilliantly for the Tampa Bay Mutiny and Roberto Donadoni, a member of the losing Italian 1994 World Cup final side, plied his trade for the New York based Metrostars.

In the first ten years of Major League Soccer Galaxy would become one of its most successful sides. After winning the inaugural Western Conference in the 1996, they would also top the league in 1998, 1999, 2001 and 2002. Their first MLS Cup came in 2002 after losing appearances in the finals of 1999 and 2001. The second came three years later thanks to a 1-0 win over the New England Revolution. They also continued to sign American internationals and as higher profile Latin American players as possible. Alexi Lalas joined in 2001 after a year away from football due to a premature retirement and then went on to make the MLS All-Stars XI in 2002. Mexican international striker Luis Hernández, holder of the country's record as the highest goalscorer in World Cups, played for the Galaxy in 2000 and 2001. Also at this time prolific Guatemalan striker Carlos Ruiz had three years in LA scoring fifty goals in just over seventy appearances.

Perhaps the most significant signing was American international Landon Donavon in 2005, again one of the national side's leading players. Already a high value player in the MLS after three years with the San Jose Earthquakes, Donavon signed in place of Ruiz who Galaxy traded despite being the previous year's league top scorer. In his first season Donavon was part of the MLS Cup winning side of 2005, scoring sixteen goals in the process. At the end of the season he found himself voted into the best MLS XI of all time as part of the league's tenth anniversary celebrations.

However by the 2007 season the Galaxy were considered to be in a mini slump. 2006 had seen the Galaxy miss out on the play-offs for the first time in their history. The year had started tragically with the sudden death of team General Manager Doug Hamilton. Highly thought of at the club and in the game as a whole, the loss was felt throughout the MLS. Struggling and stumbling through the season, head coach Steve Sampson was eventually dismissed and replaced by Frank Yallop, once of Ipswich Town as a player. Galaxy never recovered their league position significantly and their ten-season play-off run was over. A lucrative sponsorship deal ended the season on a high note for the Galaxy but on the pitch there was serious worries that the team needed an overhaul.

At the same time in Madrid a genuine superstar was unhappy. Going into the 2006-07 season with Real Madrid, David Beckham had every reason to be excited about his future with the Spanish giants. After an emotional resignation as England captain and then the shock of being told by international manager Steve McClaren that he no longer featured in his plans, playing for Madrid had become his sole focus. Fabio Capello had returned to Real to try and repeat his success by bringing them the La Liga title that had eluded them since 2003. Ruud Van Nistelrooy had also joined the club in the summer and both he and Beckham had stated how excited they were to rekindle the understanding they had struck up while playing for Manchester United. Amongst the high profile arrivals, departures and retirements, Beckham remained a popular figure at the club with fans and officials alike. Beckham's contract ended at the close of the season but fans and pundits agreed it was a formality that he would be offered a new one. The stars seemed to have aligned for the midfielder to focus on his club career and bring glory to Madrid.

Along with Van Nistelrooy Real had signed winger José Antonio Reyes on a year's loan from Arsenal. As the season began it became clear Capello was keen to strike a very different cord from the one Real fans had been used to previously. The era of Galaticos was over and Beckham was suddenly out of favour, both for his poor form and for what he represented. Capello kerbed Real's attacking instincts and preferred Reyes for his pace on the break and perceived greater goal threat. By the end of October it was clear that Beckham was no longer a starting member of Capello's team, limited to sporadic appearances from the bench and starts in games against lesser opposition. Beckham's form continued to suffer and suddenly the press were speculating that either Real were stalling on a contract offer or Beckham was refusing to sign one. When pressed by journalists Capello insisted he wanted Beckham to stay beyond the end of the season but in contrast, continued not to pick him. Sniffing blood in the water most of Europe's top clubs began to circle around the story, tempted by the revenue Beckham could generate on and off the pitch.

The story didn't go unnoticed in LA where people began drawing straight lines between the Los Angeles Galaxy and David Beckham. After playing in a pre-season game against the Galaxy in 2005 Beckham had spoken of his desire to end his career in America. As if to reinforce the statement he opened a soccer academy for teenagers in Los Angeles in the same year, the site of which was next to the Galaxy's 27,000-seat stadium in Carson. As the contract rumblings continued and Beckham himself commented on his frustration at being left out of the side, Galaxy General Manager Alexi Lalas made the first move by publicly declaring his desire to bring Beckham to LA. Careful to avoid anything that Real Madrid could cite as inducement to Beckham, Lalas spoke in broad strokes about the benefit signing him could have to American football in general.

Before any negotiation could take place a major obstacle stood in the way of any move to the MLS. In order to stem the excesses that blighted NASL, each club adhered to the draft system and worked under strict salary caps to keep the league fiscally responsible. If Beckham was to move then all three parties involved – the LA Galaxy, Major League Soccer and Beckham himself

– would have to be willing to settle for a uniquely structured deal. Recognising the world of possibilities having David Beckham in the league could bring, MLS officials met, proposed and passed the 'Designated Player Rule' or as it would go on to be nicknamed, the Beckham Rule. The rule quite simply circumnavigated the current legislation by allowing each club one player outside of the salary cap conditions. With one obstacle down it now fell to the Galaxy to finance the deal.

With new sponsorship in place and the MLS desperate to make the move happen, Galaxy had a financial ace up their sleeve. Owned by the sports conglomerate the Anschutz Entertainment Group (AEG), they sat in an extensive portfolio that included Basketball team the LA Lakers, ice hockey franchise the Manchester Monarchs and tellingly a stake in the David Beckham Soccer Academies. AEG already promoted their close relationship with Beckham and were privately and publicly very keen to finance the deal to bring him to the States.

After extensive and successful negotiation with Beckham's representatives, a deal was done and the move was on. On Thursday January 11th 2007, David Beckham made his announcement and called a press conference to coincide with the MLS Superdraft. Despite the offer of a two-year extension to his contract with Real Madrid he had agreed to move to the LA Galaxy at the end of the Spanish league season. The huge deal gave Beckham more revenue and control over his image rights than he or any other footballer had ever enjoyed before, no small matter considering 'Brand Beckham' was about to gain a foothold in the American market. By the time sponsorship, endorsements, wages and bonuses were added together, the contract was worth allegedly a potential $250m. Beckham was quick to point out that the move had appealed to him for purely footballing reasons and that moving to the U.S.A. in his mid-thirties had never been an option, but there was no denying the sheer scale of the deal. Getting Beckham into the MLS had taken a new law, Lalas's vision and the financial muscle of AEG but it was now confirmed. One of the most recognisable faces in the world was coming to America to play soccer.

As much as Beckham stood to earn from the contract, the exposure MLS generated from his signature was priceless. Suddenly the focal point of the football world became Los Angeles and the hype machine went into overdrive. LA Galaxy shirts emblazoned with Beckham's name and chosen squad number (23 in tribute to one of his sporting heroes, American basketballer Michael Jordan) went on sale worldwide along with all sorts of Galaxy/Beckham merchandise. Beckham carried out a high profile television interview on American television stating his attention to grow interest in football in the country. The deal seemed to fit everyone involved and the 2007 LA Galaxy season looked like being the most watched in MLS history.

Back in Madrid things weren't quite as optimistic. On the 13th January Capello stated that Beckham had played his last game for Madrid as his head was already in America. All the better as far as the Galaxy were concerned and a possible loan deal that would allow him to play from the beginning of the MLS season in April was mooted. Beckham still felt he had something to prove and despite not even being allowed to train with the first team at times, by early February he had forced his way back into Capello's plans. Reinvigorated by the challenge ahead he made his first appearance in Real Madrid's first team since the announcement was made against Real Sociedad. Typically Beckham played as if his life depended on it rather than someone running out an un-renewed contract.

He would stay in the first team and end the season with his first league winner's medal since moving to Spain. Real relentlessly hunted down Barcelona and many pundits suggested it was Beckham's drive and form that led to the success. Capello openly praised Beckham's professionalism, commitment and refusal to accept he couldn't force his way back into the staring line-up. Real Madrid president Ramón Calderón even claimed he was going to re-sign Beckham by getting him out of his contract with the Galaxy. Despite the claims Beckham had no intention of letting his new employers down and America eagerly awaited his debut.

By the time Beckham was saying his emotional goodbye to the Bernabéu in June, the MLS season was in full swing. Beckham was due to join Galaxy in July but an ankle injury in the last game of the Spanish season meant he wouldn't make his debut until a friendly against Chelsea at the end of the month. Only able to make the subs bench, Beckham came on for the last sixteen minutes in front of a capacity crowd and the largest ever viewing audience for an MLS team featured on ESPN. Clearly lacking fitness and protecting his ankle, Beckham played the game out safely and his American adventure had begun.

The only fly in the ointment had been the Galaxy's results so far. Carrying forward the previous year's desperate form they had struggled to break into the play-off positions. Knocked out of the Open Cup by third division Richmond Kickers and punished by a crippling fixture schedule that saw the Galaxy pushing their newfound marketability in the friendly game market, only the North American Superliga looked like bringing success. After another substitute appearance Beckham's first start for the Galaxy came in the Superliga semi-final against DC United. Producing a brilliant display after being given the captaincy straight away, Beckham scored from a free kick, set Landon

Donavan up for a goal and got himself booked as if anyone needed reminding of his commitment to football. In the final at the end of August against Mexican team Pachuca, Beckham picked up ligament damage to his knee that would keep him out for between six to ten weeks. Forced off he watched on as Galaxy lost on penalties, leaving their only chance of success a late season run at the play-off places.

Unfortunately they had left themselves too much to do. Despite some vastly improved performances Galaxy couldn't break into the top four and the play-off spots. Beckham made a substitute appearance in the last game of the season against the Chicago Fire but couldn't prevent a 1-0 defeat sealing their fate. After being injury plagued since his arrival, Beckham's first season with the Galaxy ended with only a handful of appearances and one goal.

The 2007 MLS season had been another disappointing one on the pitch for the LA Galaxy. Despite the presence of a genuinely world-class player, results didn't come and a late season surge did nothing to paper over the cracks. The real results had all been off the pitch. Consistently sold out for home games the club had also sold over 250,000 replica shirts since Beckham's signature in January. After becoming one of the biggest clubs in America since the conception of the MLS, they had now become one of the most publicised in the world. In 2008 David Beckham's LA Galaxy home shirt became the biggest selling personalised sports strip of all time. Within a year the Galaxy had recouped the money they had spent on bringing him to the States. The MLS benefited both from the exposure and the full houses at Galaxy away games, spectators lured to see the most famous player in the world playing in their league.

To say that the Galaxy mattered to football for anything to do with their results would be wrong. In 2008 they missed the play-offs again, in 2009 they lost another MLS Cup final on penalties to Real Salt Lake. What they managed to do in 2007 was to grow the MLS beyond all recognition by signing the only player in the world who could do it. Since Beckham's move the Designated Player Rule has been used to lure more quality players to the MLS, notably Swedish midfielder Freddie Ljungberg, French striker Thierry Henry, the Republic of Ireland's Robbie Keane, Argentinean international Claudio López and striker Blanco – winner of over a hundred caps for Mexico. If America is ever going to truly embrace football it will be on the back of the exposure that Beckham's stated ambition to help has delivered.

It is interesting to note that as the MLS season started in 2010 with Beckham unavailable due to a long term achilles injury, average attendance at MLS games was higher than the more established and treasured National Hockey League but also less than a hundred fans away from the American sporting giant of the NBA. Each year the figures have grown and all but three of the 2010 season's sixteen MLS teams reported attendances up year on year. It is impossible to separate Beckham from that growth and therefore, it is also impossible to separate the LA Galaxy. To what degree the Galaxy's ambitions of 2007 and the resulting effect on the game in America really matter, only time will tell.

Futbol Club Barcelona 2008–09

Honours

Primera División Champions

Copa del Rey Winners

UEFA Champions League Winners

Supercopa de España Winners

UEFA Super Cup Winners

FIFA Club World Cup Winners

		GK Valdés		
	CB Touré		**CB** Piqué	
RB Puyol (c)		**DM** Busquets		**RB** Sylvinho
	CM Xavi		**CM** Iniesta	
RW Messi		**CF** Eto'o		**LW** Henry

Barcelona's starting line-up for the 2009 champions League final against Manchester United, played 27th May at the Stadio Olimpico in Rome

Football, as with all sport, is at its heart about achievement but Holland and Brazil in the 1974 and 1982 World Cups respectively will tell you that the best teams don't always win the biggest trophies. In 2009 Barcelona were not only the best team in world football but they would go on to prove it in the most definitive terms possible by winning every major trophy available to them.

Since Cruyff had stepped down in 1996 President Núñez came under fire as the club's performances struggled to meet the standards the Dream Team had set.

It was no longer enough to win, they had to dominate and excite in equal measure. Former England manager Bobby Robson was initially handed the managers job but held it only for one season before Dutchman Louis van Gaal took over. Both achieved reasonable results but could never live up to expectations Cruyff's team had raised.

Still Barça continued to attract some of the world's best players to the club. Brazilian striking sensation Ronaldo joined his former manager Robson from PSV Eindhoven in 1996. In a brilliant spell he scored 47 goals in just 51 games and fired the club to success in the Copa del Rey and European Cup Winners Cup. After a world-record fee was brokered in 1997 he left the club for a new career at Internazionale. After Robson was moved into a new position to make way for van Gaal's arrival, a new raft of players were bought to the club to chase success. It would take two players to replace Ronaldo's goals – fellow Brazilian Rivaldo and Dutch striker Patrick Kluivert and all the while the fans still had their Portuguese hero Luis Figo to cheer.

By the turn of the millennium Núñez's popularity had fallen to such a level he decided to step down from the role of president he'd held for 22 years. He had never been given any credit for the raising of the Dream Team and had endured several attempts to remove him already. The final straw came as Cruyff spoke of the need for Núñez to step down and the Dutchmen still held the fans in the palm of his hand. Former vice-president Joan Gaspart was voted into the role and presided over three turbulent and trophyless seasons.

Gaspart only lasted until 2003 after a torrid time at the helm. Luis Figo had been sold to bitter rivals Real Madrid in 2000 and their Galaticos had been born. Los Blancos had won two more European Cups in 2000 and 2002 and assembled a side full of the world's best attacking players. In the same timescale Barça had laboured to a fourth place finish twice in La Liga, then in 2003 dropped to sixth and UEFA Cup qualification. The latest of five managers employed in Gaspart's reign – Radomir Antic – was removed. Despite relative success since taking over a club languishing in the lower reaches of the table in January, Antic's style of football didn't fit with Barça's ethos. A new president was to be elected and it was time to evolve the club once again.

Joan Laporta came from behind to win the Presidential election after a campaign based on his charisma and bold promises to buy David Beckham. While he ultimately failed to convince Beckham to come to the Camp Nou, the Englishman instead opting for Real Madrid, he did employ Dutchman Frank Rijkaard as manager and set about bringing in personnel that would fit the Barça way. Ronaldinho quickly replaced Beckham as the marquee signing the fans demanded of their new president. Barça and Rijkaard achieved the improvement they had promised and ultimately won a second European Cup in 2006 in Paris.

That team had evolved and the starting line-up for the final against English club Arsenal contained only three Spanish players – goalkeeper Victor Valdés, right-back Oleguer and central defender Carlos Puyol. All the attacking positions were taken by signings made in Laporta's reign. While Catalonia once again rejoiced in the joy of being holders of the European Cup, even with youth system graduates Xavi and Andrés Iniesta on the bench the team had an uncommonly multinational feel.

In 2008 Rijkaard's star had slipped. Without a trophy since the European Cup win, he parted company with Barcelona on good terms and with a history of success. During his five seasons in charge he'd won two La Ligas, the Champions League, and two Spanish Super Cups. After losing 4-1 to Real Madrid as the season neared its end and with rumours of players taking more of an interest in Barcelona's nightlife then their training sessions, it was announced that Rijkaard was leaving and his replacement would be coach of Barcelona's 'B' team – Josep 'Pep' Guardiola.

Guardiola had been one of the lynchpins of the Dream Team's success. A graduate of La Masia – Barça's youth academy – he'd become a Catalonian legend for his fierce pride in the region of his birth. As popular as he was with the club's fans, some reserved judgement due to his perceived lack of experience. He had been a dominant force and leader on the pitch during the course of nearly 500 appearances in a Barcelona shirt, winning 19 trophies over his 11 years in the first team. He'd only just retired from playing in 2006 after a brief spells in Italy, Qatar and Mexico. Although the sense of Catalonia was almost instantly returned to the club, was he really the man to return the discipline and success demanded by the Barcelona faithful?

Laporta was currently struggling to win universal support in his position. Prior to the 2008-09 season he received and narrowly survived a vote of no confidence. Aware of the dissent in the ranks many of his board felt compelled to resign. Laporta took a leaf from Núñez's book and held firm. After appointing Guardiola because of a belief in the man, it was also key that the decision would go down well with the majority of fans.

Barcelona's director of sport was fellow Dream Team graduate Txiki Begiristain. Between him and Guardiola they began to identify who they needed to keep and who they needed to recruit to revitalise the Catalans. Ronaldinho had been the subject of much of the speculation surrounding certain player's commitment to the club. The previous season had seen him injured and struggling for form, ultimately costing him his place as a starter. He was moved on to AC Milan and stated his desire for a new challenge. He'd been brilliant but then burnt out at the Camp Nou.The decision to deem him surplus to requirements was seen as the beginning of a new era.

Gianluca Zambrotta joined Ronaldinho on the plane to Milan as the overhaul began in earnest. Portuguese playmaker Deco had arrived from FC Porto in 2004 with a Champions League medal in his pocket, he added another in Barça's colours in 2006. Long-time admirers Chelsea gave Deco an opportunity Guardiola had made public he wouldn't. He left for London and was quickly followed by prospect Giovanni Dos Santos who moved to Tottenham Hotspur. Lillian Thuram retired with health issues, Oleguer moved to Ajax after his recent history had been blighted with injury and personal problems, and holding midfielder Edmílson could never compare to the club's greatest ever now in charge of the first team and so was moved to Villarreal. Along with the higher profile names a host of bit part players were removed from the wage bill through release or transfer and the recruitment drive began.

Defensively several key issues were identified. Gerard Piqué was born in Barcelona and raised through the youth system. Before he had the chance to break into the B team, Manchester United had signed him. Guardiola recruited Piqué who had only been on the periphery of the United first team in his career to date to play in the centre of his defence. Piqué's strength and height gave him a physical advantage over most opponents but his ability on the ball was what attracted his new manager the most. Joining him in defence was Dani Alves, a player who had become one of the hottest properties in world football after his performances for Seville. His signing gave a glimpse of Guardiola's philosophy as Alves had made his name as a very attacking full back with an eye for goal.

Also coming from Seville, Seydou Keita joined to sit at the base of Guardiola's midfield and Alexander Hleb moved from Arsenal after impressing as an attacking midfielder. A number of other signings were made mainly as cover and squad players and Guardiola promoted some of Barça's canteranos (youth players), notably midfielder Sergio Busquets and wide striker Pedro.

These new signings had to fit around the nucleus of the side already in place at the club. Defenders Éric Abidal and Sylvinho, defensive midfielder Yaya Touré and attacking players Eidor Gudjohnsen, Thierry Henry and Samuel Eto'o were all the previous regime's signings but still featured in plans for the new season. Eto'o had initially been offered for sale but after no deal could be done, had forced his way into Guardiola's plans. Besides these players Barça were also reaping the benefits of their youth system as several graduates from La Masia had established themselves in the first team.

Besides Valdes, Puyol and now Piqué defensively, Sergio Busquets fought with Keita and Touré for the holding midfield berth and made over forty appearances in the season. In the attacking midfield positions Xavi took over holes left by Deco and Ronaldinho's departure and alongside him Iniesta had proved his equal. The intelligence, passing and movement of these two players in Barcelona's midfield became a standout feature of Guardiola's team. On top of all this they had a jewel in the crown, an Argentinean capable of playing wide in attack or as a secondary striker. His performances already had people drawing the inevitable comparisons with his compatriot and national team manager Diego Maradona. His name was Lionel Messi.

Messi had arrived in Barcelona in 2000 after a unique agreement had been struck with the player and his family. Messi required a growth hormone treatment that Newell's old Boys, his club in Argentina, simply couldn't afford. After Barça agreed to pay for his treatment on the agreement that the player and his family moved to Catalonia, Messi had joined La Masia and immediately made an impact. Mesmeric dribbling skills and outstanding pace saw him make his debut in the first team at the age of just 16. Undaunted by the pressure of the perpetual label of 'next big thing', by the 2006-07 season he was a first team regular and had scored the goal of the season after a slaloming run past six players in a Kings Cup game against Getafe. As Guardiola joined in 2008 Messi was coming off the back of his best season yet in which he had attracted the tag of the best player in the world regularly. He'd scored 16 goals but also been attributed 13 assists and while it'd been an unsuccessful season, Messi had emerged as indisputably world class. At only 21 his potential was frightening.

Messi inherited Ronaldinho's prized number 10 shirt and expectation as resident genius. Guardiola had played under Cruyff's version of total football and believed in tiki-taka – the Spanish ideal of short passing, possession, movement and pressure. In Messi he had what Ajax and Holland had had in Cruyff, the player with the ability to make the system work for and around him. Messi would make up a front three for most of the season with Henry and Eto'o, all fed by Xavi and Iniesta's invention. With a system in place and a new ethic of hard work and the team above all else, Guardiola had already made his mark before the season had begun.

In La Liga Barça would be outstanding. They finished as champions, nine points clear of Real Madrid but in reality miles apart from their domestic competition. Defensively they had conceded less than a goal a game, Piqué and Puyol proving to be perfect stable mates at the heart of the Catalan's rear guard. After starting inauspiciously with a loss at Numancia and a home draw with Racing Santander, Barça won their next nine games with an aggregate score of 35-6. In that run they put four past Málaga, five past Almería and six past Valladolid, Atlético Madrid, and Sporting Gijón. Messi hit form immediately and Eto'o had already scored thirteen in the league.

After a 1-1 draw with Getafe, Barça won their next ten games and swung the title firmly in their favour. Key games were won away in Seville, at home to Valencia and in the first 'clásico' of the season against Real Madrid. At the Camp Nou Eto'o and Messi scored a goal apiece in the last ten minutes to earn all three points. Despite not breaking through until the final phase of the game, Barça had been on top throughout.

They continued to excite and dazzle in the league all their way to the title, scoring 105 goals and finishing with the outstanding goal difference of +70. The standout performance in a season full of them came in the return against Madrid at the Bernabéu. Well on their way to the title, Barça fell behind to Gonzalo Higuain's thirteenth minute header. Stung into action, a clever one two with Messi gave Henry an equaliser three minutes later. From that moment on the Catalans were outstanding, running in five more to finish with a 6-2 win at the home of their biggest rivals. Messi had bordered on unplayable and scored twice. Even captain Puyol had got in on the act with a first half header that had delighted the Barça faithful.

Deserved champions, the La Liga trophy was joined in the cabinet by the Copa del Rey after a 4-1 triumph in the final against Athletic Bilbao. The campaign had been routine and an opportunity for Guardiola to give his full squad minutes on the pitch. They had safely negotiated themselves past Benidorm, Atlético Madrid, neighbours Espanyol and Mallorca on the way to the final and now faced the Basques of Bilboa. Behind early, they quickly found their rhythm and went in at half time on level terms thanks to Touré's stunning run and finish from just outside the box. With twenty-five minutes left in the game, it was all but over as Barça had blown away Bilbao to lead 4-1, Messi, Xavi and another la Masia graduate Bojan with the goals.

Thanks to their domestic success Barça had earned the right to play for the 2009 Spanish Super Cup against Bilbao again. A 5-1 aggregate win meant that Barcelona finished 2009 as holders of all of Spain's highest level trophies – champions of La Liga, Copa del Rey holders and winners of the Super Cup.

In Europe Barça had been just as impressive. After finishing third in Rijkaard's last season, Barcelona entered the Champions League at the third qualifying stage. In Guardiola's first competitive fixtures in charge of the club they progressed thanks to a 4-1 aggregate win over Polish side Wisla Kraków. Drawn in a favourable Group C with Basel of Switzerland, Ukrainians Shakhtar Donetsk and Sporting Clube de Portugal, Barça breezed through as winners. Their only loss came in their last group game when qualification had been secured. In six games Barça scored 18 goals, Messi with 5 of them and the Catalan public dreamt of clawing another trophy back on the record of Real Madrid.

In the knockout stages the standard improved but so did Barcelona. After an edgy 1-1 draw away to much fancied French side Lyon, Barcelona put five past them in the home leg. 4-0 up by half time, they had swept Lyon aside in dismissive manner. Even better for the Catalans, Real Madrid crashed to a humiliating 5-0 aggregate loss to Liverpool. The quarterfinals bought a Bayern Munich side that had just dispensed of Sporting CP 12-1. Despite the feeling this would be their biggest test, Barcelona once again smashed four first half goals to all but settle the tie with just forty-five minutes played. After a 1-1 draw in Munich, a highly controversial semi-final with Chelsea of England waited for them.

The Londoners shut the Barça attacking machine out impressively at the Camp Nou and the second leg hung on a knife-edge after a 0-0 draw. Chelsea moved into a 1-0 lead with as little as nine minutes on the clock thanks to a truly stunning volley from Michael Essien. Barça laboured and Chelsea striker Didier Drogba missed several good chances to all but end the tie. After a couple of good Chelsea penalty appeals were turned down, Piqué appeared to blatantly handle in the area but still referee Tom Henning Ovrebo waved away calls for a spot-kick. Éric Abidal was then sent off after a debateable challenge on Nicholas Anelka and Barça looked out of it. With 93 minutes on the clock Chelsea failed to clear Alves's deep cross and the ball worked its way to Messi. The Argentine found himself confronted with a wall of blue so simply squared the ball to Iniesta who lashed in an equaliser from the edge of the box. After yet another penalty appeal for Chelsea was turned down, the final whistle sounded to boos and angry reaction from the home fans. Regardless, Barça had won on away goals and now had the chance to lift the great trophy again.

The final in Rome against Manchester United was a complete performance. Despite some early United pressure Eto'o put Barça into the lead with his first sight of goal. In a second half dominated by the Catalans efficiency and pressing, Messi added a second with a brilliant header past a stranded Edwin Van der Sar in United's goal. The trophy they craved the most was again in Barcelona's hands and Messi had completed an incredible season. In any other year Eto'o's 36 goals would have made him the club's top scorer. In 2009 Messi had scored 38 in less appearances than Eto'o, and had turned in match winning performances week in and week out for his club. He took 2009's Ballon d'Or, and the FIFA World Player of the Year to recognise his extraordinary season.

Their success in the European Cup granted them the opportunity to play for the 2009 UEFA Super Cup against UEFA Cup winner's Shakhtar Donetsk. Pedro's goal after a brilliant exchange with Messi in extra time gave Barça a narrow 1-0 win. Only one trophy was now left to cap an extraordinary year –

the FIFA Club World Cup. The semi-final against Mexican side Atlante F.C was dealt with in the manner they'd become accustomed to. 1-0 down to Guillermo Rojas's brave early strike, Barcelona rallied and found their natural interplay and movement. Sergio Busquets tapped in a leveller just before half time than inevitably, Messi put them in front with a good run and neat finish. Andres Iniesta managed to tie the whole Atlante defence up in the sixty-seventh minute before Pedro converted his lay off. A 3-1 victory secured, only Estudiantes of Argentina now stood in their way in the final.

Barcelona were visibly tense throughout the game. The weight of their potential achievement seemed to hang heavy for the first time. The Argentines grabbed a first half lead through Boselli's header and held on until the last minute. Barça pressure built and Guardiola's decision to move Piqué to support the strikers paid off as he won a header at the edge of the area. The ball spun towards Pedro who nodded in an equaliser and gave Barça the lifeline they needed.

Into the second period of extra-time the scores were still locked at 1-1. Guardiola waved his players desperately forward from the touchline as a long cross swung invitingly into the area. After a season of brilliance there could be no other player to settle it as Messi threw himself forward and chested in a winner to send Catalonia into delirium. Champions of Spain, champions of Europe and now they found themselves officially the best club team in the world.

Some teams matter for nothing more than the scope of their achievements. Six trophies in a calendar year represented an unprecedented level of success, even by the standards of one of the biggest clubs in the world. Guardiola openly wept as his team paraded the World Club Cup trophy and the outstanding nature of his first season in management really came into perspective. In Messi he had the player that made his system of intense pressure coupled with intricate passing, pace and a three-pronged attack really click. They had used total football's ideals but coupled them with defensive excellence. Tiki-Taka was football's new buzzword and Spanish football had now become a blueprint for the world to look to.

Spain 2010

Honours

World Cup Winners at South Africa 2010

GK
Iker Casillas (C)
Real Madrid

RB Sergio Ramos *Real Madrid*
CB Gerard Piqué *Barcelona*
CB Carles Puyol *Barcelona*
LB Joan Capdevila *Villarreal*

DM Sergio Busquets *Barcelona*
DM Xabi Alonso *Real Madrid*

CM Xavi Hernández *Barcelona*

RW Andrés Iniesta *Barcelona*
LW Pedro Rodríguez *Barcelona*

CF David Villa *Barcelona*

Starting line-up in 2010 World Cup Final, played on 11th July 2010 at Soccer City in Johannesburg

Barcelona's magnificent 2009 had carried on a wonderful era for Spanish football. After Real Madrid's Galaticos and Rijkaard's Barcelona emerged in the early part of the century, Spain had produced a generation of players who had proved capable of taking them to major honours. Both of the country's biggest and most successful clubs retained a spine of Spanish players in their first teams, as well as a strong and talented Spanish presence across the breadth of La Liga. The national side had been perceived as perennial underachievers but the 2008 European Championships had seen Spain expose those myths and take a major trophy for the first time since 1964.

The Spanish national team's history is one laced with triumph and despair. In the European Championships they'd enjoyed early success, qualifying for the first ever tournament in 1960 but forfeiting their quarterfinal for political reasons when drawn against the Soviet Union. Dictator Franco's animosity with the Communist ideals of the USSR and its leaders meant it was deemed unsafe and unwise to send a team to the country. Four years later they had no such issues as the tournament was held on home soil. After wins against Romania, Northern Ireland, and the Republic of Ireland in the opening rounds and then Hungary in their semi-final, the young Spanish team faced the Soviet Union at the Bernabéu for the title. Barcelona's Jesus Pereda and Real Zaragoza striker Marcelino scored the decisive goals in a 2-1 win for the home side and the Spanish tasted international success for the first time.

Their next significant appearance in the championships came in 1984 when they once again made the final. This time they found themselves against a supremely talented French side containing the likes of Michel Platini, Patrick Battiston and Jean Tigana. Despite France going down to ten men Spain froze and conspired to lose 2-0, unable to carry on the luck that saw them win their semi-final against the Danes on penalties. Quarterfinal defeats at Euros '96 and 2000 further compounded the belief that the Spanish couldn't see it through despite the obvious talent in their squads, the likes of Raúl, Fernando Morientes, Juan Carlos Valerón and Fernando Hierro available for both tournaments.

The 2008 tournament had finally dispelled that idea as a magnificent Spanish side under the leadership of Luis Aragonés marched to the trophy. With the old guard put to one side to make way for a new generation of talent, players such as Xavi, Iniesta, Fernando Torres and David Villa had flourished in a loose 4-4-2 that made the most of the brilliant midfield options at their disposal. Three wins saw them top their group, Villa scoring 4 including a hat trick in their group game against Russia. Italy were their first knockout opponents and provided a significant milestone to overcome. Spain had not beaten the Italians since the 1920 Summer Olympics in Antwerp and played out a nervy and goalless 120 minutes. Iker Casillas then proved to be the hero by saving Daniele De Rossi and Antonio Di Natale's penalties to leave Cesc

Fábregas the spot-kick to put them through. He showed no trace of nerves and sent them through to the semi-final and another game against Russia.

Their old foes proved to be no more resistant than they had been in the group game when a second half collapse saw Russia lose 3-0. Spain's midfield four of David Silva on the left, Xavi in the centre, Marcos Senna sitting deep and Andrés Iniesta on the right were just too strong for the Russians to live with. In the final they faced an emerging Germany side and opted to bring Fábregas in to keep Xavi company in the centre and leave Fernando Torres up front on his own. The change in tactics worked and Torres scored the game's solitary goal to give the Spanish the Henri Delaunay Trophy for the second time.

No one could doubt that Spain had deserved the trophy but some suggested that the Dutch had been a better side, undone by poor refereeing in their losing quarter-final with Russia. Holland had beaten France and Italy convincingly in Group C and earned plaudits for their style of play and some spectacular goals. The chance to address the question properly would present itself at the World Cup in 2010, a tournament Spain found themselves amongst the favourites for despite a poor historical record in the competition.

Spain had taken their World Cup bow in 1934, losing to hosts Italy in the second round amid accusations of home intimidation and an overly aggressive approach from the home side. The Second World War and the Spanish Civil War meant they weren't seen at the finals again until 1950 when they topped a group England had been expected to walk in Brazil. The final pool saw them finish fourth in the tournament but unable to record a single win against Sweden, Brazil or winners Uruguay.

Spain then failed to qualify for Switzerland '54 or Sweden '58 and were unable to get through their groups at Chile '62 or in England in 1966. The World Cup then failed to see a Spanish side until 1978 when again, they failed to get through their group and qualify for the second round. 1982 would be different however as the Spanish would be hosting the tournament for the first time and expectations were high. Managed by legendary Real Madrid defender José Santamaría, once again the Spanish struggled in the spotlight. Although they stumbled through their initial group despite losing to Northern Ireland and only drawing with Honduras, the second round saw them fail to record a win against West Germany or England and they were eliminated on their own soil.

1986 in Mexico saw a marked improvement but more failure. A quarter-final appearance represented their best performance since 1950 and a second round rout of a highly fancied Denmark side had brought them to the fore. Emilio Butragueño scored four of Spain's five in that game and drawn against

Belgium for a place in the semis, Spain were suddenly looking like they could spring a surprise. Once more the spotlight proved too bright and a defeat on penalties left them looking at a plane home rather than a trip to the Azteca to play Argentina. They lost to Yugoslavia in the second round at Italia '90, fell at the quarter-finals again to Italy in the USA in 1994 and in France so close to home in '98, they failed to make it out of their group.

A third quarter-final appearance and another loss, this time to hosts South Korea in 2002, gave the Spanish an all too familiar feeling – play well through a group but then blowing their lines under knockout pressure. The pattern repeated itself in Germany in 2006 but several players learned from the 3-1 loss to finalists France and took the experience into the win at Euro '08. The heart of Spain's team had been to a major tournament and failed, then been to a major tournament and won. Both would prove to be equally valuable experiences in 2010.

Luis Aragones's triumph in 2008 was to be his last act as Spain manager. He stepped down and made way for Vicente del Bosque, the man who had marshalled Real Madrid's Galaticos into twice Champions League winners. With a talented squad now experienced in winning, he oversaw an incredible run in which Spain won ten out ten matches in qualifying. Tricky away games in Turkey and Belgium were brushed aside with two routine 2-1 wins. David Villa was outstanding in the campaign, scoring seven and repeatedly profiting from that midfield guile that blessed Spain. He broke a national record by scoring twelve in one year of games for Spain and then another by scoring in six consecutive games for the national side. The team took one of football's world records by winning fifteen consecutive games and equalled another by remaining unbeaten for thirty-five. A defeat by the United States in 2009 Confederations Cup proved to be merely a blip and they marched to the 2010 South African World Cup confident and with form on their side.

The tournament was hugely anticipated as it would be Africa's first as hosts. Spain and del Bosque now largely mirrored Barça's loose 4-3-3 approach which was being lauded as the 'new' way to win. Del Bosque encouraged his team to keep passes short and precise, pressure the ball and use intelligence as much as pace as a tool to find space. They had been good to watch but were ruthless with it.

The squad contained no less than seven of Barcelona's incredible 2009 squad – Piqué, Puyol, Iniesta, Busquets and Xavi all starters, Pedro coming off the bench when required and Valdes in reserve. Real Madrid supplied the first team with its captain – goalkeeper Iker Casillas, fullback Sergio Ramos and midfielder Xabi Alonso. David Villa finished the season as a Valencia player who had scored 21 league goals for Los Che but by the time the World Cup began he had signed for Barcelona for a fee believed to be in the region of €40m. Fernando Torres joined up with the squad with an injury he was carrying from his season with Liverpool, Cesc Fábregas came from Arsenal amidst a sea of speculation linking him with the club he had been with as a boy – Barça. Like David Villa, David Silva came into the tournament in the middle of leaving Valencia, his destination was to be Manchester City. Other players would also get minutes on the pitch such as Jesús Navas of Seville and Fernando Llorente from Athletic Bilboa to further prove the depth of quality in the squad.

Drawn into Group H with Switzerland, Chile and Honduras, the Spanish had all but qualified before a ball was kicked in the eyes of the world's press. Under huge pressure to perform after their spectacular form of the last two years, Spain fell into an old trap and lost their first group game against Switzerland. Playing with Iniesta and Silva supporting Villa in attack from wide positions, the highly organised Swiss bit and snapped at the Spanish having done their homework. Managed by the tactically astute Ottmar Hitzfeld, the key moment came in the 52nd minute when Switzerland took the opportunity Spanish defensive indecision gave them. Gelson Fernandes scrambled in what would prove to be a winner and despite a response from del Bosque in bringing on Torres and Navas to support Villa in attack, the Swiss held firm to shock the watching world.

The loss left the Spanish with no margin for error. Five days later they faced Honduras and found their tempo again. Villa scored a brilliant first after showing just how dangerous he was when cutting in from the left and then added a second just after halftime. 2-0 didn't reflect the Spaniards real superiority, poor finishing and some last ditch defending all that kept the score down to a reasonable level. A final group game win against Chile saw them qualify top of the table despite the opening defeat and Villa had scored a third in the tournament overall with a chip for Spain's opener. Iniesta added a second before halftime after some intelligent movement and incisive passing presented him with the opportunity. Spain looked to be gathering momentum with each game.

The knockout draw had thrown up an Iberian derby with Portugal in the round of sixteen. La Liga team mates faced each other as Real Madrid's Cristiano Ronaldo and Pepe lined up for Portugal. Atlético Madrid's Simão and Tiago also made the Portuguese eleven well aware of what their midfield opponents Iniesta, Xavi, Alonso and Busquets could do. The game struggled through the first half with neither side willing to take a chance for fear of punishment on the break.

Into the second half and not for the first time Villa proved to be the difference. Fed by Iniesta's clever ball and Xavi's flick, Villa scored from his own rebound after Portuguese goalkeeper Eduardo saved his first effort. Portugal couldn't break down the Spanish back line with Alonso and Busquets holding effectively and the game ended with a 1-0 win for Spain. They knew they'd now face Paraguay in the quarter-final on June 3rd and their determination to break teams down would serve them well.

Paraguay proved stubborn and a dour first half ensued. The second half burst into life with the award and miss of a Paraguayan penalty. Óscar Cardozo stepped up and watched Casillas save his moment of glory. Spain launched an attack of their own straight away and after Alcaraz hauled down Villa, had a penalty of their own. Alonso scored but then had to retake due to a questionable encroachment decision. His second effort was saved and despite claims for a further penalty after a challenge on Fábregas, Paraguay survived. The stalemate lasted until the eighty-third minute when substitute Pedro broke free and raced into the area only to hit the post, the rebound falling to the feet ofVilla. He squeezed a shot in via both posts for another 1-0 win. Spain were now guaranteed their best World Cup finals finish since 1950 and faced a free scoring Germany side in the semi-final. The Germans had impressed, particularly in eliminating England and Argentina, and represented Spain's biggest test so far.

Villa was deployed as a lone striker from the off and struggled to break down a highly organised German defence. Despite having most of the possession, the Germans had opted to let Spain have the ball and concentrate on closing down and hitting them on the break. Miroslav Klose missed a couple of half chances and both sides struggled for definitive penetration. Eventually Spain won a corner with twenty minutes to go. The German defence switched off for no more that ten seconds to allow Carles Puyol to run unchecked into the area. With only defensive partner Piqué between him and the ball, Puyol rose and met Xavi's corner with a powerful header to take the lead Spanish possession had merited. Now on the brink of the country's first World Cup final, their defence held firm and they were through to face Holland for the ultimate prize in the international game.

History was to no help in picking a winner – the sides had never met in the final tournament of a major championship. With members of both countries Royal family in attendance and a pre-match appearance by Nelson Mandela delighting the crowd in South Africa, the sides lined up for the final on the 11th July at Johannesburg's Soccer City hoping to win the trophy for the first time. As the game kicked off English referee Howard Webb became the first half's biggest figure as the Dutch adopted a physical approach to intimidate and shut down the Spanish midfield. Nigel de Jong and Marc van Bommel were to sit in front of the Dutch back four and both ended the first forty-five minutes lucky to have just been yellow carded. Both sides missed half chances, Villa snapped at a half volley for the best of the Spanish attempts.

The second half saw Holland continue to use aggression to break the Spanish rhythm. Ex-Real Madrid player Arjen Robben missed a one on one with his old team mate Casillas for Holland and Sergio Ramos should have done better with a free header for Spain. The game moved into extra time and still hung on a knife-edge despite Spain's greater possession. John Heitinga received a second yellow, one of the games fourteen, to leave the Dutch a man light for the last eleven minutes.

Spain seized on the opportunity to counter-attack after Webb failed to award a clear Dutch corner and then a free kick just outside of Spain's penalty area. Breaking forward with just four minutes to go, the ball worked its way to Fábregas just outside of Holland's penalty area. His bouncing pass found Iniesta who controlled and then lashed in a half volley to send Spain into raptures. At the final whistle wild celebrations were sparked across the country as their team had just written themselves into the country's history. They flew home to a sea of red and yellow in Madrid as millions filled the streets and a nation-wide fiesta began in earnest. They had played the game the 'Spanish' way and won the biggest prizes available in European and World football.

Spain's victory mattered because it marked the evolution of Jack Hogan's and Hugo Meisl's 'whirl', through Rinus Michels' total football played with Cruyff's genius and the abandon that they would always outscore their opponents, to the Spanish triumph of possession, tiki-taka and flexibility within an organised framework. The method of playing an interchangeable three up front so effectively had started to win the biggest honours when employed at Ajax, then failed at the hands of the Dutch national side on the biggest stage. Now it had evolved through Cruyff's Dream Team with Guardiola at its heart to a breathtakingly successful Barça side with Guardiola at the helm, and then on to the national team using the system to their own ends. Ultimately the Spanish deserved to win the World Cup despite accusations of negativity – the very antithesis of Michels, Cruyff's and Guardiola's vision. The reality was that the strength of their possession was simply too much for most to live with and even when faced with total football's originators, their more structured version took the biggest prize in world football.

Your Team

Honours

Nothing to Everything

'To think of football as merely 22 hirelings kicking a ball is merely to say that a violin is wood and cat-gut, Hamlet so much ink and paper. It is conflict and art'

English novelist, playwright and broadcaster, J.B. Priestly, speaking on the subject of football

The one team that matters above all others.

Football is territorial, tribal and passionate. It is exciting, infuriating and awe-inspiring. It is the game that over the course of a season can encompass every part of the emotional spectrum from abject despair to total delight. As fans it gives us a legitimate reason to be utterly irrational all the while citing a complete lie about a lack of bias. It makes us act as we would nowhere else in polite society and yet provide some of *the* great moments of respect and responsibility in modern life. It is the game we love and we wouldn't have things any other way.

As with any sport, football is changing over time but at its heart it is still *our* game. Throw all the arguments about goal-line technology, extra officials, rule changes and club ownership at the wall, and what remains still boils down to 22 players, 1 ball, 2 goals & a desire to win. Whether we support a Manchester United and are regularly competing in top European competition and for the biggest of the domestic honours, or we support

Enfield Town and are just thankful to have a club in any capacity to support, they are still *our* club.

And that's why we keep coming back for more. Our teams may frustrate us with a lack of success or mistakes made by management but whatever the level, they can evoke feelings and passion little else other than the major loves of one's life can rival. Some people believe your club chooses you but I don't subscribe to that theory at all. For whatever the reason when you make the choice to follow a team, it lives with you and it'll never go away. Some live to regret that choice after years of trophy-less misery but in reality, they still wouldn't change their allegiance.

Whilst writing this book every football fan I have come across has given me a valid reason why their club matters and should be included. I know full well there are some glaring omissions but that is purely because it had to be capped somewhere – fifty seemed as good a number as any. I have no idea if someday there might be 'Another 50 Teams That Mattered' on a shelf next to this book but I do know one thing for certain, you could easily write about another fifty teams; you could easily write about another hundred and fifty in truth.

Football is littered with stories that are worth telling. The game has birthed some of the greatest moments in all sport and inspires a devotion often only rivalled by the most religious or committed. These teams I've selected do not necessarily matter the most and they are only in historical order, there's no implied status given by position. The point I'm trying to make is that every team matters to someone and that is what makes football the sporting colossus we love just the way it is.

Acknowledgements

This book has only been possible thanks to a great number of people and I shall attempt to mention each one here.

On a practical level Stuart Fuller has been a great source of support, inspiration, help and advice and I simply couldn't have finished this project without him. I'm also eternally grateful to Stuart for allowing me to use his photograph just as I am to both Andrew Gibney and Michael Stoffl. For assorted reasons I also want to thank Ben Shave and Jeff Livingstone, not least of those reasons is the amount of times both have covered for me when I should have been doing the day job – editing the (even if I do say so myself) excellent blog 'In Bed With Maradona'.

The research has been epic but I will forever indebted to the writing of Jonathan Wilson, Phil Ball, John Foot, Alex Bellos, Keir Radnedge, Rob Smyth, David Goldblatt and David Winner amongst many, many others for both information and inspiration. Also I need to mention Chris Mann, Adam Bate, Kieron O'Connor and Andrew Thomas who have all in one way or another made me push myself to get my fumbling word play into better shape. Kevin Day and Roy Meredith have been supportive of my work throughout and have become friends, and a special mention for Kris Hallam (@KrisHallam) who was the first person to say he liked my work and has no idea how much that meant at the time. Also they say one should never meet your heroes but having met the writer of the foreword of this book Iain Macintosh and having all expectations surpassed, I can tell you that saying is utter rubbish.

In terms of support I have to mention Danny Last, author of the wonderful European Football Weekends who occasionally lets me put nonsense on his blog and bears all consequence himself. Similarly the Magic Spongers, the Sabotage Times, Ghost Goal, Spiel Magazine, Twisted Blood and the Equaliser have all hosted articles by myself since my first humble offerings appeared on IBWM and I'd like to thank them for the chance.

There are also several people who have been no support at all but continue to be my friends as long as I'm willing to take the not so gentle ribbing associated with entering any drunken conversation with them. Among these I'll mention by name Steve Weatherill (Weatherilldinho), Michael Ramsden (Rambo), Adam Wainwright (Ladyboy), Steven Stocker (Not Fat Steve), Thomas Maher (Billy Elliot), Scott Armstrong (180), Chris Smith (Nicey), Ben McClean (B-Mac), Bobby Sharma (Boy), James Maher (Marsey) and Jan Mosalski (Janos).

Also I would never be able to wear the Revolutions blue again if I didn't mention my team mates James Evans, Craig Tyman (told you I was two-footed), Phil Pinkstone, Gareth Beardall, Lewis Evans and Matthew Evans. RTID.

I need to thank several people who I've never met to say thanks for the entertainment during the long hours writing and researching this book, namely Paul Hawksbee and Andy Jacobs on talkSPORT, the entire casts of the 'Guardian Football Weekly', 'Red, White and Blue', 'Two Footed Tackle', 'Football Pubcast', 'Cafe Calcio' and 'The Game' podcasts. Also a special mention to the Football Ramble chaps – Marcus Speller, James (or Jim) Campbell, Pete Donaldson, Lukey Moore and of course Lord Ramble (they say silence is golden Lord Ramble, you take the piss).

My family have been a huge source of pride throughout my life and have been more supportive than ever since I embarked on this book. My Mum and Dad have both been more supportive than anyone dare hope for I am eternally grateful for their strength and love. Also my brothers Adam and Paul, as well as Eve, Reuben and Oliver have also all been terrific help and I love you all. I should also mention the in-laws David and Liz, Jill, Sid, Kadie and Millie who have all been brilliant and have helped more than they'll ever know.

Last but by no means least I have to thank my beautiful wife Penny and our perfect daughter Beau. Penny, you are my world and you have shown me that I can achieve anything with you by my side. I love you and always will and hope to make soothing ocean sounds in bed next to you (aha matey…) for the rest of our lives. Beau, as I write this you are seven months old and you have already taught me more about life than I ever thought possible. I love you with all my heart and will continue to blow raspberries on your belly for as long as possible.

References & Bibliography

Club & Team Websites

www.acmilan.com
www.ajax.nl
www.arsenal.com
www.fcbarcelona.com
www.bocajuniors.com.ar
www.camlions.com
www.celticfc.net
www.colocolo.cl
www.darwenfc.com
www.clubwebsite.co.uk/afcdarwen
www.dickkerrladies.com
www.eintracht.com
www.enfieldfc.co.uk
www.etfc.co.uk
www.exetercityfc.co.uk
www.leedsunited.com
www.leytonorient.com
www.liverpoolfc.tv
www.losmillonarios.net
www.madridatleticos.com
www.manutd.com
www.mfc.co.uk
www.millonarios.com
www.nottinghamforest.co.uk
www.nycosmos.com
www.fcporto.pt
www.provercelli.com
www.queensparkfc.co.uk
www.realmadrid.com
www.sheffieldfc.com
www.torinofc.it
www.tottenhamhotspur.com
www.wba.co.uk
www.wolves.co.uk

Statistics, Fixtures & Results

www.archivio.inter.it
www.englandfootballonline.com
www.englandstats.com
www.fa-cupfinals.co.uk
www.planetworldcup.com
www.soccerbase.com
www.scottish-football-historical-archive.com
www.statto.com
www.rsssf.com
www.11v11.com

Historical, Information & Governing Bodies

www.arthurwharton.com
www.aviation-safety.net
www.avoidingthedrop.com
www.ayresomepark.co.uk
www.ayrshirehistory.com

www.bbc.co.uk
www.britannica.com
www.bundesliga.de
www.clubsincrisis.com
www.dalealbo.cl
www.DaveBrett.com
www.diegomaradona.com
www.equaliserfootball.com
www.ezinearticles.com
www.f-archiv.de
www.thefa.com
www.fcprovc.com
www.fifa.com
www.footballeconomy.com
www.football-italia.net
www.fourfourtwo.com
www.furd.org
www.grecianvoices.com
www.homepages.sover.net
www.icliverpool.icnetwork.co.uk
www.ifhof.com
www.inbedwithmaradona.com
www.kenn.com
www.le.ac.uk
www.lfchistory.net
www.miafoundation.org
www.themightyleeds.co.uk
www.nationalfootballmuseum.com
www.national-football-teams.com
www.nonleaguefootballhistory.co.uk
www.newsclick.de
www.theoffside.com
www.oldbaggies.com
www.our4fathers.com
www.runofplay.com
www.scottishfa.co.uk
www.soccerhistory.org.uk
www.soccernet.espn.go.com
www.soccerphile.com
www.spartacus.schoolnet.co.uk
www.sport.co.uk
www.supporters-direct.org
www.tagesspiegel.de
www.talkfootball.co.uk
www.thefootballramble.com
www.tomwfootball.com
www.wsc.co.uk
www.websters-online-dictionary.org
www.world-football-legends.co.uk
www.uefa.com
www.usolympicteam.com
www.ussoccer.com

Newspapers & Magazines

The Blizzard
The Daily Mail
The Daily Mirror
Express and Star
Four Four Two
The Guardian
The Herald
The Independent
The Lancashire Telegraph
The LA Times
The New York Times
The Northern Echo
The Sheffield Telegraph
Sports Illustrated
The Sunday Herald
The Sunday Times
The Telegraph
Time
The Times
USA Today
When Saturday Comes
The Yorkshire Evening Post

Books & Journals

Ball P., **Morbo: the Story of Spanish Football** *Published by*

When Saturday Comes Books, London, 2001

Bellos A., **Futebol: The Brazilian Way of Life** *Published by Bloomsbury, London, 2002*

Clough B., **Clough: The Autobiography** *Published by Corgi, London, 1995*

Crouch T. & Corbett J., **The World Cup: The Complete History** *Published by Aurum Press Ltd, London, 2010*

Davies P., **All Played Out: The Full Story of Italia '90** *Published by Jonathan Cape Ltd, London, 1998*

Downing D., **The Best of Enemies: England v Germany** *Published by Bloomsbury, London, 2000*

Foot J., **Calcio: A History of Italian Football** *Published by Harper Perennial, London, 2007*

Goldblatt D. & Acton J., **The Football Book** *Published by Dorling Kindersley Ltd, London, 2009*

Goldblatt D., **The Ball is Round: A Global History of Football** *Published by Penguin Books, London, 2007*

Hesse-Lichtenberger U., **Tor! The Story of German Football** *Published by When Saturday Comes Books, London 2002*

Hill T., **Encyclopedia of World Football** *Published by Parragon, Bath, 2009*

Maradona D., **El Diego: The Autobiography** *Published by Yellow Jersey Press, London, 2004*

Pelé (with Duarte O. & Bellos A.), **Pelé: The Autobiography** *Published by Simon & Schuster UK Ltd, London, 2006P*

Radnedge K., **2010 FIFA World Cup South Africa Official Book** *Published by Carlton Books, London, 2010*

Radnedge K., **The Complete Encyclopaedia of Football** *Published by Carlton Books, London, 2004*

Wilson J., **Inverting the Pyramid: The History of Football Tactics** *Published by Orion Books, London, 2008*

Wilson J., **The Anatomy Of England: A History in Ten Matches** *Published by Orion Books, London, 2011*

Winner D., **Brilliant Orange: The Neurotic Genius of Dutch Football** *Published by Bloomsbury, London, 2000*

Collections

High Balls, Long Balls & No Balls Complied & designed by Mike Kiely: *Published by Arcturus Publishing Ltd, London, 2009*

Sky Sports Football Yearbook 2008-2009 Edited by Glenda Rollin & Jack Rollin: *Published by Headline, Chatham, 2008*

Sky Sports Football Yearbook 2010-2011 Edited by Glenda Rollin & Jack Rollin: *Published by Headline, Chatham, 2010*

The Wit & Wisdom of Football Compiled by Guy Lloyd: *Published by House of Raven Book Services, King's Sutton, 2005*

1001 Football Moments Project Director Matthew Lowing: *Published by Carlton Books Ltd, London, 2007*

Magazines, Newspapers & Further Reading

When Saturday Comes, Four Four Two, World Soccer, The Guardian, The Times, The Financial Times, The Independent, The Daily Mail, Gazetta dello Sport, L'Equipe, Kicker, Marca, France Football, The Blizzard

Documentaries & Film

Once in a Lifetime: The Extraordinary Story of the New York Cosmos Directed by Paul Crowder & John Dower, *GreeneStreet Films, ESPN Original Entertainment, Cactus Three & Passion Pictures*

One Night in Turin Directed by James Erskine, *New Black Films & Kaleidoscope Entertainment*

ESPN Films 30 for 30: The Two Escobars Directed by Jeff Zimbalist & Michael Zimbalist, *All Rise Films & ESPN Films*

Maradona by Kusturica Directed by Emir Kusturica, *Pentagrama Films, Exception Wild Bunch, Estudios Picasso*

Zidane: A 21st Century Portrait Directed by Douglas Gordon & Philippe Parreno, *Anna Lena Films, Kanzaman, Naflastrengir, Fondazione Sandretto Re Rebaudengo, arte France Cinéma, Love Streams Productions, Canal+, CNC, & CinéCinéma*

The Damned United Directed by Tom Hooper, *Columbia Pictures Corporation, BBC Films, Screen Yorkshire, Left Bank Pictures & Screen Yorkshire Production Fund*

All production and directorial credits as per IMDB 01.09.2011